The FOURTH WAY

P. D. OUSPENSKY

A Record Of Talks And Answers To Questions Based On The Teaching Of G. I. Gurdjieff

SANAGE
PUBLISHING HOUSE

Paperback: 978-939492447-5

Printed by: Manipal Technologies Limited, Manipal

Sanage Publishing House LLP
Mumbai, India

sanagepublishing@gmail.com

Peter D. Ouspensky (1878 – 1947) was a Russian esotericist known for his expositions of the early work of the Greek-Armenian teacher of esoteric doctrine George Gurdjieff. He met Gurdjieff in Moscow in 1915, and was associated with the ideas and practices originating with Gurdjieff from then on. He taught ideas and methods based in the Gurdjieff system for 25 years in England and the United States, although he separated from Gurdjieff personally in 1924, for reasons that are explained in the last chapter of his book In Search of the Miraculous.

CONTENTS

Chances are limited and time is counted—Self-remembering and recurrence—Personality and recurrence—Study of children's minds—Origin of the idea of recurrence—Three dimensions of time—The idea of recurrence and the system—Parallel time—'Limitations of our mind—Growth of tendencies and recurrence—Possibilities of meeting a school next time— Being prepared—Is the starting-point the same for everybody?—School and the demands made in it—Death of essence—Recurrence and date of death— Recurrence of world events—The only thing is to awake.

FOREWORD

WHEN P. D. Ouspensky was asked if he intended to publish his lectures, he answered: 'What is the use? The most important is not the lectures but the questions and answers.'

This book consists of verbatim extracts from talks and answers to questions given by Ouspensky between 1921 and 1946. Chapter I is a general survey of the fundamental ideas, which in subsequent chapters are amplified subject by subject in the specific order followed by Ouspensky himself.

To achieve this order some of the material has had to be taken out of its chronological sequence; but in no case has there been any alteration of phrasing or meaning.

* * *

CHAPTER I

What the system is about—Study of psychology—Incompleteness of man —Study of the world and study of man—Principle of scale—Possible evolution—Self-study—Many 'I's—Division of functions—Four states of consciousness—Self -observation—Self remembering—Two higher functions—Wrong work of the machine—Imagination—Lying— Absence of will—Lack of control—Expression of unpleasant emotions—Negative emotions—Change of attitudes—Observation of functions—Identification —Considering—Sleep—Prison and escape—Seven categories of man— Mechanicalness—Law of Three—Law of Seven—Illusions— We cannot 'do'—Good and evil—Morality and conscience—Only a few can develop— A, B and C influences—Magnetic centre—We live in a bad place in the universe—Ray of Creation—Orders of laws.

Before I begin to Explain to you in a general way what this system is about, and to talk about our methods, I want particularly to impress on your minds that the most important ideas and principles of the system do not belong to me. This is chiefly what makes them valuable, because if they belonged to me, they would be like all other theories invented by ordinary minds, they would give only a subjective view of things.

When I began to write *A New Model of the Universe* in 1907, I formulated to myself, as many other people have done before and since, that behind the surface of the life which we know lies something much bigger and more important.

And I said to myself then that until we know more about what lies behind, all our knowledge of life and of ourselves is really negligible. I remember one conversation at that time, when I said, 'If it were possible to accept as proven that consciousness (or, as I should call it now, intelligence) can manifest itself apart from the physical body, many other things could be proved. Only it cannot be taken as proved.' I realized that manifestations of supernormal psychology such as thought transference, clairvoyance, the possibility of knowing the future, of looking back into the past, and so on, have not been proved. So, I tried to find a method of studying these things and worked on that line for several years. I found some interesting things in that way, but the results were very elusive; and though several experiments were successful, it was almost impossible to repeat them.

I came to two conclusions in the course of these experiments: first, that we do not know enough about ordinary psychology; we cannot study supernormal psychology, because we do not know normal psychology. Secondly, I came to the conclusion that certain real knowledge exists; that there may be schools which know exactly what we want to know, but that for some reason they are hidden, and this knowledge is hidden. So, I began to look for these schools. I travelled in Europe, Egypt, India, Ceylon, Turkey, and the Near East; but it was really later, when I had already finished these travels, that I met in Russia during the war a group of people who were studying a certain system which came originally from Eastern schools. This system began with the study of psychology, exactly as I had realized it must begin.

The chief idea of this system was that we do not use even a small part of our powers and our forces. We have in us, so to speak, a very big and very fine organization, only we do not know how to use it. In this group they employed certain oriental metaphors, and they told me that we have in us a large house full of beautiful furniture, with a library and many other rooms, but we live in the basement and the kitchen and cannot get out of them. If people tell us about what this house has upstairs, we do not believe them, or we laugh at them, or we call it superstition or fairy tales or fables.

This system can be divided into study of the world, on certain new principles, and study of man. The study of the world and study of man include in themselves a kind of special language. We try to use ordinary words, the same words as we use in ordinary conversation, but we attach a slightly different and more precise meaning to them.

Study of the world, study of the universe, is based on the study of some fundamental laws which are not generally known or recognized in science. The two chief laws are the Law of Three and the Law of Seven, which will be explained later. Included in this, and necessary from this point of view, is the principle of *scale*, a principle which does not enter into ordinary scientific study or enters very little.

The study of man is closely connected with the idea of the evolution of man, but the evolution of man must be understood in a slightly different way from the ordinary. Ordinarily the word evolution applied either to man or to anything else presupposes a kind of mechanical evolution; I mean that certain things, by certain known or unknown laws, transform into other things, and these other things transform into still others, and so on. But from the point of view of this system there is no such evolution at all, I do not speak in general, but specifically of man. The evolution of man, if it occurs, can only be the result of knowledge and effort; as long as *man* knows only what he can know in the ordinary way, there is no evolution for him and there never was any evolution for him.

Serious study begins in this system with the study of psychology, that is to say with the study of oneself, because psychology cannot be studied, as astronomy can, outside oneself. A man has to study himself. When I was told that, I saw at once that we do not have any methods of studying ourselves and already have many wrong ideas about ourselves. So, I realized that we must get rid of wrong ideas about ourselves and at the same time find methods for studying ourselves.

Perhaps you realize how difficult it is to define what is meant by psychology? There are so many meanings attached to the same words in different systems that it is difficult to have a general definition. So, we begin by defining psychology as *study of oneself*. You have to learn certain methods and principles and, according to these principles and using these methods, you will try to see yourselves from a new point of view.

If we begin to study ourselves, we first of all come up against one word which we use more than any other and that is the word 'I'. We say, 'I am doing', 'I am sitting', 'I feel', 'I like', 'I dislike' and so on. This is our chief illusion, for the principal mistake we make about ourselves is that we consider ourselves one; we always speak about ourselves as 'I' and we suppose that we refer to the same thing all the time when in reality we are divided into hundreds and hundreds of different 'I's. At one moment when I say 'I', one part of me is speaking, and at another moment when I say 'I', it is quite another 'I' speak. We do not know that we have not one 'I', but many different 'I's connected with our feelings and desires and have no controlling 'I'. These 'I's change all the time; one suppresses another, one replaces another, and all this struggle makes up our inner life.

'I's which we see in ourselves are divided into several groups. Some of these groups are legitimate, they belong to right divisions of man, and some of them are quite artificial and are created by insufficient knowledge and by certain imaginary ideas that man has about himself.

To begin self-study, it is necessary to study methods of self-observation, but that again must be based on a certain understanding of the divisions of our functions. Our ordinary idea of these divisions is quite wrong. We know the difference between intellectual and emotional functions. For instance, when we discuss things, think about them, compare them, invent explanations, or find real explanations, this is all intellectual work, whereas love, hate, fear, suspicion and so on are emotional. But very often, when trying to observe ourselves, we mix even intellectual and emotional functions; when we really feel, we call it thinking, and when we think we call it feeling. But in the course of study, we shall learn in what way they differ. For instance, there is an enormous difference in speed, but we shall speak more about that later.

Then there are two other functions which no system of ordinary psychology divides and understands in the right way instinctive function and moving function. Instinctive refers to the inner work of the organism:

digestion of food, beating of the heart, breathing, these are instinctive functions. To instinctive function belong also ordinary senses sight, hearing, smell, taste, touch, the feeling of cold and warmth, things like that; and this is all, really. Of outer movements, only simple reflexes belong to instinctive function, because more complicated reflexes belong to moving function. It is very easy to distinguish between instinctive and moving functions. We do not have to learn anything that belongs to instinctive function, we are born with the capacity to use all the instinctive functions. Moving functions, on the other hand, all have to be learned, a child learns to walk, to write and so on. There is a very great difference between the two functions, since there is nothing inherent in moving functions, and instinctive functions are all inherent.

So, in self-observation it is necessary first of all to divide these four functions and to classify at once everything that you observe, saying, 'This is intellectual function', 'This is emotional function' and so on.

If you practice this observation for some time, you may notice some strange things. For instance, you will find that what is really difficult in observing is that you forget about it. You start to observe, and your emotions connect with some kind of thought, and you forget about self-observation.

Again, after some time, if you continue this effort to observe, which is a new function not used in the same way in ordinary life, you will notice another interesting thing that generally you do not *remember yourself*. If you could be aware of yourself all the time, then you would be able to observe all the time, or in any case as long as you liked. But because you cannot remember yourself, you cannot concentrate; and this is why you will have to admit that you have no will. If you could remember yourself, you would have will and could do what you liked. But you cannot remember yourself, you cannot be aware of yourself and so you have no will. You may sometimes have will for a short time, but it turns to something else, and you forget about it.

This is the situation, the state of being, the state from which we have to start self-study. But very soon, if you continue, you will come to the conclusion that almost from the very beginning of self-study you have to correct certain things in yourself which are not right, to arrange certain things which are not in their right places. The system has an explanation for this.

We are made in such a way that we can live in four states of consciousness, but such as we are we use only two: one when we are asleep, and the other when we are what we call 'awake' that is to say, in this present state, when we can talk, listen, read, write and so on. But these are only two out of four possible states. The third state of consciousness is very strange. If people explain to us what the third state of consciousness is, we begin to think that we have it. The third state can be called *self-consciousness*, and most people, if asked, say, 'Certainly we are conscious!' A sufficient time or repeated and frequent efforts of self-observation is necessary before we really recognize the fact that we are not conscious.

that we are conscious only potentially. If we are asked, we say, 'Yes, I am', and for that moment we are, but the next moment we cease to remember and are not conscious. So, in the process of self-observation, we realize that we are not in the third state of consciousness, that we live only in two. We live either in sleep or in a waking state which, in the system, is called *relative consciousness*. The fourth state, which is called *objective consciousness*, is inaccessible to us because it can only be reached through self-consciousness, that is, by becoming aware of oneself first, so that much later we may manage to reach the objective state of consciousness.

So, at the same time as self-observing, we try to be aware of ourselves by holding the sensation of 'I am here' nothing more. And this is the fact that all Western psychology, without the smallest exception, has missed. Although many people came very near to it, they did not recognize the importance of this fact and did not realize that the state of man as he can be changed, that man can remember himself, if he tries for a long time.

It is not a question of a day or a month. It is a very long study, and a study of how to remove obstacles, because we do not remember ourselves, we are not conscious of ourselves, owing to many wrong functions in our machine, and all these functions have to be corrected and put right. When most of these functions are put right, these periods of self-remembering will become longer and longer, and if they become sufficiently long, we shall acquire two new functions. With self-consciousness, which is the third state of consciousness, we acquire a function which is called *higher emotional,* although it is equally intellectual, because on this level there is no difference between intellectual and emotional such as there is on the ordinary level. And when we come to the state of objective consciousness, we acquire another function which is called *higher mental.* Phenomena of what I call supernormal psychology belong to these two functions; and this is why, when I made those experiments twenty-five years ago, I came to the conclusion that experimental work is impossible, because it is not a question of experiment but of changing one's state of consciousness.

I have just given you some general ideas. Now try to tell me what you do not understand, what you wish me to explain better. Try to ask any questions you like, either in relation to what I said or your own questions. In that way it will be easier to make a start.

Q. To attain the higher state of consciousness is it necessary to be permanently aware of oneself?

A. We cannot do that, so there is no question of being permanently aware. We can only talk now about the beginning. We must study ourselves in connection with this division of different functions when we can, when we remember to do it because in this we depend on chance. When we remember, we must try to be aware of ourselves. This is all we can do.

Q. Must you be able to be conscious of your instinctive functions?

A. Only of the senses. Inner instinctive work does not need to become conscious. It is conscious for itself, independently of the intellectual function, and there is no need to increase this. We must try to become conscious of ourselves as we see ourselves, not of our inner functions. After some time, we may become aware of certain inner functions of which it is useful to be aware; but not yet. You see, we do not acquire any new feelings. We only classify better our ordinary impressions, the ordinary things we get from life, from people, from everything.

Q. Would it be correct to say that when learning anything like driving a car, intellectual function tells moving function what to do and that, when proficient, moving function works by itself?

A. Quite right. You can observe many things like that. First you learn by intellectual function.

Q. How important is the knowledge gained by watching our physical actions? Is this merely an exercise for watching our minds?

A. No, it is very important because we mix many things and do not know the causes of many things. We can understand causes only by constant watching for a long time.

Q. May we have instruction about how to work on each of the four functions?

A. All that will be explained, but for the present, and for a long time, you can only observe.

Q. Would it be an example of different 'I's working when one goes to bed late and fully decides to go to bed early next night and, when night comes, does otherwise?

A. Quite right, one 'I' decides, and another has to do it.

Q. How do we set about trying to be more conscious of ourselves?

A. This is quite simple to explain, although it is very difficult to achieve.

There are no roundabout ways. A better state can only be achieved by direct effort, just by trying to be more conscious, by asking oneself as often as possible, 'Am I conscious or not?'

Q. But how does one attain any certainty that your method is right?

A. Just by comparing one observation with another. And then we talk when we meet. People speak about their observations; they compare them.

I try to explain what they cannot understand; there are other people who help me, and in that way, one becomes sure of ordinary things, just as one knows that grass is green.

There is no question of faith or belief in all this. Quite the opposite, this system teaches people to believe in absolutely nothing. You must verify everything that you see, hear, and feel. Only in that way can you come to something.

At the same time, you must realize that our machine docs do not work perfectly; it works far from perfectly, because of many wrong functions, so that a very important part of self-study is connected with the study of these wrong functions. We must know them in order to eliminate them. And one of the particularly wrong functions, which we sometimes like in ourselves, is imagination. In this system imagination does not mean conscious or intentional thinking on some subject or visualization of something, but imagination that turns without any control and without any result. It takes very much energy and turns thinking in a wrong direction.

Q. When you say 'imagination', do you mean imagining something to be true, not drawing pictures?

A. Imagination has many aspects; it may be just ordinary daydreams or, for instance, imagining non-existent powers in oneself. It is the same thing, it works without control, it runs by itself.

Q. Each one is self-deception?

A. One does not take it as self-deception: one imagines something, then believes it and forgets that it was imagination.

Studying man in his present state of sleep, absence of unity, mechanicalness, and lack of control, we find several other wrong functions which are the result of his state in particular, lying to himself and to other people all the time. The psychology of ordinary man could even be called the study of lying, because man lies more than anything else; and as a matter of fact, he cannot speak the truth. It is not so simple to speak the truth. one has to learn how to do it, and sometimes it takes a very long time.

Q. Would you mind explaining what you mean by lying?

A. Lying is thinking or speaking about things that one does not know.

this is the beginning of lying. It does not mean intentional lying telling stories, as for instance that there is a bear in the other room. You can go to the other room and see that there is no bear in it. But if you collect all the theories that people, put forward on any given subject, without knowing anything about it, you will see where lying begins. Man does not know himself, he does not know anything, yet he has theories about everything. Most of these theories are lying.

Q. I want to know the truth that it is good for me to know in my present state. How can I discover whether it is a lie?

A. For almost everything you know you have methods for verifying. But first you must know what you can know and what you cannot. That helps verifying. If you start with that you will soon hear lies, even without thinking. Lies have a different sound, particularly lies about things we cannot know.

Q. As regards imagination, if you are thinking instead of imagining, should you be aware of the effort all the time?

A. Yes, you will be aware of it not so much of effort as of control. You will feel that you control things, they do not just go on by themselves.

Q. When you say, 'remember yourself', do you mean by that to remember after you have observed yourself, or do you mean to remember the things we know are in us?

A. No, take it quite apart from observation. To remember oneself means the same thing as to be aware of oneself, 'I am'. Sometimes it comes by itself; it is a very strange feeling. It is not a function, not thinking, not feeling; it is a different state of consciousness. By itself it only comes for very short moments, generally in quite new surroundings, and one says to oneself: 'How strange. I am here'. This is self- remembering; at this moment you remember yourself.

Later when you begin to distinguish these moments, you reach another interesting conclusion: you realize that what you remember from childhood are only glimpses of self-remembering, because all that you know of ordinary moments is that things have happened. You *know* you were there, but you do not remember anything exactly; but if this flash happens, then you remember all that surrounded this moment.

Q. Can one with observation be aware that one has not got certain things? Is one to observe things from the point of view of everything being possible?

A. I do not think it is necessary to use such a word as 'everything'. Just observe, without any guessing, and observe only what you can see. For a long time, you just have to observe and try to find out what you can about intellectual, emotional, instinctive, and moving functions. From this you may come to the conclusion that you have four definite minds not only one mind but four different ones. One mind control's intellectual function, another quite different mind controls emotional functions, a third controls instinctive functions, and a fourth, again quite different, controls moving functions. We call them centres: intellectual centre, emotional centre, moving centre and instinctive centre. They are quite independent. Each centre has its own memory, its own imagination, and its own will.

Q. In the case of conflicting desires, I presume that if one had enough knowledge of oneself, one would be able to see to it that they did not conflict?

A. Knowledge by itself is not sufficient. One can know and desires can still be in conflict, because each desire represents a different will. What we call our will in the ordinary sense is only the resultant of desires. The resultant sometimes reaches a definite line of action and at other times cannot reach any definite line, because one desire goes one way and another way, and we cannot decide what to do. This is our usual state. Certainly, our future aim must be to come to oneness instead of being many, as we are now, because in order to do anything rightly, to know anything rightly, to arrive anywhere, we must become one. It is a very far aim, and we cannot begin to approach it until we know ourselves, because, in the state in which we are now, our ignorance of ourselves is such that when we see it, we begin to be terrified that we may not find our way anywhere.

The human being is a very complicated machine and has to be studied as a machine. We realize that in order to control any kind of machine, such as a motor car or a railway engine, we should first have to learn. We cannot control these machines instinctively, but for some reason we think that ordinary instinct is sufficient to control the human machine, although it is so much more complicated. This is one of the first wrong assumptions: we do not realize that we have to learn, that control is a question of knowledge and skill.

Well, tell me what interests you most in all this and what you want to hear more about.

Q. I was interested in the question of imagination. I suppose it means that in the ordinary application of the word one was using the wrong meaning.

A. In the ordinary meaning of imagination the most important factor is missed, but in the terminology of this system we begin with what is most important. The most important factor in every function is: 'Is it under our control or not?' So, when imagination is under our control, we do not even call it imagination; we call it by various names visualization, creative thinking, inventive thinking, you can find a name for each special case. But when it comes by itself and controls us so that we are in its power, then we call it imagination.

Again, there is another side of imagination which we miss in ordinary understanding. This is that we imagine non-existent things, non-existent capacities, for instance. We ascribe to ourselves powers which we do not have; we imagine ourselves to be self-conscious although we are not. We have imaginary powers and imaginary self-consciousness, and we imagine ourselves to be one, when really, we are many different 'I's. There are many such things that we imagine about *ourselves* and other people. For instance, we imagine that we can 'do', that we have choice; we have no choice, we cannot 'do', things just happen to us.

So, we imagine ourselves, really. We are not what we imagine ourselves to be.

Q. Is there any difference between imagination and daydreaming?

A. If you cannot control daydreaming, it means that it is part of imagination; but not all of it. Imagination has many different sides. We imagine non-existent states, non existent possibilities, non-existent powers.

Q. Could you give me a definition of negative imagination?

A. Imagining all kinds of unpleasant things, torturing oneself, imagining all the things that might happen to you or other people things like that; it takes different forms. Some people imagine different illnesses, some imagine accidents, others imagine misfortunes.

Q. Is the control of your emotions a reasonable objective?

A. Control of emotions is a very difficult thing. It is a very important part of self-study, but we cannot begin with the control of emotions, because we do not understand enough about emotions.

I will explain, what we can do from the very beginning of observing the emotional function is to try to stop one particular manifestation in ourselves. We must try to stop the manifestation of unpleasant emotions. For many people this is one of the most difficult things, because unpleasant emotions are expressed so quickly and so easily that you cannot catch them. Yet unless you try you cannot really observe yourself, so from the very beginning, when observing emotions, you must try to stop the expression of *unpleasant emotions*. This is the first step. In this system we call all these unpleasant, violent, or depressing emotions by the name of negative emotions. As I said, the first step is trying not to *express* these negative emotions.

the second step is the study of negative emotions themselves, making lists of them, finding their connections because some of them are simple and some are compound and trying to understand that they are quite useless. It sounds strange, but it is very important to understand that all negative emotions are absolutely useless: they do not serve any useful purpose, they do not make us acquainted with new things or bring us nearer to new things; they do not give us energy; they only waste energy and create unpleasant illusions. They can even destroy physical health.

Thirdly, after a certain amount of study and observation we may come to the conclusion that we can get rid of negative emotions, that they are not obligatory. Here the system helps because it shows that in fact there is no real centre for negative emotions, but that they belong to an artificial centre in us, which we create in childhood by imitating people with negative emotions by whom we are surrounded. People even teach children to express negative emotions. Then children learn still more by imitation; they imitate older children, older children imitate grown-up people, and so at a very early age they become professors of negative emotions.

It is a great liberation when we begin to understand that there are no obligatory negative emotions. We are born without them, but for some unknown reason we teach ourselves negative emotions.

Q. To be free from negative emotions, must we be able to stop them arising?

A. This is wrong because we cannot control emotions. I mentioned the different speed of different functions. The slowest is the intellectual function. Next come moving and instinctive functions which have an approximately equal speed which is enormously quicker than intellectual. The emotional function should be still quicker, but generally works at about the same speed as the instinctive function. So, moving, instinctive and emotional functions are very much quicker than thought, and it is impossible to catch emotions by thought. When we are in an emotional state, they succeed each other so quickly that we have no time to think. But we can get an idea of the difference in speed by comparing thinking functions with moving functions. If, doing some quick movement, you try to observe yourself, you will see that you cannot. Thought cannot follow movement. Either you have to make the movement quite slow, or you cannot observe. This is a definite fact.

Q. By movements, do you mean physical movements?

A. Yes, ordinary things, like driving a car or writing; you cannot observe anything of that kind. You can remember, and later it creates the illusion of observing. In reality you cannot observe quick movements.

So, you see, as we are now, real struggle with negative emotions is a question of the future, not a very far future, but there are many things we need to know first and methods which we must study. There is no direct way; we must learn roundabout methods of how to attack them.

First of all, we have to change many of our mental attitudes, which are more or less in our power; I mean intellectual attitudes, or points of view. We have too many wrong points of view about negative emotions; we find them necessary, or beautiful, or noble; we glorify them, and so on. We must get rid of all that. So, we have to clean our mind in relation to negative emotions. When our mind is right concerning negative emotions, when we have ceased to glorify them, then little by little we shall find a way to struggle with them, each separately. One person finds it easier to struggle with one particular negative emotion, another finds it easier with another. You must begin with the easiest, and what is easiest for me may be the most difficult for you; so, you must find the easiest for yourself, and later come to the more difficult.

Q. Does that explain why I associate certain of my own negative emotions with people I remember back in my childhood?

A. Quite probably because many negative emotions are learned by imitation. But some may be essentially in our nature because our nature also has different inclinations one way or another way. Emotions can be divided into groups, and one person may be more inclined to one group and another to another group. For instance, some people have an inclination to different forms of fear, others to different forms of anger. But they are different and do not come from imitation.

Q. Are they the hardest to struggle with?

A. Yes, but they are generally based on some kind of weakness, because at the basis of negative emotions there generally lies a kind of self-indulgence one allows oneself. And if one does not allow oneself fears, one allows anger, and if one does not allow anger, one allows self-pity. Negative emotions are always based on some kind of permission.

But before we come to such complicated questions as struggle with negative emotions, it is very important to observe ourselves in small, everyday manifestations of the moving function and also those which we can observe of the instinctive function, that is, our sensations of pleasant and unpleasant, warm, and cold sensations like that which are always passing through us.

Q. You have not mentioned identification, but can I ask you a question about it?

A. Please. But not everybody here has heard about it, so I will just explain a little. You see, when we begin to observe emotions particularly, but really all other functions as well, we find that all our functions are accompanied by a certain attitude; we become too absorbed in things, too lost in things, particularly when the slightest emotional element appears. This is called identification. We identify with things. It is not a very good word, but in English there is none better. The idea of identification exists in Indian writings and the Buddhists speak of attachment and non-attachment. These words seem to me even less satisfactory because, before meeting this system, I read these words and did not understand or rather I understood but took the idea intellectually. I understood fully only when I found the same idea expressed in Russian and in Greek by early Christian writers. They have four words for four degrees of identification, but this is not necessary for us yet. We try to understand the idea not by definition but by observation. It is a certain quality of attachment being lost in things.

Q. You lose your sense of observation?

A. When you become identified you cannot observe.

Q. It usually starts with emotion? Does possessiveness come into it too?

A. Yes. Many things. It begins first with interest. You are interested in something, and the next moment you are in it, and do not exist anymore.

Q. But if you are thinking and conscious of the effort of thinking, does that save you from identification? You cannot do both at once, can you?

A. Yes, it saves you for a moment, but the next moment another thought comes and takes you away. So, there is no guarantee. You must be on the watch all the time against it.

Q. What negative emotions are you likely to glorify?

A. Some people are very proud of their irritability or irritation, or something like that. They like to be thought very hard. There is practically no negative emotion which you cannot enjoy, and that is the most difficult thing to realize. Really some people get all their pleasures from negative emotions.

Identification in relation to people takes a special form which is called, in this system, *considering*. But considering can be of two kinds, when we consider other people's feelings, and when we consider our own. Chiefly we consider our own feelings. We consider mostly in the sense that people somehow do not value us enough or do not think about us enough or are not careful enough about us. We find many words for that. This is a very important facet of identification, and it is very difficult to be free from it. some people are fully in its power. In any case, it is important to observe considering.

For me personally, in the beginning, the most interesting idea was that of self-remembering. I simply could not understand how people could miss such a thing. All European philosophy and psychology just missed this point. There are traces in older teachings, but they are so well disguised and placed between less important things that you cannot see the importance of the idea.

When we try to keep all these things in mind and to observe ourselves, we come to the very definite conclusion that in the state of consciousness in which we are, with all this identification, considering, negative emotions and absence of self-remembering, we are really asleep. We only imagine that we are awake. So, when we try to remember ourselves, it means only one thing we try to awake. And we do awake for a second but then we fall asleep again. This is our state of being, so actually we are asleep. We can awake only if we correct many things in the machine and if we work very persistently on this idea of awaking, and for a long time.

Q. Does bad physical pain distort one's mental ideas?

A. Certainly. That is why we cannot speak about it. When we speak about man, we speak about man in his normal state. Then we can speak about obtaining these new functions, consciousness and so on. Exceptional cases cannot be taken because they distort the whole picture.

There are many interesting things in connection with that. This group I met in Moscow used oriental metaphors and parables, and one of the things they liked to speak about was prison that man is in prison, so what can he wish for, what can he desire? If he is a more or less sensible man, he can wish for only one thing to escape. But even before he can formulate this desire, that he wants to escape, he must become aware that he is in prison. If he does not realize that he is in prison, he cannot wish to escape. Then, when he formulates this wish, he begins to realize the possibilities of escape, and he understands that, by himself, he cannot escape, because it is necessary to dig under walls, and things like that. He realizes that first of all he must have some people who would like to escape with him, a small group of people. So, he realizes that a certain number of people can perhaps escape. But all cannot escape. One cannot and *all* cannot, but a small number of people can. Again, in what conditions? He comes to the conclusion that it is necessary to have help. Without that they cannot escape. They must have maps, files, tools and so on. so, they must have help from outside.

This is exactly, almost literally, the position of man. We can learn how to use the unused parts of our machine. This prison means really that we sit in the kitchen and basement of our house and cannot get out. One can get out, but not by oneself. Without school one cannot. School means that there are people who are already escaping or, at any rate, are preparing to escape. School cannot begin without help from another school, without help from those who escaped before. From them we can get certain ideas, a certain plan, a certain knowledge these are our tools. I repeat, all cannot escape. There are many laws against it. To put it simply, it would be too noticeable, and that would immediately produce a reaction from mechanical forces.

Q. The wish to escape is instinctive, is it?

A. No. Only the inner work of the organism is instinctive. It must be intellectual and emotional, because the instinctive function really belongs to the lower, the physical functions. Still, in some conditions, there may be a physical wish to escape. Suppose it is too hot in the room and we know it is cool outside, certainly we may wish to escape. But to realize that we are in prison and that it is possible to escape needs reason and feeling.

Q. It seems difficult, without greater self-observation, to know what your objective is in escaping.

A. Yes, certainly. Prison is just an example. For us prison is our sleep, and, without metaphors, we want to awake when we realize that we are asleep. It must be realized emotionally. We must understand that we are helpless in sleep; anything may happen. We can see pictures of life, see why things happen in one way or another both big and small things and realize that it is because people are asleep. Naturally they cannot do anything in sleep.

You know, in relation to these ideas and these methods, we live in a rather strange time in one sense, because schools are disappearing quickly. Thirty or forty years ago you could find many kinds of schools which practically do not exist now or are much more difficult to find.

Q. Are they disappearing in the East as well as the West?

A. I mean the East, of course. In the West there ceased to be any long ago. But about schools I think we had better speak separately. It is a very interesting subject, because we do not know how to make the right divisions. There are different kinds of schools.

Q. When you are first trying to observe, is it better to choose a lot of short occupations rather than getting involved in long ones? Does it make a difference?

A. No. You must try to observe yourself in different conditions, not only in the same conditions.

Q. Is it good, then, to analyze afterwards?

A. No. Generally speaking, in the beginning and for a long time, there should be no analysis. In order to analyze you must know laws; why things happened in that way and could not happen in another way. So, before you know the laws, it is better not to try to analyze. Just observe things as they are and try to classify them more or less into intellectual, emotional, instinctive, and moving functions. Each of these functions has its own centre or mind through which it manifests.

In connection with functions and states of consciousness and from the point of view of his possible evolution, man is divided into seven categories. People are born only in one of the three first categories.

A person in whom the instinctive or moving function predominates, and in whom intellectual and emotional functions are less developed, is called man No. 1; but if the emotional function predominates over the other functions, he is called man No. 2; and if the intellectual function predominates, he is man No. 3. Beyond these three kinds of men, but not born as such, is man No. 4. This means the beginning of change, chiefly in consciousness but also in knowledge and capacity for observation. Next comes man No. 5 who has already developed in himself the third state of consciousness, that is, self-consciousness, and in whom the higher emotional function works. Next is man No. 6 and finally man No. 7, who has full objective consciousness and in whom the higher intellectual function works.

Q. How can one recognize a higher man than ourselves as we do not know what to look for?

A. When we know better what is lacking in us, what the things are that we ascribe to ourselves but do not possess, we shall begin to see something about it, although actually we can distinguish people of a higher level only by their knowledge. If they know something that we do not know, and if we realize that no one else knows it, and that it could not be learned in any ordinary way, that may serve as a guide.

Try to think a little about the characteristics of these seven categories of man. For instance, what could be the general characteristics of man 1, 2 and 3? First of all, sleep. Man 1, 2 and 3, before he begins to study himself in connection with some system which gives him the possibility of self-study, passes all his life in sleep. He only looks as though he is awake. he is really never awake, or occasionally he awakes for a moment, looks round and falls asleep again. This is the first characteristic of man 1, 2 and 3. The second characteristic is the fact that though he has many different 'I's, some of these 'I's do not even know one another. Man can have quite definite attitudes, definite convictions, or definite views, and on the other hand he can have quite different convictions, quite different views, quite different likes, and different dislikes, and one of them does not know the other. This is one of the chief characteristics of man 1, 2 and 3. Men are very divided, and they do not know and cannot know it, because each of these 'I's knows only certain 'I's that it meets by association; other 'I's remain quite unknown. 'I's are divided according to functions; there are intellectual, emotional, instinctive, and moving 'I's. Round themselves they know something, but beyond that they know nothing, so until man begins to study himself with knowledge of this division, he can never come to a right understanding of his functions or reactions.

This sleep of man, and absence of unity in him, create another very important characteristic, and this is, the complete mechanicalness of man. Man in this state, man 1, 2 and 3, is a machine controlled by external influences; he has no possibility to resist these external influences, and no possibility to distinguish them from one another, no possibility to study himself apart from these things. He sees himself always on the move and has a long-established and very strong illusion that he is free to go where he wills, that he can move according to his wish, and that he can go to the right or to the left. He cannot do this; if he moves to the right, that means that he could not move to the left. 'Will' is quite a wrong idea; it does not exist. Will can exist only in man who has one controlling 'I', but as long as he has many different 'I's which do not know one another he has just as many different wills; each 'I' has its own will, there can be no other 'I' or other will. But man can come to a state when he acquires a controlling 'I' and when he acquires will. He can reach this state only by developing consciousness. These are the rudiments of the principles of this system

Now I Just want to say one thing more. We begin with psychology study of oneself, of the human machine, of states of consciousness, methods of correcting things and so on; but at the same time an important part of the system is given to doctrines of general laws of the world, because we cannot understand even ourselves if we do not know some of the fundamental laws which lie behind all things. Ordinary scientific knowledge is not sufficient for this, because, just as such important points as absence of self-remembering were missed in psychology, so our science either forgot or never knew the fundamental laws on which everything is based.

As I said, all things in the world, whether big or small, on every scale, are based on two fundamental laws, which in this system are called the Law of Three and the Law of Seven.

The Law of Three, in a short description, means that three forces enter into every manifestation, into every phenomenon and every event. They are called (but these are only words because they do not express their qualities) positive, negative and neutralizing, or active, passive and neutralizing, or still more simply, they may be called first force, second force and third force. These three forces enter into everything. In many cases we understand the need of two forces that one force cannot create an action, that there is action and resistance. But generally, we are not aware of the third force. This is connected with the state of our being, the state of our consciousness. In another state we would be aware of it in many cases where we do not see it now. Sometimes we can find examples of third force in ordinary scientific study for example, in chemistry and in biology we can find the necessity of a third force in the creation of events and phenomena.

We begin with the study of psychology. Later we shall talk more about three forces, and we may find some examples of their interaction. But it is better to be prepared and get accustomed now to the idea of the need to study these three forces.

The Law of Seven must also be described briefly. It means that no process in the world goes without interruptions. To illustrate this idea let us take a certain period of activity in which vibrations are increasing, suppose they begin at 1000 vibrations a second and increase to 2000 vibrations a second. This period is called an octave, because this law was applied to music and the period was divided into seven notes and a repetition of the first note. The octave, particularly the major octave, is really a picture or formula of a cosmic law, because, in cosmic arrangements, within one octave there are two moments when vibrations slow down by themselves. Vibrations do not develop regularly. In the major octave this is shown by the missing semi-tones; that is why we are told that it is a picture of a cosmic law; but this law has nothing to do with music.

The reason why it is necessary to understand the Law of Seven is that it plays a very important part in all events. If there were no Law of Seven everything in the world would go to its final conclusion, but because of this law everything deviates. For instance, if rain began it would go on without stopping, if floods began, they would cover everything, if an earthquake began it would go on indefinitely. But they stop, because of the Law of Seven, because at every missing semi-tone things deviate, they do not go by straight lines. The Law of Seven also explains why there are no straight lines in nature. Everything in our life and our machine is also based on this law. So, we shall study it in the work of our organism because we have to study ourselves not only psychologically, not only in connection with our mental life, but also in connection with our physical life. In our physical processes we find many examples of the working of this law.

At the same time, the Law of Seven explains that, if you know how and at what moment to do it, you can give an additional shock to an octave and keep the line straight. We can observe in human activity how people start to do one thing and after sometimes do quite a different thing, still calling it by the first name without noticing that things have completely changed. But in personal work, particularly in work connected with this system, we must learn how to keep these octaves from deviating, how to keep a straight line. Otherwise, we shall not find anything.

We have to keep returning to psychology even when studying other sides of the system, because only with the help of the psychological study shall we really increase our knowledge; without it we shall only be learning words. Only when we know how to study ourselves psychologically, in relation to the working of our minds, our cognition and so on, can we begin to understand something.

I will try to give some examples of how self-study should begin. We spoke already of lying and I gave a possible definition of psychology as 'the study of lying'. So, one of the first and most important things for you to observe is lying. Very much akin to lying are our illusions, things about which we deceive ourselves, wrong ideas, wrong convictions, wrong views and so on. All these must be studied because until we begin to understand our illusions, we can never see truth. In everything we must first separate our illusions from facts. Only then will it be possible to see whether we can really learn something new.

One of the most important and most difficult illusions to conquer is our conviction that we can 'do'. Try to understand what that means. We think that we make a plan, decide, start, and achieve what we want, but the system explains that man 1, 2 and 3 cannot 'do', cannot do anything, everything just happens to him. That may sound strange, particularly now when everybody thinks they can do something. But little by little you will understand that many things we are accustomed to say about man generally could only be true about men of higher level and do not apply to men of our low level. If you say that man can 'do', that would be right about man No. 7 or No. 6. Even man No. 5 can do something in comparison with us, but we can do nothing. You might say, too, that you think man has consciousness. That would be right in relation to man No. 5, 6 or 7, beginning at No. 5, and if you were to say that man has conscience, that would be right in relation to man No. 4 but not in relation to man No. 1, 2 and 3. We must learn to distinguish to which category of man things refer, because some things are right in relation to one category but wrong in relation to another.

It is very important to understand that man cannot 'do', because this is the basis of our view of ourselves, and even when we become disappointed with ourselves, we think that other people can 'do'. We cannot accept completely and fully that things happen mechanically and that nobody gives a push to them. At first it is difficult to see this on a big scale, but you will see it very soon in yourself. In studying yourself, if you try to do certain things which generally you do not do, for instance, if you try to remember yourself, if you try to be aware of yourself, then very soon you will see whether you can 'do' something or not. And in most cases, you will find that you cannot do it.

Q. If we can do nothing with ourselves as man 1, 2 or 3, must we call in some outside agency if we want to be aware?

A. There are no outside agencies we can call in because we are mechanical. We can do nothing, but there are differences in doing and self-observation will show them; for instance, we can show some resistance. We may have some wish, some tendency, but we can show resistance to it, and we can go on resisting every day. In quite small things we have choice, so although we cannot 'do' in quotation marks there are many small things we can do now. For instance, we can try to be aware of ourselves. Certainly, we cannot do it for a long time. But do we try or not? This is the question. In observing these different actions of ours we see that, as a general principle, although man 1, 2 and 3 can 'do' nothing, if he becomes interested in something, if he begins to want something more than ordinary things, then he is not always on the same level and he can choose moments when he can start doing in a very elementary sense.

Another very important problem we must consider is the idea of good and evil in this system, because generally people's views are very confused on this subject, and it is necessary to establish for yourself how to understand it. From the viewpoint of the system there are only two things that can be compared or seen in man, the manifestation of mechanical laws and the manifestation of consciousness. If you want to find examples of what you can call good or bad, to arrive at some standard, you will see at once that what we call evil is always mechanical, it can never be conscious; and what we call good is always conscious, it cannot be mechanical. It will take a long time to see the reason for that, because these ideas of mechanical and conscious are mixed in our mind. We never describe them in the right way, so this is the next point you must consider and study.

Further, in connection with the question of good and evil, we must try to understand the relative positions of morality and conscience. What is morality and what is conscience? We can say first of all that morality is not constant. It is different in different countries, in different centuries, in different decades, in different classes, with people of different education, and so on. What may be moral in the Caucasus may be immoral in Europe. For instance, in some countries blood revenge is a most moral thing; if a man refuses to kill somebody who killed his distant uncle, he would be considered most immoral. But in Europe nobody would think that, in fact most people would think a man very immoral to kill anybody, even a relative of somebody who had killed his uncle. So, morality is always different, and it always changes. But conscience never changes. Conscience is a kind of emotional understanding of truth in certain definite relations, generally in relation to behavior, to people and so on. This is always the same; it cannot change, and it cannot differ in one nation or another, in one country or another, in one person or another.

Try to connect in your mind what I said about the study of good and evil, mechanicalness and consciousness, morality, and conscience, and then put the question, 'Is conscious evil possible?' That will require study and observation, but from the point of view of the system there is a definite principle that conscious evil is impossible; mechanicalness must be unconscious.

Q. The idea of evil being always unconscious is rather difficult to understand. Can you explain it a little more?

A. I said, first of all try to find for yourself what you call evil, not by definition but by examples. When you have a certain number of examples, ask yourself, could they be conscious? Could evil things be done consciously? Later you will see they could be done only unconsciously. Another answer is that all you call evil can happen mechanically, and it always does happen mechanically, so it has no need of consciousness.

I said that we should study the ideas of this system chiefly in connection with the evolution of man, and I explained that by evolution we must understand a conscious process and conscious efforts, continuous and connected. There is no mechanical evolution as it is sometimes understood. Evolution, if it is possible, can only be conscious, and the beginning of evolution is always the evolution of consciousness, it cannot be the evolution of anything else. If consciousness begins to evolve, other things begin to grow and evolve. If consciousness remains on the same level, everything else remains on the same level.

There are several things which it is important to understand from the very beginning in relation to evolution. First, that out of the very large quantity of men 1, 2 and 3, only very few can become No. 4, 5, 6 and 7. or even begin. That must be very well understood, because if we begin to think that everybody can evolve, we cease to understand the conditions necessary for the beginning of evolution, as I described them for you in the example of escape from prison.

Q. Have all races of men the same possibility of development?

A. That is an interesting question. I asked this question myself when I first came to this work and I was told that it had been discussed in very important schools at a very important period, and that after making all possible experiments in this connection they came to the conclusion that there is no difference, from the point of view of possible development, between the white, yellow, black, brown, and red races. At the present time, the white and yellow races have predominance, whereas in the past it was probably one of the others. For instance, the Sphinx reminds one of a negro, not a European.

Q. In connection with what you said about good and evil, could a follower of this system take part in war?

A. It is his business. There are no external prohibitions or conditions.

Q. But could he reconcile the two?

A. Again it is his business. This particular system leaves man very free. He wants to create consciousness and will. Neither consciousness nor will can be created by following certain external restrictions. One must be free.

You must understand that external things matter least of all. It is the internal things that are important, internal war.

Q. There are many things that seem to me evil which I am capable of committing.

A. You cannot take yourself because you could only take examples of evil which you have committed already. So, it is better to take the idea in general. Find all possible examples, I do not mean accidents or mistakes, because many crimes are accidental but take all that we call definite intentional evil, and you will see that it does not need consciousness; one mechanical action, and everything goes on.

Q. It creates the illusion of choice.

A. That is the greatest illusion, the illusion of 'doing' and the illusion of choice.

These things belong to a higher level. Beginning at No. 4 one already begins to have choice, but men 1, 2 and 3 have very little choice.

Q. Wouldn't you say that the study of black magic was conscious evil?

A. Do you know anybody who studied it, with the exception of people who read books with terrifying pictures and deceive themselves?

Q. If you deliberately set to work to deceive another person is not that deliberate evil?

A. Most probably you could not help yourself; there was such a pressure of circumstances or something, that you could not do otherwise.

These are all difficult problems, and they take a long time to get used to, because we are accustomed to think in the wrong way. For instance, when we look at historical events, we take as conscious just those things that cannot be conscious and the things that may be conscious, we take as mechanical, as a kind of process.

Now if we return to this idea that only a very few can develop and find hidden possibilities in themselves, the question naturally arises: What determines the difference? Why do some people have a chance, and some people have no chance? It is quite true that some people have no chance from the very beginning. They are born in such circumstances that they can learn nothing, or they are themselves defective in some way so, we exclude defective people because there is nothing to be said about them. We are interested in people who are in normal circumstances, and they themselves must be normal, with ordinary possibilities of learning, understanding and so on. Now, out of these people only a very few will be capable of making even the first step in the way of development. How and why is it so?

All people in the ordinary conditions of life live under two kinds of influences. First there are the influences created in life, desire for riches, fame and so on, which we call influences A. Secondly, there are other influences which come from outside life, which work in the same conditions although they are different, and we call these influences B. They reach man in the form of religion, literature, or philosophy. These influences of the second kind are conscious in their origin. Influences A are mechanical from the beginning. Man can meet these B influences, or he can pass them by without noticing them, or he can hear them and think that he understands them, use the words and at the same time have no real understanding at all. These two influences really determine the further development of man. If man accumulates influences B, the results of these influences crystallize in him (I use the word crystallize in the ordinary sense) and form in him a certain kind of centre of attraction which we call magnetic centre.

The compact mass of memory of these influences attracts him in a certain direction or makes him turn in a certain direction. When magnetic centre is formed in man it will be easier for him to attract to himself more influences B, and not to be distracted by influences A. With ordinary people influences A can take so much of their time that nothing is left for other influences, and they are hardly affected at all by influences B. But if this magnetic centre in man grows, then after some time he meets another man, or a group of people, from whom he can learn something different, something that is not included in influences B, and which we call influence C. This influence is conscious in origin and action and can only be transmitted by direct instruction. Influences B can come through books and works of art and things like that, but influence C can only come by direct contact. If a man in whom magnetic centre has grown meets with a man or a group through whom he comes into contact with influence C, that means that he has made the first step. Then there is a possibility of development for him.

Q. What does the first step mean?

A. It is connected with the idea of a 'path' or 'way'. What is important to understand is that the way does not begin on the ordinary level of life; it begins on a higher level. The first step is the moment when one meets with influence C. From this moment there begins a staircase with a number of steps which have to be climbed before the way can be reached. The way does not begin at the bottom, but only after the last step has been climbed.

Q. What do you call a normal man?

A. It may seem paradoxical, but we have no other definition, it means a man who can develop.

Q. Is there any relationship between influences B and influences A? When influences B come into a man, do they affect influences A and transform them?

A. They may affect them, but at the same time one necessarily excludes another. Man, lives on the earth under these two different influences; he may choose only one, or he may have both. When you speak of influences A and B, you begin to speak about facts. If you replace this expression by one or another definite fact, you will see in which relation they stand. It is very easy.

At this point the question naturally arises: Why is it so difficult for a man to start changing himself, to come to a possibility of growing? Because, you see, we must remember that man is created in a very interesting way by nature. He is developed up to a certain point; after this point he must develop himself. Nature does not develop man beyond a certain point. Later we shall learn in full detail up to what point man is developed and how his further development must begin, and we shall see why from this point of view he could never develop himself and why he cannot be developed by nature. But before that we must understand certain general conditions.

It is difficult for a man even to start any kind of work on himself because he lives in a very bad place in the universe. At first that must sound a very strange idea. We do not realize that there are better and worse places in the universe, and we certainly do not realize that we happen to be in almost the worst place. We fail to realize it because, from one point of view, our knowledge of the universe is too complicated. From another point of view, it does not take into account real facts.

If we look for the nearest place to us in the universe, we realize that we live on the earth, and that the moon is under the influence of the earth. At the same time, we see that the earth is one of the planets of the solar system, that there are bigger planets, probably more powerful than the earth, and that all these planets, taken together, must somehow affect and control the earth. Next in scale comes the sun, and we realize that the sun controls all the planets and the earth at the same time. If you think from this point of view, you will already have a different idea of the solar system, although there is nothing new in these things: it is only a question of how to relate one thing to another.

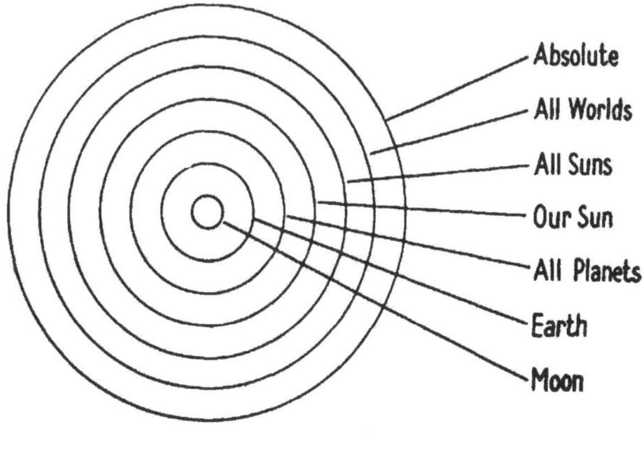

Earth is one of the planets of the solar system and the sun is one of the stars of the Milky Way. Beyond that we can take all possible worlds. This is all we know from the ordinary point of view. As a purely philosophical term we can add to that a condition or relationship of things which we call the Absolute, a state in which everything is one. Now we can express this relation of moon to earth, earth to planets and so on in a slightly different way.

- ○ **Absolute. Unknown beginning of all.**
- ○ **All Worlds. All galaxies similar and dissimilar to our galaxy.**
- ○ **All Suns. Our galaxy.**
- ○ **Our Sun. Our solar system.**
- ○ **All Planets. All planets of the solar system.**
- ○ **Earth.**
- ○ **Moon.**

Looking from the top down, we can begin to understand the vast difference in scale if we compare All Suns with our Sun, or Earth with All Planets. We can understand that they stand in a certain definite relation of scale to one another. The smallest is the Moon, and beyond the Moon we know nothing. The whole of this is called the Ray of Creation. There are other rays, because this ray does not include the whole universe, but since we live on the earth, and it passes through the earth we belong to this Ray of Creation. From this diagram it is clear what is meant by a bad place in the universe. The worst place is the moon, but the earth is almost as bad. It is like living near the North Pole, which explains why so many things are difficult on the earth. We cannot change or do anything about it, but when we know, we can adapt, and in that way, we can escape many things which otherwise we could not escape. But we must not let our imagination run away with us and tell us that we can escape altogether.

I just want to add one thing. For reasons which are difficult to explain as yet, in the Ray of Creation all these worlds are connected with each other: influences pass from higher to lower but there is a gap between Planets and Earth. In order to bridge this gap so that influences from All Planets could reach the earth a certain instrument was invented. It is a kind of sensitive film which surrounds the earth, that is to say. Organic Life on Earth. So plants, animals and men serve a definite purpose; they serve for communication between earth and planets. With the help of organic life which can receive and retain them, planetary influences penetrate to the earth. This is the meaning and reason for organic life on earth.

Q. You assume organic life only on the earth. Do you assume there is nothing on other planets?

A. No, not at all, but we are interested in organic life on earth, because we are on the earth and we are part of organic life on the earth, so we speak only about earth. All other planets we take together as a mass, but about earth we speak differently. This is the principle of scale. The nearer something is to you the nearer to full scale is your study. If you study this room you need to know how many people are coming and how many chairs will be required; you study in detail, but if you take the house only, you do not need to know such details. And if you take the street, it is again different. In the same way we study the Ray of Creation on different scales. We speak about organic life on the earth, but we do not speak about organic life on any other planet; we have no way of studying it except on the earth.

I will give you a few more details about the Ray of Creation which will explain to you what I mean when I say that the earth is a bad place in the universe. You will remember that, earlier, I said we should have to come to the study of the fundamental laws of the universe, and I said that the two laws we should study would be the Law of Three and the Law of Seven, and then I also mentioned the principle of scale. Now you have already met with this principle, and you understand that we do not study everything on the same scale. This is really the weakest point in ordinary science; scientists try to study everything on the same scale, without understanding that it is not necessary at all. In fact, quite the opposite. For all practical purposes we must learn to study things on different scales.

We must return to the Law of Three. You will remember how it was explained that everything that happens is the result of the action of three forces and that two forces by themselves cannot produce any effect. I will try to connect this idea with the Ray of Creation.

The Absolute is World 1, for the three forces in it make one. By his own will and consciousness the Absolute creates worlds. It is all intentional there and each force in it occupies each place. This is incomprehensible to us. In the next world, World 3, there are the same three forces, only they are already divided. These three forces again produce worlds of which we take one, but this World 6 is different from World 3 which is in contact with the Absolute, for it is already mechanical. World 6 has three forces from the preceding world and three of its own. The next world, World 12, has three forces from the world of the second order, six from the world of the third order and three of its own. The next world, World 24, has twenty-four forces, the one after forty-eight forces and the last ninety-six forces.

World	3	All Worlds	3
World	6	All Suns	6 (3+ 3)
World	12	Sun	12 (3+ 6+ 3)
World	24	All Planets	24 (3+ 6+ 12+ 3)
World	48	Earth	48 (3+ 6+ 12+ 24+ 3)
World	96	Moon	96 (3+ 6+ 12+ 24+ 48+ 3)

These figures refer to the number of laws governing each world. The greater the number of laws, the harder it is to change anything. For instance, man lives on earth, which is under forty-eight laws. He himself is under many more laws, but even these forty-eight laws make it very difficult for him to change anything because every little thing is governed by these laws. Fortunately, not all of the laws under which man lives are obligatory for him, so he may escape from some of them, and his possibility of evolution is fundamentally connected with escaping from certain laws. By climbing the prison wall, too, a man escapes from laws.

* * *

CHAPTER II

Man is an incomplete being—He lives below his legitimate level—Revaluation of old values—'Useful' and ''harmful'—Illusions—Man is asleep—Practical self-study—Study of obstacles—Psychology of lying— Man is a machine—Creating a permanent 'I'—Allegory of a house in disorder—Roles—Buffers—Self-remembering—Why this system cannot be popular—Prison—Formulation of aim—To be free— Sin—Repentance —Helping humanity—Attraction and repulsion—Self-observation— Division of all that belongs to man into seven categories—Knowledge and being—Their relationship—We can have more knowledge—Necessity of changing being—Understanding— Harmful functions—Expression of negative emotions—Unnecessary talk—Difference between this system and others—levels of being— Thinking in different categories—Dangers of the present situation.

I would like you to revise in your memory what I Said last time, because many things I said were not fully developed. I only gave hints, a general idea, of things we have to study; so, it is necessary to recall the order of things and their relative importance. Because some things I said were essential for the understanding of further ideas, while some I brought in merely in explanation of other things.

But first I would like to stress again one important point. This system belongs to the class of systems which regard man as an incomplete being and study him from the point of view of his possible development. Ordinary psychology is very far from reality. The man it studies is an imaginary quantity. Man is not what he is supposed to be. We ascribe to ourselves many qualities we do not possess. We are not conscious. If we are not conscious, we cannot have unity, cannot have individuality, cannot have an Ego or 'I'. All these things are invented by man to keep the illusion of consciousness. Man *can* be conscious, but at present he is not. It must be recognized that man lives below his legitimate level. There are also other things man may attain, but now I speak of what belongs to him by right, but what he does not have.

This system turns everything we know or ever thought of upside down. It cannot be reconciled with ordinary psychological ideas. We have to decide how we are to see man: as an egg or as a bird. And if we see him as an egg, we must not ascribe to him properties of a bird. When we see him as an egg the whole psychology becomes different: all human life becomes the life of embryos, of incomplete beings. And for some the meaning of life becomes the possibility of passing to another state.

It is very important to understand what is a complete being and what is an incomplete being, because if this is not understood from the beginning it will be difficult to go further. Perhaps an example will help to illustrate what I mean. Let us compare a horse-carriage with an aero plane. An aero plane has many possibilities that an ordinary carriage does not have, but at the same time an aero plane can be used as an ordinary carriage. It would be very clumsy and inconvenient and very expensive, but you can attach two horses to it and travel in an aero plane by road. Suppose the man who has this aero plane does not know that it has an engine and can move by itself and suppose he learns about the engine, then he can dispense with the horses and use it as a motor car. But it will still be too clumsy. Suppose that the man studies this machine and discovers that it can fly. Certainly, it will have many advantages which he missed when he used the aero plane as a carriage. This is what we are doing with ourselves; we use ourselves as a carriage, when we could fly. But examples are one thing and facts are another. There is no need of allegories and analogies, for we can speak about actual facts if we begin to study consciousness in the right way.

If we return for a moment to the analogy of an aero plane, what is the reason why our aero plane cannot fly? Naturally the first reason is because we do not know the machine, how to work it and how to put it in motion. And the second reason is that as a result of this ignorance the machine works at a very slow speed. The effect of this slow speed is much greater than if we compare a horse-carriage and an aero plane.

To follow the ideas and methods of the system fully, it is necessary to recognize and agree upon two points: the low level of consciousness and the practical absence of will and individuality in man. When these are accepted, it is very useful and necessary to learn the right use of two ideas, two words, 'useful' and 'harmful'; because it is rather difficult to apply these words to a psychological state and find what is useful in the psychological structure of man and what is harmful in it. But if you regard man from the point of view of his possible development, it becomes dear that what helps his development is useful, and what hinders it is harmful. It is very strange that it is necessary even to explain this, but unfortunately our ordinary thought, particularly when it meets with serious problems, docs do not use this idea; somehow, we lose the understanding of what is useful and harmful. Our thought has acquired many bad habits, and one of them is thinking without purpose. Our thinking has become automatic; we are quite satisfied if we think of and develop possible side-issues without having any idea why we are doing it. From the point of view of this system such thinking is useless. All study, all thinking, and investigation must have one aim, one purpose in view, and this aim must be attaining consciousness. It is useless to study oneself without this purpose. There are reasons to study oneself only if one has already realized that one does not have consciousness and one wishes to attain it. Otherwise, it becomes just futile. Attaining consciousness is connected with the gradual liberation from mechanicalness, for man as he is fully and completely under mechanical laws. The more a man attains consciousness, the more he leaves mechanicalness, which means he becomes more free from accidental mechanical laws.

The first step in acquiring consciousness is the realization that we are not conscious. But this illusion cannot be changed alone, for there are many others. As I said earlier, the worst of them is the illusion that we can 'do'. All our life is based on this illusion. We always think that we are doing when, in reality, we are not doing anything, everything happens.

Another illusion is that we are awake. When we realize that we are asleep we will see that all history is made by people who are asleep. Sleeping people fight, make laws; sleeping people obey or disobey them. The worst of our illusions are the wrong ideas among which we live, and which govern our lives. If we could change our attitude towards these wrong ideas and understand what they are, this in itself would be a great change and would immediately change other things.

Now, it would be good if we start in this way: you have been thinking during the week, so try to remember what was not clear in what you have heard and ask questions, and then I will develop that line of thought.

Q. If we are not conscious, are we able to judge what is useful for us and what is harmful?

A. I said that self-observation cannot be impersonal, for we are personally interested in the right work of our machine. Right work of the organism is profitable for us, wrong work is harmful. One must have a simple commercial attitude to one's life and inner functions, and one must know what is profit and what is loss, so one cannot observe oneself quite impartially like some historical events that happened a thousand years ago. When a man adopts this attitude to himself, he is ready to begin practical self- study, for practical self-study means the study of the most mechanical things. Some functions in us can become conscious, others can never become conscious. Instinctive functions, for instance, have no need to become conscious, but there are many others, our whole life is filled with them which it is very important to make conscious or, if they cannot become conscious, to stop or eliminate, for they are really harmful. They are not merely mechanical in the sense that they are automatic; they are due to the wrong work of the machine which has gone on for a long time. So, they have already caused definite harm; things have become broken or twisted or strained.

Q. In trying to study myself I can find nothing real, nothing tangible.

A. Study what is there, whether it is real or unreal. You cannot study only what is real, you have to study what is there. It is not an obstacle to self-study if you find nothing real you must study what you find. Actually, you are quite right that there is nothing real, but one must study oneself and study obstacles.

The chief obstacle to the attainment of self-consciousness is that we think we have it. One will never get self-consciousness so long as one believes that one has it. There are many other things we think we have, and because of this we cannot have them.

There is individuality or oneness we think we are one, indivisible. We think we have will, or that if we do not have it always, we *can* have it, and other things. There are many aspects to this, for if we do not have one thing, we cannot have another. We think that we have these things, and this happens because we do not know the meaning of the words we use.

There is a definite obstacle, a definite reason why we cannot have consciousness as we are. This chief obstacle in the way of development is lying. I have already mentioned lying, but we must speak more about it, for we do not know what lying means because we have never studied this question seriously. Yet the psychology of lying is really the most important part of the study of the human being. If a man could be described as a zoological type, he would be described as a lying animal.

I shall leave out all external lying and take only a man's lying to himself about himself. This is the reason why we are in the state in which we are now, and why we cannot come to a better, a higher, a more powerful, more effective state of consciousness. According to the system we are now studying we cannot know truth, because truth can be reached only in objective consciousness. So, we cannot define what truth is; but if we take it that lying is the opposite of truth, we can define lying.

The most serious lying is when we know perfectly well that we do not and cannot know the truth about things and yet never act accordingly. We always think and act as though we knew the truth. This is lying. When I know that I do not know something, and at the same time say that I know, or act as though I knew it, it is lying. For instance, we know nothing about ourselves, and we really *know* that we know nothing, yet we never recognize or admit the fact; we never confess it even to our selves, we act and think and speak as though we knew who we are. This is the origin, the beginning of lying.

When we understand this and follow this line, and when we try to connect this idea with everything we think, everything we say, everything we do, we will begin to remove the obstacles which lie on the way to consciousness. But the psychology of lying is much more difficult than we think because there are many different kinds of lying and many very subtle forms hard to discover in ourselves. In others we see them comparatively easily, but not in ourselves.

Q. If we do not know what truth is, how do we know when we lie?

A. You know that you cannot know the truth, and if you say you do know, or can know it, it would be a lie, because no one can know the truth in the state in which we are. Do not think philosophically, take it in relation to facts. People speak about everything as though they knew. If you ask a man whether there are people on the moon, he will have an opinion about it. And so, with everything else. We have opinions about everything, and all these opinions are lying, particularly about our selves. We do not know about states of consciousness, or the different functions, or the speed of functions, or their relation to one another. We do not know about how functions are divided. We know nothing, yet we think we know about ourselves. All we have is opinions, and they are all lies.

Q. If all opinions are lies, should we avoid opinions?

A. You must know their value. The first lie we tell ourselves is when we say 'I'.

It is a lie because in saying 'I' we presume certain things: we presume a certain unity and a certain power. And if I say 'I' today and say 'I' tomorrow, it is supposed to be the same 'I', when in reality there is no connection between them. We are in this present state because of certain obstacles or certain facts in ourselves, and the most important fact that we do not understand is that we have no right to say 'I', for it will be a lie. When you begin to observe yourself, you will see that it is really so: there are 'I's in you which do not know one another and never come into contact. For instance, begin to study your likes and dislikes and you will see that you can like one thing one moment and like another thing another moment, and the two are so opposed to one another that you will realize at once that those 'I's never meet. If you observe your decisions, you will see that one 'I' decides and another has to carry out the decision, and this one is either unwilling to do it or never heard about it. If you find one thing one does not lie to oneself about you will be very exceptional. Being surrounded by these lies, born and educated in these lies, we cannot be any different from what we are; we are just the result, the product of this lying.

Q. If I try to find truth and find it impossible, should I not have to separate myself from the everyday world?

A. You would then study an artificial being, not a real one. You can study yourself only in the conditions in which you are because you are the result of these conditions. You cannot study yourself apart from your conditions.

Q. Isn't there anything common to all 'I's?

A. Only one thing, that they are mechanical. To be mechanical means to depend on external circumstances.

Q. From what you said it seems very difficult to study oneself without lying to oneself.

A. No, lying must stop. You must remember the principle lies can only produce lies. Only when you know the chief types of lying will you be able, I do not say to struggle with them, but to observe them. Struggle comes later. Many things are necessary in order to struggle with something in ourselves; for a long time, we can only study. When we know the general arrangement and classification of things in ourselves, only then does the possibility come of struggling with something. Such as we are we cannot change anything, because man is a very well-balanced machine, balanced in the sense that one thing conditions another. Things look disconnected, but in actual fact they are connected, because each thing is balanced by many other things.

Q. Would you mind expounding what you mean by machine? Machines cannot have potentialities; they cannot have a hope of getting consciousness.

A. Analogies cannot be complete because they cannot be carried on indefinitely. This too is a limitation of our mind or, if you like, a limitation of our consciousness. So, the comparison with a machine cannot be carried on in every direction. But man is a machine in quite a real, quite a definite sense; he cannot produce any action from himself, he is only a transmitting station, nothing more, and as such he is a machine. If a man could have an idea or could do something without external causes acting for him, then he would not be a machine, or would not be completely a machine. As he is, he is completely a machine, particularly in the state of consciousness in which we are. And the fact that we believe ourselves to be in quite a different state makes us even more mechanical.

Our machine is not even working rightly, so if a man wants to create favorable conditions for the possibility of inner growth which is in him, he must first become a normal machine, because as he is, he is not a normal machine. When we hear about mechanicalness, we often think that, although man is a machine, not all his functions are equally mechanical, nor are all human activities equally mechanical. Everybody finds something that he thinks less mechanical, according to his views or tastes. In reality all human activities are equally mechanical, there is no difference from this point of view between scrubbing floors and writing poetry.

Generally speaking, it must be understood that a complete revaluation of all values from the point of view of their usefulness is necessary; without revaluation we can never move from the point at which we are. We have many wrong values; we have to be brave and start on this revaluation.

Q. I understand that we have to create an 'I' out of nothing. What creates 'I'?

A. First, self-knowledge. There is a very good Eastern allegory which deals with the creation of 'I'. Man is compared to a house full of servants, without master or steward to look after them. So, the servants do what they like; none of them does his own work. The house is in a state of complete chaos, because all the servants try to do someone else's work which they are not competent to do. The cook works in the stables, the coachman in the kitchen, and so on. The only possibility for things to improve is if a certain number of servants decide to elect one of themselves as a deputy steward and in this way make him control the other servants. He can do only one thing: he puts each servant where he belongs and so they begin to do their right work. When this is done, there is the possibility of the real steward coming to replace the deputy steward and to prepare the house for the master. We do not know what the real steward means or what the master means, but we can take it that the house full of servants and the possibility of a deputy steward describes our situation. This allegory helps us to understand the beginning of the possibility of creating a permanent 'I'.

From the point of view of self-study and of work to attain one 'I', we must understand the process by which we may come from this plurality to oneness. It is a complicated process and has different stages. Between the present state of plurality of 'I's and the one controlling 'I' we wish to attain, there are certain stages of development which must be studied. But first we must understand that there are certain formations in us, without knowing which we cannot understand how we eventually come from our present state to the state of one 'I', if it is possible for us.

You see, although a great many of our 'I's are disconnected and do not even know one another, they are divided into certain groups. This does not mean that they are divided consciously; they are divided by circumstances of life. These groups of 'I's manifest themselves as roles that a man plays in his life. Everybody has a certain number of roles: one corresponds to one set of conditions, another to another and so on. Man, himself seldom notices these differences. For instance, he has one role for his work, another for his home, yet another among friends, another if he is interested in sport, and so on. These roles are easier to observe in other people than in oneself. People are often so different in different conditions that these roles become quite obvious and well defined; but sometimes they are better hidden or even played only inside without any external manifestations. All people, whether they know it or not, whether they wish it or not, have certain roles which they play. This acting is un conscious. If it could be conscious, it would be quite different, but one never notices how one passes from one role to another. Or if one notices it, one persuades oneself that one is doing it on purpose, that it is a conscious action. In reality the change is always controlled by circumstances, it cannot be controlled by man himself, because he himself does not exist yet. Sometimes there are definite contradictions between one and another role. In one role one says one thing, has certain definite views and convictions; then one passes into another role and has absolutely different convictions and says absolutely different things, without noticing it, or else thinking that one does it on purpose.

There are very definite causes which prevent man from seeing the difference between one role or mask and another. These causes are certain artificial formations called buffers. Buffer is a very good name for these appliances.

Buffers between railway carriages prevent clashing, diminish the shock. It is the same with buffers between different roles and different groups of 'I's or personalities. People can live with different personalities without them clashing, and if these personalities have no external manifestation, they exist internally all the same.

It is very useful to try to find what buffers are. Try to find how one lies to oneself with the help of buffers. Suppose one says, 'I never argue'. Then, if one really has a good conviction that one never argues, one can argue as much as one like and never notice it. This is the result of a buffer. If one has a certain number of good buffers, one is quite safe from unpleasant contradictions. Buffers are quite mechanical; a buffer is like a wooden thing, it does not adapt, but it plays its part very well: it prevents one seeing contradictions.

Q. How are roles created?

A. Roles are not created; they are not conscious. They are adaptations to circumstances.

Q. Is it difficult to stop playing a role?

A. It is not a question of stopping, it is a question of not identifying.

Q. Can some roles be good?

A. We speak only about consciousness and mechanicalness. If a role is mechanical, we must observe it and not identify with it. The most difficult thing is to act yourself consciously. We start consciously and then we usually identify.

Q. You said that one could not change any of one's 'I's, because man was so well balanced a machine that to upset this balance would be harmful?

A. Yes, but I meant someone trying to change by himself, without knowledge, without plan or system. But if you work on a plan such as this system it is different. That is why you are advised to do certain things which cannot produce any harmful effects. This system is the result of experience. Besides, in the actual stopping of the expression of unpleasant emotions, or stopping imagination and things of this kind, very little can be done at first. It is more for self-observation. You think that if you decide to do a thing you can really achieve it, but it is not so. Things go on automatically, mechanically, and you do not notice it. But if you start to oppose them you begin to notice them. So, it is more for observation than for any results. It is not so easy to get results.

Q. If you are going to stop imagination, mustn't you have some point on which to fix your mind?

A. We always have enough points on which to fix our mind, the question is can we fix it? We have the power of observation, but we cannot keep our mind on what we want to. The situation is like this we teach this self-study from different sides, if we do a little at one point, and a little at another point, and a little at a third point, together they will produce some effect and make it easier to do something on a fourth point We cannot do first one thing and then another, we have to start from all sides.

As to struggle with imagination, it is suggested just as a struggle it does not mean that we can stop it. Much more energy than we possess is needed to stop imagination, we can only attempt to stop it. We can do nothing; we can only try. We can only begin something, and it we begin many things at once we will get some results. With this system it is possible to start from many sides, and then results will appear

Q. When I try to remember myself, I cannot think or do anything else.

A. Yes, it shows how difficult it is. In the beginning, at the first attempts you make to be aware of yourself you have to use practically all your mental powers, so that nothing remains. But it does not mean that it will always be like that. It is not real self- remembering, you only study how to do it. You will find later on that consciousness can exist without thought, that consciousness is. something different from thought. You use thought just to give a push, and then it begins to move in this direction, and you become conscious without thought. Then you can think about anything you like. But in the beginning, you certainly have to use this mental energy, because it is. the only controllable energy you have except movements. But you cannot make yourself conscious by turning a wheel or running, so you have to use thinking energy at first. It does not mean that you will always have to do it, you open a door.

Q. Why is this system not widely known and popular?

A. It cannot be because of its negative character. We study the way not of acquiring but of losing. If one could acquire things at once, the system would be popular. But nothing can be promised. It is. difficult to expect people to like this, for no one likes to lose illusions. People want positive things without realizing what is. possible. They want to know straight away what they can attain. But first they must lose many things. The ideas of this system can never be popular so long as they are not distorted, because people will not agree that they are asleep, that they are machines, people who consider themselves important will always oppose this idea.

The system does not want to offer ideas to people who do not want them. If people have tried other methods and realized their futility, they may wish to try this system. This system is. only for those who need it. It is. necessary to understand man's situation and also his possibilities. As I said, man is. in prison. If he realizes he is in prison., he may wish to run away. But he may be afraid that if he runs away, he may find himself in a worse position than before, and so he may reconcile himself to staying in prison. If he decides to run away, he must understand that two conditions are necessary: he must be one of a number of people who wish to run away, for they have to dig a tunnel, and one man cannot do it alone, and secondly, they must have help from those who have run away before them. So first he must realize he is in prison; second, he must wish to run away; third, he must have friends who also wish to run away; fourth, he must have help from outside; fifth, he must work to dig the tunnel. No amount of faith or prayer can dig the tunnel for him. And he does not know what he will find when he gets out of prison. There are many reasons why one man cannot escape from prison. But twenty people may. Each of them profits by the work of the rest. What one gains, all the twenty gains.

Q. Do we progress by the process of elimination rather than construction?

A. There are two processes. First there is the process of elimination, many useless mechanical functions must be eliminated. Then there is the process of construction.

Q. You said that one's aim should be acquiring self-consciousness. But this aim seems too large for me, for I do not know what self-consciousness is. How can I understand better the idea of a right aim?

A. You should be able to understand the question of aim not necessarily to be able to give a reply. Aim is one, in general, whether large or small. You should have come already to some realizations, through your trying to study yourself, and on the basis of these realizations you may be able to formulate your aim. Let us take it in this form, can we say that our aim is freedom, that we want to be free? And can we say that we are not free now? This is sufficient for a general formulation. If we start with this formulation, we shall always be able to see where we are: we shall be able to see how far we are not free, in what we are becoming more free. This idea of absence of freedom must be studied individually by every person. In other words, everybody must be able to see in what way he is not free. It is not enough to remember words 'I am not free'; it is necessary to know it definitely. One must realize that at every moment of one's life one decides to do one thing and does another, that one wishes to go to one place and in reality, is going to another place, and so on. Again, this must not be taken literally, but everyone must find his own form of lack of freedom, peculiar to him. When everybody realizes that it will be easy to speak about it. Everybody will then understand that he is a slave and will see what it is that really governs and controls him. Then it will be simple to understand that the aim is freedom; but as long as it is merely theoretical it will serve no useful purpose. It will serve our purpose of understanding what we want only if we realize this slavery individually, in our own life, through our own practical experience.

Each one of us must find in what he is not free. He wants to know, and he cannot know; either he has no time, or perhaps he has no preparatory knowledge. He wants to *be*, he wants to remember himself, he wants to 'do' in a certain way, but things happen differently, not as he wants it. When he realizes this, he will see that the aim is freedom; and to be free one must be conscious.

Q. But freedom for a few only, not for the world?

A. You can think only of yourself. You cannot give *me* freedom, so what is the use thinking about me? But perhaps you can help another person to find something that will help *him* to become free; but only when you get something yourself, only when you yourself have become more free.

Q. How can a man ever be free? Man is so weak and there are so many forces against him!

A. He can be more free than he is now, more free relative to his present state. Look at it. from the personal point of view, not philosophically, then you will see that one can be more free or less free, because there are different moments in your life at certain moments you are less free, at other moments you are more free. When you sleep at night you are less free than in daytime, and if a fire happens when you are asleep you will die because you will not be able to get out. So, in daytime you are more free. Things must be taken simply, not philosophically. Certainly, if we begin to think philosophically that there is no such thing as freedom, then there is nothing left but to die.

Q. Is it. possible to determine the influences in life that destroy our freedom more than anything else?

A The influences that increase our slavery are our illusions, and particularly the illusion that we are free. We imagine that we are free, and this makes us ten times more slaves This is the chief influence with which we can struggle. There are many other influences which have to be struggled with, but this is the beginning, this is the first our illusions about our position, about our freedom. So first of all, it is necessary to sacrifice this illusion of freedom which we think we have. If we try to sacrifice this illusion, perhaps we shall come to the possibility of actually being more free.

Q. What meaning have ordinary values like bravery, unselfishness, and cheerfulness from the point of view of the system?

A. Sometimes they have very good meaning, sometimes no meaning at all You cannot expect a permanent meaning in such values, because ordinary views always assume words to have a permanent meaning, whereas they cannot have one.

Q. Has this system anything to say about the idea of sin?

A Sin, in a general definition, is 'everything that is unnecessary'; but we must modify this definition Sin is always the result of weakness. If I have to go somewhere and promise to be there at 12.30 and I know that if I walk fast, I shall be there in time, but instead I stop on the way to look at shop windows, this would be sin against my promise to be there at 12:30 Everything must be taken from the point of view of aim or decision, in relation to the thing you set out to do at a given moment. If you have an aim in connection with the work, then everything you do against your own work is sin. It is not a sin if you have no aim. It is not a sin to stop at shop windows, but if you have to be somewhere at a certain time and stopping will make you late, then it is a sin. We can understand sin and crime when we understand them in relation to the work. Then we can take a slightly larger view and think of the people who are just coming into the work, and then of those who may come, and so on. It is necessary to approach this problem thinking in concentric circles and begin with people who are in the work or who think themselves in the work. Then everything they do against their own understanding of the work will certainly be sin because they deceive themselves. And what they do against other people in the work either by suggestion or example is sin because their aim is to help and not to hinder. So, it is possible to understand sin only in relation to the work first, and then, later, to see it outside the work.

Q. What did you mean by saying that sin is the result of weakness?

A. You see, in the work requirements grow, many things gradually become more difficult. One takes certain decisions, and one of the first is to make efforts, to go against the ordinary way which is always to avoid efforts and to make things as easy as possible. If one tries to work, one makes a decision to go against this tendency, to make things more difficult. Again, if it remains merely a mental decision, if it does not lead to any action, it is nonsense and is certainly sin against oneself

Q. Can you go from the word 'sin' to the word 'repentance'? I take it that repentance is something quite different from the usual conception of it.

A. In the work, bad things cancel many good things, but good things do not cancel bad things. Bad things can only be cancelled by repentance It does not at all mean that a man does something and then repents and says to himself, 'I will not do it again' because he will. If one has done a thing, the trace of it remains, so that it is easier to do it a second time, and this creates momentum. One can sometimes overcome this momentum by repentance, which means suffering

Q. You call it repentance in so far as it does overcome momentum?

A Repentance may be good, but not strong enough to overcome momentum. But, if it does overcome it, then it is 'repentance'. Sincere repentance is a big force in the work. Our tendencies always make us do things which are against the work. They do not necessarily assume the same form, which makes it deceptive I could do something in one form and then follow it up not in the same form but in the same way. But if I repent rightly and at the right moment, I can stop this tendency

Q. Then real repentance necessarily means change of being?

A. I would not call it change of being, but simply stopping a tendency.

Q. Is there no way in which we can help humanity?

A. We always start with the idea that things should be put right. But suppose some man acquires power and begins to put things right. He may make them so bad that some higher power may have to come to put them right again, and this may mean destroying the earth. This explains another thing, the difficulty of acquiring what we may call higher powers. It is as though some definite conscious mind prevents one from acquiring higher powers, because immediately one would want to abuse them. It looks as though you can get these powers only when these higher minds or conscious beings are sure that you will not interfere. But there is no conscious observer, there are laws, and they are in you. They are sort of automatic brakes in you which will prevent your interfering.

Q. What is the good of having these powers if you cannot use them?

A. Evidently at a given moment forces in the world have to fight it out among themselves, and higher powers do not want to interfere, evidently for a certain definite reason. If the positive side, the one opposed to chaos is sufficiently strong, it will conquer. If it is weak, it has to be destroyed, and then perhaps something new will appear. There are many allusions to this idea in the Bible or maybe they are only allegories. It all shows that things have to be fought out on one level, so there can be no interference.

Q. You said that a man has no will. Then what do you call it when a person makes a very real effort to overcome a habit, or not to do what he would like to do?

A. It is either attraction to something, or repulsion from something. Either he is afraid of something, or dislikes something, and that creates repulsion; or someone told him he could get something and that creates attraction. It is not in him; it is in things. Things either attract or repel him, but he calls it his will.

Q. You regard it as quite valueless then?

A. It is mechanical; it is of no value. It may have an objective value, in the sense that he may get something from it in the material sense. But that is not the effort I speak about. Effort begins only from one thing, the effort to awake.

Q. Can man develop consciousness by his own efforts?

A. No, he cannot do it by his own efforts alone. First of all, he must have a certain knowledge, and a certain explanation of methods; and there are many other difficulties besides. Man is a machine, a machine which works under external influences. This machine of man 1, 2 and 3 does not know itself, but when a man begins to know himself, he already becomes a different machine; this is how development begins. But he cannot get the necessary knowledge by himself.

Q. When you say that self-observation is the way towards self-consciousness, must one observe during the exact experience?

A. As much as one can. In the beginning it may be difficult, but very soon you will find it possible. When you realize that you can think with one part of your mind and observe with another part there will be no complication or confusion.

Q. Is the first step to try and realize completely that we know nothing at all?

A. Very useful if you can, but we cannot do that, we are so sure of many things.

Q. Is it a thing to aim at?

A. We can aim at it as much as we like, but we can never achieve it in the ordinary way. If we learn new things about ourselves, things we did not know before, then we can compare what we knew before and what we have learned now. Without comparison we can achieve nothing.

Last time I explained the division of man into seven categories. This division, connected with the idea of man's possible evolution, gives a very good method for understanding the differences or divisions of many things. For instance, from the beginning we take different manifestations of man in different fields of activity, in religion, science, art and so on, and try to look at them from the point of view of this division into seven categories. You will see at once that if there are seven categories of man there must be, correspondingly, seven categories of everything that belongs to man. We do not know about man No. 5, 6 and 7, but we know the difference between man 1, 2 and 3, and so we can easily understand that religion of man No. 1, whatever it may be called, will be a primitive religion, simplified in all senses. Gods are simple, virtues are simple, and sins are simple everything is simple, because man No. 1 does not like to think much. Sentimental, emotional religion, full of illusions and imagination, will be the religion of man No. 2. And religion composed of theories, words, and definitions for everything will be the religion of man No. 3. These are the only kinds of religion we know, although if men of higher levels exist, there must also be religion of man No. 5, religion of man No. 6 and religion of man No. 7.

It is the same with art, there is art No. 1, art No. 2 and art No. 3, and we know nothing else. But there are some works of art remaining from very old days which evidently belong to men of higher consciousness. If we find such works of art, we will see that we do not understand them, they are beyond our level. From this point of view all ordinary art, art of man No. 1, 2 and 3, is called subjective art, for it is based only on a subjective understanding or subjective feeling of things.

In science it is even easier to understand the difference. Certainly science No. 1, 2 and 3 is all we know. It uses man's present state of consciousness and present functions as an instrument for getting certain results. Science No. 4 will begin with improvement of instruments. If you have to work in any particular branch of science, you have a certain instrument for this work and get certain results. But suppose you can have a better instrument; you will immediately get better results. So, science No. 4 is connected with improving the instrument of knowing, with improving man's functions and state of consciousness.

Q. Can you tell us more what man 1, 2 and 3 means?

A. This refers to the centre of gravity at moments of important decisions. Man

No. 3 would act from theory, man No. 2 on the basis of emotional likes and dislikes, man No. 1 on the basis of physical likes and dislikes.

Q. To understand examples of conscious art one must have knowledge that an average person has not got?

A. Not only knowledge, but knowledge and being. There are two sides of us which must be developed.

In speaking about knowledge and being it is necessary to start from the beginning. Try to think how you look at it yourself, what your attitude to those two ideas was before you met this system. We are all in the same position. We want knowledge, but we do not realize that there are obstacles in ourselves that prevent us from acquiring this knowledge.

I will start with myself. Before I met the system, I read a great deal and made many experiments. From these experiments I got interesting states, understood several laws, and I naturally wanted a continuation of these states. But I saw that for this more knowledge was necessary. Then I met this system. In the system particular stress was laid on *being*. According to this system no more knowledge is possible until one's being is changed.

Soon after we heard about knowledge and being our groups divided into two camps. The first camp thought that the whole thing was change of being, that with change of being we would get more from the knowledge we already have. The second camp (to which I believe I alone belonged) said that even in our present state of being we can get much more knowledge than we have, that we are not so saturated with knowledge that we cannot absorb more.

Later I understood that both are necessary. Take an example of two men: one knows the four rules of arithmetic, the other does not. Naturally the first will be in a better position, although their level of being is the same. The more a man knows about mathematics, the better is his position in a certain profession. So, knowledge can increase even with the same being. And he may know more not only in mathematics; he may know many other things, have more psychological knowledge.

On the other hand, you notice that you give two people knowledge (I am speaking of psychological knowledge), and one gets it, while the other cannot. Evidently his being is not prepared. So, people are not in the same position in this respect.

The relationship of knowledge and being is a very big question. I want you to think about it and follow what I have just said. Try to find your own examples. Knowledge can lead very far. The question is, can one take it? Can one absorb it? One kind of knowledge we can get, another kind we cannot, so we cannot speak in general about it. For instance, take psychological knowledge: such as we are we can learn very much, and certain things can become much dearer. But every moment a man's know ledge depends on his being. This is what we do not understand.

A man can get only as much knowledge as his being allows, otherwise his knowledge will be just words. If knowledge is given to several people, one of them gets it, others do not. Why? Evidently because their being is different.

Q. I do not understand clearly what 'being' is.

A. It is you, what you are. The more you know yourself, the more you know your being. If you have never learnt that you have being, the being of all people will be the same to you. Someone who has never heard of self-remembering, if you ask him, will say that he can remember himself. This is one being. Another knows he does not remember himself; this is a different being.

A third is beginning to remember himself, this is a third being. This is how it must be taken.

We understand the difference of objects, but in ordinary thinking we do not understand the difference of being. What do we learn in this system? First that we are not one, that we have many 'I's, that there is no central 'I' in control. This is the state of our being. The result is mechanicalness, we are machines. If we manage to be less mechanical, less divided in ourselves, if we manage to have more control of ourselves, it will mean that our being has changed.

When I met this system, it showed me that change of being was necessary, because we are not what we think ourselves to be. If we were what we think we are, if we had consciousness, will, if we could 'do', then only knowledge would be necessary. But we all think of ourselves differently from what we are in reality. And it is exactly this difference between what we are and what we think we are that shows what is lacking in our being. So, two things are necessary: change of knowledge and change of being.

Q. But we are constantly changing!

A. No, we are in one room, running from one corner to another, not changing. In one corner we think we are one thing; in another we think we are different. We cannot change just because we have gone from one comer to another. What looks like change is change through imitation, change of conditions, likes, and dislikes.

This state of consciousness in which we are now always moves up and down. 'Down' means that we are nearer to sleep, 'up' means that we are nearer to the possibility of awakening. We are never in exactly the same state, but these small changes only mean marking time on the same spot.

So, you see, evolution of man is quite possible, but it is possible only by changing knowledge and changing being; and changing being means acquiring consciousness. It cannot come by itself, it cannot 'happen'.

Q. Does one acquire knowledge of oneself through self-observation?

A. Self-observation is connected with certain definite practices. If you just start observing how things happen, you will miss many things, but if you try to struggle against some of the things you see, for instance against small habits, you will at once begin to see many things which ordinarily you do not notice. Everyone has many small habits, habits of walking, habits of moving their hands, habits of sitting, standing, speaking in a certain way. This struggle is not for any particular results but merely for self-observation. Perhaps later you will find that you have to get rid of certain habits, but at present this struggle should be merely for self-study

At the same time, if we want to develop consciousness and improve our functions, almost from the very beginning of self-observation we are advised to try and stop some of our functions which are not only useless but definitely harmful. For instance, in observing yourself, particularly in observing the emotional function, try to stop as much as possible all expression of negative emotions. Many people's lives practically consist of that, they express negative emotions at every possible moment, on any occasion, whether suitable or unsuitable, they can always find something wrong in everything. The chief tendency of man 1, 2 and 3 is to express immediately all his negative emotions. If he makes an effort to stop this expression it gives him material for observation, and he sees himself from quite a different angle. If he makes serious efforts in this direction, very soon he will become convinced that he has no will, because it is a most difficult thing to stop this expression of negative emotions. At the same time, it is necessary.

Another useless function is talk; we talk too much. We talk and talk and talk, and we never really notice it. Generally, we think we talk very little, much too little, but particularly those people who talk most think that they never talk. This is a very useful subject for watching. You will see how your day passes, how many mechanical things you say in certain conditions, how many other mechanical things in other conditions. Or you will notice that you just talk and talk because it gives you pleasure or fills your time. It is necessary to watch it and stop at least some of this unnecessary talk. Talk, imagination, lying and expressing negative emotions. are in fact our chief functions.

Now if you want to ask me anything I will try to explain. We must try not only to study these ideas in the form in which they are given but also to apply them in connection with different problems. They give good keys for the solution of many of them.

Q. When you speak about lying are you referring to what we say or to our thoughts too?

A. At present it is quite enough to take only what we say. Later we shall have to study our thoughts too, that would be lying to ourselves. It is the same thing, but we have to begin with the actual things we say, and in the beginning lying will need a certain effort to verify. It is always speaking about things we do not know. We do not call it lying that is our escape, we give it some good name, and then we can accept it.

Q. I should like to know more exactly what is meant by being. I understood it is something more permanent as opposed to a sort of shirting collection of 'I's.

A. Do not make it too complicated. All of you is your being. Knowledge is separate. You can visualize separately all that you know, but all that you *are*, apart from what you know, is your being. In this division you consist of two things: what you know and what you are. From the point of view of development, the idea is that work on knowledge without work on being is not sufficient. Knowledge is limited by being. In the state in which you are, if you get more knowledge, you will not be able to use it, to understand it, to connect it. Development of knowledge is not sufficient, for at a certain moment it has to stop, and instead of leading you forward it will lead you backwards, because if your acquiring of knowledge is not followed by change of being, all your knowledge will become distorted in you. Then the more knowledge you acquire, the worse off you will be.

Q. What part does being play in the attainment of knowledge?

A. Being is your state. In one state you can acquire certain knowledge, but if another state develops you can acquire more knowledge. If you are divided into different 'I's all contradicting one another, it is very difficult to acquire knowledge because each part will acquire it by itself and understand it by itself, so you will not have much understanding. If you become one, then certainly it would be easier to acquire knowledge, to remember it and understand it. Being means state, inner conditions, all together, not separate.

Q. Does not our being grow with knowledge?

A. No, being cannot grow by itself. Knowledge, even very good knowledge, cannot make being grow. You have to work on knowledge and being separately, otherwise you will cease to understand the knowledge you acquire. Work on being is different work, a different effort is necessary.

Generally speaking, we know more about our knowledge than we know about our being. We know how little we know about ourselves.

we know how, at every moment, we make mistakes about everything.

we know how we cannot foresee things, how we cannot understand people, how we cannot understand things. We know all that and realize that it is all the result of our insufficient knowledge. But we do not understand the difference between people's being. It is useful to take a piece of paper and write down what constitutes our being. Then you will see that it cannot grow by itself. For instance, one feature of our being is that we are machines; another that we live in only a small part of our machine; a third this plurality that was spoken about in the first lecture. We say 'I', but this 'I' is different every moment. We have many 'I's all on the same level and there is no central 'I' in control. This is the state of our being. We are never one and never the same. If you write down all these features you will see what would constitute a change of being, and what can be changed. In each particular feature there is something that can change; and a little change in one feature also means a change in another.

The more you know yourself, the more you know your being. If you do not know yourself, you do not know your being. And if you remain on the same level of, being you cannot get more knowledge.

Q. In order to work on being, is it necessary for us to occupy all our time during the day, not to have any spare time?

A. You begin with the impossible. Begin with the possible; begin with one step. Try to do a little, and results will show you. There is always a limit, you cannot do more than you can. If you try to do too much, you will do nothing. But, little by little, you will see that right thinking, right attitudes are necessary. It needs time, because for so long people have been in the power of negative emotions, negative imagination, lying, identification, and things like that. But little by little these will disappear. You cannot change everything at once.

You must always think about the next step, only one step. We can understand the next step as being a little more collected than now. When we have understood that we can think of it as being still more collected but not completely, not finally.

Q. Shall we be able to judge the change of our being without deceiving ourselves?

A. Yes, but before you are able to judge the change, you must know your being as it is now. When you know most features of your being, you will be able to see changes. We can judge the level of our being by the instability of our 'I' what we call 'I' because one moment one part of us says 'I', another moment another part. If you observe well, you will find how different you are, even in the course of one day. One moment you decide to do one thing, another moment another thing. It is this constant changing even in the course of twenty-four hours that really shows the level of our being.

Q. On what does the difference in level among ordinary sleeping people depend?

A. On reliability. There are more reliable people and less reliable people. This is also true in the work. Unreliable people cannot get much.

Q. Do we all start on the same level?

A. More or less, but there are variations. The chief thing is reliability.

Q. How does one develop one's being?

A. All that you have learnt, all that you have heard about the possibility of development, all refers to being. First of all, development of being means awakening, since the chief feature of our being is that we are asleep. By trying to awake we change our being; this is the first point. Then there are many other things: creating unity, not expressing negative emotions, observation, study of negative emotions, trying not to identify, trying to avoid useless talk, all this is work on being. It is true that in this way you acquire certain knowledge, but if it is simply intellectual knowledge, it is put separately. Being is power, power to 'do', and power to 'do' is power *to be different*.

Q. I do not understand this distinction of knowledge and being working together. It seems that in self-study they are so mixed that it is hard to see which is which.

A. Yes, but at the same time it is possible. We know what knowledge means. We know that knowledge is relative and depends on our capacities, actually we can acquire a sufficient amount of knowledge to start with in our present state;

but very soon we realize that in order to acquire more knowledge, deeper or larger knowledge, of things we really want to understand, we must change our being, for our present capacities for acquiring knowledge are very limited. So even from the point of view of acquiring knowledge we come to the necessity of changing being, otherwise we will only have words and will not know what they mean.

Q. Have the ideas of the system any value from the point of view of change of being?

A. Ideas by themselves cannot produce change of being your effort must go in the right direction, and one thing must correspond to another. You make an effort on one line, and you must make an effort on the other line. You can change nothing without a system; even with a system it is difficult.

Q. What is meant by 'work'?

A. 'Work' in the sense we use this word in the system means work for acquiring knowledge and for the study of change of being. You have to have some clear objective and work for it, so 'work' includes acquiring knowledge and self-control in order to reach your objective.

Q. Why has nature made man incomplete, left him half-way?

A. It is a good question only as long as you do not understand what a man can acquire. When you do, you will realize that those things can only be acquired by man's own efforts. What can be developed in man is consciousness and will, and they can be developed only if man realizes that he does not possess them. When he realizes that, he will see that they can only be got, not given. Man is created in the only way he can be created. All that can be given is given; no more can be given. Otherwise, it would be the same as to take a man from the street and make him a general; he would not know what to do. This is a subject for discussion; we cannot be given those qualities; we must earn or buy them. This is the only way to acquire them.

Real knowledge, objective knowledge is knowledge which comes from higher mind. Such knowledge shows us how to study man, how to study the universe, and also how to study the one in relation to the other. With objective knowledge it is possible to know the real world by making use of the principles of relativity and scale and by knowing the two fundamental laws of the universe: the Law of Three and the Law of Seven.

The approach to objective knowledge is through the study of objective language. You remember, I said that the study of this system begins with the study of a new language, and I gave you several examples: centres, division of man into No. 1, 2, 3, 4, 5 and so on, identifying, considering, self-remembering. These are all expressions of this language.

The next step is the study of oneself, the study of the human machine, and the understanding of man's place in the universe. This knowledge of oneself is both an aim and a means.

But as I said, if a man wants to develop, knowledge alone is not sufficient; he must also work to change his being. Only, change of being is so difficult that it would be almost impossible if knowledge were not there to help him. So, knowledge and being must grow side by side, though the one is quite separate from the other. Neither knowledge nor being separately can give right understanding because understanding is the resultant of a simultaneous growth of knowledge and being.

Growth of knowledge means a transition from the particular to the general, from details to the whole, from the illusory to the real. Ordinary knowledge is always a knowledge of details without knowledge of the whole, a knowledge of leaves, or the veins and serrations of the leaves, without knowing the tree. Real knowledge not only shows a given detail but the place, the function, and the meaning of this detail in relation to the whole.

Q. If knowledge exists on different levels, then we can only have the knowledge belonging to our level?

A. Quite right, but if we had all the knowledge that we could get on our level, our level would change. The point is, we do not have all the knowledge possible to us on our level, we have too little.

Q. Is knowledge only given in direct connection with the work?

A. From the very beginning you are given certain ideas and told certain things about the human machine; for instance, about the four functions, about different states of consciousness, about the fact that we live in a state which goes up and down, sometimes nearer to self-consciousness, sometimes nearer to sleep. When you heard this, you were also told to prove it for yourselves. If you only hear about these things, or read about them, they remain merely words. But when you begin to verify them for yourselves, when you understand each function in yourselves and find out your own feelings and sensations connected with each of them, then it becomes knowledge.

Being is something quite separate. You can make all possible efforts in your present state, yet you will feel that there is more to be got out of your knowledge, but your being is not adequate. So, it is necessary to work on being, make it stronger, more definite. Then from the same words you will be able to extract more knowledge.

Q. If understanding is the resultant of knowledge and being, I cannot see how they combine.

A. Any moment you understand something, your understanding is a combination of your knowledge and your being. Understanding is the result of experience: a certain experience in being and a certain experience in knowledge.

Q. It is still not clear to me what you mean by being and state of being.

A. Instead of looking for definitions, try to find illustrations. The being of a man is all that he is. Many things enter into being. You can be more conscious or more asleep, more divided or more whole, more interested in some things and less interested in other things; you can lie more or lie less, dislike lying or lie without any embarrassment, be more consistent or less consistent, have a feeling of mechanicalness or not; you may have no great conflicts in yourself or you may consist of conflicts, have comparatively few negative emotions or be immersed in negative emotions. Generally, state of being means a greater or lesser consecutiveness of actions. When one thing contradicts another too much, it means weak being. We do not realize that if a man is very inconsistent it makes his knowledge unreliable. Development of one line only, either knowledge or being, gives very bad results.

Being includes all your power to 'do'. Knowledge is only auxiliary; it can help. But in order to change our being and this is where knowledge comes in, we must first realize and understand our present state. As we begin to understand the state of our being, we begin to learn what to do with ourselves.

Q. What did you mean when you said that development of either knowledge or being alone gives bad results?

A. It may help if I tell you how I first heard about it. If knowledge develops beyond being, the result will be a 'weak Yogi', a man who knows everything and can do nothing. If being develops beyond knowledge, the result is a 'stupid saint', a man who can do everything and does not know what to do.

If you compare this system with others, you will find that it is precisely in the importance it gives to this idea of being that it differs from other systems, philosophical and otherwise. Other systems are concerned with knowledge or conduct. They assume that such as we are, we can know more or behave differently. In religious systems 'faith' and 'conduct' are generally regarded as being voluntary. One can be good or bad, it is arbitrary. But this system has the idea of different levels of being. On our present level of being there is one knowledge, one conduct, one faith, all determined by being. But first comes knowledge, how little we know. You begin to study yourselves: you realize that you are machines but that you can become conscious. The machine starts on a certain level of being. All it can or cannot do is dependent upon this level. Try to understand what is meant by being, levels of being, change of being. This system says that everything forces, energies, different kinds of activity, they all depend on the level of being. We cannot know more because of our level of being. At the same time the slightest difference in the level of being opens up new possibilities for knowledge and for 'doing'. All our powers are determined by our level of being.

Q. I understood we were all on the same level?

A. Yes, in comparison with man No. 4. But there are people who are further away from the level of man No. 4 and others who are nearer to it. As in everything else there are degrees. There is a big distance between the two levels, but there are intermediate states. It is the same in ourselves:

each of us can be different at different moments.

There is a slight difference between people, but it is not enough to measure being. All normal people are born on the same level and have the same possibilities. No one can be born higher than the ordinary level. We cannot attain anything without special training. The slight differences between people are differences in functions, but real difference of being is difference of state of consciousness. Difference in functions is a one-sided difference.

Q. Could you explain more about the degrees that exist between us and man No. 4? I want to understand.

A. This is a right question; and you can understand it by observing other people and yourself. There are men No. 1, 2 and 3 who are not at all interested in the possibility of development or in acquiring knowledge, or in anything like that. Then there are those who have the possibility of a certain understanding, but it moves from one thing to another, it is not a directed interest. Then there may be directed interest, the beginning of magnetic centre, meeting with influence C and so on. So, man 1, 2 and 3 can be very different, he may be nearer to possibilities of development, further from these possibilities, or even without any possibilities.

Q. How can one understand other people's knowledge unless one is on the same level?

A. Do you mean who can teach, whom one can trust and so on? On the level where we are we can judge about people's knowledge, but not about their being. We can see without mistake who knows more. But about being mistakes are easily possible. Suppose you meet someone who knows more than you do but you suspect that his being is lower. You will be wrong because it is not your business to Judge his being. Leave his being alone and try to learn from him. We are not capable of seeing levels of being higher than our own; we can judge about the level of being only on the same level as ours or lower. It is important to remember this principle.

Q. Is this system a system of knowledge?

A. This system is not so much a system of knowledge as a system of thinking. It shows how to think differently, what to think differently means, why it is better to think differently. To think differently means to think in different categories.

One thing is in our way, we do not know what it means 'to know'. We must try to understand what to know means; this will help us to understand what it means to think in new categories.

Q. What is the origin of this system?

A. I will not speak of details, but of the principle of what must be its origin in principle. To serve a useful purpose, to have any weight, a teaching must come from men of a higher mind than ours, otherwise it will not help, and we will remain on the same level. If a teaching comes from a higher level, we can expect something. If it comes from the same level as ours, we can expect nothing. We have enough material for evaluation. We can ask ourselves: was it invented on the same level as ours or on a different level? If the amount of material we have does not enable us to judge, we must wait. But only we ourselves must judge. If I say anything about it, you cannot verify it. It is useful to think about this; only you must find answers for yourselves.

Q. Has it been handed down for ages?

A. How can you verify it?

Q. I will take your word for it.

A. You must not believe anything.

Q. Can you tell us where to look for its origin and traces?

A. In yourself. Has it given you something you did not have before?

Q. Surely it is impossible to understand the system until one reaches the level it was originated on?

A. Understanding is relative. We can understand many things on our level: only then can we move on. We cannot jump. Certainly, with the help of this system we can understand better about ourselves and about life than with any other system I know. If we can say that we got from it what we could not get in any other way, then we must continue to study it. We must have valuation. After a very short time one can tell. Personally, I learnt very much from this system in a short time, and with its help, I even began to understand things I had met with in other systems and had not understood. For instance, take 'sleep' in the New Testament. People do not notice it, yet it is constantly spoken of there, it is constantly said that people are asleep, but can awake, though they will not awake without efforts. The system explains not only itself but also what is true in other systems. It explains that if people want to understand one another, under standing is possible only among people who are awake. In ordinary life everything is a hopeless tangle; people are not meant to understand one another in ordinary life. If that were meant, people would be created differently. Man must complete himself by his own efforts. We can realize this if we realize the nature of will and consciousness. Capacity to understand is connected with this. If people begin to work with the aim of gaining consciousness and will, they will begin to understand one another. In life, with the best intentions, there are only blunders. People are machines: they are not made to understand one another.

Q. Is it possible to understand the reason of this muddle? What is the purpose of being made so?

A. To see the danger and to try and begin to understand our situation. People never understood one another, but in our time the situation in life is becoming more and more complicated and dangerous. At the same time, such as they are, people serve the purposes of the moon and the earth. But of this we will speak later.

It is a mistake to think of our times as being like any other. Now there are exceptional difficulties and exceptional facilities.

Q. The difficulties are likely to be increased with time?

A. Yes, but not beyond a certain limit, beyond this limit it becomes an impossibility.

It is important to realize, not in theory but through seeing facts, that people do not understand one another, and that the situation is becoming more and more complicated. If people have machine-guns, it is more dangerous. And they have machine-guns in many senses. So, each misunderstanding becomes more deep and more complicated.

Q. What is the end?

A. We cannot say that would be fortune-telling. Certainly, we cannot expect any good from that.

You see, all our ordinary views of things are no good, they do not lead anywhere. It is necessary to think differently, and this means to see things we do not see now, and not to see things we see now. And this last is perhaps the most difficult because we are accustomed to see certain things:

it is a great sacrifice not to see the things we are accustomed to see. We are accustomed to think that we live in a more or less comfortable world. Certainly, there are unpleasant things, such as wars and revolutions, but on the whole, it is a comfortable and well-meaning world. It is most difficult to get rid of this idea of a well-meaning world. And then we must understand that we do not see things themselves at all. We see like in Plato's allegory of the cave only the reflections of things, so that what we see has lost all reality. We must realize how often we are governed and controlled not by the things themselves but by our ideas of things, our views of things, our picture of things. *This* is the most interesting thing. Try to think about it.

* * *

CHAPTER III

Self-study and improvement—States of consciousness and functions— Degrees of consciousness—Division of functions—Self-remembering— Mechanicalness—Study of functions of the four centres—Subdivision of centres—Attention—Formatory apparatus—Wrong work of centres— Four kinds of energy—Stopping leaks—Negative emotions—Stopping the expression of negative emotions—Change of attitudes.

In this system, which studies man as an incomplete being, particular stress is laid on self-study, and in this sense the idea of self-study is necessarily connected with the idea of improvement. As we are, we can use very little of our powers, but study develops them. Self-study begins with the study of states of consciousness. Man has the right to be self-conscious, even such as he is, without any change. Objective consciousness requires many changes in him, but self-consciousness he can have now. Yet he has not got it, although he thinks he has. How has this illusion started? Why does man ascribe self-consciousness to himself? He ascribes it to himself because it is his legitimate state. If he is not self-conscious, he lives below his legitimate level, uses only one-tenth of his powers. But as long as he ascribes to himself what is only a possibility, he will not work for the attainment of this state.

Next the question arises: why does man not possess self-consciousness if he has all the necessary arrangements and organs for it? The reason for this is his sleep. It is not easy to awake, for there are many causes of sleep. The question is often asked: do all people possess the possibility of awaking? No, not all: very few are capable of realizing they are asleep and of making the necessary efforts to awake. First, a man must be prepared, he must understand his situation; second, he must have enough energy and a sufficiently strong desire to be able to get out.

In all this strange combination that is man, the one thing that can be changed is consciousness. But first he must realize that he is a machine, so as to be able to tighten some screws, loosen others, and so on. He must study; that is where the possibility of change begins. When he realizes that he is a machine, and when he knows something about his machine, he will see that his machine can work in different conditions of consciousness and so will try to give it better conditions.

We are told in this system that man has the possibility of living in four states of consciousness but that as he is, he lives only in two. We also know that our functions are divided into four categories. So, we study four categories of functions in two states of consciousness. At the same time, we realize that glimpses of self-consciousness happen, and that what prevents us from having more of these glimpses is the fact that we do not remember ourselves, that we are asleep.

The first thing necessary in a serious study of oneself is to understand that consciousness has degrees. You must remember that you do not pass from one state of consciousness to another, but that they are added to one another. This means that if you are in the state of sleep, when you awake, the state of relative consciousness or 'waking sleep' is added to the state of sleep; if you become self-conscious, this is added to the state of 'waking sleep'; and if you acquire the state of objective consciousness, this is added to the state of self-consciousness. There are no sharp transitions from one state to another state. Why not? Because each state consists of different layers. As in sleep, you can be more asleep or less asleep, so in the state in which we are now, you can be nearer to self-consciousness or further from it.

The second thing necessary in a serious study of oneself is the study of functions by observing them, learning to divide them in the right way, learning to recognize each one separately. Each function has its own profession, its own specialty. They must be studied separately, and their differences clearly understood, remembering that they are controlled by different centres or minds. It is very useful to think about our different functions or centres and realize that they are quite independent. We do not realize that there are four independent beings in us, four independent minds. We always try to reduce everything to one mind. Instinctive centre can exist quite apart from other centres, moving and emotional centres can exist without the intellectual. We can imagine four people living in us. The one we call instinctive is a physical man. The moving man is also a physical man, but with different inclinations. Then there is the sentimental or emotional man, and the theoretical or intellectual man. If we look at ourselves from this point of view, it is easier to see where we make the chief mistake about ourselves, because we take ourselves as one, as always, the same.

We have no means of seeing centres, but we can observe functions: the more you observe, the more material you will have. This division of functions is very important. Control of any of our faculties can only be obtained with the help of knowledge. Each function can be controlled only if we know the peculiarities and the speed of each.

Observation of functions must be connected with the study of states of consciousness and degrees of consciousness. It must be clearly understood that consciousness and functions are quite different things. To move, to think, to feel, to have sensations, these are functions; they can work quite independently of whether we are conscious or not; in other words, they can work mechanically. To be conscious is something quite different. But if we are more conscious it immediately increases the sharpness of our functions.

Functions can be compared to machines working in varying degrees of light. These machines are such that they are able to work better with light than in darkness; every moment there is more light the machines work better. Consciousness is light and machines are functions.

Observation of functions requires long work. It is necessary to find many examples of each. In studying them we shall unavoidably see that our machine does not work rightly; some functions are all right while others are undesirable from the point of view of our aim. For we must have an aim, otherwise no study will give any results. If we realize we are asleep, the aim is to awake; if we realize we are machines, the aim is to cease being machines. If we want to be more conscious, we must study what prevents us from remembering ourselves. So, we have to introduce a certain valuation of functions from the point of view of whether they are useful or harmful for self remembering.

So, there are two lines of study: study of the functions of our centres, and study of unnecessary or harmful functions.

Q. Is the method of this study observation?

A. One can find many things in that way, and it can prepare the ground for further study, but it is not sufficient by itself. By self-observation one cannot establish the most important divisions in oneself, divisions both horizontal and vertical, for there are many different divisions; one cannot know the different states of consciousness and separate one's functions. One must know the chief divisions, otherwise one will make mistakes and will not know what one observes.

Man is a very complicated machine; he is really not a machine, but a big factory consisting of many different machines all working at different speeds, with different fuels, in different conditions. So, it is not only a question of observation but a question of knowledge, and man cannot get this knowledge from himself, for nature did not make this knowledge instinctive, it has to be acquired by the mind. Instinctively man can know what is sour or sweet and similar things but instinctive knowledge ends there. So, man must learn, and he must learn from somebody who has learned before him.

If you make a serious effort to observe functions for yourself, you will realize that ordinarily, whatever you do, whatever you think, whatever you feel, you do not remember yourself. You do not realize that you are present, that you are here. At the same time, you will find that, if you make sufficient efforts for a sufficiently long time, you can increase your capacity for self-remembering. You will begin to remember yourself more often, you will begin to remember yourself more deeply, you will begin to remember yourself in connection with more ideas, the idea of consciousness, the idea of work, the idea of centres, the idea of self-study.

But the question is how to remember oneself, how to make oneself more aware? The first step is to realize that we are not conscious. When we realize this and observe it for some time, we must try to catch ourselves at moments when we are not conscious and, little by little, this will make us more conscious. This effort will show how little conscious we are, because in ordinary conditions of life it is very difficult to be conscious. Here you put yourselves in artificial conditions, you think about yourselves 'I am sitting here' or 'I am myself' and even then, you cannot do it much. But in ordinary conditions when you are thinking about something, or talking, or working, everything distracts you, and you cannot remember yourselves. This expression 'remembering oneself' is taken intentionally, for in ordinary conversation we often say, 'he forgot himself' or 'he remembered himself in time'. We use this expression only in relation to extreme forms of negative emotions, but in actual fact we always forget ourselves, and with the exception of very rare moments we never remember ourselves in time.

Q. Is self-remembering the initial process of this system?

A. It is the centre of the initial process, and it has to go on, it must enter into everything. At first this sounds improbable, because you may try to remember yourself, and then you find that for long periods of time it does not come to your mind; then again you begin to remember about it. But efforts of this kind are never lost; something accumulates and at a certain moment when in the ordinary state you would have been completely identified and submerged in things, you find that you can stand aside and control yourself. You never know when it will be or how it comes. You must only do what you can observe yourself, study, and chiefly try to remember yourself; then, at a certain moment, you will see results.

Q. How does one begin to use memory in the sense of self-remembering?

A. Self-remembering is not really connected with memory; it is simply an expression. It means self-awareness, or self-consciousness. One must be conscious of oneself. It begins with the mental process of trying to remember oneself. This capacity to remember oneself must be developed, because in self-observation we must try to study our functions separately from one another intellectual function separately from the emotional, instinctive separately from moving. This is very important but not easy.

Q. Do you mean we should practice observing these different functions?

A. Yes, at certain moments of the day we must try to see in ourselves what we think, how we feel, how we move and so on. At one time you can concentrate on the intellectual function, at another time on the emotional, then on the instinctive or the moving. For instance, try to find out what you are thinking about, why you think and how you think about it. Try to observe physical sensations such as warmth, cold, what you see, what you hear. Then, every time you make a movement you can see how you move, how you sit, how you stand, how you walk and so on. It is not easy to separate instinctive functions, because in ordinary psychology they are mixed with the emotional; it takes some time to put them in their right place.

Q. Would there be any sense in breaking down certain habitual actions, such as going to bed at a certain time at night?

A. Mechanical changes of that kind may be useful in the very beginning of self-study, but they cannot produce any lasting effect. They may help you to see something that you would not have seen otherwise but, by themselves, they cannot produce any change. Change must begin from inside, from change of consciousness, from the moment when you begin to remember yourself or even earlier, when you begin to realize the possibility of self-remembering and that it is really important. Only unfortunately it often happens that people start well and then lose the line of efforts.

Q. Does observing mechanicalness impair mechanicalness? I was thinking of physical work.

A. Without work on consciousness all the sides of us that can be conscious will become more and more mechanical. Only very uniform work without any variations is totally mechanical. If work is a little more complicated, then the more mechanical it is the worse it is... In no work is mechanicalness useful one has to adapt, to change methods in order to produce good work, and for that one has to be aware of what one is doing. Being efficient in physical work does not mean mechanicalness. Training does not make us more mechanical. Being an. expert means being intelligent about one's work.

Q. The moving and instinctive centres seem to work more evenly and normally than the intellectual and emotional. Why is this so?

A. Because otherwise people would go to the left instead of going to the right and never get where they want to go. And if the instinctive centre were like the intellectual and the emotional centres are now, a man would soon poison himself. A certain degree of normality is obligatory for the instinctive and moving centres. Other centres can go mad without immediate harm.

In order to understand man's mechanicalness, it is very useful to learn to think about him as a machine, to study the functions of this machine and to understand the chief divisions of functions not only in general, not merely in theory, but to study them in their activity, to learn how they work. This division into four functions is only a preliminary division, because each of them is again subdivided. All this has to be studied and understood by observation, because theoretical study does not give the same result, does not lead to the same conclusions, does not show the same truth. For instance, very few systems recognize the existence of the instinctive centre or instinctive mind, and no system I have heard of recognizes the existence of an independent moving mind. Yet moving mind plays a very important part in our life, so the absence of this division spoils to a great extent the results of ordinary observation of man, particularly in modem psychology, for, since this fact is not recognized, many things are ascribed to a wrong origin. Moving centre is very important to study and observe, because it has other functions besides movement in space, such, for instance, as imitation, which is a very important function in man No. 1. Besides, moving centre also controls dreams, and not only dreams at night, but dreams in waking state daydreams. And since most of our life passes either in real dreams or in daydreams, study of the moving function is most important. We think that the intellectual and emotional side is more important, but actually most of our life is controlled by instinctive and moving minds. So, moving centre has many useful and many useless functions.

Q. Is there a connection between behaving mechanically and moving Centre?

A. No, moving Centre only means the mind whose legitimate function is to control movements. So 'moving' and 'mechanical' are not the same. Every Centre may be mechanical; every function can be more mechanical or less mechanical, more conscious, or less conscious. Certainly, there are some mechanical processes in us for which there is no need to become conscious, such as the physiological processes which are arranged and controlled by their own mind. But it is our actions as a whole, both in relation to ourselves and to other people, that can become harmful if they are left to themselves.

Q. Is talking always mechanical? I often talk before I have time to stop it.

A. In most cases. This is one of the first things one has to observe and struggle with. It is very difficult to observe and difficult to struggle with, but it must be done.

Q. I used to think that by talking about my observations I was formulating them. But now I feel there is a danger of observation evaporating in talking.

A. There may be very different talking; you can talk for the sake of talking, or you can *make* yourself talk, with effort. Talking can be awakening, and it can be sleep.

Q. Could we be told of some way of making more efforts to observe?

A. If you put yourself in a more difficult position, for instance if you assume an unaccustomed posture, you won't be able to stop observing. We do not observe ourselves because life is too easy. If you are hungry, cold, tired, you will observe yourself. But with civilization there are no strong physical sensations. We smooth out all things before they reach a degree that will make us observe.

Q. Is this the kind of observation you want us to practice? I thought it was observation of our inner states.

A. everything is useful. The study of the machine is also necessary, as well as the psychological side. You cannot study one side without the other. You must know how the machine works

Q. How do you know how many centres there are?

A. By observation. In the ordinary way you can observe four different functions which obviously come from different sources, controlled by different principles. Self-observation shows this quite clearly and after some time you cannot mix them.

Q. Why haven't modern psychologists come to that conclusion?

A. Because they do not know about it. This division of centres looks very simple, yet the fact that it is not known shows that ordinary mind cannot discover it. Ordinary mind, if you take existing psychology, just feels something different but cannot definitely say that this is one thing and that is another thing. This idea comes from schools, just as does the complete idea of the division of four states of consciousness. You can find this last idea in literature, but the description is quite different, so again it comes from schools and must be explained orally. There are things which can be described in books and there are other things which can never be rightly described.

Q. So the idea of centres is an old idea?

A. It is very old, but we cannot discover it until we are told about it. If we are told, we can observe ourselves and find that it is true, but by ourselves we cannot discover it Facts prove this, for it has not been discovered.

Q. Where are the centres situated?

A. It does not matter because each Centre occupies the whole body There is not a single cell in our body that is not controlled by all centres. This must not be taken too literally; for instance, you cannot say that intellect controls every cell, so there are limitations, but speaking generally, each Centre controls the whole body in a different way. But we cannot know the physical side by ordinary observation; we can study functions, however, and that gives all the material that is necessary.

Q. Then one can observe with the intellect?

A. You can do nothing else; that is the only part of us, which is to a certain extent under our control, so we can use the mind for observation. Later perhaps you can train other centres to make observations, but that cannot come for a long time. Naturally, other centres must not be in the way. For instance, if you identify emotionally with something, it will prevent your observing; you want to think about one thing, but it will constantly bring you other thoughts, other associations. For a long time, we have to work from the intellectual Centre, but at the same time we must understand that we cannot go far with it because it has definite limits; it will bring you to a certain point after which you cannot go further unless you can use the emotional Centre. But the emotional Centre has to be trained first. You must learn not to express negative emotions, and only if you do that for a sufficiently long time can other things be explained.

Q. You cannot let your emotions guide you without your intellect, can you?

A. Normally you could, but then we are not quite normal, so they may guide us in a right way or a wrong way. There is no guarantee that they will guide us in the way we want, we may want to go to one place and our emotions may lead us somewhere else.

Q. Emotions would have to develop an intelligence of their own?

A. I quite agree with you, but what does it mean? It means first of all that you must learn to control the expression of all unpleasant emotions; only then can you know emotionally what to do next.

Q. You say that the thinking and the emotional functions are completely separate, but isn't it very difficult to tell the difference?

A. No, it is not difficult at all, only a little patience and observation are necessary; after a short time, you will see quite clearly what is thinking and what is feeling.

Q. Are the three centres often working simultaneously?

A. Yes, but 'simultaneously' may have different meanings. It is very rarely that they work simultaneously on the same subject. All the four functions can and do happen simultaneously, but they can work on different things. An example of all the four functions working simultaneously on the same subject would be artistic creation. Owing to their working simultaneously centres often get very mixed, yet it is possible to distinguish them. This is the beginning of self-observation and self understanding; we have to understand the different functions and then begin to divide them.

Q. Why is it that moving Centre can stop imagination? For instance, I find gardening or any physical work some help to stop it.

A. It means that the same Centre was occupied with imagination that is occupied with gardening. It only proves that imagination is a function of moving Centre.

Q. I cannot see the importance of the stress laid on centres.

A. It is very important to see that our mind is divided into four minds, that there is no unity in us, that the four minds or functions are quite different. This alone gives one a different picture of oneself.

Q. How can one distinguish between emotion and instinct?

A. It is a very important question and must be solved by one's own observation and study. Instinctive emotions are always connected with something physical. Since modem psychology does not separate instinctive emotions from other emotions there is bound to be some difficulty in understanding the difference. But when you know that they are different, it is possible to distinguish between them.

Q. Is there anything that can control unruly organs or cells?

A. Yes, instinctive Centre. Do you think we would be alive for half an hour if instinctive Centre did not work? It knows the right and the wrong work of each organ. It always tries to make them work rightly. We think organs work by themselves; this is imagination. They are controlled by instinctive Centre. This is 'instinct' in the real sense in relation to man.

Q. Has the quality of intellect any bearing on the acquisition of consciousness?

A. Yes, because we must begin with intellect. Our intellectual Centre is better developed, or more under its own control. The emotional Centre is more irresponsible. So, since we have more command of our intellectual Centre, we have to use it until either we become more conscious or learn to use other functions more efficiently and control them better than we do now. At present we have no control over instinctive and emotional functions, and only a little over the moving function. External influences move them. We cannot be glad or angry without cause, and a cause means something external. Later work must be in the emotional Centre because the chief energy is in it. Intellectual Centre is only auxiliary, but at present it is all we have.

I want to tell you a little more about centres which will help you to understand the situation. Some centres are divided into two halves positive and negative. This division is very clear in the intellectual and the instinctive centres. In the intellectual Centre it is 'yes' and 'no', affirmation and negation. All the work of the intellectual Centre consists of comparing. The division in the instinctive Centre is quite plain: pleasure pain. All instinctive life is governed by this. At a superficial glance it seems that the emotional Centre also consists of two halves pleasant and unpleasant emotions. But it is not really so. All our violent and depressing emotions and, generally, most of our mental suffering has the same character it is unnatural, and our organism has no real Centre for these negative emotions; they work with the help of an artificial Centre. This artificial Centre, a kind of swelling is gradually created in us from early childhood, for a child grows surrounded by people with negative emotions and imitates them.

Q. Are instinctive emotions not negative?

A. They may be negative, but they are rightfully so. They are all useful. The negative half of the instinctive Centre is a watchman warning us of danger. In the emotional Centre negative emotions are very harmful.

Then each half of a Centre is divided into three parts: intellectual part, emotional part and moving or mechanical part. The moving part of each Centre is the most mechanical and the most often used. Generally, we use only the mechanical parts of centres. Even the emotional parts are used only occasionally; as to the intellectual parts, they are very seldom used in ordinary conditions. This shows how we limit ourselves, how we use only a little part, the weakest part, of our organism.

It is very easy to distinguish these three parts when we begin to observe ourselves. Mechanical parts do not need attention. Emotional parts need strong interest or identification, attention without effort or intention, for attention is drawn and kept by the attraction of the object itself. And in the intellectual parts you have to control your attention.

When you get accustomed to control attention, you will see at once what I mean. First the character of the action will show you which Centre you are in, and then observation of attention will show you the part of Centre.

It is particularly important to observe the emotional parts and to study the things that attract and keep the attention, because they produce imagination Study of attention is a very important part of self-study, and if you begin to observe this division of centres into parts, in addition to the division of centres themselves, it will give you the possibility of coming to smaller details and will help you to study attention.

Q. Is it possible for us as we are to give attention to something without being identified?

A. Certainly Only you must distinguish attention from identification. Attention can be controlled; identification is mechanical.

Q. Did you say we have three kinds of attention?

A. No. Attention is one, there is no other attention but sometimes you can act without attention, you can do many things, even normal, logical things without any attention. In other cases, attention is drawn and kept by the attraction of the thing itself, and in the third case attention is controlled.

Q. I find that if I control my attention for even a short time I cannot imagine.

A. Quite right, because imagination goes on in mechanical parts of centres, without attention. If attention is fixed on something, imagination stops.

Q. Is it only when one is self-remembering that one can give controlled attention?

A. It is more or less on the same line, but at the same time-controlled attention is possible in ordinary life Sometimes people can control their attention and do interesting work without knowing anything about self-remembering Although controlled attention is very close to self-remembering, there is a difference. Attention can be in only one Centre, whereas self-remembering needs the work of three or even four centres.

Q. Isn't it very easy for controlled attention to become identification?

A. No, they are quite different. One is the maximum of control; the other is the minimum of control. There is no possibility of control in identification.

Q. Can one encourage the intellectual Centre to work?

A. Cultivate attention. You will see that then it gives different results. Think with attention. Do not let yourself think mechanically. Mechanical thinking transforms itself into imagination.

Q. What is the difference between doing things consciously and intentionally?

A. We cannot speak about doing things consciously because we are not conscious. As to doing things intentionally, if you do some work and have to give your attention to it, then, even without your noticing it, part of your effort will be connected with keeping attention on what you are doing. But if it becomes quite mechanical, you may be thinking of something else, yet your hands will be still doing it. That will be the mechanical part of the Centre. If your work needs constant thinking, invention, adaptation, you have to work with intellectual parts.

The mechanical part of the intellectual Centre has a special name. Sometimes it is spoken of as a separate Centre, and in that case, it is called the formatory Centre or formatory apparatus. Most people use only this part.

they never use the better parts of the intellectual Centre. But ideas of this system or similar ideas cannot be understood by formatory apparatus at all. Formatory apparatus has very definite limitations. One of its peculiarities is that it compares only two things, as though in any particular line only two things existed. Then formatory Centre likes thinking in extremes; for instance, it either knows everything or it knows nothing. Another of its peculiarities is immediately to look for the opposite. You can find many examples of formatory thinking. For instance, if I say, you must do this or you must do that, people say, 'But you said we cannot do!' If I say this needs will-power, they say, 'How if we have no will?' If I speak of being more conscious or less conscious, people say, 'But we have no consciousness!' These are all examples of formatory thinking.

Q. Can you give an example of formatory apparatus rightly used?

A. If the intellectual Centre works normally, that is, if other parts do their work, formatory Centre does its work quite all right. It is a registering apparatus. We are concerned only about its wrong work. This refers not only to the formatory apparatus but to all the mechanical parts of centres. Only when they begin to work wrongly do they become dangerous. So, there is no need to worry about their right work; what you must try to do is eliminate their wrong work. The mechanical part of the emotional Centre wants to do the work of the higher part, and it is the same with the formatory Centre, it wants to do the work of the intellectual Centre and as a result the moving part of the Centre includes all the intellectual life of an ordinary person.

Q. How do you account then for people occasionally living in the higher parts of the Centre? One can occasionally have an idea.

A. Certain combinations of ideas may 'happen', but we want control, not an explanation of things that happen by themselves. Anything may happen once or twice, but it has no practical value or meaning, just as once or twice one can find money in the street, but one cannot live on it.

Q. I do not understand what acting mechanically means, because one seems to spend half of one's life doing things mechanically, like writing. Has all this got to be undone?

A. That is moving Centre, I do not mean that. Many things are mechanical and should remain mechanical. But mechanical thoughts, mechanical feelings that is what has to be studied and can and should be changed. Mechanical thinking is not worth a penny. You can think about many things mechanically, but you will get nothing from it. In a mechanical way you can use only a small part of your intellectual Centre, the formatory apparatus, and it is not worth spending your time on.

There is one thing you must understand about parts of centres, and that is that the intellectual parts differ much less from one another than the other parts. This division into intellectual, emotional, and moving is very clear and sharply denned in the lower parts of centres, but it becomes much less apparent in the higher parts.

Q. Do only different centres interfere with each other, or can one part of the same Centre interfere with another part?

A. It may be anything. Supposing you work with moving Centre then instinctive Centre may interfere, or emotional Centre, or another part of moving Centre. Or if you feel in one Centre and then start speaking, you pass into another Centre and may even forget what you wanted to say.

Q. Does the sum of the intellectual parts of different centres make up the intellectual Centre or are they separate?

A. No, they can all work separately, but certainly if one could control the intellectual parts of all centres and make them work together, that would be the way to higher centres. Intellectual parts will not make up a Centre by themselves, but their combined work will produce better work than they can do separately.

Q. Does work on oneself diminish the functions of the mechanical parts of centres?

A. It will diminish the work of the mechanical parts in the sense that it will diminish mechanicalness where attention and consciousness are useful. The mechanical parts will then do their own work for which they are intended, and perhaps do it better than at present, because now they are too occupied with things that do not concern them. This will enable the better parts of centres to work.

Q. Is mechanicalness to be looked upon as a fact to be observed or as an evil to be fought against?

A. You see, you will never understand mechanicalness if you speak in this way, in relation to small things. But when you see, or find in your memory, how quite mechanically you can do the most abominable things, which later you cannot understand how you could have done, then you will know what mechanicalness is. All our life we do mechanically what we would never do consciously. That is what we must understand. If we look through our life, year by year, month by month, we see things we would never have done consciously, or things we did not do which we would have done if we were conscious. This is the way to think about mechanicalness.

Q. Is formulation a proper function of the intellectual Centre?

A. Quite right. There may be different degrees, but at present we can only speak about formulation and formation. In this connection it is important to understand the right meaning of the word 'formatory'. There are two methods of mental conclusions: 'formation' and 'formulation'. 'Formation' is a conclusion arrived at by the way of least resistance, avoiding difficulties. It is easier because it makes itself ready-made phrases, ready-made opinions, like a stamp. It is generally defective with the exception of the simplest cases. 'Formulation' is a conclusion arrived at on the basis of all the available material; it needs effort and is sometimes difficult, but it means the best we can do.

Q. How is it possible for us to formulate? Will not certain 'I's distort the evidence?

A. If they distort, they will distort the formulation. But certainly, it is necessary to learn to distinguish formulation from formation. Formation is, so to speak, just one glance, sometimes quite wrong, and formulation, as I said, is when you collect all you know about a given subject and try to make some deduction from it.

Q. Why is it that sometimes I find lectures interesting and sometimes not?

A. Because you are in different centres. In one Centre you can be interested in another Centre you are not interested. Suppose you are in instinctive Centre; it cannot be interested in esoteric ideas it is interested in food and things like that. But if you are in the intellectual or partly in the emotional Centre, you can be interested. You know that we have four rooms in our house, and it depends on which room we are in whether we are interested or not.

Q. I find in typing routine work one types more quickly. In typing intelligent work, one types more slowly.

A. Because two centres work. Complicated work needs two centres. But even in copying, intellectual Centre enters. Moving Centre cannot be trusted much; it controls imagination and dreams. So, when it works, intellectual Centre watches. If one works wholly with moving Centre, one is half asleep. All co-operation of centres is a certain degree of awaken ness. What does falling asleep mean? Disconnection of centres.

Q. Speech comes under two centres, doesn't it?

A. More, even. Generally, it is partly instinctive, partly moving, partly intellectual, and it may be emotional, so it may include all four functions.

Q. Is the intellectual part of each separate Centre the better part, and the one to try and maintain, as against the emotional and mechanical parts of each Centre?

A. All parts are equally necessary, but each part must do its own work. Parts are not wrong in themselves, each of them has its own function, but if they replace one another, their work becomes wrong.

You see, the idea that we do not use the whole of our brain but only part of it is not a new one, but psychological systems do not explain what we don't use, because parts of centres are not on the same level, they are really different machines. This system gives a real anatomy of our brain and generally of our whole mentality. So, this is a very important point, and if one begins to observe oneself from the point of view of attention, one can study the different values of one's mental processes. This is the key to these machines.

Q. What is the difference between the moving part of the intellectual Centre and the intellectual part of the moving Centre?

A. They are completely different. Intellectual part of moving Centre can control all our most complicated movements when we have to invent new movements. Suppose one invents a very complicated machine, or works with a very difficult machine, or does very intricate handwork which needs constant attention and constant self-remembering even, in order not to break the whole thing; that would be the work of the intellectual part of moving Centre.

And the moving part of the intellectual Centre is the registering or formatory apparatus, a card-index system in the brain. It is quite useful in its place, but it is used for wrong purposes. Suppose, for instance, that one throws those cards in the air and tries to make deductions from the way they come down; that would be wrong work of the formatory apparatus and that is what we usually do.

Q. When you spoke about adjusting things, did you mean trying to make centres work better? What will guide them to this better working?

A. All work on yourself self-study, self-knowledge, self-remembering. First, we have to know the machine and then we have to learn to control it. We have to readjust functions so that each does its own rightful work. Most of our activity consists of one Centre doing the work of another Centre. Our incapacity to reach our normal level lies in our inability to make our centres work rightly.

Many inexplicable things we observe are due to wrong work of centres.

Q. Does wrong work of centres mean interference with one another?

A. There are two forms of wrong work of centres. Either they interfere, that is, one works instead of another, or one takes energy from another.

Sometimes centres have to work for each other. If, for some reason, one Centre stops working, the machine is so arranged that another Centre can continue its work for a time to avoid an interruption. The original idea of such an arrangement is quite right, but in actual life it has become the cause of mental and physical disturbances, because one Centre cannot work properly for another. And in the state of identification, they like to do wrong work instead of their own work. It has become a kind of bad habit, and by mixing functions the centres begin to mix energies, trying to get more potent energies for which they are not adapted.

Q. I find it difficult to see instances of wrong work of centres. My only observation is that I often experience a sensation of unnecessary excitement.

A. You can see examples when people become unnecessarily emotional in relation to things which would be better done without any emotion.

Q. How can one stop this interference?

A. Our functions are at present conditioned by our state of consciousness. There is a slight variation: we can be a little more conscious than we are, a little more or much less. That affects functions, for if you are more awake functions produce better results, if you are more asleep, they produce worse results. This we can observe, but as a principle you must understand that functions and states of consciousness are independent of each other and exist by themselves. The state of consciousness affects functions, and increased consciousness will create new functions. Complete, real awakening will produce new functions which we do not have now.

Q. The thing to aim at is a perfect adjustment of the four centres?

A. Yes, this is the starting point. After that a man can think about creating higher states of consciousness about being conscious of himself and then about being conscious of things outside himself. This will correspond to the working of higher centres.

One Centre cannot be improved by itself. All must be improved, must come to normal working. You see, the human machine is very cleverly made and everything in it can be used for the same purpose. But on the ordinary level the work of centres is not fully coordinated, they live too independently, and at the same time they hinder one another and use one another's energy.

Every Centre is adapted to work with a certain kind of energy, and it receives exactly what it needs; but all the centres steal from one another, and so a Centre that needs a higher kind of energy is reduced to working with a lower kind, or a Centre suited for working with a less potent energy uses a more potent, more explosive energy. This is how the machine works at present. Imagine several furnaces one has to work on crude oil, another on wood, a third on petrol. Suppose the one designed for wood is given petrol: we can expect nothing but explosions. And then imagine a furnace designed for petrol, and you will see that it cannot work properly on wood or coal.

We must distinguish four energies working through us: physical or mechanical energy for instance, moving this table; life energy which makes the body absorb food, reconstruct tissues, and so on; psychic or mental energy, with which the centres work, and most important of all, energy of consciousness.

Energy of consciousness is not recognized by psychology and by scientific schools. Consciousness is regarded as part of psychic functions. Other schools deny consciousness altogether and regard everything as mechanical. Some schools deny the existence of life energy. But life energy is different from mechanical energy and living matter can be created only from living matter. All growth proceeds with life energy. Psychic energy is the energy with which centres work. They can work with consciousness or without consciousness, but the results are different, although not so different that the difference can be easily distinguished in others. One can know consciousness only in oneself.

For every thought, feeling or action, or for being conscious, we must have corresponding energy. If we have not got it, we go down and work with lower energy lead merely an animal or vegetable life. Then again, we accumulate energy, again have thoughts, can again be conscious for a short time.

Even an enormous amount of physical energy cannot produce a thought. For thought a different, a stronger solution is necessary. And consciousness requires a still quicker, more explosive energy.

Q. If no amount of psychic energy can produce conscious energy, what difference does it make how much psychic energy I use?

A. You want psychic energy for quite different purposes. For instance, you have to think with psychic energy.

Q. I have found that trying to keep attention fixed uses a great deal of energy. Does it mean I do it in a wrong way?

A. No, you have to use energy to keep attention. This is work, and work needs energy, although on the other hand it saves energy, it saves waste of energy in another direction. If you are doing things without attention, it will mean a much greater loss.

Q. Why is it so difficult to control attention?

A. Lack of habit. We are too accustomed to let things happen. When we want to control attention or something else, we find it difficult, just as physical work is difficult if we are not accustomed to it.

Q. Why should moments of consciousness be so rare? Is it a question of energy?

A. No fuel. If you have no electricity, or if you have a pocket torch with a bad battery, you may have a flash and then nothing. Consciousness is light, light is the result of a certain energy; if there is no energy there is no light.

Q. Does the secret of all development of consciousness lie in the conservation and control of energy?

A. No, not all the secret, though conservation and increase of energy is very important. But in itself it is not enough; one has to know how to control it. Energy is the mechanical side of consciousness. We cannot begin with the idea of control. In order to control one small thing, we must know the whole machine. First, we have to stop waste of energy.

second, collect it by self-remembering; then, adjust things. We cannot begin in any other way.

Q. Can energy be stored?

A. Yes, energy can be stored when you are able to store it. But at first the question is not about storing but about not wasting. We would have enough energy for everything we want to do if we did not waste it on unnecessary things. For instance, the reason why we are so formatory is that we are too dull, we do not feel enough. We think we feel, but this is an illusion. And the reason why we feel so little is because we have no energy available for the emotional centre.

Leaks of energy were already spoken about, but the worst of all is expressing negative emotions. If you can stop the expression of negative emotions, you will save energy and never feel the lack of it.

We can only hope to become conscious beings if we use in the right way the energy that is now used in the wrong way. The machine can produce enough energy, but you can waste it on being angry or irritated or something like that, and then very little remains. The normal organism produces quite enough energy not only for all centres but also for storing. Production is all right, but expenditure is wrong. These leaks have to be studied, because with some kinds of leaks it is not worth going on until they are stopped, for the more one accumulates energy, the more will leak out. It would be like pouring water into a sieve. Certain negative emotions precisely produce such leaks. In certain situations, some people go through a whole range of negative emotions so habitual that they do not even notice them. It may occupy only five minutes or five seconds, but it may be sufficient to spend all the energy their organism produced for twenty-four hours.

I want particularly to draw your attention to this idea of negative emotion and the state of negative emotion. This is really the second important point; the first referred to consciousness that we are not conscious and that we can become conscious. It is necessary to realize that there is not a single useful negative emotion, useful in any sense. Negative emotions are all a sign of weakness. Next, we must realize that we can struggle with them; they can be conquered and destroyed, because there is no real Centre for them. If they had a real Centre, like instinctive emotions, there would be no chance; we would remain forever in the power of negative emotions. So, it is lucky for us that they have no real Centre; it is an artificial Centre that works, and this artificial Centre can be abolished. When this is done, we will feel much better for it. Even the realization that it is possible is very much, but we have many convictions, prejudices and even 'principles' about negative emotions, so it is very difficult to get rid of the idea that they are necessary. Try to think about it, and if you have any questions, I will answer them.

Q. You said we had no positive emotions?

A. We have no positive emotions; we call positive emotion an emotion that cannot become negative, and all our emotions, even the best we can have in our present state, can become negative at any moment. Also, by their scope, our emotions are too small for positive emotions. Positive emotions include very much, whereas our emotions are very narrow. So, at present we have no positive emotions, but negative emotions are there.

Q. And if we become free of negative emotions?

A. Then we can have positive emotions. Some negative emotions can be simply destroyed, but some others we can dispose of only by transforming them into positive. Only, that is very far from us now; we cannot do it at present; now we can only prepare the ground for that, chiefly by creating right attitudes, for mental work comes first. We create right mental attitudes by understanding that negative emotions serve no useful purpose and by realizing how much we lose by allowing ourselves the pleasure of having them. Then perhaps we will have enough energy to do something about them.

Q. To do something about them is to stop them?

A. We have to begin with right understanding, right attitude. As long as we think negative emotions are unavoidable, or even useful for self-expression, or something like that, we can do nothing.

A certain mental struggle is necessary to realize that they have no useful function in our life and that at the same time all life is based on them.

There are many strange things in us. First, there are things that could be conscious and are not; and second, we spoil our life by negative emotions for which nature has not even provided a Centre, so that we must make one artificially. What is mechanical? What is not normal, what is unnatural, is most mechanical.

Q. Can you always tell a negative emotion from a genuine one?

A. You can tell it by identification, because two things are always present in negative emotions identification and negative imagination. Without negative imagination and identification negative emotions cannot exist.

Q. When you are in the middle of having a negative emotion such as bad temper, you cannot stop it just by thinking?

A. No, but you can prepare the ground beforehand. If you can create a right attitude, then after some time it will help you to stop the negative emotion in the beginning. When you are in the middle of it you cannot stop it; then it is too late. You must not let yourself get into a bad temper; you must not justify it.

Q. From what you say it seems to me you are presupposing an 'I' higher than others who can do this?

A. Not higher, but some intellectual 'I's are free from the emotional Centre and can see things impartially. They can say 'I had this negative emotion all my life. Did I get a penny? No. I only paid and paid and paid. That means it is useless.'

Q. Have we emotions that are not negative?

A. Certainly, but not positive. They are not negative yet but can turn negative the next moment.

Q. But it seems to me there are circumstances that simply induce one to have negative emotions!

A. This is one of the worst illusions we have. We think that negative emotions are produced by circumstances, whereas all negative emotions are *in us, inside us*. This is a very important point. We *always* think our negative emotions are produced by the fault of other people or by the fault of circumstances. We always think that. Our negative emotions are in ourselves and are produced by ourselves. There is absolutely not a single unavoidable reason why somebody else's action or some circumstance should produce a negative emotion *in me*. It is only *my* weakness. No negative emotion can be produced by external causes if we do not want it. We have negative emotions because we permit them, justify them, explain them by external causes and in this way, we do not struggle with them.

Q. Is there any reason why we are so anxious to keep them?

A. Habit. We are too accustomed to them; and we cannot sleep without them. What would many people do without negative emotions? This habit is so strong that special work is necessary to get rid of them.

But in the beginning work on negative emotions is two-fold: studying and trying not to express them. Real work on negative emotions comes later. You cannot study them if you express them. If you try to stop expressing them, then you can see and study them.

Q. Is not changing one's points of view a method of struggling with them?

A. Quite right, only it is not sufficient by itself. Real struggle begins with struggling with identification. If you destroy identification, negative emotions will become weaker by themselves. But of course, change of points of view is also very necessary.

Q. I understood you to say that struggling with negative emotions is useless, but we must study and observe them. Is this correct?

A. Struggle with negative emotions needs very many efforts; the habit is too strong. At first you must simply study and attempt to struggle with the expression of negative emotions. Now, if you struggle with one emotion you may create two instead. In time, indirectly, one can gain mastery over emotions. But the first step is study.

Q. Can one have negative emotions and be in good health?

A. The word 'health' must be taken in a broader sense, from the point of view of the system. We cannot take it in the ordinary sense of physical manifestations actual absence of physical illness because one of the first necessities of health is right work of centres. People whose centres work wrongly are not healthy. The idea of health must be enlarged, it cannot be taken narrowly.

Q. About right work of centres, I do not see how you can prevent emotional Centre interfering with the work you are trying to do with the intellectual.

A. It interferes all the time. You can do nothing about it until you have conquered negative emotions and have learned not to identify. When you cease to identify, negative emotions cease to have power, because they work only on the basis of identification.

Q. When you feel an unpleasant emotion, why is it necessary not to express it?

A. It is the same as in relation to unnecessary talk. Ask yourself: is it useful, is it necessary to express them? The idea is to create resistance, otherwise we cannot observe. And this creation of resistance is the introduction to the study of emotions. We cannot see them without it.

Q. Why is it that if you try to resist them it brings about a complete stop of thought?

A. Lack of practice. In the beginning everything stops.

Q. If you do not express unpleasant emotions, is it good bottling them up?

A. Try. You must not believe anything. If you find that it is good to express them, we will argue. I will then say that you cannot control this expression and that, if you observe, you will find it better not to express them. The question is, can you refrain from expressing them? Much time and many other things besides are necessary in order really not to express unpleasant emotions.

Q. Why is it that it gives a feeling of relief to express anger or irritation?

A. There is a worm in you that wants to express itself. Then, when it expresses itself, you feel relief but, in this way, it becomes stronger and has more and more control over you. When you realize that nobody else is responsible for your irritation, little by little you will begin to feel differently. We have much more power over expression of negative emotions than we think, and we *can* learn not to express them. Even in ordinary life we do not always express negative emotions; in certain conditions we know that it would be dangerous. And if we can control the expression of them in certain conditions, we can control it in all conditions, if we try.

Q. May not restraint from expressing negative emotions, commonly described as 'letting off steam', have a harmful effect?

A. There is no danger. We cannot produce a restraint sufficiently strong to harm ourselves. 'Letting off steam' as a relief is an illusion. It makes us lose energy. Expression of negative emotions is always mechanical, so it can never be useful. But resistance to it is conscious.

Q. If we must not have negative emotions, this will abolish all emotional life!

A. Quite the opposite. *Now* we have no emotional life, but only an imitation. The idea is to have an emotional life. Real possibilities of knowing are in the emotional Centre.

Q. The same amount of exhaustion is incurred by controlling as by releasing. What then can I gain by trying to control the expression of anger?

A. It is quite a wrong assumption that it is the same amount of energy because control increases energy. It may be that you have to expend a certain amount of energy to control some emotion, but next moment, since you do not spend energy on this useless emotion, control will increase your energy. This is the chemical action of control.

Q. My experience is that suppressing the expression of a negative emotion makes one tired.

A. You can become tired if you only suppress the expression. But I never said suppress, I said, 'Do not express, find reasons for not expressing'. Suppression can never help, because sooner or later the negative emotion will jump out. If you merely suppress, you keep the identification and only shut off the external expression. It is a question of finding reasons, of thinking rightly, because expression of negative emotion is always based on some kind of wrong thinking.

Q. I should like to get more help about tackling negative emotions.

A. It must be your own effort, and first of all you must study your negative emotions and classify them. You must find which negative emotions you chiefly have, why they come, what brings them, and so on. You must understand that your only control over emotions is by mind, but this is not immediate. If you think rightly for six months, then it will affect negative emotions. If you begin to think rightly today, it will not change your negative emotions tomorrow.

Q. When I think about negative emotions, I do understand very clearly that they are in ourselves, and yet, soon after, I continue to express them. Is it simply because I am not one?

A. First, because you are not one, and second, because you do not try in the right way. It is a question of long work, as I said, and this cannot be changed at once. If one has constant negative emotions, recurring negative emotions of the same kind, one always falls in at the same point. If one observed oneself better, one would know that this was coming, or had come, and if one had thought rightly beforehand, one would have some resistance. But if one has no right attitude, if one does not think rightly, then one is helpless, and the negative emotion happens again at the same time, in the same way. This is one of the methods of controlling emotions through the intellectual Centre. But attitudes must be created not at the moment of emotional explosion but long beforehand. Then, little by little, emotional explosions will come under the control of the intellect. Thoughts can be more permanent than feelings, and in that way, thoughts can influence feelings. You can create permanent thoughts, permanent attitudes which will affect feelings in time. But before this can become possible a certain discipline must be introduced into our emotions, and a certain knowledge must be acquired in order to work on the emotional mind.

Q. I have noticed that nearly all the time I hardly feel any emotion or have any vividness of experience. Is this sleep?

A. Partly sleep, partly living in moving and instinctive centres. Then, exactly as you describe, we hardly feel any vividness of experience.

Q. In some cases the negative emotion of fear seems useful, otherwise people would cross the road at any time without looking.

A. You speak about instinctive fear; emotional fear is different; it is based on imagination.

Q. Do negative emotions have a harmful effect on other functions?

A. You must find that out for yourself. For instance, if you are agitated or irritated, or something like that, notice other things. Can you remember well? Can you think well, work well? You will see that all your faculties are diminished. This observation will by itself show you many other things to observe.

Q. Why is it that negative emotion appears to affect the functioning of the instinctive Centre to such a degree?

A. Negative emotion affects all centres. Centres are so connected that you cannot have a strong or violent negative emotion and with the help of identification they all become strong without affecting all centres. You cannot have a negative emotion and at the same time do something else right or even think rightly. You eat wrongly, breathe wrongly, walk wrongly, work wrongly everything.

Q. Are negative emotions a wrong use of the instinctive Centre?

A. No, but all emotions have their origin in the instinctive Centre. In a small child centres are not divided. Negative emotions are created from material taken from the instinctive Centre. This material legitimately belongs to the instinctive Centre and is wrongly borrowed from it. We are in a very strange state, because positive emotions do not belong to our ordinary emotional Centre but to the higher emotional Centre, and negative emotions do not belong to the ordinary emotional Centre but exist in an artificial Centre. The emotional Centre borrows material from the instinctive, and with the negative half of the instinctive Centre and the help of imagination and identification, it creates negative emotions. Destroying them is a very difficult work; but you must realize that as long as negative emotions exist no development is possible, because development means development of all there is in man. Negative emotions cannot develop.

it would be very disastrous if they could. So, if one is trying to create consciousness, one must at the same time struggle with negative emotions, for either you keep them or you develop, you cannot have both together.

Q. Would a way to controlling negative emotions be trying to understand why a thing happened, to understand cause and effect?

A. It may be in some particular case, but at present there is no question of destroying or controlling, the question is of studying. The strongest method for controlling negative emotions is learning not to express them. So, we must first struggle with the expression of negative emotions and, second, with such emotions as we can struggle with. When we learn not to express them, we will speak of the next step. You cannot control negative emotions as long as they have free expression.

I want you to understand that stopping the expression of negative emotions and struggle with negative emotions themselves are two quite different practices.

Trying to stop the expression comes first. If you express a negative emotion, you are in its power, you can do nothing at that moment. When you have learnt not to express it, you can try not to identify, to create a right attitude, and to remember yourself.

Q. I can sometimes manage not to express a negative emotion to begin with, but it goes on trying to come out.

A. That means you only stopped the external manifestation, and you must try to stop the cause of it. I do not mean the emotion itself, but the cause of the expression. There is a difference. Emotion is one thing, expression is another. Try to find the difference.

Q. Does trying to control unpleasant emotions gradually eliminate them?

A. Certainly, because many of them can exist only when there is no control; the moment control begins, many of them become easy to eliminate.

Q. If one's early training has been such that it is natural not to express unpleasant emotions, is it not equally mechanical?

A. This is an academic question; it is necessary to verify whether you can do it in all circumstances. One may be trained not to express negative emotions in certain circumstances, but in other circumstances one will express them.

Q. Is not the point not to feel unpleasant emotions?

A. That comes later, it is quite a separate question. You come to that by not identifying.

Q. By what means can one check where one's unpleasant emotions come from, what causes them and how we are to get over our tendency to deceive ourselves? Is this only possible through a school?

A. At present it is not important to learn where they come from, but important to stop their expression. Many things about negative emotions can be learned afterwards. As to what causes them identification is the general cause of all negative emotions. You cannot struggle with them without help, many people tried. If you realized how small our possibility is, you would understand that one must have every possible help in order to achieve something.

Q. Must negative emotions always be mechanical?

A. What is opposite to mechanical? Conscious. Who will have negative emotions consciously? When one knows that one can give them up, nobody would have them. So certainly, they are mechanical.

Q. Could we hear more about right attitude as a weapon against negative emotions? It must mean more than just not identifying.

A. Certainly, it means more; it means right thinking on a definite subject. For instance, almost all our personal negative emotions are based on accusation; somebody else is guilty. If, by persistent thinking, we realize that nobody can be guilty against us, that we are the cause of all that happens to us, that changes things, not at once certainly, because many times this realization will come too late. But after some time, this right thinking, this creating of right attitude or point of view can become a permanent process; then negative emotions will only appear occasionally. Exactly by being permanent this process of right thinking has power over negative emotions, it catches them in the beginning.

Q. I find that much of my time is passed in a negative state, not very definite, and I don't seem to be able to do anything about it.

A. Yes, but you must have realized that it is generally connected with some kind of identification or imagination. When you find different manifestations of this negative state, you can struggle with it, because this struggle is in the mind. You can refuse some points of view and accept other points of view, and very soon you will see a difference.

This is connected with a very big question, because from one point of view we are so mechanical that we can do nothing; but from another point of view there are several things which we can begin to do. We have certain possibilities in us, only we do not use them. It is true that we cannot 'do' anything in the sense that we cannot change what *we, feel* at any given moment, but we can make ourselves *think* about a subject at a given moment. This is the beginning. We must know what is possible and begin from that, because then the possibility to do something, instead of letting things happen, will gradually increase.

We do not realize what enormous power lies in thinking. I do not mean that as a philosophical explanation of power. The power lies in the fact that, if we always think rightly about certain things, we can make it Permanent, it grows into a permanent attitude. You may find some inclination to wrong emotional manifestations of some kind. Just at that moment you can do nothing, you have educated in yourself the capacity for this kind of reaction by wrong thinking. But if you start from right thinking, then after some time you will educate in yourself the capacity for a different reaction. Only this method has to be understood, and this understanding must be quite deep.

You can apply this method to many different things. This is really the one thing you can do. You can 'do' nothing else. There is no direct way to struggle with negative manifestations because you cannot catch them and there is no way to prevent them except by being prepared for them beforehand. But a passing realization that they are wrong will not help, it must be very deep, otherwise you will have an equally difficult process to prepare the ground for another manifestation. You do not realize how much you lose by these spontaneous manifestations of a negative character. They make so many things impossible.

Q. Even if I begin to think rightly, I find imitation starts when I hear somebody grumbling, and I begin to do the same.

A. The fact that you begin to think rightly will not change anything straight away. It is necessary to think rightly for a long time; then results will come but not at once. It is a question of months or years to create right attitudes. By creating right attitudes, you consolidate the fact that you have really and seriously decided not to give way to negative manifestations. We do not realize how much we lose in this way. We lose exactly what we want to get.

But first of all, you must stop the habit of expressing negative emotions. This is why, in the very first lectures, when you hear about self-observation, it is explained that you must learn not to express negative emotions. Everybody knows how not to show what they feel, I do not mean in exceptional cases, but in ordinary cases. All negative Ness is based on identification, imagination and on one particular feature, namely, allowing oneself to express it. You always believe you cannot stop it and therefore feel it is quite right to show what you feel. So first you must get rid of this illusion. You can stop the manifestations of negative emotions. If you say, 'I don't want to', I will believe you, but not if you say, 'I cannot'.

I have given you many suggestions about work on emotions, such as study, struggle with identification, struggle with the expression of negative emotions, right thinking about negative emotions. Four practices. If you really use all that is given, very soon you will see quite perceptible results. Real control of emotional Centre needs self remembering, a new state of consciousness, so it is a long way off; now we must use auxiliary methods. The most important of them in the beginning is a right attitude.

* * *

CHAPTER IV

Language—Different divisions used in the system—Essence and personality —A, B and C influences—Magnetic centre—Wrong magnetic centre— Deputy Steward—Law of accident—Law of fate— Law of will—Law of cause and effect—Escape from the law of accident—Centre of gravity— Why schools are necessary—For whom schools are necessary—What constitutes a school—Degrees of schools—Way of Fakir, Way of Monk and Way of Yogi—The Fourth Way—Difference between the Fourth Way and the traditional ways— All ways lead to the same goal—Level of school depends on the level of students—Inner circles of humanity.

The Study of the methods used in this system by which man can come to a higher consciousness begins with the study of a new language. This language is based on different principles which you do not know yet; but as you go on with your study you will very soon begin to understand them. With this language it is possible to come nearer to truth, possible to speak with greater precision than we do now, and two people who understand this language will never misunderstand each other in simple things. You have already heard certain expressions of this language, such as self-remembering, identifying, considering and so on. It is very important to understand the different divisions the system uses, which are part of this language. Man is a very complicated machine, and he can be studied in divisions. In ordinary language we do not use these divisions and so people do not understand one another.

Try to understand what I am saying, because it is rather difficult to express. If you take a town, you can understand that it can be divided into north, south, east, and west; it can be divided into districts and quarters, and then divided into different streets. It can also be studied from the point of view of its population, for it has people of different nationalities, people of different professions, belonging to different classes and so on. None of these divisions will coincide with one another, each must be studied separately. You cannot make a general map, including them all, you must make a series of different maps.

It is the same with man. For instance, I have already given you certain divisions. The first is the division of centres or functions, so that each man consists of four men, each living his own life in the same man, with his own associations, his own likes, and dislikes. Then I showed you the division into different 'I's. This is a very useful division; man is not one, he is plural, a crowd, consisting of people who do not know one another and who fight with each other. This division into many 'I's was supplemented by the different roles a man plays in different circumstances. Then there was the division into knowledge and being what a man knows and what he is. I have also given you the division of man into seven categories:

man No. 1, 2, 3, 4, 5, 6 and 7.

Now we come to another, a quite different division, not parallel with any of the others, the division into essence and personality. Essence is what is born in you, personality is what you acquire. Essence is your own, personality is not your own. All man's inner life, all his perceptions and reactions are divided into those two parts. There are certain things which are born with you, such as certain physical features, state of health, certain kinds of predispositions, inclinations, tendencies and so on. They belong to essence. Personality is what you acquire in the course of your life: views, opinions, words. It is easier to understand the difference between essence and personality if you find some examples. Although the two are always mixed in life, it is easier to distinguish personality and essence in other people than in oneself, because personality changes very often with the change of conditions, but essence remains the same. This division is very important to understand, because many things that we speak about in man refer to essence, while others refer to personality.

Q. If essence is what we are born with, can it be added to? Can it increase?

A. Yes, but it can be done only if personality becomes educated and ceases to press upon essence. Personality is too heavy, too strong; it surrounds essence like a shell, so nothing can reach it directly, everything has to pass through personality. Essence cannot grow in these conditions, but if personality becomes more transparent, impressions and external influences will penetrate through it and reach essence and then essence will begin to grow.

Q. So a strong personality prevents impressions from reaching one's essence?

A. Yes, but what does a strong personality mean? It means a strong influence of what is not your own, of what you have acquired other people's words, other people's views, and theories. They can form such a thick crust round essence that nothing can penetrate it to reach you, to reach what you are.

Q. Is it possible to break this shell or destroy it?

A. Before destroying this shell of personality, or breaking it, it is necessary to prepare other defenses. If for some reason this shell falls off, people find themselves without any defenses against many very difficult influences which they cannot control. Personality keeps you from certain distant influences: if you weaken it, you will be under many influences which could not reach you before, so you will have even less control than you have now. But there are many things which we could control and do not control now. This is the right way of thinking about it.

Q. Can you give an example of such influences?

A. For instance, a simple example would be atmospheric changes or the change of seasons, they affect essence very much, and if one is surrounded with personality, one is less affected. Change of seasons is a very serious thing for people whose essence is more open to influences. I give you this simply as an example of things that people do not take into account and about which they have no idea. There are many other things; for instance, old books on magic warn people about how dangerous this is and how one must be prepared beforehand; and in many cases they are right, because the opening up of essence may be good, but it may be accompanied by many dangers. Personality is created on many wrong bases, but it is also a kind of defense.

Q. Is it possible for us to go through life without ever observing essence?

A. It depends whether it is in schoolwork or not. In ordinary life we do not even know about the existence of those two principles. In self-study one is told of this division, but essence and personality are so mixed that for a long time this division remains theoretical, for it is impossible to say which is which by observation, except in extreme cases. Then, as one works, one gradually begins to see that one thing is more ingrained, goes deeper, another less. In this way, little by little, one can see essence. All permanent or more permanent qualities must depend on essence. When personality is educated and becomes less heavy, many qualities pass into essence and become permanent. This is how essence develops. In personality things jump up and disappear, but what passes into essence remains.

Q. Is essence more or less the same as being?

A. It cannot be put like that. Being is life, it is a process. Essence is an object.

Q. Is essence in a child more developed than personality?

A. At a certain very early age essence may be stronger than personality, but they are both undeveloped. And there are different children and different circumstances.

Q. How can we struggle against personality?

A. It is not a question of struggle but only of controlling and educating. Personality must not have too much freedom. It must be educated in a certain way, act according to certain principles, work in a certain direction. At present our personality is all wrong. There is too much lying, deceiving oneself, imagination, negative emotions. All these things must be put right; only then can the machine work as it should. We have to work through personality; for a long time, essence can have no practical meaning for us. If we begin to work on it consciously, certain things will influence essence, but not at once.

Q. Can we do what we want with personality?

A. If you work, if you study, you will gradually change it and your work on personality will reflect on essence. Either you control personality, or personality is controlled by thousands of different 'I's, each of whom has its own ideas, its own views, and desires. We must realize what an enormous work it is to acquire unity when, as we are now, one part decides to work, and another part does not know about it or does not agree. When you have educated your personality, when it has become obedient to your aim and begins to serve it, then it is useful and right. But if you have an aim in a certain part of you and your personality works against this aim, then, naturally, it is not right.

Q. It was said that there is good in personality as well as in essence, but I cannot find anything in it useful for my ultimate aim.

A. What do you mean when you say there is no good in personality? Even if you observe and find out things about yourself, it is good. This too is in personality. The part that wishes to know, to work, to change is part of personality. There may be many things that are wrong in our personality, and these things have to be studied and eliminated. Personality is developed by study and by diminishing useless functions. Through this it becomes better and cleaner. In school conditions essence must be more important than personality, and if personality dominates it too much, development becomes impossible, because real development is in essence, and if personality hangs too heavily on its essence cannot breathe. But personality is also very important. The possibility of change is really very complicated, because it consists of many things. There must be a certain quality in essence, for if this quality does not exist, nothing is possible; there must be certain material, certain acquisitions in personality, and there must be a certain kind of circumstances.

Q. Has personality to allow itself to be second? Does it step back of its own accord?

A. It does not step back, it becomes different. If it oppresses essence, it is abnormal. In our present state personality is pathological, unhealthy. With work it simply becomes healthy.

Q. I do not understand how personality can influence essence if essence is what we are born with.

A. Take the intellectual Centre: its contents are not born with us thoughts, ideas, convictions, opinions, these are all acquired. As to how personality can influence essence, suppose in your personality you come to a certain conclusion, and you find yourself by observation to have some essential habit, say, some kind of unpleasant emotion that always comes up in certain circumstances. You realize that it is not useful in any sense, it wastes energy and makes your life more difficult. How can you struggle with it? You find that this negative state feeds on self-justification, that in your ordinary habitual state you always justify it and think it is somebody else's fault, or say that you did not mean it, or that people do not understand you, or something like that. This allows it to exist. If you change your point of view, if you cease justifying it and create instead a permanent idea in yourself that this emotion is wrong, that it is not justifiable, then this point of view may eventually become permanent.

Q. Does heredity count for anything in essence?

A. Heredity practically does not exist in man. Wrong qualities may be hereditary but good qualities cannot be inherited. Animals are under different laws from man; in them good and bad qualities are equally transmitted, but in man what may be transmitted, apart from physical qualities, are only features of degeneration, otherwise there is nothing to transmit. Physical features can be inherited, but not features like self-consciousness. Essence cannot be inherited.

Q. Is the tendency to negative emotion in the essence or is it entirely acquired in personality?

A. There may be a tendency even in the essence, a certain disposition to it, but we can take it that it all refers to personality, because if there were a really strong tendency to negative emotion in the essence it would almost mean insanity.

Q. If there are defects in essence, can they be altered?

A. Yes, but, as I said, personality must change first; essence does not change so easily. Changing features in essence is very difficult work; it needs knowledge and sufficient energy, and we are weak and have no knowledge. It is done only when it is necessary, and only with the help of school methods. Suppose one has a lazy essence and one wants to awake one can change it after a long period of self-study, but one must have help, school help. So, it is lucky for us that work on essence comes second, that we have to start with work on personality. But by working on personality, we already work to a certain extent on essence. Sleep, awakening, consciousness all this does not refer to personality, it refers to essence. So actually, you work on essence from the very beginning, and personality, by changing, will produce a certain pressure on essence and change it too.

Q. Is one always born with essence?

A. Yes, but often essence remains undeveloped, on the level of a small child.

Q. Is essence the reliable part in us?

A. Even in personality there are reliable and unreliable things. For instance, imagination is unreliable. Imagining that you can swim when you cannot and knowledge of the multiplication table are both in personality; one is reliable, the other is unreliable.

Q. Does the level of being dependent on growth of essence?

A. Certainly, and this is the relation between them. Only you cannot measure being in that way, for the division into essence and personality is at present merely theoretical. But it is useful to remember that these two principles are in you, because, as I said, if you do not know this division it will prevent you from understanding certain other things you will hear.

One thing you must realize about essence and personality is that essence is one, whereas personality consists of several groups of 'I's. So, we can say that we have not a personality but personalities in the plural, for there are five or six, sometimes ten personalities in one person. Magnetic Centre, for instance, is also in personality, for we are not born with it, it is created in life. It is a group of 'I's which can, to a certain small extent, control other groups of 'I's. Some of these personalities are all right, but some will always be in your way and have to be controlled or eliminated.

Q. What work can one do on personality?

A. It can be controlled by mind. That is all that can be expected. In your mind you formulate your aim and personality must work in accordance with this aim.

Q. What is desire to awaken due to? Is it in essence?

A. This is connected with magnetic Centre. You will remember that in the first lecture I spoke about magnetic Centre and the different influences under which man lives. This brings us to the question of why some people are interested in these ideas, while others are not, what creates this desire to know, the energy to seek; why people who live in similar conditions are so different, for one person is satisfied with ready-made theories and clichés, while another wants to find truth for himself. What is it that explains this difference in people in relation to new ideas, for some people meet with the possibility of acquiring new knowledge and are not interested, while for others it may change the whole trend of their lives?

People come to these and similar ideas in different ways. Some understand something, others take them on an ordinary level. The cause of this difference is that man lives in mechanical life under two kinds of influences. What does it mean? It is connected with the idea explained in the beginning, that man is a machine controlled by external influences, by things around him. He may be receptive to one kind of influences and not receptive to another kind. Most of these influences are created in life itself, by people like himself. But among them, mixed with them, there are other influences which are not created in life but come from a different source, from people of a higher mind. They come in the form of religions, science, philosophical systems, esoteric doctrines, art, all sorts of teachings, and so on. They cannot be distinguished from influences of the first kind outwardly, so it depends on the man whether he discriminates between them or not. Man can live only under influences A, that is, influences of the first kind, and disregard influences B, not be interested in them. But if he is interested in these influences of the second kind and has absorbed them in sufficient quantity, a certain process takes place in him. Results of these influences B, the memory of them, collect separately in a special compartment and form what is called a magnetic Centre. Magnetic Centre is a combination of certain interests and emotional associations which makes him turn in a definite direction. It is a certain cycle of ideas and a certain cycle of emotions. This is the origin of interest in this kind of ideas.

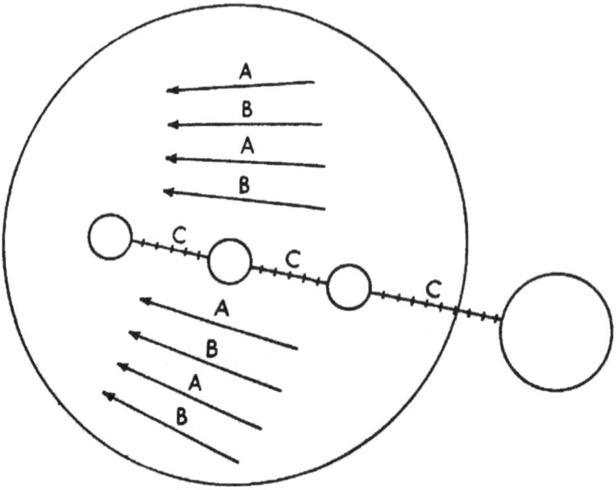

Q. If we are mere machines, are we to conclude that you are trying to lead us, machines, in a certain desirable direction, or are we capable of discriminating between truth and falsity? If so, with what faculty?

A. With magnetic Centre. Men *are* machines, there is no question about that; only they are not quite the same machines as an engine or something of that kind. You have heard already that man can live in four states of consciousness, but that in ordinary life he lives only in two. These two other states of consciousness can be developed in man, but they cannot develop by themselves, they have to be developed through knowledge and effort. And the faculty that helps man to understand and discriminate is the magnetic Centre.

Now we are speaking about man before he meets a school. He lives in life under ordinary conditions. Conditions may be very different, but, in any conditions, he lives under the two kinds of influence I was speaking about. What are influences A? All interests of life, struggle for existence, desires, excitements, possessions, riches, amusements and so on. They are created without intention and are mechanical both in their origin and their action. But at the same time man also lives under influences originally created in schools but thrown into the general turnover of life. These influences B are as it were a life apart. They are arranged for a certain purpose, to serve as 'lights on the way' The rest depends on man himself. All his interests may concentrate only on influences of the first kind, or part of him may remain interested in influences created in life, while another part may be interested in this other kind of influences. If a man notices and studies them, they may accumulate in him. The memory of these interests may begin to collect in him from a very early age and form a certain group of 'I's out of the many 'I's in him. After some time, this group of 'I's or magnetic Centre begins to control and determine his general direction in life and the trend of his interests, or of a part of his interests Magnetic Centre means looking for definite things and being on the level of certain things. But it a man does not notice these influences; they will produce no effect This is why people are so different. One person may be very intellectual, may have studied philosophy, art and so on and at the same time he has no chance if he has no magnetic Centre. If he comes in contact with a school, he will not recognize it. And another man may be insufficiently educated, may not have read so much, may not know so many words, yet if he meets a school he may become interested at once.

Q. What makes us different in this sense?

A. It is a combination of what we are born with and outside circumstances that makes us what we are, it is all mechanical, all under the law of accident. It is useless to deny that people are born different; but that we cannot change, in any case in the beginning. We have to take it for granted that people have different capacities, but not for awakening, this is where people make a mistake. Awakening does not depend on what is born, it depends on the magnetic Centre, and magnetic Centre depends on what one is interested in. One person is interested in one thing and another in another thing, but on what that depends, we do not know, and it will not help us to investigate this question, because it will only be theories. In our state of consciousness, we can only know some things and we must concentrate on the things we can know without wasting time on the things we cannot know

Q. Does not our magnetic Centre depend very largely on mechanical causes?

A. Not quite. As I said, it is a certain combination of interests, and not only interests but also of ideas a man has acquired, a certain knowledge, a certain understanding It all enters into the magnetic Centre. It is mechanical like everything else, but influences B are different in their nature, although in the beginning they come mechanically. This is not important. The important point is whether there is interest in B influences or not. This is how out of mechanicalness comes struggle with mechanicalness. Magnetic Centre helps a man to see, understand and distinguish certain things.

A man cannot appreciate the difference between ideas, he cannot say which is better and which worse, which suits him, which does not suit him, without the help of magnetic Centre. Accumulation of knowledge does not help to create a magnetic Centre; magnetic Centre is good taste with the help of which a man can have a new evaluation of the ideas that come his way. The question is, in this stream of life, to distinguish the two kinds of influences, to feel the difference between them. If a man does not feel it, if he takes influences B in the same way as influences A, then they produce the same effect and magnetic Centre is not formed.

Then, there are many dangers, because some of these ideas which make up the second kind of influences are so distorted that they can form a wrong magnetic Centre. Magnetic Centre must be very uniform and very sane to lead somewhere, otherwise it is only an embarrassment and nothing else.

Q. How does one know whether one is under influences B?

A. Influences B are always there. They come originally from the inner circle of life, from that part of life which has become free from the law of mechanicalness, but they may pass through many stages before they reach man and may be so distorted and so disguised that it is difficult to recognize them, just as it is difficult to recognize ideas of an esoteric origin which come to us in the form of legends and myths, or even superstitions and things like that. Sometimes they have an esoteric origin and then they are influencing B.

Q. Suppose one only imagines that one is working under influences B?

A. One does not know about it and one does not 'work' under influences B. One can be interested in influences B just for one's own personal advantage, profession, fame or something like that; then one loses all the profit one can get from them. But if a man values them for themselves, not selfishly, not only for his own gain, if he is interested in their meaning, then he may get something from them. Definitions are very difficult and mostly wrong, for our ordinary language has so many different associations that sometimes a more precise definition spoils the possibility of understanding. For instance, you can say, though I do not guarantee that it will always be right, that the chief characteristic of influence A is that it is always selfish, whereas influence B is unselfish. But people understand these words so differently that it does not convey much. You can also say that influences A need identification and influences B can exist without identification and that if there is identification with influences B it spoils them. In fact, the more identification there is with influences B, the more they become influences A. But all this is not sufficient to explain the difference between them.

Q. Is total immersion in influences B and complete rejection of influences A a correct attitude to life? Can we altogether dispense with influences A?

A. Why should we? Influences A may be quite legitimate interests in life. If you do not disappear in them, they are quite harmless. One has to accept everything that comes, only not identify. Influences A are not dangerous in themselves, only identification is dangerous. So, there is no question of dispensing, there is only the question of having some interest in influences B, of not being entirely under the power of influences A. If people have an interest in these influences B, they have a magnetic Centre; if not, they have no magnetic Centre.

After some time, with the help of magnetic Centre, a man may find a school, or if he comes near one, he may recognize it. But if he has no magnetic Centre, he will not notice it, or will not be interested. And if he meets a school or a man who transmits another kind of influence, influence C, magnetic Centre helps him to recognize this new influence and absorb it. If he has rot first absorbed enough influences B, and so has no magnetic Centre, or if his magnetic Centre is wrong or too weak, a man will not recognize influence C. Or he may meet a wrong school and have wrong instruction and instead of becoming better become worse; instead of acquiring, lose. Influence C differs from influences B in that it is conscious, instead of being accidental, both in its origin and its action, whereas influences B are conscious in their origin but accidental or mechanical in their action. Influence C is school influence.

Q. Must one be adult to recognize C influence?

A. There is no general rule about age. But one must have enough experience, enough temptations from influences A and enough time to accumulate influences B. Otherwise influence C will serve as influence B; in other words, it will do the work of a more simple instrument and will not have its full value. When people have tried and have realized that ordinary means do not satisfy them, do not give them what they want, they value influences C. But if they come before that, they take influences C on the same level as the other influences and influences C lose their power. It is very important to understand that.

Q. When you recognize influence C, is it bound to be the right one for you?

A. No, not at all, you may be right or wrong, it depends on your magnetic Centre. If the magnetic Centre is right, you are bound to recognize the right things; if it is wrong, you may find quite a wrong school. This happens every day. Why do so many quite unfounded and wrong schools exist, with no material whatever? Because people have a wrong magnetic Centre. The case is possible, for instance, when a man with a wrongly formed magnetic Centre may come upon a school which pretends to be connected with esotericism, while in actual fact no such connection exists. In this case influences which should have been influences *of the third kind* become influences of the first kind, that is, leading nowhere.

Q. Isn't there a way in which one can find out?

A. Only by results. But even if people have wrong results, if they have a wrong magnetic Centre, they persuade themselves that the results are good. One can deceive oneself about anything.

Generally speaking, there is very little chance of finding a right school and many possibilities of wrong schools, because a school must have influences C, that is, ideas that come direct from higher mind. What does 'direct' mean? It means coming not through books, not through ordinary learning accessible to everybody. These ideas must come from another school, and to that school again from another school, and so on, until one comes to the original source. If there are no ideas of that kind, it is only an imitation school. This does not mean that a school must be directly connected with the source, but it must at a certain time have received this kind of ideas, and then people can work on them. But if it has no ideas different from ordinary ideas, it is not a school; then, at best, it is a school on the level of B influences, that is, a philosophical or scientific school. It can be called a school only if, through it, one may be able to find the direction towards becoming man No. 4 (although there is no guarantee of attaining it). So, through the school you can find the right direction only if you have a right kind of school. If you come to a wrong kind of school, you lose what you can learn by yourself.

Q. What becomes of magnetic Centre when one has come to a school?

A. We can say that it becomes that part of a man which is interested in schoolwork. It lives on influences B, but now it receives better material, more concentrated knowledge than before. Besides, many things a man has learned before may be useful to him when he has joined a school, particularly after he has thrown away all that is useless. In ordinary life man does not know what to learn and what to discard. For instance, many things in which people believe have no meaning, but a man often cannot recognize this and takes them all on the same level both those that have meaning and those that have not. But in studying himself according to school methods he learns to recognize imaginary values in himself and, through this, to discover imaginary values outside himself. And then, much later, after long work, the group of 'I's or the personality which was the magnetic Centre develops into 'deputy steward'.

When the magnetic Centre is right and a man meets with true influence C, it begins to act on the magnetic Centre. And then, at this point, man becomes free from the law of accident. The bigger the magnetic Centre the more man is free from the law of accident. This means that he becomes free from this law only at the point through which he is connected with influence C.

Q. You said that, after bringing us into contact with the system, magnetic Centre becomes deputy steward; is he the seed of permanent 'I'?

A. What was magnetic Centre before you met the work may later become deputy steward, which means a personality that conquers other personalities and leads them but that does not come at once. Deputy steward is much higher than magnetic Centre. Magnetic Centre forms itself from B influences, while deputy steward is formed from one's efforts. Magnetic Centre is the seed, the germ of deputy steward.

Q. What is meant by the law of accident?

A. The life of man-machine, of man who cannot 'do', who has no will or choice, is controlled by accident, for things in ordinary life happen mechanically, accidentally; there is no reason in them. And just as man's external life is controlled by accidental external influences, so is his inner life also controlled by both internal and external influences which are equally accidental. You will understand that, if you realize what it means that man is asleep, that he cannot 'do', cannot remember himself; when you think of the constant unconscious flow of thoughts in man, of daydreaming of identifying and considering, of mental conversations that go on in him, of his constant deviation towards the line of least resistance. People think that accidents are rare, but in actual fact most things that happen to them are accidental.

What does accident mean? It means a combination of circumstances which is not dependent on the will of the man himself nor the will of another person, nor on fate, as do, for instance, conditions of birth and upbringing, nor on the preceding actions of the man himself. An accident happens when two lines of events cross one another. Suppose a man stands under the roof of a house, sheltering from rain, and a brick falls and hits him on the head. This would be an accident. There are two separate lines of cause and effect. Take the line of the man's movements and the fact that he happened to stop under the roof of that particular house; every small thing in it had a cause, but the brick did not enter into this line of cause and effect. Suppose the brick was negligently set and the rain made it loose and at a certain moment it fell. There is nothing in the life of the man or the life of the brick to connect them. The two lines of cause and effect meet accidentally.

Q. If accidents pull the strings, what makes accidents?

A. Other accidents. Nobody makes accidents; take it in an ordinary simple way.

Things happen in human life according to three laws:

1. The law of accident, when an event happens without any connection with the line of events we observe.

2. The law of fate. Fate refers only to things with which man is born:

parents, brothers, sisters, physical capacities, health, and things like that. It also refers to birth and death. Sometimes things can happen in our life under the law of fate, and at times they are very important things, but this is very rare.

The law of will. Will has two meanings: our own will, or somebody else's will. We cannot speak of our own will, since, as we are, we have none. As regards another person's will, for the purposes of classification, every intentional action of another person may be called the result of this person's will.

3. In studying human life, it becomes clear that these definitions are not sufficient. It becomes necessary to introduce between accident and fate the law of cause and effect which controls a certain part of events in man's life, for the difference between events controlled by accident in the strict sense of the word and events resulting from cause and effect becomes abundantly clear. From this point of view, we see a considerable difference between people in ordinary life. There are people in whose life the important events are the result of accident. And there are other people in whose case the important events of their life are always the result of their previous actions, that is, depend on cause and effect. Further observation shows that the first type of people, that is people depending on accident, never come near schoolwork, or if they do, they leave very soon, for one accident can bring them and another can just as easily lead them away. Only those people can come to the work whose life is controlled by the law of cause and effect, that is who have liberated themselves to a considerable extent from the law of accident or who were never entirely under this law.

Q. You said that man is a machine moved by external influences. Where then does control come in?

A. There is no control. We must change to have control. Things happen all around us and we are affected by them. At every moment our life is intersected by other lines, so that accident controls most events. The action of one machine affects another machine. We are surrounded by possibilities of accident; if one does not happen, another does.

We must understand our situation. In men 1, 2 and 3 there is no control; practically everything in their life is controlled by accident. There are some things which are the results of their own actions, but they are all on the same level. Control begins on a different level, and it starts with ourselves: control of our reactions, states of consciousness, functions and so on. Then, little by little, we may come to some measure of control in the sense of avoiding one influence and approaching another. It is a very slow process.

Q. When do we cease to be under the law of accident?

A. When we develop will. To be completely free from the law of accident is very far, but there are different stages between complete freedom and our present position. In ordinary conditions accident is opposed to *plan*.

A man who in one or another case acts according to plan escapes in these actions from the law of accident. But actions conforming to plan are impossible in ordinary life except in conditions where the combination of accidental happenings chances to coincide with the plan.

The reasons why it is impossible to fulfil a plan in life are, first of all, the absence of unity and constancy in man himself, and the new lines which continually enter man's line of actions and cross it. This can be easily verified if a man tries to follow a plan in anything that does not *happen* or is opposed to the general trend of momentums operating in his life; for instance, if a man tries to remember himself, to struggle with habits, to observe himself, and so on. He will see that his plan is not being fulfilled and the result is quite different from what he intended, or that everything stops altogether and even the initial impulse, and the understanding of the necessity and usefulness of these attempts vanishes. But if he continues to study himself, to make efforts, to work, he will see that his relation to the law of accident gradually changes. Our being subject to the law of accident is a definite fact that cannot be changed completely. Such as we are we will always be under a certain possibility of accident. Yet little by little we can make accidental happenings less possible.

The theory of accidents is very simple. They happen only when the place is empty; if the place is occupied, they cannot happen. Occupied by what? By conscious actions. If you cannot produce a conscious action, at least it must be filled by intentional actions. So, when work and everything connected with it becomes in truth the Centre of gravity of man's life, he becomes practically free from the law of accident.

Q. What do you call a Centre of gravity?

A. The idea of Centre of gravity can be interpreted in many different ways. It is a more or less permanent aim and the realization of the relative importance of things in connection with this aim. This means that certain interests become more important than anything else one acquires a permanent direction, one does not go one day in one direction and another day in another; one goes in one direction, and one knows the direction.

The stronger your Centre of gravity, the more you are free from accident. When you change your direction every moment, then every moment something new may happen and every accident can turn you one way or another way. But if your intentional activity, such for instance as self-remembering, becomes so definite, so intense, and so continual as to leave no place for accidents, accidents will be much less likely to happen, because accidents need space and time. So, we have to add more causes which will produce results and, in this way, simply exclude accident, because the more our time is occupied with conscious work the less room will be left for accidental happenings.

Q. If one does not identify, if one does not consider, if one does not have negative emotions, would this be creating new causes?

A. Naturally. But since we always identify, always consider, and have negative emotions, we cannot experience that. We must see that even to have one negative emotion less would be a new cause.

Q. How is it possible to live under two such different laws as the law of accident and the law of cause and effect?

A. I see no contradiction. Cause and effect in relation to the laws under which man lives means result of your own actions, and 'accident' means something happening to you without relation to your action.

Q. Can we direct or mould the law of accident now, or must we wait till we have full consciousness?

A. There is no question of waiting: if one waits, one never gets anything at every moment one must do what one can. At the present moment we can to a certain extent mould the law of accident only by moulding ourselves. The more control we have of ourselves, the more the law of accident changes and, as I said, later accidents may even practically disappear, although theoretically the possibility will always remain.

Q. How do we create new causes? Does it mean making plans?

A. No, you usually make the same plans you have made all your life and expect to have new causes.

Q. I should like to know how to lessen the effect of accident upon one's work. When I make a plan for the day, it is often spoiled by people coming unexpectedly.

A. Leave such cases alone. What is important is people or 'I's in us coming in and stopping our work. For instance, a negative emotion comes in and stops work. That is what we must prevent.

Q. Accident need not always be a bad accident? It can also be a happy one, can't it?

A. Quite right. But our aim is to get rid of accident, and after some time, if we work, we may become free of both good and bad accidents. Ask yourself whether it will be better. Try to understand how much we expect from good accidents and how difficult life would become if we had to 'do' everything and if nothing 'happened'.

Q. Is one partly free from the law of accident if one is in a school?

A. No, this would be too simple. Just being there does not change anything. I have just explained that one begins to get out from under the law of accident if one acquires what we call a Centre of gravity, which means that work on oneself becomes especially important, sufficiently important to occupy a big place in man's life. This creates a certain kind of balance and, little by little, dispenses with accident.

Q. Did you mean that when we are more conscious, we are no longer affected by the law of accident?

A. Again, it is not being conscious that does it by itself. When inner accidents stop in us, it will make us more free from external accidents. There are too many accidental things in ourselves and, as I said, we can get rid of these accidental things only by creating a Centre of gravity, a certain permanent weight, weight in the sense that it keeps us more balanced. And for this we need a school.

Q. Why are you so sure that one cannot develop except through a school?

A. There are so many difficulties. If you try to understand these difficulties you will see that without method, and without help, one cannot move one will remain what one is, or rather one will go down, for nothing remains in the same state. If one does not develop, one goes down. In life, in ordinary conditions everything goes down, or one capacity may develop at the expense of another. All capacities cannot develop without the help of school, for system and method are necessary.

But before speaking of why schools are necessary it must be realized for whom they are necessary, because schools are not necessary at all for the vast majority of people. They are necessary only to those who already realize the inadequacy of knowledge collected by the ordinary mind and who feel that, by themselves, with their own strength they can neither resolve the problems which surround them nor find the right way. Only such people are capable of overcoming the difficulties connected with schoolwork, and only for them are schools necessary.

And in order to understand why schools are necessary one must realize that the knowledge which comes from men of higher mind can be transmitted only to a very limited number of people simultaneously and that the observance of a whole series of definite conditions, without which knowledge cannot be transmitted *correctly*, is necessary.

The existence of these conditions and the impossibility of doing without them explains the necessity of an organization. The transmission of knowledge demands efforts both on the part of him who receives it and on the part of him who gives it. The organization facilitates these efforts or makes them possible. These conditions cannot come about by themselves.

A school can only be organized according to a certain definite plan worked out and known long ago. There can be nothing arbitrary and improvised in schools. But schools can be of different types corresponding to different ways. I shall speak about different ways later.

Q. Can it be explained in what these conditions consist of?

A. These conditions are connected with the necessity of a simultaneous development of knowledge and being. As I said before, the development of one without a corresponding development of the other gives wrong results. Schools are necessary to avoid such one-sided development and the undesirable results connected with it. The conditions of school teaching are such that from the very first steps work progresses simultaneously along two lines, the line of knowledge and the line of being. From the first days at school a man begins to study mechanicalness and to struggle against mechanicalness in himself, against involuntary actions, against unnecessary talk, against imagination, against the expression of negative emotions, against day dreaming and against sleep. In making a step along the line of knowledge a man must make a step along the line of being. The principles of schoolwork, all the demands made upon him, all help him to study his being and to work to change it.

Q. If there is no hope of attaining a higher degree of consciousness without a school, this would exclude so many who, through no fault of their own, never come into contact with the right school and yet who urgently desire to progress?

A. It is impossible to account for these things, because man lives to such an extent under the law of accident, and individual man is so small and insignificant. We think we are very important, but in reality, we are not important at all. In order to become important, we must become something first, for such as we are we are practically nothing. Who could be interested in our development except ourselves? So actually, meeting a school that corresponds to one's type for one may meet a school that does not correspond to one's type or one's development is to a great extent a matter of luck.

Q. Would it not be a case of wanting sufficiently, for it is said, 'seek and ye shall find'?

A. With the exception of very difficult circumstances, when fate, accident and cause and effect are all going against a man, if a man really seeks, he can find. He will look for a school with the help of his magnetic Centre; but if magnetic Centre is not formed, he cannot start.

Q. Where are the schools leading?

A. This is an interesting question because it also answers other questions about the differences in men. With the help of a school, you can attain what you want, but first you must formulate what you want.

A question was asked earlier about whether a school leads machines to what is good for them. If it is a real school, it will not lead machines anywhere, because machines have their own fate in the universe, and no one can do anything for them. But a school can help people who are tired of being machines.

it can show them the way to cease to be machines and teach them how it can be done.

That is all that a school can do, and without a school it cannot be achieved.

Q. What constitutes a school?

A. Speaking generally, a school is a place where one can learn something. There can be schools of modern languages, schools of music, schools of medicine and so on. But the kind of school I mean is not only for learning but also for *becoming different*. It was explained before that nobody can work alone, without a school. Also, it must be clear to you by now that a group of people who decide to work by themselves will arrive nowhere, because they would not know where to go and what to do.

So, we can say that a school is an organization for the transmission to a certain number of prepared people of knowledge coming from higher mind. This is the most essential characteristic of a school. Another very important fact is the selection of students. Only people of a certain preparation and a certain level of understanding are admitted to a real school.

A school cannot be open to all, it cannot be open to many. Schools can be of very different levels depending on the preparation and the level of being of the students. The higher the level of the school, the greater the demands made upon the students. So, from this point of view schools are divided into degrees. There are schools where men No. 1, 2 and 3 learn how to become No. 4 and acquire all the knowledge that will help them in this change. The next degree are schools where men No. 4 learn to become No. 5. There is no need for us to speak of further degrees since they are too far from us. But even in schools of the lowest degree the beginning of schoolwork already means a certain preparation. One cannot pass straight from the absurdity of ordinary life to school. Even if a school does all that is possible to give a man something, if he is not prepared, if he does not know how to take it, it cannot be given.

Q. What does being prepared mean?

A. It is first of all necessary to be ready for any level on which one can begin, not only from the point of view of knowledge, but also from the point of view of being. One must realize one's situation, know what one cannot do by oneself, realize that one needs help, and many other things. It depends on what a person needs in a school. Nobody needs a school as such, but if one does need something, then one needs a school in order to get it. Being prepared means that one must already know oneself to a certain extent; one must know one's aim; one must know the value of one's decisions; there must be a certain elimination of lying to oneself; one must be able to be sincere with oneself.

Unfortunately, C influence very often becomes B influence if people come to a school unprepared. Later, perhaps after a long time, they may hear the same things that they heard when they first came and discover a new meaning in them. Then this becomes C influence. There are many ideas which, if understood rightly, can become C influence.

Besides, one can only enter a school when one has already lost, or is prepared to lose, at least a certain amount of self-will. Self-will is the chief obstacle to entering a school because a school means not only learning but also discipline. And some people may find discipline boring, or unnecessary.

Q. Is there a form of examination that one must pass before one can enter a school?

A. Examination is almost continuous, it goes on all the time, and not only before one enters a school but also when one is in the school.

Q. There must be a reason why some people see the possibility of change and others do not.

A. Yes, there are reasons. It is a kind of previous training of the mind. Most people have the same chance, but some accumulate material and are prepared for change, and others not. But even if they are prepared, they need help and have to make efforts.

Q. Can people wish to change and find it impossible?

A. Sometimes resistance is too great; for instance, imagination may be too strong, and they may refuse to give it up. Or, as I said, sometimes magnetic Centre may be formed in a wrong way. There are people with two or more magnetic centres looking in different directions. Then they can never be interested in the same thing for long. But if one has a rightly formed magnetic Centre, all these interests become connected, and it may be a very powerful thing.

Q. You say that if people are unprepared C influence becomes B influence for them. Is it because they have nothing to judge it by?

A. Not only because of that; it is because they have no valuation of ideas, they take all ideas on the same level.

Q. Do negative emotions prevent one taking in C influence?

A. If you have a great deal of negative emotion, it forms a cloud which prevents not only C influence but even A influence getting to you. It has been established long ago that, although C influences exist, one cannot get them by oneself. This means that there is something one has to conquer in order to understand, and in order to understand more one has to conquer something else. This is why school is necessary. In school you cannot deceive yourself and it can be explained to you why you do not understand.

As I said, there are many degrees of schools. Schools that begin on the ordinary level of life are very elementary. In them there are necessarily certain rules and conditions. If one forgets them, or makes excuses for oneself, one cannot really consider oneself as being in a school.

Q. Can one be disciplined to school life without being disciplined to ordinary conventions?

A. School discipline is based on understanding, it is quite different.

Q. Isn't there a danger of taking discipline as escape from responsibility?

A. Then one will fail.

Q. To what extent can one develop being without a school?

A. No real development of being is possible without schools, or rather, it is possible to a certain extent, but it is generally incomplete. Right development of being is impossible without schools because one cannot look after oneself, one cannot be sufficiently strict with oneself. And it is not only a question of being strict one simply cannot remember things at the right time, but one will also forget, or one will make things easy for oneself. If it were possible to work by oneself, schools would be a waste of time and systems would not be necessary; but since they exist, it means that it is impossible without them. One can have no plan, no system by oneself. How can one develop without a plan or system? How can any work be done? How can one get the necessary knowledge, understand one's position, know what to do? One cannot even get preliminary knowledge with which to start.

Q. Do schools necessarily contain people of higher consciousness?

A. Not contain, we cannot expect that, but, as I said, a school cannot be started without knowledge coming from men of a higher mind.

Q. Will a school help me to make decisions that will affect the future?

A. All that I can say is that what you do today will make tomorrow, so tomorrow depends on what you do to-day. You can change the future now that is what must be understood. In ordinary life you cannot change anything, but when you begin to know more you have more power to change.

Schools are not all the same. For some kind of people one kind of school is necessary, for another kind of people there is another kind of school. There is no universal school for all kinds of people. This brings us to the subject of different ways. But before speaking about the ways it is necessary to realize that thousands of years ago people came to the idea that man can change, that he can acquire something he has not got. What he can acquire was expressed differently and approached from different angles, but the general idea was always the same that man can develop, that he can acquire something new. So, there were formed three ways corresponding to the division of man into man No. 1, No. 2 and No. 3.

The first way is the way of the Fakir. It is a long, difficult, and uncertain way.

A fakir works on the physical body, on conquering physical pain.

The second way is the way of the Monk. This way is shorter, more sure, and more definite. It requires certain conditions, but above all it requires faith, for if there is no faith a man cannot be a true monk.

The third way is the way of the Yogi, the way of knowledge and consciousness. When we speak about the three ways we speak about principles. In actual life they are seldom met with in a pure form, for they are mostly mixed. But if you know the principle, when you study school practices you can separate which practice belongs to which way. When we speak of yogis, we really take only Jnana-Yoga and Raja-Yoga. Jnana-Yoga is the yoga of knowledge, of a new way of thinking. It teaches to think in different categories, not in the categories of space and time and of causality. And Raja-Yoga is work on being, on consciousness.

Although in many respects these ways are very efficient, the characteristic thing about them is that the first step is the most difficult. From the very first moment you have to give up everything and do what you are told. If you keep one little thing, you cannot follow any of these ways. So, although the three ways are good in many other respects, they are not sufficiently elastic. For instance, they do not suit our present mode of life. The Fakir is an exaggerated No. 1 man with a heavy predominance of instinctive-moving Centre. The Monk is an exaggerated No. 2 man with the emotional Centre developed and the others under-developed. The Yogi is an exaggerated No. 3 man with the intellectual Centre developed and the others not sufficiently developed. If only these three traditional ways existed, there would be nothing for us, for we are too over-educated for these ways. But there is a Fourth Way which is a special way, not a combination of the other three. It is different from others first of all in that there is no external giving up of things, for all the work is inner.

A man must begin work in the same conditions in which he finds himself when he meets it, because these conditions are the best for him. If he begins to work and study in these conditions, he can attain something, and later, if it is necessary, he will be able to change them, but not before he sees the necessity for it. So, at first one continues to live the same life as before, in the same circumstances as before. In many respects this way proves more difficult than the others, for nothing is harder than to change oneself internally without changing externally.

Then in the Fourth Way the first principle is that man must not believe anything; he must learn; so, faith does not enter into the Fourth Way. One must not believe what one hears or what one is advised, one must find proofs for everything. If one is convinced that something is true, then one can believe it, but not before. This is a brief outline of the difference between the four ways.

Q. Why is it wrong to believe?

A. People believe or disbelieve when they are too lazy to think. You have to choose; you have to be convinced. You are told that you must remember yourself, but it would be wrong for you to remember yourself because you are told. First you must realize that you do not remember yourself and what it means, and then if you really realize that you need it and would like to remember yourself, you will do it in the right way. If you, do it simply by copying somebody, you will do it in a wrong way. You must realize that you are doing it *for yourself,* not because somebody told you.

Q. Is the Fourth Way for any special type of man?

A. Yes, if you like for a type of man who cannot follow the other ways.

Q. Does it take much longer?

A. It can be the shortest of all because more knowledge enters into it. The Fourth Way is sometimes called the way of the 'sly man'. The sly man knows about the three traditional ways, but he also knows more than they do. Suppose people in all the ways work to get into a certain state necessary for some particular work they have to do. The sly man will produce this state in the shortest time of all; but he must know how to do it, he must know the secret.

Q. What is the special meaning attached to the words 'sly man'?

A. What do you understand by slyness?

Q. Indirectness.

A. Yes, many things one cannot get direct. This idea is very largely used in the New Testament, only it is not called being 'sly'. There are situations that are so difficult that one cannot go straight, it is necessary to be 'sly'.

Q. Can anybody go by the Fourth Way?

A. No, because it needs understanding and efforts. One must be prepared for making efforts.

Q. How can anybody tell whether he has got the right way for him?

A. By results. You meet a system and begin to work. After some time, you must be able to say what you have got from it. It is not very difficult. Certainly, in most cases it will look at first like intellectual acquisitions, for you acquire new ideas, new knowledge.

But it is so arranged that acquiring new ideas in the system is connected with a certain change in understanding, in attention, in will and so on. One cannot get new ideas in a right way without a certain change.

Q. If the four ways are ways towards the same objective, what is the factor, or main quality, common to them all?

A. What is similar in all the ways is the possibility of changing being. If you think of all that makes up being, such as wrong work of centres, identification, considering, negative emotions, absence of unity and so on, you will understand that all this can be changed in each of the four ways: in the way of the Fakir by conquering physical suffering, in the way of the Monk by creating religious emotion, in the way of the Yogi by acquiring knowledge and working on consciousness. Ways are the same, but people are different; a man who can go by one way cannot go by another. There are four definite categories of people in our times according to which the ways are divided. I do not mean that it has always been so, but it is definitely so now. This division is connected not so much with people being No. 1, 2 or 3 as with there being one-Centre people, two-Centre people, three-Centre people, four-Centre people. This means people in whom one Centre is fully developed while the others are underdeveloped, or two centres developed and the others not developed, or three centres developed and the fourth under-developed, or four centres developed more or less equally. This makes the division into four ways.

Q. Is this system the Fourth Way?

A. This is a wrong formulation. You can ask yourself: 'Does this system belong to the way of the Fakir, the way of the Monk, or the way of the Yogi? No, but it may belong to the Fourth Way.' You cannot say this system is the Fourth Way; the Fourth Way is very big, and this system is very small by comparison.

Q. Is it only in relation to schools that magnetic Centre operates?

A. In the religious way a different magnetic Centre is necessary.

A magnetic Centre that brings one to a Yogi school or a monastery is different from the magnetic Centre that brings one even to a group that may possibly lead to a Fourth Way school. With that kind of magnetic Centre, one would not be able to work here: people would not have enough initiative. In the religious way they must obey. In this way people must have broader minds, they must understand. In Yogi schools and the religious way one can go on for a long time without understanding, just doing what one is told. Here, results are proportionate to understanding.

Q. The magnetic Centre of different people may be attracted by different ideas? Is the starting point connected with that?

A. Yes, it may be very different, but in relation to this system there must be a certain similarity of magnetic centres, so that people can work together; because in a certain period, class and education, people have more or less the same material.

Q. Does the Fourth Way embrace the three other ways?

A. No, this is a wrong description, because the Fourth Way does not have many of the things which enter into the first three ways, and it has many other things that do not enter into the three ways. The idea of the Fourth Way is that it discards from the three ways all that is unnecessary in them, because besides the necessary things the three ways have other things which have remained there purely through tradition, imitation and so on.

In the Fourth Way all the sides that can develop, develop at the same time, and this makes it different from other ways where you first develop one side and then go back and develop another, then again go back, and develop a third side. In the Fourth Way all the four centres must be more or less alive, on the surface, open to receive impressions, otherwise long preliminary work to open them is necessary before one can begin.

Q. Is not the Fourth Way actually very much the most difficult, owing to the continual choice entailed under conditions of maximum outside distractions?

A. It depends on what you call most difficult. The other three ways need a very big decision right at the beginning, when you really know nothing. You have to renounce everything absolutely. If you can do that, and if you have other qualities that are needed, you can go by the way of the Monk, or the way of the Yogi, if you can find a Monk or a Yogi school. But if you do not know such schools and if you find that you cannot give up even small things, then certainly this is the only way possible for you. It is not a question of more or less difficult;

it is a question of which is most possible. Then, if you think, you will find that there is only one way that is possible.

Q. Is there anything in the schools of the Fourth Way equal to prayer state, and if so, does it come with self-remembering?

A. Yes, in all the ways one has to pass through the same experiences, only in a different order. Certainly, self-remembering, non-identifying and several other practices will give exactly the same personal sensations as high emotions of a religious or an intellectual order. You remember that man was compared to a house with four rooms. What does development mean? It means working in the four rooms, only the order of rooms in which a man works is different in different ways. In the Fourth Way work is done in all the four rooms at once.

Q. Is this organization a school?

A. This is an interesting question: can we call ourselves a school? To a certain extent we may, because we acquire a certain knowledge and at the same time, we learn how to change our being. But I must say in relation to this that in the beginning of our work, in St. Petersburg in 1916, we were made to understand that a school, in the full sense of the term, must consist of two degrees, that is, it must have two levels in it: one level, where men 1, 2 and 3 learn to become No. 4 and the other level where men No. 4 learn to become No. 5. If a school has two levels, it has more possibilities, because a double organization of this kind can give a larger variety of experience and make the work more quick and more sure. So, although in a certain sense we can call ourselves a school, it is better to use this term for a bigger organization.

Q. Did I understand from what you said that this is not exactly a school?

A. For some people it may be a school, for others not. It is always like that. It cannot be definite and cannot be the same for everybody.

Q. If it is not yet ready to be called a school, what can make it so?

A. Only work of its members on their own being, understanding of the principles of schoolwork and discipline of a certain very definite kind. If we want to create a school, because we have come to the conclusion that we cannot change by ourselves without it, we must take part in the building of the school. This is the method of the Fourth Way. In the religious way schools already exist, but here, if we want a school, we must take part in the building of it. But first you must learn. When you know enough, you will know what to do.

Q. You said that one can learn how to escape only from those who have escaped before?

A. Quite right in the allegory of prison. And this means a school can only start from another school. This system can have value only if it comes from higher mind. If we have reason to believe that it only comes from an ordinary mind, like ours, it can have no value and we cannot expect anything from it. Then better sit down and write your own system.

Q. Would it be possible for everyone in a school to progress from No. 4 to No. 5, or only for a few?

A. There is no limitation in principle. But you must understand that there is an enormous difference between man No. 4 and man No. 5. Man No. 4 is a man who has acquired a permanent Centre of gravity, but in everything else he is an ordinary man. Man No. 5 is very different. He already has unity, a permanent 'I', the third state of consciousness. This means that he is awake, he can always remember himself when he needs it, and the higher emotional Centre works in him which gives him many new powers.

Q. Is it worse not to be able to go on with the system than not to have started?

A. If you have started, nobody can stop you, except yourself.

Q. How can one reconcile this with what you said about their being no guarantee?

A. It depends on your work. How can I guarantee your work? What we can get depends on our own efforts, and one must work at one's own risk but after some time one begins to see: 'I got this that I did not have before' and 'I got that that I did not have before'. So little by little one can be more sure.

Q. What does a school study?

A. It studies possibilities of the development of inner qualities in man. It begins with the idea that not all the qualities can develop equally in order that certain qualities should develop, other qualities have to be restrained and some others have to go. Suppose you have a hundred qualities. Out of these, suppose thirty can develop and seventy cannot Then you have to restrain those seventy in order that the thirty may develop. And in schools they have a certain knowledge about which qualities can and which cannot develop, which conditions are good, how to restrain certain qualities, how to develop other qualities. Different schools teach in different ways. For instance, this kind of school says simply: develop only consciousness and all the rest will be added unto you, and for that one must struggle with negative emotions, lying, identification, considering, imagination and so on.

Q. You said we must verify everything, but if we can only know what we ourselves have experienced, does it not limit us to a very small world?

A. We know not only what we experience ourselves, we know what other people have experienced the whole idea of school is study on the basis of the experience of other people, not people such as we are, but people of higher mind, otherwise there can be no school. If a school is limited only to what we know ourselves, then it is not a school.

Q. Isn't it the belief that there exists something beyond what we know that makes us seek for it?

A. There are many things beyond, only we must understand that our possibility of knowing, *actually* knowing, is very limited in present conditions. We can formulate problems, we can make theories, but we cannot find answers for them, or we can find merely theoretical answers so that one answer is as good as another. But we can hope and expect that if we change our state of consciousness and perfect our inner machinery we shall perhaps know more.

Q. Does school stand for self-initiation?

A. What does self-initiation mean? It is all words. What would it mean to be initiated into the Chinese language? It would mean to learn it, to be taught. You cannot be initiated into Chinese by laying hands on you. Initiation is work. Two people can be in the same school, and for one it will be a school of one level and for another a school of another level. And for a third it may not be a school at all. It depends how deep one is in it. The highest school can be on very low level, and one and the same school can be on different levels, depending on the people in it. It requires work and remembering of aim.

Q. If schools are so important, why do they not have more influence in the world?

A. Schools can only act through people who are interested in them. They can do nothing if they are surrounded by people who are indifferent. The possibility of schools influencing life is conditioned by the general attitude to schools. In order to have influence, schools must have people who are interested and who would obey. But this must come from below, it cannot be produced by schools. Schools can throw B influences into the world, but if people are not interested in them, they can do nothing. They cannot use violence.

Q. Can a school lose by giving away its knowledge?

A. A school can lose in many different ways. We shall come to this question later on. It depends on whom it gives to. If it gives just in general and does not receive anything, certainly it will lose. If one has money and begins to give it to everybody, whether they deserve it or not, certainly one will lose one's money.

Q. You said that if we want a school, we must take part in building it. How can we do that?

A. You must remember that the level of a school depends on the level of being of the people who constitute it. If there are not enough people with magnetic Centre, there can be no school. But it is not simply coming to lectures and accepting what one hears that shows the presence of a magnetic Centre.

Q. Would the spreading of school ideas and school language among other people be of any help from the point of view of the school?

A. Ideas cannot be spread in the right form, it is important to understand that. It would be very good if it could be done, but it cannot. Words would remain, but the ideas themselves would be different. If it were enough to spread them, why are schools necessary? The language will spread itself, maybe even in our lifetime, but the ideas will enter into the general currency in a wrong form. For instance, there would be no distinction between 'doing' and 'happening'.

Q. We talk of schools and different levels. Is it not rather confusing? What do higher levels mean?

A. Why do you find the idea of higher levels confusing? For instance, we can take this idea of levels quite simply in relation to ourselves: using all our mental capacities we can think only up to a certain level, but if we could use higher centres, for instance higher emotional Centre which already needs more or less complete self-remembering, then certainly on the same subject we could think quite differently and find many more connections in things which we do not notice now. That shows different levels of thinking, and sometimes we actually have glimpses of a higher level of thinking, so we may have some material for observation, because even now we can think differently on the same subject.

And as regards different levels of people, we meet with results of work of people obviously belonging to higher planes; we cannot say that our experience of ordinary life is limited to results of work of people like ourselves. Take the New Testament, and there are also works of art, esoteric writings, Christian literature and so on which obviously cannot belong to ordinary people. The existence of people of higher development is not imagination, not a hypothesis, but an actual fact. So, I do not understand in what way it is confusing; I do not see how one can think without recognizing this fact. It is a definite fact that people live not only on the level on which we are but can exist on different levels.

From this point of view humanity can be regarded as divided into four concentric circles. The three inner circles are called Esoteric, Mesoteric and Exoteric. The fourth is the outer circle where men 1, 2 and 3 live. Schools act as gates through which man No. 4, who is between the outer and the Exoteric circle, can pass. Man No. 5 belongs to the Exoteric circle, man No. 6 to the Mesoteric and man No. 7 to the Esoteric or the innermost circle. The outer circle is also called the circle of the confusion of tongues, for in this circle people cannot understand one another. Understanding is possible only in the inner circles.

All this means there are degrees.

A man who lives in the outer circle is under the law of accident, or, if he has a strongly expressed essence, his life is more governed by the laws of his type or the laws of fate. But when a man begins to work towards consciousness, he already has direction. This means a change, perhaps not perceptible, but nevertheless cosmically a change. Only individual effort can help man to pass from the outer circle into the Exoteric circle. What refers to a man in the outer circle does not refer to a man who begins to work. He is under different laws, or rather, different laws begin to touch a man who begins to work. Each circle is under different laws.

* * *

CHAPTER V

Possibility of man's further development—Absence of consciousness— Cognition of truth—Study of degrees of consciousness—Self-remembering and self-observation—Impossibility of defining what self-remembering is— Self-remembering as method of awakening—Approach to self-remembering through the intellectual Centre—Reconstructing thoughts—Stopping thoughts as a method of bringing self-remembering—Remembering oneself in emotional moments—Ignorance and weakness—Identification and struggle with it—External and internal considering—Negative emotions—Quiet place in oneself.

It would be good if, from time to time, you tried to summarize in your mind what you have heard so far; because after some time of coming to lectures and talks one begins to forget the chronology of the ideas, and it is important to remember the order in which they are given.

Out of all you have heard, the most important idea is that with certain knowledge and certain efforts man can develop, he can complete himself. The development of man, if it is a process (it is not obligatory at all), passes through certain definite stages or steps. If you return to the beginning, you will remember what was said about the absence of consciousness in man and the fact that when a man realizes it, this realization gives him the possibility of acquiring consciousness, and you will see that this is the direction in which man can develop. As long as he does not realize that he is simply a machine and that all his processes are mechanical, he cannot begin to study himself, for this realization is the beginning of self-study. So, study must begin in this way: we must realize that we do not possess self-consciousness, that we cannot be aware of ourselves at moments of action or thought. This is the first step. The second step is to realize that we do not know ourselves, we do not know our machine and how it works. And the next step is to realize that we have to study methods of self-study. We observe ourselves all our life, but we do not know what self-observation means. Real self-observation must be based on facts.

So, one of the first points is: how to remember oneself, how to be more conscious? It is not enough to admit this absence of consciousness in oneself; one has to see it in actual fact, to verify it from personal observation.

We do not realize what consciousness is and what it implies. If one becomes conscious for half an hour, it is incredible what one can see and learn. So, it is an aim in itself, because of what it brings, and it also means a step towards objective consciousness.

It is necessary to speak a little about this, about what is meant by the four degrees of consciousness man can possess. If we take it from the point of view of cognition of truth, then in sleep we cannot know the difference between what is true and what is not true. Things we see in dreams all look alike. In the waking state we already have more opportunity to recognize the difference between things: the shape of things is made out by our eye, the surface of things by touch and, to a certain extent, we can orientate ourselves by the perceptions of our instruments of sense. So, there is an objective element, but we ourselves remain subjective to ourselves. When we become self- conscious, we become objective to ourselves, and in objective conscious we can know objective truth about everything. These are the degrees of consciousness.

Q. Must we change our knowledge in order to see things as they really are and know the truth?

A. No, in this state of consciousness we cannot come to things as they are; we have to change our state of consciousness. But we can take off some layers of lying. Things are surrounded by lying. We can take off one, two or three skins and come nearer to real things.

Q. I am not clear about higher consciousness. Could we at least know how to think about it?

A. We realize the possibility of higher consciousness when we realize that we are not conscious at all. We are conscious only at rare moments, without possibility of control. Now we are in two states, in sleep and half-awake. Theoretical comparisons of states of consciousness and descriptions in words will not help; but when we begin to awake, we realize the state in which we are now. It is necessary to find moments of self-remembering and then, at these moments, you will see the difference. By studying yourself you will see that you can be very near to sleep, or you can be near to self-consciousness. So, study begins with the study of these different states in ourselves. For instance, when we take ourselves as one or do not think about it then we are nearly asleep. But when we begin to divide ourselves and know that at every moment it is only one 'I' or one group of 'I's speaking, then we are nearer to self-consciousness, nearer to objective facts.

There are different ways of studying consciousness in oneself. In the beginning the first thing is the realization that one cannot be conscious when one wants to. The best time to realize this is after you have been speaking or doing something. Suppose you have been talking about some important business, or writing a letter; then ask yourself, 'Was I conscious at that time?' The second thing, in the beginning, is the realization that you are not one, that you have many different 'I's.

Q. How is one to recognize when one is self-conscious?

A. You will know; it is quite a different feeling. If you try to be conscious for a moment and then compare it with another moment when you did not try to be conscious, you will see the difference. It cannot be described. One moment you are aware of yourself, another moment you are not: you do things, you speak, you write, and you are not conscious.

Only you must remember that it is said from the very beginning that we must study not only states of consciousness but also obstacles to consciousness. So, we must study them, and then remove them. All these obstacles are in ourselves. External circumstances we cannot change, we have to take them as they are and change inwardly in these circumstances.

Q. If you observe yourself for a moment, are you conscious at that moment?

A. Not necessarily; it may be quite mechanical. But if you are conscious at the same time that you observe, the line of your attention will resemble two arrows, one showing attention directed on the thing you observe and another on yourself.

Q. I cannot understand the link between self-observation and self-remembering. How to begin, what to do?

A. Self-remembering is an attempt to be aware of yourself. Self-observation is always directed at some definite function: either you observe your thoughts, or movements, or emotions, or sensations. It must have a definite object which you observe in yourself.

Self-remembering does not divide you; you must remember the whole, it is simply the feeling of 'I', of your own person. They may come together, particularly at later stages, and then you will be able to do both at the same time observe something definite, or recognize manifestations in yourself, and remember yourself; but in the beginning the two things are different. You begin with self-observation that is the normal way and through self-observation you realize that you do not remember yourself. When you realize that, and that at very rare moments you do remember yourself, then any person who is not definitely prejudiced will be able to understand that it is possible to increase these moments of self-remembering. And then you try to do it.

Q. I find it difficult to decide whether I really observe myself or only remember things afterwards.

A. In the beginning there is no particular necessity to worry about which is which; just do what you can, either observe at the moment, or remember it immediately, or remember after some time. But later you will catch particular moments when you can be aware of yourself at the actual moment when things happen. That will be self-remembering.

Q. How do you know of the miraculous results which will follow self-remembering?

A. You see, this is connected with the whole idea of development, with the possibility of changing being. This is one of the first things we must understand: that man is not bound to remain as he is; he can change. There are different degrees of man that can be attained after long and persistent work. If we can be more conscious, this will make higher centres work. The functioning of higher centres will be in many ways miraculous. The idea of self-remembering enters into many systems and school teachings, but it is not in the right place, it is never put first. But this system says that you do not remember yourself and that if you understand that you do not remember yourself, you may be able to achieve something. Self-awareness is the greatest change possible, because in ordinary conditions of life nobody is aware of himself, and yet people do not realize this. Everybody sitting here, if they ask themselves sincerely whether they are aware of themselves, will have to answer that they are not. Nobody is aware. The whole idea is to be aware of yourself in this place, at this moment. This is the beginning, for one has to begin somewhere. Later it may take different forms, many other things may be included in it.

Nothing can describe this: it is material for observation and study. Descriptions will not help; one has to practice. Normally nobody remembers himself, nobody is aware of himself. This is the ordinary state of a human being, of a man-machine. But if he knows about it, if he realizes it and thinks about it, it becomes possible. Only, in the beginning self-remembering is very slow in coming and very small, with long lapses of not remembering.

Q. Is the essential feature of a state of self-remembering the ordinary state of alertness of mind?

A. No, you cannot take it like that, it is too small. It is a different state, more different from our present state than our present state is from physical sleep but even comparing sleep with the ordinary state gives you some possibility of understanding the difference. When you are asleep, your world is limited by actual sensations, but when you wake up and find yourself in the objective world (although you see this world in subjective categories) it is much less limited. But when you realize that this is not full awakening, that you are actually less than half-awake, you will understand that if you awake fully, you will find yourself in a still richer world and will see and understand many of its characteristics which now pass unnoticed.

Q. I want to know whether self-remembering, at any rate at an early stage, should be expected to consist of a sterile cessation of attention to any-thing other than oneself?

A. At an early stage it can only be a realization that you do not remember yourself. If we realize how little we are aware of ourselves and how tiny the moments are when we are aware, when we remember that and feel that and realize what it means, then we can understand what self-remembering means. If you realize the importance of this fact and all that it implies, it will not be sterile. But if you do not realize it, you are quite right, it will be sterile. Then it will simply be a strange exercise that does not lead anywhere.

Q. Does self-remembering come automatically when you realize that you do not remember yourself?

A. This is self-remembering. You cannot make the next step without realizing where you are. It is the same process, the same thing. The more you realize how unpleasant and dangerous it is to be a machine, the more possibility you have to change.

Q. How?

A. There is always something we can do at certain moments. You must know these moments, and what to do, and how. We are studying doors. Self-remembering is a door. If realization that we do not remember ourselves becomes continuous, then we can remember ourselves. Every day you can find time to realize that you do not remember yourself; this will gradually bring you to self-remembering. I do not mean to remember that you do not remember yourself but to *realize* it.

I repeat, it is not useful to look for definitions, they would only make understanding more difficult. What is really useful for understanding Is comparing the different degrees of consciousness within our ordinary state, for even in our ordinary state of relative consciousness there are different degrees, different levels: we can be nearer to awakening or further from it. We can see such big differences in ourselves, when we really learn to observe, that it will show us the possibilities we have. It is the one unmistakable thing. We are always moving between two shores between sleep and awakening. Moving more towards one shore or more towards the other creates two different possibilities: one is development, the other is decay.

Q. You asked us not to accept anything without questioning it. Have you, knowledge that these higher states of consciousness have actually been reached?

A. Oh yes. In the first place you can find many descriptions in literature of how mystics and religious people came to the same things. The similarity of descriptions of these experiences is the best proof. All sorts of people in different countries, thousands of years apart, living in different conditions, have come to the same kind of experience by certain ways. Then you can find many people who have personal experience of this kind which proves that quite different states of perception and reaction exist. So, it is not a hypothesis.

Q. I have recently had a very strange experience. I was talking to someone and trying to be aware of myself. Suddenly I saw my friend very clearly and realized that before this I had not really seen her at all.

A. This is a very good observation; it actually happens that way. When you tried to be aware of yourself, for a moment you became conscious and saw things you had not seen before. If you could keep this consciousness for, say, ten minutes, you would see many things which would astonish you. We look with our eyes and do not see; but if we become conscious, we begin to see things about which we have no idea. This is quite normal, if only you do not let imagination enter into it.

Q. Working to attain consciousness on the lines of the system, does there comes a sudden change or illumination?

A. Sudden? No. What does sudden mean? You see, in the process of growth of unity, when this process has gone on for a long time, at some difficult moment you may feel different. It may look sudden, but it is not really so. It is the result of previous efforts.

Q. If potentiality for objective consciousness is the normal condition of man, how is it that only a few can develop?

A. When you try to make the first step towards objective consciousness, which is gaining self-consciousness, and you see how difficult it is and how many forces work in you against it, how many obstacles there are, you will have no doubt that only a few can attain it, that it is a possibility, but a very remote possibility. There are too many obstacles laziness, lying, inertia. We like to sleep.

Q. How and why did man come to be this being of false values?

A. What do you mean by false values? It is a relative concept: from one point of view, they may be false, from another true. You can only find out for *yourself* whether man's development is an abstract idea or the truth. You must *yourself* come to one or another point of view. If you realize that change is only possible through awakening, then it becomes a fact, because you can see small degrees of awakening in yourself.

Q. If man does not remember himself, does it mean he has no consciousness?

A. *You* do not remember yourself; not man but you. If you try and fail, it does not mean you have no consciousness, but that you have not enough. Your own experience, however limited, can alone show the degree.

When we use the word 'self-consciousness' we mean a certain degree, beyond our ordinary amount of consciousness. We have a certain amount of consciousness, but it is not sufficient for getting out of our state. If we had not a drop of consciousness, we would remain as we are.

Q. How is it possible to recognize self-remembering if we ever do?

A. First it must be understood by mind what it means and what it would mean to have it; and then it must be understood that one can be at different distances from it. Suppose one is not sure, but the distance between the state of self-remembering and your present state changes, and after a time you realize that one day it is five thousand miles and another day only three thousand miles.

There is a difference. We cannot speak about several degrees at the same time; we can only speak about the next degree we can produce.

Q. I want to find out about the next degree.

A. This is all material for observation. You want to put labels on them, but you cannot; they change all the time. One moment it is almost self-consciousness, the next moment you are asleep. You must observe and see results. In one state you can understand certain things, in the next you cannot. In one state you identify, in another you have control; the more control there is, the nearer you are to self-consciousness. Talk will not help much, it will remain formatory. It is necessary to touch the emotional Centre, and you can do that only by trying different things. Work is not simple: from the very beginning you must try to do impossible things impossible in the sense that they do not happen by themselves. There cannot be a textbook telling you to do first one thing, then another thing, and so on.

At the same time questions about self-remembering must always be asked, because, for a long time, many mistakes are possible about it. So, these questions must never be suppressed, for they are most important.

Q. Is there a connection between self-remembering and awakening?

A. Self-remembering is a method of awakening. What you are doing now is only preparation, only the study of the method. You must do as much as you can in your present state; then, when your inner situation changes, you will be able to use all the experience which you now acquire. But to reach the real meaning of self remembering is possible only in very emotional states. Since you cannot create these emotional states, you cannot know what self-remembering is, but you can prepare for this experience; then when it comes you will know how to deal with it. Very high emotional energy is necessary for self-remembering. Now you are only practicing, but without this practice you will never get the real state.

Q. When you say 'asleep' and 'awake', is there a definite line between the two?

A. No, they are transitory states. At the same time there is a line beyond which we never pass.

Q. Is it a question of training?

A. It is more training of mind. We must learn to think in a different way, and above all to think more practically. We do not think practically as a rule, we think mostly about things that do not concern us.

Q. Is then self-remembering a function of the intellectual Centre? It appears to be an intellectual effort.

A. Self-remembering is the beginning and the Centre of the system and the most important thing to understand. You cannot describe it as an intellectual action or intellectual idea. You have to begin studying what self-remembering means intellectually, but in actual fact it is not intellectual because it is a moment of will. It is necessary to remember yourself not at a quiet moment when nothing happens but when you know that you are doing something wrong and not do it. For instance, when you are identified, you must be able to feel it and then stop it and at the same time remember yourself, be aware that you are doing it, that mechanicalness causes you to be identified and that you are stopping it. That will be self-remembering.

Q. How can one start practicing self-remembering?

A. You remember I gave the example of varying degrees of light in a room and a typewriter. The typewriter can be taken as the intellectual Centre, and light as consciousness. Only, in the case of consciousness there is a certain connection between all centres, for in full light not only one but all centres work differently. Real self-remembering requires emotion, but we have no control over the emotional Centre. So, by a certain understanding we can make the intellectual Centre, over which we have a certain control, work in the dark as though it were light, and this will produce self-remembering. Self-remembering means a form of thinking or intellectual work which corresponds to awakening, and in this way, it induces a moment of awakening.

Then, when one awakes for a moment, one realizes that generally one is asleep, that one is not conscious, and how dangerous it is. The more you put into it, the more you understand it, the better the result will be. If you realize what you lose by not remembering yourself and what you gain by remembering yourself, you will have a greater incentive for making efforts to self-remember. You will see that not remembering yourself is like finding yourself in an aero plane, high above the earth, and fast asleep. This is in fact our situation, but we do not wish to realize it. If a man does realize it, then naturally he will make efforts to awake. But if he thinks he is just sitting in an easy chair and nothing particular is happening, he will think that there is no harm in sleeping.

Q. What is meant by putting one's thoughts in a form in which they would correspond to awakening?

A. As I said, thoughts are the only thing we can control. To a certain extent we can control movements, but in ordinary conditions, without special instruction, we can do nothing with movements. As regards thoughts, first of all we must throw out all thoughts connected with identification and think about the ideas of the system. This is preparation for self-remembering, because at every point we come to the necessity to remember ourselves. If you cannot remember yourself, try to revive the ideas of the system in your mind. The whole system, the study of man and the universe, is all help to self-remembering. This thinking will by itself remind you and create an inner atmosphere for it. But first you must eliminate all thoughts that stand in the way. If at this stage you cannot control thoughts, you can do nothing further. You may not control your temper, or your imagination, or your lying, but you must control your thoughts. At quiet moments you must be able to see when you are wrong. If you cannot, it means that you have not begun yet; but sooner or later one must begin.

Q. Should we, each of us, know what stands in our way?

A. Yes, certainly everyone must know. It is generally connected with some form of negative Ness, or laziness, or fear.

Q. I still do not see what it means to try and think as we would think if we were more conscious.

A. Try to imagine yourself conscious that would be the right use of imagination. We develop this power of imagination in an absolutely wrong and useless way which is always making trouble for us. But now, for once, try to use it and imagine yourself conscious. Try to think how you would act, think, speak and so on.

At first self-remembering is an effort on functions. You begin to remember yourself simply by forming your mental processes in a certain way, and this brings moments of consciousness. You cannot work on consciousness itself: you can make one or two spasmodic efforts, but no permanent efforts. But you can make efforts on thoughts, and in this way, you can work on consciousness in a roundabout way. This is the most important part of the method. Try to understand the difference between remembering yourself in this way and being conscious. It is the same mental process that you use in everything, in reading, writing and all that you do, so you have a certain control over it. Even if we put the same amount of energy into self-remembering that we put into the study of a foreign language we would acquire a certain amount of consciousness. Unfortunately, we do not want to put even that amount of energy into it; we think that these things must come by themselves, or that it is enough to try once, and it must come. Self-remembering needs effort, so, if you continue to make these efforts, moments of consciousness will come more often and will stay longer. Then, gradually, self-remembering will cease to be purely intellectual, it will have an awakening power.

Q. What will self-remembering be then, emotion and sensation?

A. Emotion is a function and sensation are a function, but self-remembering is not. It is an attempt to create in oneself a state of consciousness without any relation to functions. From the very beginning we must understand that functions are one thing and states of consciousness another. You are now in a certain state of consciousness, and by trying to remember yourself you try to create an approach to the third state of consciousness. You do this by a certain *reconstruction*. You reconstruct a certain form of thinking which you have in higher states of consciousness. You cannot keep a flash of consciousness unless your thoughts are in a certain form. It is quite simple: you remember the example of the line of attention with two arrows? Attention is directed both on myself and on the thing I see. This double attention is the form of thinking corresponding to another state of consciousness.

Q. Is not self-remembering itself a state of consciousness?

A. It can be taken like that. At the same time, it can be taken as a method for inducing self-consciousness.

Q. What is the relation of thought to consciousness?

A. It is very difficult to answer briefly. Thought is a mechanical process, it can work without, or with very little consciousness. And consciousness can exist without perceptible thought.

Q. If self-remembering can be taken either as a state of consciousness or as a method for inducing it, are there different kinds of self-remembering? Is it brought about by different qualities of thought?

A. One has to do many things besides thinking, one has to make efforts. It is not only thinking. The difference is only that at first, we can do very little. We have to begin from where we are. Then, if we continue, self-remembering will gradually become more emotional. It is not different qualities of thought that make the difference; it is different qualities of effort and underlying realization. Self-remembering is effective only if one realizes that one does not remember oneself, but that one can remember oneself.

Q. Is not the act of giving attention a method of changing the state of consciousness?

A. A certain control of attention is necessary even in ordinary life. But attention can be drawn, or it can be controlled, and that is of quite a different value.

Q. I understood that we have a certain control of our thoughts in the sense of stopping certain kinds of thinking. But I have never heard before about constructing our thoughts.

A. We have the power not only not to think but also to think about this and that. So, we can do both: we can eliminate useless thoughts and we can also put in the Centre of our thinking the realization of 'I', 'I am here', 'I am thinking'.

Q. Why is it that an accident or a violent crisis brings self-remembering?

A. Every kind of emotional moment, emotional shock, makes you realize 'I am'. You realize it without any theory behind it: if you find yourself in a very unexpected place, you have a feeling of 'I' and 'here'; when you are in unusual circumstances it always reminds you of your existence. But in customary conditions we always forget.

Q. Is self-remembering the only strength the system hands out to us?

A. It is the only way to reach all the rest because it is the first thing that is lacking in us. We are always forgetting ourselves from one moment to another, and this state must be changed. One must remember oneself this is the beginning and the end of the whole thing, because when one has that one has everything.

Q. What is the distinction in the meaning of attention and consciousness?

A. Attention can be regarded as the elementary beginning of consciousness, the first degree. It is not full awareness for it is only directed one way. As I said, consciousness needs double attention.

Q. What is the object of attaining this higher consciousness to live more fully?

A. One thing depends on another. If we want to have will, if we want to be free instead of being marionettes, if we want to awake, we must develop consciousness. If we realize that we are asleep and that all people are asleep, and what it means, then all the absurdities of life are explained. It is quite clear that people cannot do anything differently from what they do now if they are asleep.

Q. As we are, would we ever be able to be conscious when we want to be, or does it always come accidentally?

A. Nothing comes in its full state at once. The first step is to be more conscious;

the second step is to be still more conscious. If, with effort, you can now make yourself be conscious for a minute, then, if you work on it and do all that is possible to help, after some time you will be able to be conscious for five minutes.

Q. Is it wrong when it is accidental?

A. You cannot rely on it. As we are, higher states cannot last; they are just flashes, and if they last, then it is imagination. This is a definite fact because we have no energy for lasting higher states. Flashes are possible, only again you must judge and classify them by what material they bring.

Q. Cannot they last in memory even?

A. The memory that we can command, control and use is only intellectual, and intellectual memory cannot keep them.

Q. It seems to me quite impossible to self-remember at will, although it seems not quite so difficult to observe myself.

A. You must try methods that will produce it. Try this method of stopping your thoughts, to see for how long you can keep your thoughts down, to think about nothing, if you know about self-remembering. But suppose a man who does not know about self-remembering tries this, he will not come to the idea of self-remembering in this way. If you already know, that will create a moment of self-remembering for how long will depend on your efforts. It is a very good way. This method is described, for instance, in some books on Yoga, but people who try it do not know why they are doing it, so it cannot produce good results. Quite the opposite, it may produce a kind of trance state.

Q. When you said, 'knowing about self-remembering', did you mean if you have it in your head as an aim, or if you had a taste of it?

A. There are different degrees. You see, we speak about self-remembering all the time; we always come back to it; so, you cannot say you do not know about self-remembering. But if you take a man who has studied ordinary psychology or philosophy, he does not know about it.

Q. Is it possible to have done self-remembering before one met this system? I ask because I have tried to self-remember and the results seem to correspond to what I used to do before, without knowing what I was doing.

A. That's the thing. You can study it to understand the principle that if you do a certain thing knowing what it is, it gives one result, and if you do almost the same thing without knowing what it is, it gives a different result. Many people came very near to self-remembering in practice, others came very near to it in theory but without practice either theory without practice, or practice without theory and neither from the one nor from the other did they come to the real truth. For instance, in the so-called Yoga literature there are many near approaches to self-remembering. For example, they speak about 'I am' consciousness, but they are so theoretical that you cannot get anything out of it. Self-remembering was never mentioned in any literature in an exact, concrete form, although in a disguised form it is spoken about in the New Testament and in Buddhist writings. For instance, when it is said, 'Watch, do not sleep', this is self-remembering. But people interpret it differently.

Q. Is emotional Centre the chief Centre that works in self-remembering?

A. You cannot control emotions. You simply decide to remember yourself. I have given you a very simple, practical method. Try to stop your thoughts but, at the same time, do not forget your aim that you do it in order to remember yourself. That may help. What prevents self-remembering? This constant turning of thoughts. Stop this turning, and perhaps you will have a taste of it.

Q. What centres work in self-remembering?

A. Self-remembering needs the best work you can produce, so the more centres that take part in it the better the result. Self-remembering cannot be produced by slow, weak work, the work of one or two centres. You may begin with two centres, but it is not sufficient, because other centres can interrupt your self-remembering and stop it. But if you put all centres to the work there is nothing that can stop it. You must always remember that self-remembering needs the best work you are capable of.

Q. You said real self-remembering needs emotion, but when I think of it, I do not experience any emotion. Can one remember oneself without emotional experience?

A. The idea is to remember oneself, to be aware of oneself. And what comes with it you just notice; you must not put any definite demands upon it. If you make it a regular practice to try and remember yourself three or four times a day, self-remembering will come by itself in the intervals, when you need it. But that you will notice later. You must make it a regular practice to try and remember yourself, if possible, at the same times of the day. And, as I said, the practice of stopping thoughts will produce the same effect. So, if you cannot remember yourself, try stopping thoughts. You *can stop* thoughts, but you must not be disappointed if at first you cannot. Stopping thoughts is a very difficult thing. You cannot say to yourself 'I will stop thoughts', and they stop. You have to use effort all the time. So, you must not do it for long. If you, do it for a few minutes it is quite sufficient, otherwise you will persuade yourself that you are doing it when instead you will just sit quietly and think and be very happy about it. As much as you can you must keep only one thought, 'I do not want to think about anything' and throw all other thoughts out. It is a very good exercise, but only an exercise.

Q. Is it bad to stop breathing when one tries to stop thoughts?

A. This question was asked once in our old groups and Mr. Gurdjieff asked: 'For how

long?' The man said for ten minutes. Mr. Gurdjieff answered: 'If you can stop breathing for ten minutes it is very good, because after four minutes you die!'

Q. Are self-remembering and stopping thoughts the same thing?

A. Not exactly; they are two different methods. In the first you bring in a certain definite thought, the realization that you do not remember yourself. You must always start with that. And stopping thought is simply creating a right atmosphere, right surroundings, for self-remembering. So, they are not the same thing, but they bring the same results.

Q. Is one's work more accurate if one is remembering oneself and the work one is doing?

A. Yes, when you are awake you can do everything better, but a long time is necessary for that. When you get accustomed to self-remembering you will not be able to understand how you ever worked without it. But in the beginning, it is difficult to work and to remember oneself at the same time. Still, efforts in this direction give very interesting results; of that there can be no doubt. All experience of all times shows that these efforts are always rewarded. Besides, if you make these efforts, you will understand that certain things one can only do in sleep and cannot do when one is awake, because some things can only be mechanical. For instance, suppose you forget or lose things: you cannot lose things on purpose, you can lose them only mechanically.

Q. While performing on the piano, when I thought 'I am here' I did not know what I was doing.

A. Because this is not being conscious, it is thinking about self-remembering. Then it interferes with what you are doing; just as when you are writing and suddenly think 'How is this word spelt?' you cannot remember. This is one function interfering with another. But real self-remembering is not in centers, it is above centers. It cannot interfere with the work of centers, only one will see more, one will see one's mistakes.

We must realize that the capacity for remembering oneself is our right. We do not have it, but we *can* have it; we have all the necessary organs for it, so to speak, but we are not trained, not accustomed to using them. It is necessary to create a certain particular energy or point, using this word in an ordinary sense, and this can be created only at a moment of a serious emotional stress. Everything before that is only preparation of the method. But if you find yourself in a moment of very strong emotional stress and try to remember yourself then, it will remain after the stress is over, and then you will be able to remember yourself. So only with very intense emotion is it possible to create this foundation for self-remembering. But it cannot be done if you do not prepare yourself beforehand. Moments may come, but you will get nothing from them. These emotional moments come from time to time, but we do not use them, because we do not know *how* to use them. If you try sufficiently hard to remember yourself during a moment of intense emotion, and if the emotional stress is strong enough, it will leave a certain trace, and this will help you to remember yourself in the future.

Q. So what we are doing now is a sort of practicing?

A. Now you are only studying yourselves, you can do nothing else.

Q. What is this preparation you are speaking about?

A. Self-study, self-observation, self-understanding. We can change nothing yet, nor make a single thing different. It all happens in the same way as before. But there is a difference already, for you see many things you could not have seen before, and many things 'happen' differently. It does not mean you have changed anything: they happen differently.

Q. Is our life long enough to attain results?

A. You come to the understanding of this point through self-remembering. When you reach certain results in it, if it comes often like seeing oneself in a mirror, then there comes another form of self-remembering, remembering one's life, the time-body. This increases possibilities. There are also other steps, but we can only speak of one step ahead, otherwise it would be imagination. We must understand that we must not touch certain questions without self-remembering. It is a question of perfecting our instrument of cognition. Our mind is very limited by our state of consciousness. We can hope that certain things will become comprehensible if our state of consciousness changes.

Q. Can self-consciousness give knowledge?

A. No, consciousness does not, by itself, give knowledge. Knowledge must be acquired. No amount of consciousness can give knowledge and no amount of knowledge can give consciousness. They are not parallel and cannot replace one another. But when you become conscious you see things you have not seen before. If you keep it long enough it produces an enormous effect. The whole world would be different if you could keep it up for, say, fifteen minutes. But one cannot be aware of oneself for fifteen minutes without a very strong emotional element. You must produce something that makes you emotional; you cannot do it without the help of the emotional Centre.

Q. It does not come by itself?

A. It is a question of destroying obstacles. We are not sufficiently emotional, because we spend our energy on identification, negative emotions, critical attitude, suspicion, lying and things like that. If we manage to stop this waste, we will be more emotional,

Q. In endeavoring to remember myself I find that I should avoid too much effort. I feel that one can swamp the effect by excessive effort.

A. What you mean is not too much effort, but a wrong kind of effort. Muscular effort will not help you to remember yourself. It is necessary for each person to find for himself the moment to make this particular big effort, especially at moments when all instinctive and emotional tendencies go against it. This is the moment to make effort. If you manage to remember yourself then, you will know how to do it.

Q. How can one prevent regular efforts becoming just formal; how can one stop the meaning slipping out of them?

A. Self-remembering cannot become formal; if it, does it mean deep sleep. Then it is necessary to do something to wake oneself up. But you must always start with the idea of mechanicalness and the results of mechanicalness. You are quite right. Everything slips away and disappears, and you find yourself again with nothing. Again, you start with some conscious effort, again it slips away. The question is how to prevent it disappearing. In our ordinary ways of thinking and feeling there are many mechanical tendencies which always turn us in the usual way. We want to think in another way, we want to be different, to work in another way, to feel in a new way, but nothing happens, because there are so many old tendencies which turn us back. We must study these tendencies and try to throw light on them. Above all, we must overcome the inertia of mind; then, if we do, twenty-four hours will not be sufficient, and life will become very full. It is difficult to begin and yet it is not so difficult.

Q. How can one conquer this inertia?

A. By effort: effort to self-remember, to observe, not to identify. Consciousness is a force, and force can only be developed by overcoming obstacles. Two things can be developed in man consciousness and will. Both are forces. If man overcomes unconsciousness, he will possess consciousness; if he overcomes mechanicalness he will possess will. If he understands the nature of the powers he can attain, it will be clear to him that they cannot be given; these powers must be developed by effort. If we were made more conscious, we would remain conscious machines. Mr. Gurdjieff told me that in some schools they could, by some special methods, make a sheep conscious. But it just remained a conscious sheep. I asked him what they did with it, and he said they ate it. The idea of the conscious sheep is this: suppose a man is made conscious by someone else; he will become an instrument in the hands of others. One's own efforts are necessary, because otherwise, even if a man is made conscious, he will not be able to use it. It is in the very nature of things that consciousness and will cannot be given. If someone could give them to you, it would not be an advantage. This is the reason why one must buy everything; nothing is given free. The most difficult thing is to learn how to pay. But if it could be explained in a few words, there would be no need to go to school. One has to pay not only for consciousness but for everything. Not the smallest idea can become one's own until one has paid for it.

Q. Self-remembering seems to be a very sad and cheerless experience. Is it a sad system?

A. There are no sad systems as far as I know, only sad people and sad attitudes, sad understanding. And I do not understand why self-remembering should be cheerless and sad. It is the realization of the fact that one is asleep. If one realized that one was asleep and there was no chance of awakening, then indeed it would be a cheerless realization, I quite agree. But the system does not say you should stop at that; it says that you should try to awake. And this is quite another thing. I remember, when I first heard this idea, I saw many quite new things, because it was an answer to all the questions I had when I studied psychology. So, I realized at once that psychology begins at this point. I understood that man does not remember himself but could remember himself if he made sufficient efforts. Without self-remembering there can be no study, no psychology. But if a man realizes and bears in mind that he does not remember himself, and that nobody remembers, and yet there is a possibility of self remembering, then study begins. This is how it must be understood.

Certainly, there can be no joy in realizing that one is a machine and asleep. But we do not speak about joy or suffering, we speak about control. We realize that we are machines, and we do not want to be machines. We realize that we are asleep, and we want to awake. Real joy can only be connected with awakening or with something that helps awakening.

Q. But so many people are self-conscious in a bad sense of the word. Isn't that a form of self-remembering too?

A. Not at all. What is called being self-conscious in English is a form of embarrassment or shyness; it has nothing to do with self-remembering.

As I have explained, if you are not awake you cannot make yourself awake; but you have some control over thoughts, and you must construct them in such a way as to bring you to awakening.

Q. Is a child nearer to self-remembering than a grown-up person? One has such vivid memories of childhood.

A. No, not quite; it is not self-remembering. Self-remembering means conscious work, I mean intentional work. Vivid memories of childhood are due to the activity of the emotional Centre. In a child it is more active, and moments of consciousness come by themselves. But self-remembering is a moment of consciousness that comes by *your own effort*. Suppose a child has flashes of consciousness without the possibility of using these moments? It does not help at all.

Q. Would it not help us to try to get back to those states we had in childhood?

A. How? That is the question. If we could stop identification, we would have many moments like that, but we do not know how to begin to stop identification. If we could destroy negative emotions, if we could remember ourselves, then those things would be in our hands, under our control, not accidental.

Q. When well washed and carefully dressed I feel it is much easier to self-remember.

A. It is not at all prohibited. This is not a fakir way.

Q. What is the relationship between self-remembering and negative emotions?

A. When negative emotion appears, self-remembering becomes impossible. So, to remember oneself one must have a certain control of negative emotions. As a matter of fact, people are not equal in this respect:

some have more, some less control even of the expression. And not only of the expression, for some people have more control of their emotions, some can control only certain emotions. And certainly, only those who have a certain control of negative emotions can work on self-remembering and get good results. At the same time this control can be attained; one can begin from different sides, and if certain self-remembering is created, this immediately helps one to struggle with negative emotions; and struggle with negative emotions helps self-remembering.

Q. Does it always take a long time to awake?

A. I can only say how much time it takes to know this system, but I cannot say how much time it takes to awake. Awakening is the result of personal work, so it is difficult to foretell. It goes by degrees. Complete awakening means a very big change, and that needs time, because it means acquiring new psychic functions. So, we can only study degrees or steps which a man must pass through. One can be shown the way, but one must work for oneself. By itself learning is a small thing, for man can change himself only through the *application* of the knowledge he gets. Man *can* become conscious of himself at a given moment. This consciousness of himself is awakening, one of the attributes of another state of consciousness.

Q. Could a person wish to wake up and fail to do so?

A. Maybe for a long time he will fail, but if he is capable of awakening, he can awake; it is a long process. But certainly, he may fail. We have only one good feature in our situation, we have nothing to lose. So, if we fail, we will be in the same position as before, but if we succeed, we gain something new.

Q. Does any great effort tend to make one more conscious at the time?

A. That depends on the effort, because if one just makes a great effort to do something in a state of identification, one will not be more conscious.

Q. Does self-remembering automatically stop identification?

A. There is nothing automatic in self-remembering every moment is effort. If it is sufficiently deep and sufficiently long it is one thing, but if it is just a flash it is not sufficient. Also, if you remember yourself to the exclusion of everything else, it is one thing, and if you remember yourself and at the same time remember your aim and what you are doing, it is another thing. It depends on how much enters into self- remembering.

Q. Would you call it self-consciousness?

A. Self-consciousness is a permanent state. Self-remembering is an experiment; one day it may be successful and another day unsuccessful. It may be deeper or less deep.

Q. Can we be told about the things that may be keeping us back?

A. We are talking about just those things. There are two things that are keeping us back ignorance and weakness: we do not know enough, and we are not strong enough. The question is how to know more. By self-study that is the only method. Then comes the struggle with identification and imagination, the chief causes of weakness. Only, in individual cases these things take on a different color. What looks one color for one person looks a different color for another person. But the things that keep us back are more or less the same.

Q. Is there nothing between self-awareness and identifying?

A. They are on different levels, you cannot compare them. You cannot identify and be aware of yourself; the presence of one means the absence of the other. All things are connected, not a single manifestation is separate; they are all connected with a certain order of things.

Q. I think I have not got the right idea about identification. Does it mean that things control us and not that we control things?

A. Identification is a very difficult thing to describe because no definitions are possible. Such as we are we are never free from identifying. If we believe that we do not identify with something, we are identified with the idea that we are not identified. You cannot describe identification in logical terms. You have to find a moment of identification, catch it, and then compare things with that moment. Identification is everywhere, at every moment of ordinary life. When you begin self-observation, some forms of identification already become impossible. But in ordinary life almost everything is identification. It is a very important psychological feature that permeates the whole of our life, and we do not notice it because we are in it. The best way to understand it is to find some examples. For instance, if you see a cat with a rabbit or a mouse this is identification. Then find analogies to this picture in yourself. Only, you must understand that it is there every moment, not only at exceptional moments. Identification is an almost permanent state in us. You must be able to see this state apart from yourself, separate it from yourself, and that can only be done by trying to become more conscious, trying to remember yourself, to be aware of yourself. Only when you become more aware of yourself are you able to struggle with manifestations like identification.

Q. I find when I am identified it is nearly always with things inside me.

A. Perhaps you are right; perhaps you are not right. You may think you are identified with one thing when in reality you are identified with quite a different thing. This does not matter at all; what matters is *the state of identification*. In the state of identification, you cannot feel right, see right, judge right. But the subject of identification is not important: the result is the same.

Q. So what is the way to overcome identification?

A. That is another thing. It is different in different cases. First it is necessary to see; then it is necessary to put something against it.

Q. What do you mean by 'put something against it'?

A. Just turn your attention to something more important. You must learn to distinguish the important from the less important, and if you turn your attention to more important things, you become less identified with unimportant things. You must realize that identification can never help you; it only makes things more confused and more difficult. If you realize even that, that alone may help in some cases. People think that to be identified helps them, they do not see that it only makes things more difficult. It has no useful energy at all, only destructive energy.

Q. Is identification mainly emotion?

A. It always has an emotional element, a kind of emotional disturbance, but sometimes it becomes a habit, so that one does not even notice the emotion.

Q. I realize that it is important to be emotional in the right way, but when I feel something emotionally in the work, I soon destroy the whole thing.

A. Only identification is destructive. Emotion can only give new energy, new understanding. You take identification for emotion. You do not know emotion without identification, so, in the beginning, you cannot visualize an emotion free from it. People often think they speak about an emotional function when in reality they speak about identification.

Q. Is it possible for us, as we are now, to have any feeling at all without identifying?

A. Very difficult, unless we begin to watch ourselves. Then easy kinds of identification, I mean easy individually will respond to treatment. But everyone has his own specialties in identification. For instance, it is easy for me not to identify with music, for another it may be very difficult.

Q. Is love without identification possible?

A. I would say love is impossible *with* identification. Identification kills all emotions, except negative emotions. With identification only the unpleasant side remains.

Q. Non-identifying does not mean aloofness?

A. On the contrary, aloofness needs identification. Non-identifying is quite a different thing.

Q. If you are identified with an idea, how can you stop it?

A. First by understanding what identification means and then by trying to remember yourself. Begin with simple cases, then later you can deal with the more difficult.

Q. As you develop self-remembering do you acquire a sort of detached attitude, more free from identification?

A. Detached attitude in the sense that you know your attitudes better; you know what is useful to you and what is not useful. If you do not remember yourself, it is easy to make a mistake about it. For instance, one can undertake some kind of study that is really quite useless. Self-remembering helps understanding and understanding always means bringing everything to a certain Centre. You must have a central point in all your work, in all your attitudes, and self-remembering is a necessary condition for that.

We must talk more about identifying if it is not clear. It will become more clear when you find two or three good examples. It is a certain state in which you are in the power of things.

Q. If I look closely and think deeply, does it mean I have become identified?

A. No, identifying is a special thing, it means losing oneself. As I said, it is not so much a question of what one is identified with. Identification is a state. You must understand that many things you ascribe to things outside you are really in you. Take for instance fear. Fear is independent of things. If you are in a state of fear, you can be afraid of an ashtray. This often happens in pathological states, and a pathological state is only an intensified ordinary state. You are afraid, and then you choose what to be afraid of. This fact makes it possible to struggle with these things because they are in you.

Q. Can we have any understanding with identification?

A. How much can you understand in deep sleep, which is what identification is? If you remember your aim, realize your position, and see the danger of sleep, it will help you to sleep less.

Q. What is the difference between sympathy and identification?

A. It is quite another thing; it is a normal and legitimate emotion and can exist without identification. There may be sympathy without identification and sympathy with identification. When sympathy is mixed with identification, it often ends in anger or another negative emotion.

Q. You spoke of losing oneself in identification. Which self?

A. All, everything. Identifying is a very interesting idea. There are two stages in the process of identifying. The first stage denotes the process of becoming identified, the second a state when identification is complete.

Q. The first stage is quite harmless?

A. If it attracts too much attention and occupies too much time, it leads to the second.

Q. When you desire something, can you desire it without identification?

A. Identification is not obligatory. But if you desire to hit someone, you cannot do it without identification; if identification disappears, you do not want to any longer. It is possible not to lose oneself; losing oneself is not a necessary element at all.

Q. Is it possible to identify with two things at once?

A With ten thousand! It is necessary to observe and observe. From one point of view struggling with identification is not so difficult, because, if we can see it, it becomes so ridiculous that we cannot remain identified. Other people's identification always seems ridiculous and ours may become so too. Laughter may be useful in this respect if we can turn it on ourselves.

Q. I cannot see why identification is a bad thing.

A. Identification is a bad thing if you want to awake, but if you want to sleep, then it is a good thing.

Q. Would not everything we do suffer if we kept our minds on keeping awake instead of attending to what we are doing?

A. I have already explained that it is quite the opposite. We can do well whatever we are doing only as much as we are awake. The more we are asleep, the worse we do the thing we are doing, there are no exceptions. You take it academically, simply as a word, but between deep sleep and complete awakening there are different degrees, and you pass from one degree to another.

Q. If we feel more awake, we should not overtax these moments, should we?

A. How can we overtax them? These moments are too short even if we have glimpses. We can only try not to forget them and act in accordance with these moments. This is all we can do.

Q. Can you say that identification is being in the grip of something, not being able to shake off some idea in mind?

A. Being in the grip of things is an extreme case. There are many small identifications which are very difficult to observe, and these are the most important because they keep us mechanical. We must realize that we always pass from one identification to another. If a man looks at a wall, he is identified with the wall.

Q. How does identification diner from associations?

A. Associations are quite another thing; they can be more controlled or less controlled, but they have nothing to do with identification. Different associations are a necessary part of thinking; we define things by associations, and we do everything with the help of associations.

Q. I cannot see why an 'I' changes. Can the cause always be seen in some identification?

A. It is always by associations. A certain number of 'I's try to push their way to the front, so as soon as one loses oneself in one of them it is replaced by another. We think that 'I's are just passive, indifferent things, but emotions, associations, memories, always work. That is why it is useful to stop thinking, even occasionally, as an exercise. Then you will begin to see how difficult it is to do it. Your question simply shows that you have never tried, otherwise you would know.

Q. Is concentration identification?

A. Concentration is controlled action; identification controls you.

Q. Is concentration possible for us?

A. There are degrees. Intentional concentration for half an hour is impossible. If we could concentrate without external help, we would be conscious. But everything has degrees.

Q. Is the beginning of a new observation identification with the object you observe?

A. Identification happens when you are repelled or attracted by something. Study or observation does not necessarily produce identification, but attraction and repulsion always do. Also, we use too strong a language, and this automatically produces identification. We have many automatic appliances of this sort.

Q. What can I do about identification? I feel that I always lose myself in whatever I do. It does not seem possible to be different.

A. No, it is possible. If you have to do something, you have to do it, but you may identify more or identify less. There is nothing hopeless in it so long as you remember about it. Try to observe; you do not always identify to the same extent; sometimes you identify so that you can see nothing else, at other times you can see something. If things were always the same, there would be no chance for us, but they always vary in degree of intensity, and that gives a possibility of change. Everything we do, we have to learn in advance. If you want to drive a car, you have to learn beforehand. If you work now, in time you will have more control.

Q. Why is it wrong to be completely absorbed in one's work?

A. It will be bad work. If you are identified, you can never get good results. It is one of our illusions to think that we must lose ourselves to get good results, for in this way we only get poor results. When one is identified, one does not exist; only the thing exists with which one is identified.

Q. Is the aim of non-identifying to free the mind from the object?

A. The aim is to awake. Identifying is a feature of sleep; identified mind is asleep.

Freedom from identifying is one of the sides of awakening.

A state where identifying does not exist is quite possible, but we do not observe it in life, and we do not notice that we are constantly identified. Identifying cannot disappear by itself; struggle is necessary.

Q. How can anyone awake if identification is universal?

A. One can only awake as a result of effort, of struggle against it. But first one must understand what to identify means. As in everything else, so in identification there are degrees. In observing oneself one finds when one is more identified, less identified, or not identified at all. If one wants to awake, one must and can get free from identification. As we are, every moment of our life we are lost, we are never free, because we identify.

Q. Can you give an example of identification?

A. We identify all the time, that is why it is difficult to give an example. For instance, take likes and dislikes, they all mean identification, especially dislikes. They cannot exist without identification and generally they are nothing but identification. Usually, people imagine that they have many more dislikes than they actually have. If they investigate and analyze them, they will probably find that they only dislike one or two things. When I studied it, there was only one real dislike that I could find in myself.

But you must find your own examples; it must be verified by personal experience.

If at a moment of a strong identification you try to stop it, you will see the idea.

Q. But I still do not understand what it is!

A. Let us try from the intellectual side. You realize that you do not remember yourself? Try to see why you cannot and you will find that identification prevents you. Then you will see what it is. All these things are connected.

Q. Is non-identifying the only way to know what identifying is?

A. No, as I explained, by observing it because it is not always the same. We do not notice the temperature of our body except when it becomes a little higher or lower than normal. In the same way we can notice identification when it is stronger or weaker than usual. By comparing these degrees, we can see what it is.

Q. In struggling with identification is it necessary to know why one is identified?

A. One is identified not for any particular reason or purpose, but in all cases because one cannot help it. How can you know why you identify? But you must know why you struggle. This is the thing. If you do not forget the reason why, you will be ten times more successful. Very often we begin struggling and then forget why.

There are many forms of identification, but the first step is to see it; the second step is to struggle with it in order to become free from it. As I said, it is a process, not a moment; we are in it all the time. We spend our energy in the wrong way on identification and negative emotions, they are open taps from which our energy flows out.

Q. Can one suddenly change the energy of anger into something else? One has tremendous energy at these moments.

A. One has tremendous energy, and it works by itself, without control, and makes one act in a certain way. Why? What is the connecting link? Identification is the link. Stop identification and you will have this energy at your disposal. How can you do this?

Not at once, it needs practice at easier moments. When emotion is very strong you cannot do it. It is necessary to know more, to be prepared. If you know how not to identify at the right moment, you will have great energy at your disposal. What you do with it is another thing; you may lose it again on something quite useless. But it needs practice. You cannot learn to swim when you fall into the sea during a storm, you must learn in calm water. Then, if you fall in, you may perhaps be able to swim. I repeat again: it is impossible to be conscious if you are identified. This is one of the difficulties that comes later, because people have some favorite identifications

which they do not want to give up, and at the same time they say they want to be conscious. The two things cannot go together. There are many incompatible things in life, and identification and consciousness are two of the most incompatible.

Q. How can one avoid the reaction which comes after feeling very enthusiastic? Is it due to identification?

A. Yes, this reaction comes as a result of identification. Struggle with identification will prevent it from happening. It is not what you call enthusiasm that produces the reaction, but the identification. Identification is *always* followed by this reaction.

Q. Is a bored man identified with nothing?

A. Boredom is also identification one of the biggest. It is identification with oneself, with something in oneself.

Q. It seems to me I cannot study a person without losing myself in him or her, yet I understand that this is wrong?

A. It is a wrong idea that one cannot study a person or anything else without losing oneself. If you lose yourself in anything, you cannot study it. Identifying is always a weakening element: the more you identify the worse your study is and the smaller the results.

You may remember that in the first lecture I said that identifying with people takes the form of considering. There are two kinds of considering: internal and external. Internal considering is the same as identifying.

External considering needs a certain amount of self-remembering; it means taking into account other people's weaknesses, putting oneself in their place. Often in life it is described by the word 'tact'; only tact may be educated or accidental. External considering means control. If we learn to use it consciously, it will give us a possibility of control.

Internal considering is when we feel that people do not give us enough, do not appreciate us enough. If one considers internally, one misses moments of external considering. External considering must be cultivated, internal considering must be eliminated. But first observe and see how often you miss moments of external considering and what an enormous role internal considering plays in life.

Study of internal considering, of mechanicalness, of lying, of imagination, of identification shows that they all belong to us, that we are always in these states. When you see this, you realize the difficulty of work on oneself. Such as you are you cannot begin to get something new; you will see that first you must scrub the machine clean; it is too covered with rust. We think we are what we are. Unfortunately, we are not what we are but what we have become; we are not natural beings. We are too asleep, we lie too much, we live too much in imagination, we identify too much. We think we have to do with real beings, but in reality, we have to do with imaginary beings. Almost all we know about ourselves is imaginary. Beneath all this agglomeration man is quite different. We have many imaginary things we must throw off before we can come to real things. So long as we live in imaginary things, we cannot see the value of the real; and only when we come to real things in ourselves can we see what is real outside us. We have too much accidental growth in us.

Q. If one retired from the world, surely one would overcome identification, considering and negative emotion?

A. This question is often asked, but one cannot be at all sure that it would be easier. Besides you can find descriptions in literature of how people attained a very high degree of development in seclusion, but when they came in contact with other people, they at once lost all they had gained. In schools of the Fourth Way, it was found that the best conditions for study and work on oneself are a man's ordinary conditions of life, because from one point of view these conditions are easier and from another, they are the most difficult. So, if a man gets something in these conditions he will keep it in all conditions, whereas if he gets it in special conditions, he will lose it in other conditions.

Q. Could you, please, say again which is internal and which external considering?

A. External considering is a form of self-remembering in relation to people. You take other people into consideration and do, not what is pleasant *to you*, but what is pleasant to *them*. It means you must sacrifice yourself, but it does not mean self sacrifice. It means that in relation to people you must not act without thinking. You must think first, and then act. Your thinking will show you that, more often than not, if this person would prefer you to act in one manner and not in another, it is all the same to you, so why not do what he likes? So, the idea of sacrifice does not enter into it. But if it is not the same to you, it is quite a different question. What is better for you, what is better for them, who those people are, what you want from them, what you want to do for them, all this must enter into it. But the idea is that in relation to people things must not happen mechanically, without thinking. You must decide your course of action. It means you do not walk over people without seeing them. And internal considering means that you walk over them without noticing. We have too much internal and not enough external considering. External considering is very important for self-remembering. If we have not got enough of it, we cannot remember ourselves.

Q. Is it the same as understanding people?

A. No, you can understand people only as much as you understand yourself. It is understanding their difficulties, understanding what they want, watching the impression you produce on people and trying not to produce a wrong impression.

Q. Would you say that kindness is external considering?

A. What you knew in life is not external considering. It is necessary to understand the principle and create standards for oneself. With the help of external considering, you control the impression you wish to produce. With internal considering you wish to produce one impression and produce a different one.

Q. External considering seems to me very far away.

A. It must be here today. If it remains far away, you remain far away yourself.

Q. Does external considering involve the ability to play a conscious role?

A. Yes, but there are different degrees. External considering is only the beginning; to play a conscious role means much more.

Q. And what is internal considering?

A. Feeling that people do not pay you enough; making accounts; always feeling cheated, underpaid.

Q. I find it very difficult to stop inner considering. Is there any special technique to be employed against it?

A. No, there is no special technique only understanding and right points of view. Observe more. Perhaps you will find moments free from considering and see how to begin struggling with it and studying it. It is mechanical, a mechanical attitude, the same as identification.

Q. Is self-justification always a manifestation of internal considering?

A. It is connected with it, but it is another thing. Internal considering does not need any justification. One must have a reason for justifying, but if one is in internal considering, one always justifies it. Internal considering means identification: external considering means struggle with identification. Internal considering is mechanical; external considering means at least attention. So, by practicing non-identifying, by trying to control attention, you find many opportunities of studying external considering and, if you find examples, perhaps you will find methods of struggling with internal considering and transforming it into the practice of external considering. For instance, you are talking to somebody from whom you want to get something. Say he knows something, and you want him to tell you what he knows. Then you must speak in the way he would like, not argue, not oppose him. External considering is always practical.

Q. Does inner considering mean considering oneself too much?

A. It always takes the form of inner bargaining, of thinking that other people do not consider you enough. It is very important to understand inner considering. There are so many subtle forms of it we do not notice, and yet our life is filled with it.

Q. Is desire to be noticed considering?

A. Both desire to be and not to be noticed is considering. There are many psychological states that ordinary psychology cannot explain or describe which depend on identifying and considering.

Q. How is it best to think of inner considering?

A. You must try in free moments to have a right mind about it. When you are considering, it is too late. You must think of typical cases of considering, of what produces it, and then have a right point of view about it, realize how useless and ridiculous it is. Then compare it with external considering and try not to forget it. If you do this you may remember it when a moment of considering comes, and perhaps it will not come. What is really important is to think about considering when you are free from it, and not justify or hide it from yourself.

Q. The more I try to work, the more I seem to consider internally. It seems the most difficult thing to deal with.

A. Considering cannot grow if you work, it only becomes more visible. And that means that it diminishes, for it cannot be seen without it diminishing. The fact that you notice it proves that it has become less strong. This is a natural illusion, the same as when one feels that one does not understand whereas before one understood. This means that one begins to understand. The first doubt about one's understanding already means a certain understanding.

Q. Can one think of identification as a negative state that can only be caused by negative emotions?

A. No, not quite like that. Identification is a necessary element in every negative emotion; you cannot have a negative emotion without identification. So, the study of identification and struggle against identification are very powerful weapons in the struggle with negative emotions. Sometimes you cannot struggle with a negative emotion directly, but by trying not to identify you diminish its power, for all the power of negative emotions lies in identification and imagination. So, when you separate identification and imagination, the negative emotion practically disappears, or at any rate changes.

Q. So to fight against negative emotions themselves we have to observe more and work against the strong identification with emotion?

A. Yes. Later we will speak about methods of struggling with emotions themselves, because there are many and very definite methods, different for different emotions; but first you must struggle with negative imagination and identification. This is quite sufficient to destroy many of the usual negative emotions in any case, to make them much lighter. You must start with this, because it is only possible to begin using stronger methods when you can struggle with identification to a certain extent, and when you have already stopped negative imagination. That must be stopped completely. It is useless to study further methods until that is done. Negative imagination you can stop; and even the study of identification will already diminish it. You must try to avoid identification as often as you can, not only in relation to negative emotions but in relation to everything. If you create in yourself the capacity of not identifying, that will affect these emotions and you will notice that they begin to disappear. Identification is the atmosphere in which negative emotions live, and they cannot live without it.

Q. Can we have some rules or guidance to keep to in ordinary life conditions?

A. Try to remember yourself, try not to identify. This will immediately produce an effect in ordinary life. What does life consist of? Negative emotions, identifying, considering, lying, sleep. The first point is: how to remember oneself, how to be more aware? And then you will find that negative emotions are one of the chief factors which make us unable to remember ourselves. So, one thing cannot go without the other. You cannot struggle with negative emotions without remembering yourself more, and you cannot remember yourself more without struggling with negative emotions. If you remember these two things, you will understand everything better. Try to keep these two ideas, which are connected, in mind.

Q. I had a problem which was worrying me. I tried to self-remember and for a short time I got into a state in which it was no longer possible to worry, and at the same time my sense of values generally changed. This state did not last long, but the problem, when it returned as one, did not again assume the importance it had before. I find it very difficult to recapture this state.

A. Quite right. Continue to observe and you will find that there is a place in you where you are quiet, calm, and nothing can disturb you only it is difficult to find the way there. But if you, do it several times you will be able to remember some of the steps, and by the same steps you may come there again. Only you cannot do it after one experience, for you will not remember the way. This quiet place is not a metaphor, it is a very real thing.

Q. Is it the state you get to when you self-remember, because everything seems peaceful then and one really seems to be aware of oneself?

A. Yes, you can take it like that.

Q. I have tried to reach it again by trying to self-remember but could not find it.

A. If you find yourself in it again, try to remember how you got there,

for sometimes it happens that one finds this place and loses the way there,

then again one finds it and again loses the way. It is very difficult to remember the way to this place.

* * *

CHAPTER VI

Understanding as the chief requirement in this system—Relativity of under-standing—How to increase understanding—A new language—Right and wrong attitudes—Attitudes and understanding—Necessity of aim and direction—Difficulty of finding out what one wants—Our aims are too remote— Good and evil—Morality and necessity of moral sense—Necessity of finding a permanent standard of right and wrong—Development of conscience as aim of the system—Seeing contradictions—Buffers as the chief obstacle to development of conscience—Preparation for breaking down buffers—Inner disharmony and happiness—Need to establish an inner balance—Standards of conduct in life—Consciousness and conscience—How to recognize truth— Need for sincerity with oneself—Mechanicalness

I wish to remind you that this system is based on understanding. Understanding must occupy the first place in this system. The more you understand, the better the result of your work will be.

Understanding is a relative term. Everyone understands something at every moment in his own way, but understanding may be larger, and larger, and still larger in this system we call understanding a certain possible maximum on a certain level of knowledge and being. As a rule, this maximum is too low; people's understanding is usually limited to only one room, and they never get out of that room. But the understanding of these ideas is very much beyond this one room.

What I wish you to think about refers to the whole thing. People do not ask 'why' sufficiently often, and if they do, this 'why' is generally very small. You should think of why you come here, what you want from this system and why, what you can learn from it, why this system exists, why I talk of this system, what I wish to achieve by talking about it. One has to have a certain point of view about it all; it may be a wrong one, but still, one must have some idea.

As it is, almost every idea given remains unopened, unexplored. There are boxes and boxes that may be opened, the contents read, and many new things added. But mostly we deal with unopened boxes. One box knowledge, another being, a third understanding, and so on. We do not even open the boxes. First, we have to learn the contents of the boxes. No need to limit yourself to a definite question in this respect. This is an organic system: in it you can start with anything. Start where you like, only do something with the ideas you hear. It is not enough simply to sit on those boxes of books.

Open the box with knowledge and the box with being. It is the relation between knowledge and being that is important.

There are many things that you can understand now, although, of course, they will be surrounded by things you cannot understand yet; but if you begin with those you can understand, you will understand many other things. Every moment of understanding, every realization, sheds light not only on the thing we are thinking about but on many other things as well.

Q. Is a moment of understanding a moment of self-remembering?

A. It depends. It may be connected with it or not.

Q. Could there be real understanding not connected with self-remembering?

A. There is no 'real' understanding. Understanding is relative. It is like temperature, it may be five degrees, ten degrees, fifteen degrees. You see why ordinary language is not good and why we have to study a different language? Because in ordinary language all words are taken as absolutes. In reality there are different degrees of understanding. As I said, we can understand better, and still better. Then, if we want to understand still better, we must change our being. If we can bring higher emotional Centre into play, we can understand much better. To understand still more needs higher mental Centre.

You see, definitions can seldom help and, as a matter of fact, we can have very few definitions. This conviction that in order to understand something it is necessary to define it is quite wrong, because most things we cannot define, and the few that we can, we can define only relatively with the help of other things. So, among an enormous quantity of things we cannot define at all there are small islands of things we can define.

Q. Is self-remembering less relative than understanding?

A. Even if we take it as an absolute term, the question is, for how long? Whether you remember yourself in the best possible way for half an hour or for five minutes makes a very big difference.

Q. How is one to bridge the gap between self-remembering and merely thinking about it? Is it a question of understanding?

A. You have to break a certain wall, and you do not know how to do it. Learning to do something means acquiring a certain skill. For a long time, you cannot do it well, you do it clumsily; then one day you find that you can do it properly. It is the same with self-remembering; not quite, but near enough.

Q. Is there any way to increase one's understanding?

A. Not one way; there are thousands of ways. All that we have spoken about from the first day is about ways to increase understanding. But the first way is by observing and studying ourselves, because these increases our capacity to understand. That is the first step. If you could understand the ideas that have been given, your knowledge would increase. But you only understand on the surface and apart from desire. Or you may have quite a strong desire, but the machine does not work. Yet inside our machine we have better parts which at present we do not use. We can use them only by increasing consciousness. This is the only way.

Q. Can memory of what we heard help?

A. Memory, the best memory we may have, is not sufficient, because in this system we remember not by memory but by understanding. On the contrary, memory may be a hindrance. You hear something which has a right place in the system, and if you can put it where it belongs, you cannot forget it and it will remain there; but if you just remember what was said without putting it into its right place, it is quite useless. Each small thing you hear you must try to understand, and to understand means to find the place where it belongs among other ideas. You must have a general idea of the system and everything new must have its place in it, then you will not forget, and every new observation you make will find its place. It is as though you have a drawing without details and observation fills in the details. If you have no drawing, the observation is lost.

But chiefly you must struggle with obstacles which prevent you from understanding. Only by removing these obstacles can you begin to understand more. But obstacles, with the exception of the general description of identification and so on, are individual. You must find your own; you must see what stands in your way, what keeps you from understanding. When you find it, you must struggle with it? It needs time, for it cannot be found at once, although in some cases it may be very clear almost from the beginning. For a long time, all the work must be concentrated on understanding, for it is the only thing by which one can be guided. Our chief difficulty is that we want to 'do' before we even know what it is all about. But in this system, one must understand first. When you understand things better, many other things will become possible, but not before.

Q. You said that in order to understand this system one has to increase one's being to the same extent as one's knowledge, and, of the two, the most difficult is increase of being?

A. Both are equally difficult.

Q. But it seems to me easy to increase one's knowledge?

A. Not as easy as you think, because knowledge without understanding will be useless, it will merely be more words.

We must work on change of being, but if we work on that as we do everything in ordinary life, life will not be long enough. It is possible to get a durable change of being only if we use the perfected methods of schoolwork, otherwise our attempts will be too scattered. The first condition of such work is not to believe anything, to verify everything one learns; and the second condition is not to do anything unless one understands why and for what purpose one is doing something. So, it depends on understanding; all short-cuts depend on understanding.

Q. I did not understand the difference between being and understanding.

A. You see, they are two different things. Understanding is a combination of knowledge and being. What is the limiting factor in ourselves? It is definitely our being, which means our capacity for understanding. What is understanding? It is connecting one bit of knowledge with another bit of knowledge. For instance, you will see that understanding depends on being if you take the elementary idea of being. Man is divided into different 'I's or groups of 'I's which are unconnected with one another. Then if one 'I' knows one thing, a second 'I' another thing, a third 'I' yet another, and they never meet, what kind of understanding is possible?

From one point of view, it may look as though a man has enough knowledge, but since these 'I's never meet, this knowledge can never be brought together. This is the state of an ordinary man's being, and it proves that as he is, he cannot have understanding. Understanding always means connecting things with the whole, and if one does not know the whole, how can one connect?

In this system you must try to understand; only what you understand gives positive results. If you do something without understanding it will not give much, for only what you understand is valuable.

Q. I find it difficult to understand the idea that one does not need faith. Do you not have to have faith in the system ideas?

A. No, faith will not help. You have to accept or not accept the ideas on the basis of your preparation. You come to these ideas with certain material, and with the help of this material you decide whether to accept them or not, according to whether you understand them or not. For yourself you can use the word 'accept', but we use the word 'understand'; and if you can understand, you do not need faith. There is absolutely nothing in the preliminary ideas that needs faith, because in some cases, as on the psychological side, you can verify everything, and in some other cases, as in studying the universe, there is the idea of scale. I do not see a single idea in this system which requires faith and where faith would help. On the contrary, I think faith would make things more difficult and stop you instead of helping you.

Q. If for a moment I see mechanicalness and go against it, I sometimes see and understand something new. What gives that understanding?

A. It is a matter for observation. You will get an answer to your question only if you observe facts and see the internal and external conditions which accompany understanding and the conditions which accompany lack of understanding.

Q. Is there anything else one can do, except self-observation, to further one's understanding?

A. Yes, one must understand what one is doing and why one is doing it. The more one understands, the more one can get from the same efforts.

But the chief thing is to remember oneself. The more you remember yourself, the better you will think, for you will find new machines. If you are conscious of yourself, you will find you will not need this mind. This mind will serve you for thinking about tables and chairs, but if you want to think about greater things, you will be able to use better machines.

Q. Why cannot I understand the least thing when I think about it, but sometimes understanding suddenly comes?

A. Understanding always comes that way you understand, and then you cease to understand. But if all attempts to understand something go wrong, try not to think about it but try to remember yourself, that is, to be emotional, and in time you will understand. Understanding does not become permanent at once; as in everything else there are many steps and you can understand something one day and not understand it the next day, for you may be more conscious in the same circumstances one day and more asleep the next. So many days may pass before it becomes your own.

Q. Does one understand through the emotional Centre?

A. Understanding is a combined function of all centres. Each Centre separately can only know; when they combine all their knowledge, this gives understanding. To understand something, one needs at least three centres.

Q. Did you mean that one must understand every side of a thing?

A. No, I meant that first you must have an idea on which line, on which scale, of which whole you are thinking. And then, if you speak or think about some separate thing, you must understand this separate thing in relation to the whole. Only this is understanding: finding the place of this thing, the meaning of this thing, the relation of this thing to yourself and to other things. Try it, but you will find that it is not as easy as it seems.

Q. Do we understand nothing, however limited?

A. Yes, simple things, sometimes, we understand; but if something is a little more complicated, we lose ourselves and do not understand. We want to understand big things without realizing that in actual fact we cannot understand the simplest things. If we begin with them, then gradually we will begin to understand more. But if we begin with big things and refuse to think of or observe small things, we shall never understand anything properly.

Q. Isn't it ever possible to understand emotionally, without understanding intellectually? You sometimes feel a thing that you cannot understand.

A. Then it is feeling, not understanding. Emotional understanding is very good sometimes, only you cannot verify it. But if you can look at a thing from the point of view of one Centre, another Centre and a third Centre, then you really understand. And even the direction of center's is not sufficient by itself, for knowledge is necessary. Only when knowledge is connected with the direction of centers is it understanding

Q. How can an intellectual understanding pass into emotional under-standing?

A. As I have just said, understanding very seldom works with one Centre The work of one Centre can be information or feeling, but not under-standing, which is the function of several centres two, three, four, maybe more.

Q. Is there a way in which I can test my understanding of a thing?

A. You ask without indicating the thing you mean, and this shows that you do not yourself understand what you are asking, because for every separate understanding there is a definite test. Suppose you say that you understand how to get here from where you live' then, if you take your car (if you have a car) and arrive here, this would mean that you have a test for your understanding. In everything else only practical application will show whether you understand or not.

Q. If we reach a certain stage of understanding, shall we be of more use to the world?

A. First we must be of use to ourselves. When we reach the first stage, we can think about the second stage. If we are asleep, we cannot be of use to anyone, not even to ourselves. How can we understand other people when we do not understand ourselves? Men 1, 2 and 3 cannot understand one another, on this level understanding is simply accidental. If we move in the direction of man No. 4, we begin to understand one another.

Q. What do you mean by understanding one another?

A. When people speak, try to explain their views they cannot. They cannot even repeat correctly what they have heard, they change things. And misunderstanding grows and grows. One invents a theory, immediately five others are invented to contradict it.

Thousands of years have passed from the beginning of creation, and in all this time people never understood one another. How can we expect that they will now?

So first we must understand ourselves. We do not see our situation and realize our mechanicalness. We do not see that this not understanding is a law.

Q. How can I understand better my mechanicalness and see that I am a machine?

A. We can do nothing without trying If you want to make sure whether you are a machine or not, try to do something that a machine cannot do. Try to remember yourself, for a machine cannot remember itself. If you find that you can, it will mean that you are not a machine; if you find that you cannot, it will prove that you are a machine. And then, if you realize that you are a machine and want to find out whether you can cease being a machine, again the only method is to try.

Q. Did you say that only people of equal being can understand one another?

A. This is not understood quite rightly, because if two people have an equally wrong being, they will not understand one another. It is not equality which brings understanding between people, but a certain level, not only of being but also of knowledge. Different levels, such as men No. 5, No. 6 and No. 7, presuppose levels of both knowledge and being. Men No. 5 are supposed to understand one another; men No. 6 understand better and men No. 7 understand fully. Even men No. 4 understand one another as compared with us, but *we* cannot understand one another, or understand only occasionally for a moment and at another moment cease to understand. We cannot rely on such understanding. People who know one another very well may work together for years and at certain moments do not understand one another. This is why the place or the conditions where we are is called the place of confusion of tongues because we all speak different languages. For this reason, in a right school, you first of all learn the language in which you can speak with other people in the school and then, using this language, if you use it in the right way, you will understand one another. That is why a new language is necessary. If you do not learn this language, or if the language is wrong, you will never understand one another.

Q. Can the same word have a different quality of meaning according to the level of people who use it?

A. Yes, it may have. Words begin to acquire objective meaning starting from the level of man No. 4. Men 1, 2 and 3 are purely subjective and everyone understands every word in his own way. But if people know *this* language, or even a few words of it, they can use it in the same meaning.

Q. If you understand one word completely, would that mean you had got to the stage of man No. 7?

A. No, you cannot understand one word completely and another incompletely. You have to know them all on a certain level, and then your being changes, and you find many more divisions. So, your language will become more and more complicated. And at a certain level perhaps you will need new words, new forms, because old forms will no longer be sufficient.

Q. Does understanding of a term or word vary in relation to the degree of being? Would the word 'love', for instance, mean one thing to man No. I and another to man No. 4 or 5?

A. Certainly. We can see already how the same word means one thing for man No. I, another thing for man No. 2 and yet another for man No. 3. But on the level of man I, 2 and 3 this is mechanical, in the sense that people cannot help it. They understand according to their level, their capacity, not according to the meaning of things.

Q. What are the indications of a change from one level to another say from No. 3 to No. 4 or 5?

A. Man No. 5 is one, he has unity. He does not live in this constant conflict of egos that we have. He has self-consciousness. He has control of higher emotional Centre. So, he will know himself what the change is. Other people will know only what he shows them because he can control himself. Man No. 4 knows his aim and how his aim can be attained. He goes with his eyes open, while we go without eyes shut.

Q. What did you mean by saying in one of your lectures that understanding cannot be different?

A. If people reach the highest level, they cannot understand things differently. This refers to the highest level, but since we aspire to reach it, we must take it as a principle. If people understand things differently, it means that they are all wrong. In a small way you can find examples of it even now. If two people really understand something, for instance if they can do something equally well, they will understand one another. But we lost the habit of judging things from the practical side, we judge them theoretically, by words.

Q. Cannot you have some understanding before you have complete understanding?

A. We cannot speak in absolutes when we speak about ourselves. We can only speak of relative values. Complete understanding is very far, but we can speak of less understanding and more understanding. If you continue trying to remember yourself and not to identify, understanding will grow.

Q. Could you explain more what you mean when you say that understanding means understanding a part in relation to the whole?

A. If you understand only a part, it is not understanding. It would be like blind men trying to explain the elephant, one by its tail, another by its trunk, and so on. Understanding means connecting parts with the whole. One can begin from parts, or one can begin from the whole. But whatever one begins from, the more connected things are, the better one understands if the connections are made rightly and are not merely an illusion.

Q. If you understand something in the system, do you use higher centres?

A. No, only higher parts of centres. Higher centres mean higher consciousness. But there are many different states of understanding, and one can made very interesting investigations of understanding. For instance, there are things one does not understand one moment and another moment one does, and then again one loses it. Then there are things, such as many sentences in the New Testament, which have many meanings. For instance, the sentence about little children has about forty different meanings, but one can never keep them all in mind. I could never understand more than three meanings at once. I wrote down about twenty, but then they became just words. It is necessary to know our limitations.

Right understanding requires a right attitude. We must understand that we have no control, that we are machines, that everything happens to us. But simply speaking about it does not change these facts. To cease being mechanical requires something else and first of all, it requires a change of attitude One thing over which we have a certain control is our attitudes, attitudes towards knowledge, towards the system, towards work, towards self-study, towards friends and so on We must understand that we cannot 'do', but we can change our attitudes.

Attitudes can be very different For the moment we will take only two positive and negative, not in the sense of positive and negative emotions, but referring to the positive and negative parts of intellectual Centre; the part which says yes and the part which says no, that is, approval and disapproval These are the two chief attitudes It is very important to think about attitudes because very often we take a negative attitude towards things we can understand only with a positive attitude For instance, it may happen that people take a negative attitude towards something connected with the work. Then their understanding stops, and they cannot understand anything until they change their attitude. We must have positive attitudes in some cases and negative attitudes in others, because often lack of understanding is caused by a wrong attitude There are many things in life that you cannot understand unless you have a sufficiently good negative attitude towards them, for if you look at them positively you will never understand anything If a man studies life, he must come to negative conclusions, for there are too many things wrong in life. Trying to create only positive attitudes is as wrong as having only negative attitudes. Yet some people can have a negative attitude towards anything and everything, and some others try to cultivate a positive attitude towards things that need a negative attitude on the other hand, as I said, the moment you have a negative attitude towards things that refer to the work, to the ideas, methods, and rules of the work, you cease to understand. You can understand, according to your capacity, only as long as, you are positive.

But this refers only to intellectual attitudes. In emotional Centre, negative emotional attitudes mean identifying.

Q. I am not sure I understand what a negative attitude is.

A. It means a suspicious or unsympathetic attitude, there are many variations, an attitude of fear sometimes. Take it in the ordinary sense of accepting or not accepting.

Q. Isn't an attitude the same as identification?

A. Certainly not. Attitude means point of view You can have a point of view without being identified. Very often, identifying is the result of a wrong attitude.

Q How can one change one's attitude?

A. First, by studying oneself and life on the lines of this system. This changes the attitude. This system is a system of different thinking, or rather of different attitudes, not merely of knowledge. Then, a certain valuation is necessary; you must understand the relative value of things. We do not speak about doing yet, we speak about study. We must study and come to understand things which are only words for us now, and often words used in a wrong sense and in a wrong place. It is necessary to understand and remember certain fundamental principles. If you do this, you will start in the right way. If you do not understand or remember them, things will go wrong. Generally, there are three or four chief stumbling-blocks, and unless you understand and remember the fundamental principles you will fall over one or another of them.

Q. I find that I greatly value the system with my mind, but how am I to increase my emotional valuation so as to make greater efforts?

A. By better understanding and by trying to remember yourself. Understanding cannot be only in the mind; I explained that it means the working of several centres at the same time, and the part that the emotional Centre plays in it is very important because there can be no deep understanding without emotional energy.

Q. Can you explain more why a certain attitude is necessary in order to understand a thing?

A. Try to think about it; try to see for yourself why it is necessary and try to find what an attitude or point of view means. It is a process of thinking, putting things together, all the things we already know, all the ideas and principles we have learnt, and being able to see facts from a new point of view. To think in a new way is a very difficult thing, for the old way of thinking is kept up by old habits of thinking, old associations, attitudes, and the influence of things themselves. Suppose you have a certain attitude towards something, and this thing itself is trying to keep this attitude in you by all possible means. Then, if you change it, if you direct it, you will make a big step.

Q. We have been told that real work on being requires a realization of how to get right understanding. You also said that we must understand what we want?

A. There are several reasons for that. Understanding is the strongest force we have which can change us. The more understanding we have, the better the results of our efforts. As to knowing what you want just to imagine yourself going to a big shop with many different departments. You must know what you want to buy. How can you get something if you do not know what you want? But first of all, you must know what is in the shop, otherwise you may ask for things they do not sell. This is the way to approach this problem.

It is necessary always to remember why you started. Do you want to get things you can get from ordinary life or different things? Is it worth while trying? Our capacity for imagination, generally used so wrongly, can help in this case. But you must control it all the time and not let it run away with you. We call it imagination if it runs away with us, but if you control it, you can use it to see what a thing means, what it implies. So, if you use it, it may help you to see whether you really want what you say you want or not, because very often we want something different, or we do not realize that one thing brings another thing with it. You cannot want one thing by itself; if you want one thing, you get many other things with it. Only when you know what you want will you know where you are going and know it rightly. It is necessary to know. It may be quite fantastic, quite impossible from the ordinary point of view, and yet it may be right. Or it may look very simple and right and yet be impossible.

Q. Can you tell me what one should aim at? I mean, what it is possible to acquire through the work?

A. As a general answer, the only aim is change of being. The aim is to reach higher states of consciousness and to be able to work with higher centres. All the rest is for that, in order to achieve that. It is necessary to do a thousand things that seem to have no relation to it, but they are all necessary, because we live below the normal level. First, we must reach the normal level, and second, we must try to develop new things and possibilities. No one can help you in this, only your own work and your own understanding. You must begin with understanding. These lectures and this system are to give understanding. The next step depends on your own efforts. Change of being can be achieved only if you remember all that was said and if you do not make exceptions for yourself and leave out things you do not like. If you do this, you will not have a right relation to what was said, and even if you try to remember it, it will change nothing.

Q. What do you mean when you say that we live below our normal level? What is normality?

A. Normality is capacity for development. Usually, people are below normal. Only from the level of ordinary man does the possibility of development begin. But there are many states below that of the ordinary man. People who are too identified, or hypnotized by formatory ideas, or who lie too much are more machines than an ordinary man. To be an ordinary man is already a relatively high state, because from this state it is possible to move.

Q. I have often tried to think what I want, but I only find a muddle of many things.

A. That's it. I want you to realize how difficult it is to define what one wants. Suppose you are given full choice to have what you want: you will not know what to say. But it is important that you should understand and know it; you must be able to formulate it. About certain things you can be sure that you cannot get them in any ordinary way, but there is no guarantee that you will get them in this way either. For instance, the order may be wrong. There is a certain order in which one can get things, which we do not know. You can be quite certain that you can get *some* things, but it maybe you will get not what you think you want but something else. And even if you do not get the things you want, you may be quite sure that you could not have got them in any other way.

The strange thing is that as a rule people do not know their aim. Aim can be formulated only if one already knows something about one's position. If a man does not realize his position, all his aims will be imaginary. So, I advise you to think about your aim: what you thought about it before and how you would describe what one can get and what one must try to get. It is useless to describe an aim which you know you cannot attain. But if you have an aim that you can hope to attain, your work will be conscious, serious.

In the beginning people usually set before them aims that are too abstract and remote.

A person's aim is at first like a light which he sees afar off while walking by night along a dark road. He makes this light his aim and goes towards it. On the way to it he sees another light, between him and the first light, and he understands that first he should go to the nearest light, and he goes towards it. After a certain time, he sees a third light, again between him and the light towards which he is going, and so on. This is repeated several times until, at length, the man sees the light nearest to him, that is, the aim he is able to get to from where he is.

So, do not have too big a view of things; do not look too far; look nearer. You cannot start working for some remote future; you work for tomorrow. You find something wrong today. Why? Because yesterday was wrong. So, if you make today right, tomorrow will be right. And only with an aim is it possible to remember what you did yesterday and what you do today, what corresponds to your aim and what does not.

The motive power in all our actions is of two kinds: something attracts, or something repels us. We cannot know what we can attain in the remote future, but we know very well the situation in which we are. If we understand it, it will give us a definite aim. The aim will be to get out of this situation. We can know certain things in us from which we must try to get free.

Aim must be clearly formulated, understood, and remembered. Only then is it possible to come to results. If the aim is forgotten every moment, no results are possible. How can a man who realizes his position formulate his aim? He will see that the Centre of gravity of his position is sleep, then his aim will be to awake. Or if he sees his mechanicalness, his aim will be to get rid of mechanicalness. Both come to the same thing. You see, it is a simple and practical view.

Q. I see more clearly that what hinders progress is not wanting to escape mechanicalness sufficiently. How can one intensify the desire to escape?

A. This is one of the constantly recurring questions which it is almost impossible to answer. You have to try, and you have to compare things as they are and as they should be. More understanding is necessary, and if you want a complete explanation, self-remembering, because it is the only real answer. If self-remembering increases, all the rest increases.

Q. You mentioned obstacles that have to be got over before attaining one's aim. Since then, I saw so many obstacles in myself that I do not see any possibility of getting anything.

A. That means you identify with them. You must see that you are always on the move, you never remain in one place; sometimes you are closer to your aim and sometimes further from it. It is necessary to observe yourself, to catch moments when you are nearer your aim. If you formulate your aim, you will know when you are closer to it and when you are further from it. If your aim is formulated rightly, you cannot be always at the same distance from it.

Q. I find that I work for immediate results. Is it a wrong aim?

A. There is no question of right and wrong: there is only the question of knowing your aim. Aim must always be in the present and refer to the future. No result is possible if there is no aim, no effort, and no decision.

Q. How can one see how to make big efforts?

A. By making small efforts.

A big effort depends on circumstances, situation, understanding, on many things. You cannot begin with big efforts. You must begin with small efforts, like, for instance, trying to remember yourself, or trying to stop thoughts three times a day. It is quite a small effort, but if you do it regularly, the need or the possibility of a big effort may come, and you will be able to make it at the right moment.

Q. When I first came to lectures, I had a very large aim, but now it has got much smaller.

A. Yes, aims shrink very much when you begin to work. They start enormous like balloons and then they become quite small, so that you can put them in your pocket.

Q. I suppose, in our present state, we cannot appreciate the difference between right and wrong?

A. Quite the opposite: we can appreciate this difference, and not only can but must. Wrong or evil begins to be comprehensible from the moment we have a direction. If we have no direction, then there is no particular evil, because it is all the same.

Q. By direction you mean aim?

A. Yes. Aim means direction, a certain line. If my aim is to go home from here, it will be right for me to turn to the right and wrong to turn to the left. This is how the principle of good and evil can be established. There can be no definition of good and evil, or right and wrong, without first establishing an aim or direction. When you have an aim, then what is opposed to your aim or takes you away from it is wrong, and what helps your aim is right. It must be your personal aim. If it corresponds to the possibilities of development, then the system explains these possibilities. And if you understand that what keeps us from reaching our aim is mechanicalness and what helps us is consciousness, it will follow that consciousness represents good and mechanicalness evil. So, instead of 'good' and 'evil' the system uses the words 'conscious' and 'mechanical'. This is quite sufficient for all practical purposes.

If there are any questions we may go further, only you must always remember this practical definition, because it is the only sure ground we can have: what is right for us is what helps our development, our awakening, and our struggle with mechanicalness; and what is wrong for us is what encourages our mechanical tendencies, what prevents our changing, what hinders our development. If we start from that, then later we will find many more criteria for discrimination.

Q. Is everything mechanical evil?

A. It does not necessarily mean that all that is mechanical is evil; but evil cannot be conscious, it can only be mechanical. You must ask yourself:

Can evil be conscious in *we*? Everything else is philosophy. If there is something that from your subjective point of view you consider good, and if you try consciously to do what you consider bad, you will find that either you cannot do it, or you will lose all pleasure in it. In exactly the same way you cannot be negative consciously, without identification. Negative emotions are the best conductors of evil, because they are one of the most mechanical things we have.

Q. There are many things one has to do in life that are against one's aim.

A. Why against aim? You can say that many things do not correspond to your aim, but I do not see that one *has* to do many things against one's aim. In doing things that one must do in ordinary life, the most one can do is lose time. But there are many things that one *does not have to do* that are much worse than merely wasting time. If something is unavoidable, one can always make work out of any activity. Other things are much worse, such as imagination, negative emotions, and so on. They are not unavoidable. Things we are obliged to do, do not contradict work. But without being in any way obliged we do many things that do contradict work. Actions that go definitely against one's aim can only be mechanical, and many of them interrupt one's advance towards one's aim.

Q. Is the aim of consciousness to be in complete control of the machine, so that, for a conscious man, all that is mechanical could not exist?

A. Leave conscious man. You can understand evil only in relation to yourself, the rest is too general. In yourself you find features and tendencies that go against consciousness, that help resistance. That evil is in yourself. You will see that evil can be manifested only mechanically.

A long time is necessary to understand that fully. You may often be mistaken, you may take for evil what is not evil, or take something mechanical for conscious.

Q. Can we easily do something wrong if we just act according to our upbringing, mechanically? Would it be better to act against it?

A. To act against it would be equally mechanical, you will only oppose one mechanicalness to another mechanicalness. If you do something against what you are accustomed to, it will not necessarily be right. Besides, it does not mean that everything you are taught or accustomed to is wrong. That would be too simple. Take some examples of your actions and you will see that when things happen, when you let them happen, they may be right, or they may be wrong. But if you were conscious you could choose; that would be quite a different situation.

Q. Must we find ordinary standards of conduct, or find new ones in the work?

A. Very often we excuse ourselves or find excuses for not remembering ordinary standards, because we think that we must have new ones. When we are in the process of acquiring new ones, at a certain moment we have none, so you must understand that you have to follow ordinary standards until you have new ones. If you take the essence of ordinary moral laws, you will find nothing particularly different from what you can see in the system. For instance, take ordinary rules of relationship with people. They are very simple: do not do to others what you do not want done

to yourself. It is quite logical and clear and is fully accepted in the system.

Q. Should we not find out for ourselves what is right and wrong, and not be told?

A. How can you find it out for yourself? People have looked for an answer to this problem from the creation of the world and have not found it yet. If you could find for yourself what is right and wrong, you could find out everything else. No, you have to learn this, like many other things that have to be learned. Only when you appreciate the value of self-remembering, do you begin to have right values and can judge and weigh.

Q. There are many things one does deliberately, knowing that they are wrong, but one is not strong enough to stop it.

A. Certainly, because if you are mechanical in everything, you cannot become conscious in only one thing. Besides, deliberately does not mean consciously; things just happen. If everything happens, one thing cannot not happen; it has to happen also.

Q. Is there a moral standard peculiar to this system?

A. Yes, certainly, but, as I have just said, in relation to this system it is very easy to understand. It is the relation of mechanical to conscious. This means that certain things are mechanical and should remain mechanical, but certain other things that are now mechanical must become conscious.

You see, one of the most difficult things is to recognize right and wrong, or good and evil. Our mind is not accustomed to think about it in relation to consciousness. We think that there must be a permanent external definition that can be accepted, remembered, and followed, and we do not realize that there can be no external definition. But there are inner qualities of actions which determine things.

This idea of the relation of good and bad to conscious and unconscious is a very useful thing to think about, particularly when you begin to find right analogies; not only because it gives you a certain definite understanding, but also because by keeping your mind on this and similar ideas you hear in the system, you keep it on the highest level possible for us, that is, in the intellectual parts of centres. You cannot profitably think about such things with the lower, mechanical parts of centres, for nothing would come of it. In order to get some understanding, you have to use intellectual parts of centres, and not only one, but two or three at the same time.

What is morality? Understanding of the laws of conduct? It is not sufficient. If we say, like a savage, 'If you steal from me, it is bad, but if I steal from you, it is good', it is not morality; it is merely savage conduct. Because morality begins when one has a feeling of good and bad in relation to one's own actions, and is capable of renouncing what one considers bad, and doing what one considers good.

What is good? And what is bad? Generally, at this first stage, man borrows moral principles from religious, philosophical, or scientific ideas, or simply adopts conventional taboos. He believes that some things are good, and some other things are bad. But this is subjective morality, and the understanding of good and evil is purely relative. In all countries and at all epochs certain moral codes were accepted which tried to explain what is good and what is bad. But if we try to compare the existing theories, we shall see that they all contradict one another and are full of contradictions in themselves. There is no such thing as general morality.

there is no such thing even as Christian morality. For instance, Christianity says you must not kill, but nobody takes this seriously. Many moralities have been built on the basis of killing. For instance, as I said in the first lecture, in some countries it is considered a most immoral thing to refuse blood revenge. And why in one case can a man kill and in another not? All that is known about ordinary morality is full of inconsistencies.

So, if you think about this problem, you will understand that in spite of hundreds of moral systems and teachings man cannot say what is right and what is wrong, for moral values change, there is nothing permanent in them. At the same time, according to their attitude to the idea of right and wrong people can be divided into two categories. There are people who have no feeling of right and wrong at all; all they have instead of moral sense is the idea of pleasant and unpleasant, profitable and unprofitable. And there are other people who have a feeling of right and wrong, without actually knowing *what* is right and what is wrong. People who belong to the first category cannot be interested in the system; it is not for them. People of the second category may be interested.

What must be understood from the beginning is that man must start with a certain sense of right and wrong, otherwise nothing can be done. Then he must be sufficiently skeptical about ordinary morality and must understand that there is nothing general or stable in ordinary moral principles, for they change according to conventions, place, and period. And he must understand the necessity of objective right and wrong. If he understands these three things, he will find a basis for distinguishing what is right and what is wrong in relation to each separate thing, because, if he starts rightly, he will find that there are definite standards with the help of which good and bad cease to be relative and become absolute. The whole thing is to start from a right attitude, a right point of view. If he starts from a wrong point of view, he will not find anything.

Q. How can we trust our own sense of right and wrong?

A. You cannot trust or mistrust; it is there. So that is not the question. You can only hesitate and be in doubt in relation to the object. Certainly, without knowledge, without development, without consciousness you cannot say definitely whether something is right or wrong; but you may be on the way to it. Morality is always different, but moral sense is permanent. If people have no moral sense, it is no use speaking to them. But the feeling of right and wrong is one thing, and the definition, the contents, is quite another. Two people may have a very strong feeling of right and wrong, but what is right for one will be wrong for the other. Feeling does not presuppose definition, so a man can have the feeling of right and wrong and have wrong ideas about it.

Q. Would the standard to apply be whether a particular thing helps or hinders consciousness?

A. The standard must be connected with a system. Without a system (I do not mean *this* system, but one must have a system) you cannot judge.

This system begins with the possibility of objective consciousness, and objective consciousness is described as a state in which we can know truth. If, when we reach it, we can know truth, we shall also know what is right and wrong. Consequently, the same way which leads to objective consciousness leads also to the understanding of right and wrong. As we have not got objective consciousness, we consider everything that helps us to develop it as right and good, and everything that hinders us in this as wrong and bad.

In our ordinary understanding objective truth refers more to the intellectual side of life, but a man may want to know it also on the religious side, the moral side, the aesthetic side, and so on. The system explains that men 1, 2, 3, 4, 5, 6 and 7 are all in a different position in this respect. There is religion No. 1, No. 2, No. 3, No. 4 and so on, and there is morality No. 1, No. 2, No. 3, No. 4, No. 5 and so on. It does not mean that one or another of them is wrong, but that one cannot be explained by another. For instance, Christ did not preach inquisition, and if his teaching is distorted by men 1, 2 and 3 to be used for criminal purposes, this cannot be attributed to Christ.

Since we are men 1, 2 and 3, there are many things about which we can find no visible indications as to whether they help or hinder the development of consciousness. So, we must look for other principles, and we can find these other principles only if we think about concrete cases of conduct. In the system one can find many sufficient indications which show how to look at one or another thing.

Q. Do you think that in the course of time a new belief and morality can spring from this system?

A. From this system, no. That is quite a different thing. These ideas are not for the masses, not for the multitude. You must remember that this is school teaching, and school teaching can exist only for schools. In favorable circumstances perhaps schools can increase, but that is quite a different thing; it is not the same as the appearance and growth of a religion.

The aim of the system is to bring man to conscience. Conscience is a certain faculty that exists in every normal man. It is really a different expression of consciousness, only, consciousness works more on the intellectual side, and conscience more on the moral side: it helps to realize what is good and what is bad in one's conduct. Conscience is a state in which one cannot hide anything from oneself, and it must be developed in man. This development is parallel and simultaneous with the development of consciousness. We cannot say that we do not have it, so it does not mean a special development of something that does not exist in us, only in our life it is behind the scenes, buried very deep down in us and asleep. It may awake for a moment in ordinary life, and when it does, particularly at first, it always brings suffering, for it is very unpleasant to face the truth about oneself.

Conscience in relation to emotions is the same as consciousness in relation to ideas. It may be easier for you to understand what conscience is if you think of the etymological meaning of the word's consciousness and conscience. Consciousness means all knowledge connected together. But we cannot speak of all knowledge because it would be too high; we can only speak of all knowledge we may have relating to the same subject. It must be connected with self-awareness, so consciousness must be yourself, connected with all you know about some particular thing. Conscience is the same thing, only in relation to emotions. To have a moment of conscience is to feel at once all that you feel about somebody or something. If you can feel all that you ever felt in relation to the same person, country, house, book, or anything else together, this would be a moment of conscience and you will see how many contradictions there are in your emotions. Unless you have had this experience, you cannot imagine how many different feelings you can have. In a state of conscience, we see them all at once. This is why it is such an unpleasant state. Conscience is not very far, only we have many methods of dealing with it to prevent ourselves feeling it, such as imagination, negative emotions, justifying and so on, for it is too uncomfortable.

Q. You said that conscience is feeling all our emotions at the same time. I cannot quite see how we can feel them all together.

A. No, I never said that. I said that in a moment of conscience, whether you wish it or not, you will feel all your emotions on the same subject at once. But it is not a definition of conscience. Conscience can be defined as an emotional feeling of truth on a given subject. As I said, conscience is the same thing as consciousness, only it looks different to us. We are subjective, so we take things from a subjective point of view. When we think about consciousness, we think about a certain force, a certain energy or state in connection with intellectual appreciation. The same energy, the same force can manifest through emotions, and this may happen to quite ordinary men in ordinary conditions. Sometimes people may have an emotional feeling of truth some more, others less. This is conscience. Lack of consciousness, absence of self remembering and many other things such as identification and imagination, shut us off from these moments of conscience which otherwise would be more possible. Try to think about it in this way. Seeing contradictions and conscience are connected, but they are not the same thing, and if you take them together you will never get anywhere.

Our consciousness, such as we can have in our state, cannot manifest through the intellectual Centre, because the intellectual Centre is too slow, since it works mostly only with the formatory part. But it can at times manifest through the emotional Centre, and then, as I said, it is called conscience. Consciousness, to manifest, needs long preparation, intellectual capacities, and things like that, but conscience works more often and more easily than fall consciousness. Full consciousness needs much knowledge connected with the realization of one's existence, but it must be a constant realization; it is not enough to realize it to-day and forget tomorrow.

At first, when conscience manifests itself in us, it turns against us, and we begin to see all our inner contradictions. Usually, we cannot see them because we are always in one or another small compartment, but conscience can see from the top and show us that here we felt one thing, there another thing, and here again quite a different thing, all on the same subject.

For instance, if we take the work, we must realize that at one moment we feel one thing about it, at another moment quite a different thing, at a third moment again a different thing. And we never feel it all together. If we could feel at the same time all that we ever felt about the work, we would have a great shock. That would be conscience. All our life, all our habitual ways of thinking, have only one aim to avoid shocks, unpleasant feelings, unpleasant realizations about ourselves. And this is the chief thing that keeps us asleep, because in order to awake we must not be afraid; we must be brave enough to see the contradictions.

Even quite apart from the question of conscience, it is important to find in yourself that, when you have strong emotions (it does not refer to small emotions), when you feel strongly about some particular thing, you may be practically certain that at another moment you will have a different emotion about the same thing. If you cannot see it in yourself, see it in other people. When you realize the existence of these contradictory emotions, it will help you to understand your mechanicalness and your lack of understanding of yourself lack of self-knowledge. So long as we feel different emotions at different times, what are we like? One moment we trust, another moment we are suspicious; one moment we like, another moment we dislike. So, the aim is to bring those different emotions together, otherwise we will never know ourselves. If we always feel only one emotion at a time and do not remember other emotions, we are identified with it. When we have another emotion, we forget the first; when we have a third, we forget the first and the second. Very early in life, by imitation and in different other ways, we learn to live in a kind of imaginary state to save ourselves from unpleasantness, so people develop in themselves this capacity to see only one emotion at a time.

Remember to work. Remember yourself in one mood, then remember yourself in another mood. Try to connect them together and you will see.

Q. If we have different compartments, do they express themselves?

A. As I just said, one at a time. For instance, we love somebody one moment, and wish them dead the next. Only we do not see it. Yet sometimes moments come when we can feel all our emotions on the same subject together. Only you must wait until you get a taste of such a moment, because without a taste of it you will never get any further in understanding what a moment of conscience means. Conscience can be very strong and definite. But in most cases, it is asleep, because, since most people are asleep, everything in them is asleep.

So, conscience must be awakened. We must learn to understand truth emotionally in certain cases, and we can do this only by not being afraid to face contradictions in ourselves.

We have special appliances in us that prevent us from seeing these contradictions. These appliances are called buffers. Buffers are special arrangements, or a special growth if you like, which prevent us from seeing the truth about ourselves and about other things. Buffers divide us into sort of thought-proof compartments. We may have many contradictory desires, intentions, aims, and we do not see that they are contradictory because buffers stand between them and prevent us from looking from one compartment into another. When you are in one compartment, you think it is the whole thing, then you pass into another compartment, and you think that this is the whole thing. These appliances are called buffers because, as in a railway carriage, they diminish shocks. But in relation to the human machine, they are even more: they make it impossible to see, so they are blinkers as well. People with really strong buffers never see; but if they saw how contradictory they were, they would be unable to move, because they would not trust themselves. That is why buffers are necessary in mechanical life. Such extreme cases mean wrong development, but even in ordinary people, in one or another line there are always deeply hidden buffers.

Q. When one recognizes a buffer in oneself, can one do anything to get rid of it?

A. First you must see it; before you see it, nothing can be done. And whether you can do anything after you have seen it depends on the size of the buffer and on many other things. Sometimes it is necessary to take a hammer and break it; and sometimes it disappears if you throw light on it, for buffers do not like light. When buffers begin to disappear and become less strong, conscience begins to manifest itself. In ordinary life it is kept down by buffers.

Q. Could you explain a little more what you mean by buffers?

A. Buffers are very difficult to describe or define. As I said, they are a kind of partitions in us that keep us from observing ourselves. You may have different emotional attitudes (they always refer to emotional attitudes) towards the same thing in the morning, at midday, and in the evening, without noticing it. Or in a certain set of circumstances, you have one kind of opinions and in other circumstances another kind of opinions, and buffers are walls that stand between them. Generally, each buffer is based on some kind of wrong assumption about oneself, one's capacities, one's powers, inclinations, knowledge, being, consciousness and so on. They differ from ordinary wrong ideas because they are permanent; in given circumstances one always feels and sees the same thing; and you must understand that in man 1, 2 and 3 nothing must be permanent. The only chance he has of changing is that there is nothing permanent in him. Opinions, prejudices, preconceived ideas are not buffering yet, but when they become very firm, and always the same, and always have the same trick of shutting things off from our sight, they become buffers. If people have some kind of constant wrong attitude, based on wrong information, wrong work of centres, negative emotion, if they always use the same kind of excuse, they prepare buffers. And when a buffer is established and becomes permanent, it stops all possible progress. If buffers continue to develop, they become fixed ideas, and that is already insanity, or the beginning of insanity.

Buffers can be very different. For instance, I knew a man who had a very interesting buffer. Every time he did something wrong, he said that he did it on purpose, as an experiment. This is a very good example of a buffer. Another man had a buffer that he was never late; so, with this buffer firmly established he was always late but never noticed it, and if his attention was drawn to it, he was always astonished and said, 'How can I be late? I am never late!'

Q. When a buffer has gone down, and you see something that seems unbearable, what is the next step?

A. All the work is preparation for that. If one does not work but only thinks that one works and a buffer suddenly disappears by some accident, one finds oneself in a very unpleasant situation, and one also sees that one only pretended to work. Buffers help us to pretend instead of really working. This is why people in the ordinary state cannot have conscience, because if conscience suddenly came, they would go mad. Buffers are useful in this respect; they help to keep us asleep; for if other sides are not developed, if everything is not brought into a certain balance, one would not be able to bear oneself, as one is. So, it is not even advisable to destroy buffers before one is ready. One must be ready first. We can bear ourselves only because we do not know ourselves. If we knew ourselves as we are, it would be unbearable.

Q. Yet one sees oneself intellectually without feeling strongly.

A. Intellectual self-study is only preparation; but when you try to remember yourself and not to identify, you begin to feel emotional.

Q. Do we all have buffers?

A. Yes. We could not live without them; we would have to be sincere all the time and see everything all the time.

Q. What is the cause of this inner disharmony which one usually has?

A. This disharmony is the normal state of man No. 1, 2 and 3.

A sleeping man cannot be harmonious; if he were harmonious there would be no incentive for development and there would be no possibility.

Q. But if one tries to be more awake, one becomes more aware of one's disharmony; then, having seen this, could one become more harmonious?

A. This is a theoretical question. One ceases to be disharmonious when one ceases to be what one is now. As one is now, one is disharmonious, then aware of one's disharmony, then again disharmonious, again aware of it, and so on.

Q. So one can never be happy?

A. Happiness means balance, and balance in our state is impossible, taking balance in the sense of harmoniousness. We are always balanced in a certain way, but a wrong way. If we were harmonious in our present state, there would be no reason for us to change so, nature arranged it very well that we cannot be harmonious such as we are, in order that we should not be happy in this state. Happiness is harmony between external circumstances and internal manifestations, and for us it is impossible, if by happiness you understand harmony.

Q. Work seems to make one more unhappy.

A. Study of the system, acquiring more control, cannot make one more unhappy. There is no abnegation in it. What one has to lose is imagination. Anything that is real is not an obstacle to awakening. It is the imaginary things that keep us asleep, and those we have to give up.

Q. Are buffers due to education and surroundings?

A. To many things; but the best buffers are created by self-education.

Q. Does the system teach us to get rid of buffers?

A. Yes, the system teaches us first to find them. Then, having found them, you may find methods for getting rid of them. You cannot begin to work on them before you know them.

Q. How can one find buffers?

A. One cannot find them unless one observes oneself in the right way. You must look for contradictions.

Q. Must you find your own buffers, or must you be shown?

A. In any case you cannot be shown until you have done all you can for yourself. Otherwise, people never believe it; they say, 'Anything but that!'

Q. Is saying to oneself, 'I will do it to-morrow' a buffer?

A. It is not a buffer, but a very good method of keeping the buffers going well.

Q. You say that one must look for inconsistencies. I do see many of these, but I put them down to different 'I's?

A. Yes, that is quite right. But when we are in one of these inconsistencies, we are generally identified with one of these views and cannot see the other. When you are in neither, when you stand aside, you can say, 'Sometimes I look at it in this way and sometimes in that way', but when you are identified you cannot do that. You must try to break this identification.

Q. Is to want and not to want at the same time a buffer?

A. It is not a buffer.

A buffer often takes the form of a strong conviction. For instance, one man I used to know was convinced that he loved all men. In reality he loved no one, but on the strength of this buffer he was free to be as unpleasant as he liked. It is a very safe and reliable buffer.

Q. Can one learn about buffers by observing others?

A. Yes, because that may help you to see buffers in yourself. But as things are seldom repeated literally, one would always see them only in others and not in oneself. But if one is prepared for it by finding these things in oneself first, by realizing one's mechanicalness, one could begin to see buffers.

Q. When you see buffers, sometimes you seem to create others to justify yourself.

A. You cannot create buffers so easily. You can create lies and imaginings, but buffers are solid things, and creating them is a long process.

Q. Can conscience only be understood when we experience higher emotion?

A. No, as I said, conscience is a feeling possible for quite ordinary men without any school. It is a kind of inner feeling of truth in connection with one particular thing, or another thing, or a third thing. The connection may be wrong, but the feeling itself will be quite right.

Q. Surely conscience is more than awareness of all one's emotions at a particular time, because it may alter one's resulting action. It seems to strengthen some emotions and weaken others.

A. That is because you see them. This is the biggest of all possibilities, because when you see your different emotions about the same thing, and see them constantly, you will be horrified.

Q. Isn't what we call conscience sometimes one 'I' disapproving of another?

A. This is a very good observation of conscience in the ordinary sense of the word. But what I call conscience is a certain state in which we can be later. What is called conscience in ordinary life is simply certain associations. We are accustomed to think and do things in a certain way, and if for some reason we act in a different way, we have an unpleasant feeling which we call conscience. In reality conscience is a much deeper and stronger feeling, and when real conscience appears, you will see that it is not like anything you call conscience now.

Q. Then the feeling we call conscience is wrong?

A. Not necessarily wrong, but it is not the same thing. It can be attached to quite trivial things which have no particular moral value. Morality is always relative, conscience is absolute. Conscience is a special positive emotion. In our present state we have a very small trace of this emotion, sufficient to have a general feeling that something may be right and something else may be wrong, but insufficient to say definitely what is right and what is wrong. This has to be developed. At present the state of conscience we can have does not distinguish the big from the small, but later conscience may become quite a different method of cognition, an instrument of discrimination.

Before conscience can be opened fully, we must have will, we must be able to 'do', to act according to the dictates of our conscience, otherwise, if conscience awoke fully in man in his present state, he would be a most miserable being he would not be able to forget, not able to adapt to things, and not able to change anything. Conscience destroys buffers, so that man finds himself defenseless against himself, and at the same time he has no will, so he cannot change, cannot do what he knows is right. So first he must develop will, otherwise he will find himself in a very unpleasant situation, beyond his control When he acquires control, he may allow himself the luxury of conscience, but not before that.

Q. What is the feeling of remorse which comes from having committed an action one feels is wrong? Is it conscience?

A. No, conscience is different, more powerful, more all-embracing but even if one remembers moments of remorse, it is useful Only it is necessary to know on what the remorse is based

Q. Is there a connection between essence and conscience?

A There is a big connection, for both consciousness and conscience come from essence, but not our essence Our essence is simply mechanical.

Q. I suppose self-remembering does not necessarily bring with it moral uplift?

A. It certainly brings another understanding, because when one becomes conscious, one understands the moral side of things better, for the opposite of morality is mechanicalness If one becomes more conscious, one will be able to control one's conduct

Q. Can one's moral sense be useful or reliable in connection with one's conduct?

A. It is difficult to speak in general, but the more you study the system the more you will see yourself There are many things that you can think are quite right, but which from the point of view of the system are quite wrong There are many things we do not know We can do much harm to ourselves, thinking that we are quite moral actual harm, and not only in a moral sense The system, particularly in the later stages, has a much stricter code of rules, and at the same time it is perhaps more free than anything else But, as I said, you can always begin from the point of view of what is mechanical and what is conscious.

Q. I am still not clear what the function of conscience is?

A. If the question is asked in this way, without adding anything else, all I can say is that if one does not have a definite aim, if one does not work for a certain definite purpose, the function of conscience is only to spoil life for a person who is unlucky enough to have it But if he works for a definite purpose, then conscience helps him to attain his aim.

Q. Is it not possible that, by acquiring certain knowledge and power through self remembering and other practices, man can use this power for evil purposes?

A. You see, an inevitable part of the process of self-development is the awakening of conscience, and the awakening of conscience will prevent any possibility of using new powers for any wrong aim or purpose This must be definitely understood from the very beginning, because conscience, when it awakes, will not allow one to do anything selfish or contrary to other people's interests, or harmful to anybody nothing, in fact, that we may consider wrong or evil And conscience has to be awakened, because with un-awakened conscience one will always make mistakes and will not see contradictions in oneself.

Q. Does the following of a moral code in a sleeping state help us?

A. We are not always equally asleep, and at moments when we are less asleep, we can make certain decisions; and even in our sleeping state we can follow these decisions more or follow them less, or not follow them at all and be absolutely in the power of our sleeping state. Besides, if one follows certain conscious ideas, by this very process one becomes more awake.

Q. When one is conscious, one can realize the contradictions. Does not that, to a certain extent, annihilate them?

A. No, that would be too simple; you can see them and yet they will remain. It is one thing to see and another thing to do something, one thing to know and another to alter.

Q. Is absolute truth only possible with objective consciousness?

A. Truth exists without us, but one can know truth only in objective consciousness. Not 'absolute' truth, but simply truth, for truth does not need qualifications. In our state we cannot know truth with the exception of very simple things, and even then, we make mistakes.

Q. How can one recognize truth on our level?

A. By coming to simple things. In simple things one can recognize truth.

one can recognize what is a door and what is a wall, and one can bring every difficult question to the same thing. It means that you have to recognize a certain quality in quite simple principles and verify other things by these simple principles. This is why philosophy just discussion of possibilities or the meaning of words is excluded from this system. You must try to understand simple things, and you must learn to think in this way; then you will be able to bring everything to simple things. Take for instance self-remembering. You are given all the material; if you observe yourself, you will see that you did not remember yourself at that moment; you will notice that at some moments you remember yourself more and at some moments less, and you will decide that it is better to remember yourself. This means that you have found a door, that you see the difference between a door and a wall.

Q. How to prolong states of conscience?

A. First we must think not about how to prolong but how to create, because in our ordinary state we have not got it. When we create or awake it, it is certainly useful to keep it longer, although it is very unpleasant. But there are no direct methods for inducing it, so it is only by doing all that is possible that one can get this taste of conscience. Generally, one of the first conditions is a great sincerity with oneself. We are never sincere with ourselves.

Q. How can one learn to be sincere with oneself?

A. Only by trying to see oneself. Just think about yourself, not in emotional moments, but in quiet moments, and do not justify yourself because generally we justify and explain everything by saying that it was inevitable, or that it was somebody else's fault, and so on.

Q. I have been trying to be sincere, but I see now that I do not really know what to be sincere means.

A. In order to be sincere it is not enough only to wish it. In many cases we do not wish to be sincere; but even if we wished we could not be. This must be understood. Being able to be sincere is a science. And even deciding to be sincere is very difficult, for we have many reservations.

Only sincerity and complete recognition of the fact that we are slaves to mechanicalness and its inevitable results can help us to find and destroy buffers with the help of which we deceive ourselves. We can understand what mechanicalness is and all the horror of mechanicalness only when we do something horrible and fully realize that it was mechanicalness in us that made us do it. It is necessary to be very sincere with oneself to be able to see it. If we try to cover it, to find excuses and explanations, we will never realize it. It may hurt dreadfully, but we must bear it and try to understand that only by fully confessing it to ourselves can we avoid repeating it again and again. We can even change results by full and complete understanding and by not trying to hide it.

We can escape from the tentacles of mechanicalness and break its force by big suffering. If we try to avoid suffering, if we are afraid of it, if we try to persuade ourselves that nothing bad really happened, that, after all, it is unimportant and that things can go on just as they were going before, not only shall we never escape, but we shall become more and more mechanical, and shall very soon come to a state when there will be no possibility for us and no chance.

* * *

CHAPTER VII

Plurality of our being and absence of permanent 'I'—Five meanings of the word 'I'—Different personalities and likes and dislikes—Useless and useful personalities—Magnetic Centre and Deputy Steward— Division of oneself into 'I' and 'Mr. X'—False personality—What is 'I'?—Study of false personality as means of learning to remember oneself—Efforts to struggle against false personality—Need of control—False personality and negative emotions—What is reliable and what is unreliable in oneself —Suffering and its use—Not saying 'I' indiscriminately—False personality distorts the ideas of the system—Chief feature or features—Necessity of knowing one's weaknesses—Static Triad—Valuation—Danger of becoming two— Crystallization.

Q. When we ask how to be less mechanical, we are told to be more awake. When we ask how to wake up, the answer is not to identify, and when we ask how not to identify, the answer is to self-remember. This seems to be a circle, each method being a counterpart of the other. Can we get any further help to attempt any or all of these?

A. It is not exactly right, because each of these attempts has its own peculiar feature and taste. They are all different. It is necessary to try from all possible sides in order to break the wall. It is a very high and very hard wall that we have to break.

But we do not begin with that, we begin with our plurality. When I first spoke of the many 'I's in us, I said that new 'I's jump up every moment, control things for a brief time and disappear, and many of them never meet. When you realize that you are not one, that you are many, that you may know something for certain in the morning and know nothing about it in the afternoon, then this realization is the beginning. I do not mean that if we realize this plurality, we can change it and become different; but this realization is the first step.

Q. I do not see why different likes should mean different 'I's or groups of 'I's?

A. Because the same 'I' would be identical. When you say 'I', you think of the whole thing. In reality it is only a small part of you. We can exist only because we cannot put our whole capital into each 'I', otherwise we would be bankrupt. We only put pennies. Our 'I's are pennies. Suppose you have a certain amount of money, all in pennies. Every moment you say 'I' you use a penny. That is a mistake; even such as we are we are worth more than a penny.

In this system the word 'I' can be spoken of in five ways, on five different levels. Man in his ordinary state is a multiplicity of 'I's: this is the first meaning. When a man decides to work, an 'observing I' or group of 'I's appears (shown in black on the diagram); this is the second meaning. The third meaning, indicated by the smallest circle, is when Deputy Steward appears. He has control over a number of 'I's. The fourth meaning, indicated by the middle circle, is when the Steward appears. He has control over all 'I's. The fifth meaning is that of the Master. He is drawn as the big circle outside, as he has a Time-body. He knows the past and also the future, although there must be different degrees of this.

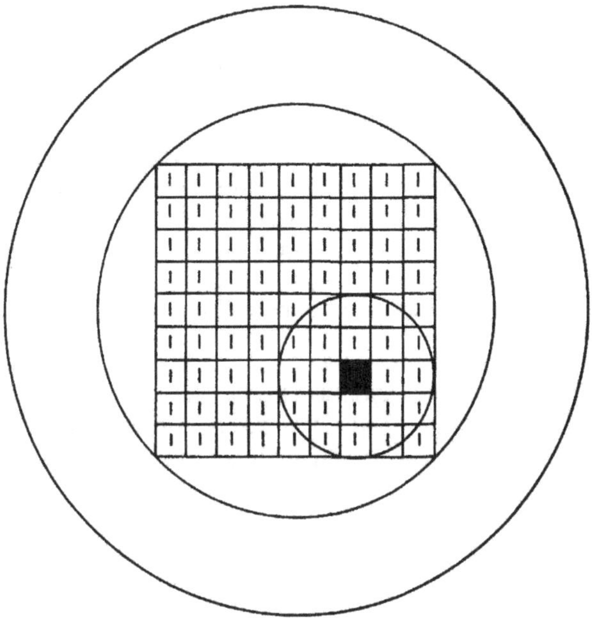

Q. Is it possible to increase the number of 'I's interested in the work?

A. We have enough 'I's, they increase themselves. The aim is to connect them and help them become one 'I' interested in the work. If many different 'I's are interested and do not know one another, one 'I' or group of 'I's can do one thing and another thing, without knowing. You can say 'I' am speaking about yourself only in relation to your work for a definite aim: self-study, study of the system, self-remembering and so on. In other things you must realize that this is not really you, but only a small part of you, mostly imaginary. When you learn to distinguish that, when it becomes almost a habit (in the sense of being constant), you will feel yourself in the right way. But if you always say 'I' to everything without discrimination, it only helps your mechanical tendencies and strengthens them. And what a quantity of things we do without wanting to do them at all! We have to do this and that, think about this, feel about that, and so one thing after another takes all our energy, and nothing remains for real work.

I said in the first lecture that these hundreds and hundreds of 'I's form certain groups in which several 'I's work together. Some of these groups are natural, others are artificial, and some are even pathological. The first natural division of 'I's is according to functions: intellectual, emotional, instinctive, and moving. But apart from these there are many other divisions which can be called different personalities.

Q. What is the difference between personalities and 'I's?

A. You can say that personalities consist of different 'I's. Everyone can find several personalities in himself, and real self-study begins with the study of these different personalities, because we cannot study 'I's there are too many of them. But with personalities it is easier, for each personality or group of 'I's means some special inclination, a special tendency, or sometimes a disinclination.

Q. Are there any special observations one can make to see personalities?

A. Study of your particular likes will help. For instance, if you find something you definitely liked throughout your life from childhood, you will see that there is a certain personality built round it. We are creatures of likes; we like all sorts of things, but we only have a certain number of genuine likes. By studying them one finds personalities.

Q. Are all personalities bound up with likes and none with dislikes?

A. I do not think normal people have such strong dislikes. Dislikes are usually accidental, so do not trust them. But there are things you have always liked and there are some you just imagine you like.

Personalities can be very different. Some are based on real facts and real tastes and inclinations, while others are based on imagination and on wrong ideas about oneself. So, it is necessary to separate personalities that can be used in some way from those that cannot be useful for self-development and so have to be destroyed, or at least subdued.

Q. It seems to me that some personalities disappear for quite a long period of time.

A. They do not disappear, they may just go behind the scenes. If they are merely occasional 'I's they may disappear, but personalities do not disappear so easily, although they may be hidden from view. Or they may be sacrificed, for sometimes in order to manifest one personality one has to sacrifice several others.

Q. How to find out which personalities are more real and which imaginary?

A. Life provides tests for personalities. Suppose you think you like something very much and then life puts you into conditions where you can enjoy what you thought you liked, but you find instead that you do not enjoy it at all, you only imagined that you liked it. Then you can see that this personality was imaginary.

Q. What determines that a personality or group of 'I's is useless and should be eliminated?

A. Personalities can be divided. Self-development begins with magnetic Centre, that is, a group of 'I's or personality interested in certain things. When a man meets a school, his magnetic Centre begins to accumulate practical and theoretical knowledge and experience which come from the study of being, and in this way, it eventually becomes Deputy Steward. Besides this personality there are other personalities, some of which can develop, and some that do not agree with it at all. So, some personalities can join in the work, others are neutral and, so long as they are not in the way, can be allowed to remain for some time, and some have to be eliminated. When magnetic Centre becomes transformed into Deputy Steward, you make certain decisions, formulate a certain aim, undertake a certain work. Then he can find out which personality can work with him, and which cannot. If a personality is against your aim and can harm it, or does not want it, or does not know about it, then obviously it cannot work with the Deputy Steward. So, they can be sorted out, but first one must know them. Then, when personalities are put in order and are grouped round magnetic Centre which means Deputy Steward, they will produce an effect on essence just by their existence.

Q. Is Deputy Steward conscience?

A. Conscience takes part in forming the Deputy Steward, but you cannot say it is Deputy Steward, because conscience is much bigger.

Q. Is there a connection between magnetic Centre and consciousness?

A. Yes, but not a direct one: there are several different states between them. It is better to say that magnetic Centre is the ground from which permanent 'I' grows. Through several transformations magnetic Centre becomes permanent 'I' much later. It is the seed of permanent 'I', but only the seed it has to become something quite different first.

Now try to understand the most important division of all for practical use. It is the division into 'I' and (for me) 'Ouspensky'. What is 'I'? We have no permanent 'I' as opposed to 'Ouspensky'. But all our interest in the system, all our efforts in self-study and self-development, and what is sometimes called the 'observing I'—all this is the beginning of 'I'. All the rest is 'Ouspensky' or 'false personality'. 'Ouspensky' is our imaginary picture of ourselves because we put into it all that we think of ourselves, which is generally imaginary. All study comes down to the study of this imaginary picture and to separating ourselves from it. So, at present you can call 'I' your valuation of the system. This is 'you'. From your attitude to the system, work in the system, interest in the system, 'I' can grow. On this basis you can separate 'I' from false personality. There is no guarantee that it will be absolutely right, but this method has a great practical value.

False personality is always against the work for self-development and spoils the work of all other personalities. It can never be useful.

Q. What is the difference between real personalities and false personality?

A. You mix two divisions which are quite different and on a different scale, so they cannot be compared. Personalities (in the plural) are spoken of in relation to essence, for I said that personality can be divided into different personalities which compose it. The division into essence and personality is at present merely theoretical and is only useful as a principle, for it is difficult to see it in oneself. We do not know our personalities, so we begin to study from two ends. We study first that personality which is connected with the work, and which has developed from the magnetic Centre and then we study false personality, on quite a different scale. False personality is opposed to 'you', it is your wrong idea of yourself exactly what you are not. This division is practical, for it is necessary to know definitely what your false personality looks like.

So, you must not confuse false personality with personalities, because, although they are not very real, personalities may be based on real inclinations, real tastes and likes, whereas false personality is all false and may even pretend to like something that 'you' dislike or to dislike something 'you' really like. When you speak about false personality, you take 'you' as existing and false personality as not; when you speak about personalities, you leave false personality out of the conversation and discuss different divisions of what you consider to be 'yourself'.

False personality must not become just a word. Everybody who speaks about it must have some picture of himself in the power of false personality. Only if this term is used like that can it give some result.

Q. Could you say more about what 'I' is?

A. 'I' is only presumed; we do not know what 'I' is. But 'Ouspensky' I know, and I can study him in all his manifestations. So, I must begin with 'Ouspensky'. 'I' is elusive and very small; it exists only as a potentiality.

if it does not grow, false personality will continue to control everything. Many people make the mistake of thinking that they know which is which. They say, 'this is I', when in reality it is false personality. This is generally connected with our capacity to play roles. It is a very limited capacity.

we generally have about five or six roles, whether we observe it or not. We may notice a certain, quite misleading, similarity between these roles and then, consciously, or unconsciously, come to the conclusion that behind them there stands a permanent individuality. We call it 'I' and think that it is behind all manifestations, when in reality it is an imaginary picture of ourselves. This picture has to be studied. It is impossible to have a practical knowledge of oneself if one does not know one's false personality. As long as we think we are one, all our definitions are wrong. Only when a man knows that all his intentions, desires and so on are not real, that they are false personality, only then can he get something. This is the only practical work possible, and it is very difficult False personality has to disappear, or at least be rendered powerless to hinder our work. But it will defend itself and will not give in easily. Work is struggle with false personality which will fight back, chiefly through lying, for lying is its strongest weapon.

Q. If you say that what we call 'I' is imaginary, what do you mean by 'self consciousness'? What 'self' can be conscious?

A. Self as different from not-self. 'I' and this table. When I said that 'I' was imaginary I meant it in the sense of a mental picture we have of ourselves, of what we think of ourselves When I say 'Ouspensky', it is an ornamented 'Ouspensky', made to look what he is not. I attribute to him many things he does not possess; I do not know his weaknesses The condition of growth of real 'I' is to get rid of 'Ouspensky', not to be identified with him.

Q. Is 'I' never real unless it is connected with effort?

A. 'I' can only be in the state of self-consciousness, and every moment in the work of creating self-consciousness means effort Nothing can 'happen' by itself If we change our being, things will be different, but in this state nothing can be different.

Q It seems to me that false personality is the only thing that can adapt to some new circumstance, it can play a new role and make it more comfortable.

A. False personality does not really adapt. To adapt in the ordinary sense means, more or less, a controlled action False personality reacts in a different way, according to what it is, but it cannot adapt. And it does not necessarily make things more comfortable, you cannot rely on it You must understand that you have not the slightest control of false personality. When we begin to see it, we realize that it controls everything, and nothing can control it. So, you cannot call it adaptation. You must separate in yourself what, you can control and what you cannot control What you cannot control belongs to false personality, and what you can control belongs to you.

Q. How can one deal with the conceit of false personality?

A. You must know all its features first and then you must think rightly. When you think rightly you will find ways to deal with it You must not justify it; it lives on justification, and even glorification, of all its features.

At any moment of our life, even in quiet moments, we are always justifying it, considering it legitimate and finding all possible excuses for it. This is what I call wrong thinking.

In studying false personality, we begin to see mechanicalness more and more. Parallel with the realization of our mechanicalness we study how to get out of it by means of creating something that is not mechanical. How can we do it? First, we must think about what we want, separate the important from the unimportant. Work on oneself, desire to know oneself and the ideas of the work, struggle to create consciousness, are not mechanical, that we can be sure of. And if we look from this point of view, we will see many imaginary things in ourselves. These imaginary things are false personality imaginary emotions, imaginary interests, imaginary ideas about ourselves. False personality is utterly mechanical, so it is again the division into conscious and mechanical. This mechanical part of us is chiefly based on imagination, on wrong views of everything, and above all on a wrong view of ourselves. We must realize how much we are in the power of this false personality and invented things which have no real existence, and we must separate what we can really depend on from what is not dependable in ourselves. That may serve as the beginning.

When we know ourselves better, this will help us to awake.

Q. Do you mean we must study our false personality by collecting material, observations?

A. By dividing yourself, by not saying 'I' to everything. You can really use the word 'I' only in relation to the more conscious part of yourself desire to work, desire to understand, realization of not understanding, realization of mechanicalness; that you can call 'I'. 'I' starts growing only in connection with study, with work on oneself; otherwise, it cannot grow and there is no change.

A permanent 'I' does not come all at once. All illusory 'I's disappear little by little and real 'I' gradually grows stronger and stronger, chiefly through self-remembering.

Self-remembering in the sense of just awareness is very good, but little by little when you go on it becomes connected with other interests, with what you want to get. At present, one moment you remember it, and then for a day or a week you forget it; but it is necessary to remember it all the time.

Q. Is the object of self-remembering the gradual discovery of permanent 'I'?

A. Not the discovery; it is preparing the ground for it. Permanent 'I' is not there. It must grow, but it cannot grow when it is all covered with negative emotions, identification, and other such things. So, you begin by preparing the ground for it.

But first of all, as I said before, it is necessary to understand what self-remembering is, why it is better to self-remember, what effect it will produce, and so on. It needs thinking about. Besides, in trying to self- remember it is necessary to keep the connection with all the other ideas of the system. If one takes one thing and omits another thing for instance, if one seriously works on self-remembering without knowing about the idea of the division of 'I's, so that one takes oneself as one (as a unity) from the beginning, then self-remembering will give wrong results and may even make development impossible. There are schools, for instance, or systems which, although they do not formulate it in this way, are actually based on false personality and on struggle against conscience. Such work must certainly produce wrong results. At first it will create a certain kind of strength, but it will make the development of higher consciousness an impossibility. False personality either destroys or distorts memory.

Self-remembering is a thing that must be based on *right* function. At the same time as working on it you must work on the weakening of false personality. Several lines of work are suggested and explained from the beginning, and all must go together. You cannot just do one thing and not another. All are necessary for creating this right combination, but first must come the understanding of the struggle with false personality. Suppose one tries to remember oneself and does not wish to make efforts against false personality. Then all its features will come into play, saying, 'I dislike these people', 'I do not want this', 'I do not want that', and so on. Then it will not be work but quite the opposite. As I said, if one tries to work in this wrong way it may make one stronger than one was before, but in such a case the stronger one becomes, the less is the possibility of development. Fixing before development, that is the danger.

Q. Is that something that one should be on guard against?

A. Certainly. Only a little part of you wants to self-remember, and other personalities, or 'I's, do not want it at all. It is necessary to find them and expose them, to see which are useful for this work, which are indifferent, and which are so asleep that they do not know anything about it. The aim is to have control over one's 'I's, or personalities, to be able to bring one or another up, to arrange them in a certain way. The 'I' that has control will not be one of these you have now. This idea of the formation of real 'I' is most important; it cannot be formed accidentally. In most cases we are satisfied with a philosophical idea of 'I'.

we believe that we have it and do not realize that actually we pass from one 'I' to another.

Q. In considering likes and dislikes, how can one separate what is real and what is false personality?

A. Start by realizing that it is all false personality, and then try to find out what is not. You cannot do the second before the first. First you must understand that all is false personality, and when you become convinced of that, you may find what is 'yourself'. Go on observing. Work begins f**rom the moment one realizes that one is not. When it enters into everything**, when it becomes a realization, then it is productive work. But when one thinks of oneself as 'I' (the whole), then it is not productive work.

You must understand that false personality is a very elusive thing. It is one, it does not consist of different personalities; but at the same time, it contains contradictory and incompatible features, features that cannot manifest themselves at the same time. So, it does not mean that you can see the whole of your false personality at one moment. Sometimes you can see more of it, at other times certain features of it manifest themselves separately.

Also, it must be remembered that false personality is often rather attractive or amusing, particularly for other people who live in their false personalities. So, when you begin to lose your false personality, when you begin to struggle with it, people will not like you. They will tell you that you have become dull.

Q. How can one tell what is *not* false personality?

A. One thing false personality cannot do is make efforts. This is the easiest way to know if you are in doubt. False personality always tries to make everything as easy as possible, always chooses what requires least effort. But you must understand that you cannot learn anything or change anything without effort. So, when you find an 'I' or a group of 'I's which are ready to make efforts, it means that they do not belong to false personality.

Q. Can one acquire a new false personality with regard to the system?

A. If one does not think about or understand false personality and if one deceives oneself, thinking that one works, one will not acquire a new false personality, but false personality will grow. So, it must be kept out, if not destroyed, soon after the beginning.

Q. My idea of myself often makes me think I am not properly valued and therefore I suffer because of my picture of myself.

A. Quite right, but do not think about the picture; you must only remember the direction. You may be mistaken in your ideas about yourself, but it is not important. Only, the direction must be right; you cannot go somewhere without knowing where you are going. You can see your imaginary picture of yourself only from the right point, and the right point is the direction. There is no other point from which you can see it.

Q. Could you say again what takes the place of real 'I' at present?

A. Desire to know. From this, real 'I' will grow, if it does. In the beginning it is difficult to define, it is the aim. If you connect yourself with a certain work, with a certain system, it begins to grow; but it cannot grow by itself merely through happy circumstances. It is quite simple to establish that we have no permanent 'I'. Try to remember yourself for fifteen minutes; this will show the degree of your being. If you had a permanent 'I', you would be able to remember yourself for fifteen hours I It is all very simple, really, only we have no keys to our machine. If we had the keys, it would be easy to open it and see what is inside, and then separate the imaginary from the real. But even that we have to learn we are too used to the unreal. So, the subject of our study must be false personality, which is always there. Only if you know it in all its manifestations can you separate what is 'I'. We are identified with our imaginary picture of ourselves, and it is a very dangerous form of identification.

Q. How can one begin to distinguish what is real?

A. You cannot. But you can distinguish what is unreal, just in the same way as you distinguish truth and lying. There is no need of philosophy, take it simply. We must first apply discrimination to simple things. Imagination plays a very important part in our life because we believe in it. The real can grow only at the expense of the imaginary. But in ordinary life the unreal grows at the expense of the real.

Q. I do not quite understand the division between work and ordinary life.

A. The relation of personal work to life is precisely this relation of permanent 'I' to false personality. Work is permanent 'I' in the essence, and ordinary life is false personality. When you understand what permanent 'I' is, when you are conscious of yourself and have permanent control, this is work. At present you live in false personality.

Q. I find it difficult to see the difference between 'I' and 'Miss B.'.

A. As I have just said, in the division of 'I' and 'Miss B' practically all is 'Miss B'. 'You' can outgrow 'Miss B' only from your interest in the system, because real 'I' cannot grow from anything else. All the material that is there will never come to anything without these ideas, without this interest, because it keeps it on a certain line, in a certain direction. At first you study, observe yourself and so on, then, after some time, if you work, 'I' will appear for a second from time to time, but you will not be able to keep it and it will disappear again. This will go on for some time, and then, at a certain moment, it will appear and stay long enough for you to recognize and remember it. This is the way of all new things; at first, they come for very short moments, then they stay longer. It is the natural way of growth; it cannot be otherwise. We have in us too many momentums of mechanical habits of thinking and too many other wrong things. Real 'I' appears and is immediately squashed.

When you understand more about false personality you will realize that you are surrounded by it. You cannot see anything without the eyes of false personality, you cannot hear without the ears of false personality or speak without the voice of false personality. Everything goes through false personality, and the first step is to know it, because then you will know how much of your life it occupies.

Q. Since false personality is imaginary, does it really exist?

A. It does not really exist, but we imagine it exists. It exists in its manifestations, but not as a real part of ourselves. It is a combination of 'I's that have no real foundation, but they act and produce certain effects. Do not try to define it, or you will lose your way in words, and we must deal with facts. Negative emotions exist, yet at the same time they do not exist, since there is no real Centre for them. It is the same with false personality. It is one of the misfortunes of our state that we are full of non-existent things.

You must understand that you cannot even begin to work on the level you are you have to change certain things first. You can find what to change only as a result of your observations. Sometimes it becomes very clear, and only then does the fight begin, because false personality begins to defend itself.

You must know false personality first. All that we speak about now, refers to the first stage understanding that we do not know false personality, that in order to know it we must study, that all the work we do is done at the expense of false personality, that all the work we can do on ourselves means diminishing the power of false personality, and that if we begin to try and work, leaving false personality without disturbing it, all the work will come to nothing.

I repeat again, you must understand that false personality is a combination of all lies, features and 'I's that can never be useful in any sense, either in life or in the work just like negative emotions. Yet false personality always says 'I' and always ascribes to itself many capacities, such as will, self-consciousness and so on, and if it is not checked it remains an obstacle to all the work.

So, one of the first and most important factors, in trying to change oneself, is this division of oneself into 'I' and whatever your name may be. If this division is not made, if one forgets it and continues to think of oneself in the usual way, or if one divides oneself in a wrong way, work stops. Work on oneself can only progress on the basis of this division, but it must be the *right* division. It often happens that people make a wrong division: what they like in themselves they call 'I' and what they dislike, or what in their opinion is weak or unimportant, they call false personality. This is quite a wrong division; it changes nothing, and one remains as one was. This wrong division is simply lying, lying to oneself, which is worse than anything, because the moment one meets with the smallest difficulty it will show itself by inner arguing and wrong understanding. If one uses a wrong division, it will not be reliable and will fail one in a moment of need.

To make a right division of oneself one must understand what is 'I' and what is 'Ouspensky', 'Brown' or 'Jones', in other words, what is lying and what is oneself. As I said, even if you admit this possibility of dividing yourself, you are bound to call what you like in yourself 'I' and what you dislike 'Not I', for the right division cannot be found at once.

you must find some indications in connection with the work which will help. For instance, if you say that your aim is to be free, it is first of all necessary to understand that you are not free. If you understand to what extent you are not free and if you formulate your desire to be free, you will then see in yourself which part of you wants to be free and which part does not. This would be a beginning.

Q. Can one see false personality without help?

A. There is nothing against it theoretically, only I never saw such a case Even with help, people will not see it. You can show a man a mirror, and he will say, 'This is not me, it is an artificial mirror, not a real mirror. It is not a reflection of me.'

Q. How can one eliminate false personality?

A. You cannot eliminate it. It is just the same as trying to cut your head off. But you can make it less insistent, less permanent If your false personality is there for twenty three hours out of the twenty-four, when work begins it will be there only twenty-two hours and 'you' will be present an hour longer. If, at a certain moment, you feel the danger of a manifestation of false personality and you find a way to stop it, this is what you have to begin with. The question of elimination does not enter at all, it is connected with quite different things. You must have control.

Q. Isn't the study of false personality analyzing oneself? I thought it was a bad thing.

A. To a certain extent it is analyzing. What was said about refraining from analysis was in the first lecture. I said then that analysis was impossible because you do not know enough. Analysis means establishing causes and effects. So, at first, I said that you have to abstain from analysis and just observe, observe, observe, nothing more, because the time for analysis would come when you knew the laws. Now we are studying these laws, so certainly you have to analyze more and more. You see, rules for observation and thinking in the first lecture are one thing, but with the passing of time they change and modify. What one cannot do in the first month one already must do in the second month. Both difficulties and possibilities increase all the time. Analysis must be used carefully, when it is necessary, not for everything. Sometimes it is only a waste of time.

Q. Would you say that false personality is sometimes built up by other people for instance, when people say in front of a child that they hate strangers?

A. Quite right. False personality is built up from many sides, and certainly to a great extent by suggestions from other people.

A. child gets many suggestions, especially about his likes and dislikes.

Q. I don't quite follow how to find the 'I's that object to the work. Does it mean we should sift out what the 'I's are?

A. You must not think theoretically about it. Try to find what in you objects to the ideas of the system or try to find the 'I's (or you can call them anything you like) which are indifferent to it. Suppose you have certain definite tastes in food. These 'I's which are interested in food cannot be interested in self-remembering. Then there is other 'I's interested in things opposed to self-remembering. There are many things you can do with pleasure only if you do not remember yourself, and naturally these 'I's will be very inimical to self-remembering, because it will only spoil their pleasure. Try to find them in that way. Theoretical approaches will not help.

Q. What is the origin of these artificial groups of 'I's?

A. They may be formed by imitation, desire to be original, to be attractive, to be admired by people and so on.

Q. When you find a group of 'I's which do not want to self-remember, what do you do about it?

A. Leave it alone. If it does not want to, what can you do with it? If there are groups of 'I's that want to, work on them. Those 'I's which realize the necessity to self-remember must work with other 'I's that also want to. They must not spend their time in persuading other 'I's.

Q. Is it to be expected that some 'I's in a man would be frightened of the idea of separating 'I' from 'Mr. A'?

A. Certainly all 'I's which constitute false personality will be frightened, because it is death to them. But you must understand that they may show their fear only for some time and, after that, they may disguise themselves in order not to die. You may seriously think that you have finished with false personality, whereas it is only concealing itself inside some feature, ready to appear. This feature is always weakness. So long as it remains it takes all energy, but it may be very well disguised, and in that form, it may even become stronger, growing parallel with the growth of real 'I'. So, the realization of the necessity of this division into 'I' and 'Mr. A' is not sufficient to destroy it. You must remember that false personality *defends itself.*

Q. Is false personality based on negative emotions?

A. There are many other things in false personality besides negative emotions. For instance, there are always bad mental habits; false personality, or parts of false personality are always based on wrong thinking. Although to a certain extent you are right: in some cases, if you take negative emotions away from false personality it collapses, for it cannot live without them. On the other hand, some false personalities can function on most pleasant emotions. There are very cheerful false personalities, and, in this way, your false personality can deceive you and make you believe that you are struggling with negative emotions. It can deceive you in many different ways.

Q. Do all negative emotions spring from false personality?

A. How could it be otherwise? It is, so to speak, a special organ for negative emotions, for displaying, enjoying, and producing them. You remember that there is no real Centre for negative emotions. False personality acts as a Centre for them.

Q. Is identification always a manifestation of false personality?

A. False personality cannot manifest itself without identification, the same as negative emotions and many other things in us, such as all lying, all imagination. One identifies, first of all, with one's imaginary idea of oneself. One says 'this is I' when it is nothing but imagination. It is the same with lying one cannot lie without identification; it would be very poor lying and nobody would believe it. So, it means that first one must deceive oneself, and then one can deceive other people.

Study of false personality is one of the quickest methods for self-remembering. The more you understand your false personality, the more you will remember yourself. What prevents self-remembering is, first of all, false personality. It cannot and does not wish to remember itself, and it does not wish to let any other personality remember. It tries in every possible way to stop self-remembering, takes some form of sleep, and calls it self-remembering. Then it is quite happy.

You must not trust your false personality its ideas, its words, its actions. You cannot destroy it, but you can make it passive for some time and then, little by little, you can make it weaker.

Q. You say one must not trust anything connected with false personality, but it seems to be all there is?

A. It cannot be so. There is one thing you, and there are imaginary 'I's. You is what really is, and you must learn to distinguish it. It may be very small, very elementary, but you should be able to find something sufficiently definite and solid in yourself. If we are entirely false personality, then nothing happens.

There are people who are only false personality. Other sides of them are so subdued, so weak, that they cannot resist false personality. These people will not study themselves because they would be afraid of seeing what they are. False personality does not like it at all. Generally, if they begin, they very soon leave off, explain it in some way, for they are unable to continue self-study. But if one has the energy to go on studying false personality, this shows that one has something besides it. As I said before, this work is every day, not once a month or once a year. It is an examination every day.

Q. Would you say false personality is more inclined to leave you as you grow older?

A. No. If you do nothing against it, it grows. Tastes may change, but it grows. This is the only 'development' that happens in mechanical life. False personality is the most mechanical part of us so mechanical that there is no hope for it. So, it must not be allowed to enter into the work.

Q. Presumably really great people, the saints for instance, conquer false personality?

A. It depends on the degree. Saints describe the devils they have to struggle with. All devils live in false personality.

Q. How can I remember my realization that much of emotional suffering is in false personality?

A. Only by self-remembering. Suffering is the best possible help for self-remembering if you learn how to use it. By itself it does not help; one can suffer one's whole life and it will not give a grain of result, but if one learns to use suffering, it will become helpful. The moment you suffer, try to remember yourself.

Q. There are two kinds of suffering: one is due to seeing my own mechanicalness and weakness, and the other is suffering from seeing someone you are fond of ill or unhappy. How to work against it or use it for the work?

A. The question is, can you do something or not? If you can, you can, but if you cannot, it is another thing. If we begin suffering about everything we cannot help, then we shall certainly never cease suffering. The chief thing is to find how much imagination there is in it. We may be perfectly sure there is none, but if we make one more effort, we often see that it is all imaginary. We have a wrong picture of ourselves, and at the same time we ascribe to this wrong picture real features. But if this picture is false, then everything about it is bound to be false, and its suffering is also false. It may be very acute, but this does not make any difference. Imaginary suffering is generally more unpleasant than real, because with real suffering you can do something, but with imaginary suffering you can do nothing. You can only get rid of it, but if you are fond of it or proud of it, then you have to keep it.

Q. I still do not see how to start understanding false personality?

A. You must know what it is, place it, so to speak; this is the first step. You must realize that all identification, all considering, all lies, all lies to oneself, all weaknesses, all contradictions, whether seen or unseen, all these are false personality. It is like a special breed of dog. If you do not know it, you cannot speak about it. Even to see little bits of it is quite enough, for every small part of it is the same color. If you see this dog once, you will always know it. It barks in a special way, walks in a special way. . . .

In the beginning you cannot know which is 'I' and which is false personality. What you call 'I' is a complicated structure, and so is false personality. You cannot know *everything* about either of them; but if you take from one side something you have no doubt about that it is false and from the other side something you have no doubt about that it is true, you can compare them.

Q. Sometimes I observe myself identifying or considering and find that I do so because of a picture I have of myself. Can I in this way come to know false personality and, by observing it, weaken it?

A. Yes, it is the only way, but only if you do not get tired of it, because, in the beginning, many people start eagerly, but soon get tired and begin to use 'I' indiscriminately without asking themselves 'which I'? Our chief enemy is the word 'I', because, as I said, we have really no right to use it in ordinary conditions. Much later, after long work, we can begin to think of the group of 'I's that correspond to Deputy Steward as 'I'. But in ordinary conditions, when you say, 'I don't like', you must ask yourself, 'Which of my "I"s does not like?' In this way you constantly remind yourself of this plurality. If you forget once, it will be easier to forget next time. There are many good beginnings in the work, and then, after some time, *this* is forgotten and people start to slide down, and in the end become more mechanical than before. The beginning of self-knowledge is understanding who speaks in you and whom you can trust.

Q. Does one's capacity for work increase just as much as one is able to weaken false personality?

A. Work begins with struggle against false personality. Everything one can get one gets only at the expense of false personality. Later, when it is made passive, one may get much at the expense of other things, but for a long time one has to live, so to speak, off false personality. False personality is very difficult to find in ordinary life, because, since there is no action against it, there is also no resistance. But when a person begins to work, resistance to work appears, and this resistance is false personality.

Q. Cannot false personality be interested in, or attracted by, system ideas?

A. Yes, very much. Only then you will have the system in the light of false personality, and it will be quite a different system. The moment false personality takes the system to itself it only grows stronger and weakens the system for you. It adds one word here and another there, and you cannot imagine in what an extraordinary form some of the ideas come back to me. One word omitted from some formulation may make an idea quite different. False personality always knows better and is always fully justified in doing what it likes. This is where the danger lies.

The system means all that is said, in the sense in which it is said. If one corrects it, consciously or unconsciously, then it cannot be called the system, it will be pseudo system, falsification of the system. The moment it becomes incorrect, or something is forgotten or left out, it will give wrong results.

Q. I ask these questions because I sometimes doubt the genuineness of my interest in the work, I may be lying to myself.

A. Only you can answer that; and there again only if you do not forget the fundamental principles and say 'I' about something which is only one of the 'I's. You must get to know other 'I's and remember about them.

To forget about this is very dangerous, because then a knock, a slight change in something can be enough to put everything wrong.

Until now, when we spoke about man, we spoke about general human features common to all people. But at a certain moment in the work, besides understanding the general principles, one must try to find one's own peculiarities, for one cannot know oneself for practical purposes if one only knows the general characteristics. Each man has his own individual features, his own weaknesses when he is unable to resist things that happen. These features or weaknesses may be very simple or very complicated. One man may be able to resist everything except good food, another all except talk, or he may be lazy, or too active. It is very important at a certain stage of self-study to find one's chief feature, which means chief weakness. People's chief weaknesses are very different, and if we can resist something that another man cannot resist because it happens to be his chief feature, this difference in weaknesses gives us the illusion that we can 'do'. Chief feature or chief weakness is in false personality. In some cases, it is possible to see definitely one, two or three features or tendencies, often linked together, which come into everything like an axis round which everything turns. This is chief feature. Sometimes it is very clear and apparent, but sometimes it is difficult to describe. Our language has often no words, no forms to describe it and it can only be indicated in a roundabout way. It is interesting that one can hardly ever find one's own chief feature, because *one is in it*, and if one is told, one usually does not believe it. But we can find what stands side by side with it, although it is not it.

It is sometimes useful to collect opinions of friends about oneself, for this often helps in discovering one's features. It is very important to find out what creates obstacles to our work. Until one has found it, a chief feature means constant loss of energy, so we must find this leak and stop it.

Q. Can one ever find the chief feature by oneself?

A. At a certain moment in organized work it will come out, or you may be told. But if you are told, you will not believe it. Or sometimes it is so obvious that it is impossible to deny it, but with the help of buffers one can forget it again. I have known people who gave a name to their chief feature and for some time remembered it, and then forgot. You must come near to it yourself. When you feel it yourself, you will know? If you are only told, you may easily forget. When you find many manifestations of your false personality, you may find your feature.

Q. Is it what you call a buffer?

A. No, but buffers hide the chief feature; it is helped by buffers.

Q. If we find out our chief features, can we correct them? You said we cannot change anything.

A. In the ordinary way we cannot. But here it means using the result of experience and knowledge that does not belong to ordinary life.

Q. But an ordinary man changes too.

A. Of course he changes, he becomes more mechanical, narrower, more set. There may be exceptions, but as a rule things do not progress in ordinary life. Personalities change, particularly if circumstances change, but it is mechanical, accidental change. We often base our opinion on exceptions, whether we observe them rightly or wrongly. Exceptions are easier to notice than rules.

Q. Having observed a certain tendency in oneself, one decides that it shall not happen.

A. Usually after one has decided it still goes on happening. Or if it does not happen, generally another tendency appears in its place. As a rule, only one thing stops things fear.

Q. Do chief features vary during life?

A. If they are clearly delineated, they go on throughout the whole life.

Q. Yet I can see things that I had that do not exist now.

A. Possibly. Our knowledge of ourselves is very defective. One can observe many things in life and make great mistakes if one does not know how to verify. And generally, as I said, it is difficult to see chief feature.

Q. Could you tell me what my chief feature is?

A. I do not think so. You see, this is not necessary for starting to work. In the beginning, what is important is not the chief feature itself but what is produced by it, and that you can study in the form of attitudes. We do not know our attitudes because we have never thought about ourselves in the right way. We have too many imaginary ideas. What we must study now is all our points of view, habitual emotions, the way we think, what we invent. These are all results of chief feature or chief features, for there may be two or three features which are the most important, not necessarily only one. Think about false personality; this is quite sufficient for practical purposes. As a theory, false personality in most cases turns round one axle and that axle is chief feature. If a man has one big weakness, from one point of view it is an advantage, because if he can conquer this feature or weakness, he can in one stride achieve many things. It is an advantage when things are concentrated, many things coming together at one point. Then efforts at this point produce better results than if one works at different points. But chief feature is not always definable. Sometimes you can put your finger on it, sometimes not; in one person you can see it, in another not. But false personality you can see.

Q. Is chief feature a food for false personality?

A. Chief feature is not food. It is false personality; it is something on which false personality is based and which enters into everything.

Q. Does chief feature always make decisions at important moments?

A. This is the best definition for it, that it always makes decisions.

In connection with chief feature, it is better to think first on general lines, why you came to the system, what you want from the system. It often happens that people come to lectures for years and forget why they came. If you remember why you came, the system can answer your questions, but not without that. You may not remember about mechanicalness; you may forget about the very keen conviction in every person that he can 'do', and that if he cannot it is because he did not think about it or did not wish to. It is necessary to struggle with this idea, and understand that we are mechanical, that we can do nothing, that we are asleep, that we have many 'I's all these things. This will help you to see false personality, for all these things we ascribe to ourselves are standard examples of imagination. And imaginary personality, or false personality, is chief feature for everybody.

Q. Is false personality always selfish?

A. If you think of yourself as false personality and try to find what is not, you may be fairly sure that all that is selfish is false personality. But the more you think about it, the less you will see it. It may appear very unselfish, and that is the worst of all!

Q. Are there many varieties of chief feature?

A. There are strange varieties and there are classical ones. One very common feature, described in many places in the New Testament, is when we see other people's faults but not our own. Then certain kinds of self-pity are very common. And there are also curious combinations for which it is sometimes difficult to find a psychological definition.

Q. Is self-remembering the only way to defeat chief feature?

A. Without self-remembering we can do nothing. It is the only way.

Q. Is it not possible to have different features when one is with different people?

A. No, these are roles. Features do not change so quickly.

Q. Is blaming other people a feature?

A. It may be a feature. But what is it based on? On lack of understanding. If you begin to study psychology, you find that all causes are in yourself.

there can be no causes outside yourself. You do not remind yourself of this often enough. One little part understands that causes are in you, but the larger part continues to accuse other people. At the bottom of every favorite negative emotion, you will find self-justification which feeds it. You must stop it in your mind first, and then after some time you will be able to stop it in the emotion too. Lack of understanding is the first cause, lack of effort the second.

Q. Did you say that laziness can be a chief feature?

A. Laziness is for some people three-quarters of their lives or more. Sometimes laziness is very important and is the chief feature of false personality, and then all the rest depends on laziness and serves laziness. But you must remember that there are different kinds of laziness. It is necessary to find these different kinds by observing yourself and observing other people. For instance, there are very busy people who are always doing something, and yet their *mind* may be lazy. This happens more often than anything else. Laziness is not only desire to sit and do nothing.

Q. What is the best way to struggle with false personality?

A. Always do something which false personality does not like and very soon you will find more things it does not like. If you continue, it will get more and more irritated and will show itself more and more clearly, so that soon there will be no question about it.

But first your struggle must be based on knowing you must know its features, find what it particularly dislikes. One false personality dislike one thing, another dislikes another thing. You must have enough strength in yourself to go against it.

Now let us speak about the relation of false personality to other parts of man. In every man, at every moment, his development proceeds by what may be called a Static Triad. This triad can be called static because things at the apex of the triangle always stay in the same place and act as neutralizing force while the other forces change very slowly. Man is divided into four parts: body, soul, essence, and personality. We have already spoken about essence and personality. The term 'soul' is used in the system in the sense of life-principle. The soul may be described as a cloud of fine matters or energies connected together and bound to the physical body. As long as it is in the body, the body is alive, and body and soul make one thing. When they separate, we say that the body dies. It is this that distinguishes a piece of dead meat from living flesh. When a Centre is working well, the soul is concentrated there. But in an ordinary man the soul has no psychic qualities, nor is it any use you're knowing anything more about it.

I only tell you this from a theoretical point of view; it is simply material, although of a finer materiality than the body.

This diagram may be useful, because it shows what we are, if we can see it. It shows the changes in our development, what we are now and what we can become. When you learn to use this diagram, it will help you to determine definite stages in the work.

The first triangle shows the state of man in ordinary life; the second shows his state when he begins to develop. There are long periods between the state shown in the first and the state shown in the second triangle and still longer between them and the third triangle. Actually, there are many intermediate stages, but these three are sufficient to show the way of development in relation to false personality.

It is necessary to remember that none of these states is permanent. Any of them may last for half an hour and then another state may come, then again, a different state. The diagram only shows bow development goes.

It would be possible to continue the diagram beyond permanent 'I', because permanent 'I' again has many forms.

The triad is made by the body, the soul, and the essence at the apex. At the second point is 'I', taken in the sense of many 'I's which are the person, that is to say, all feelings and sensations which do not form a part of false personality. The third point of the triangle is held by false personality, that is, by the imaginary picture of oneself.

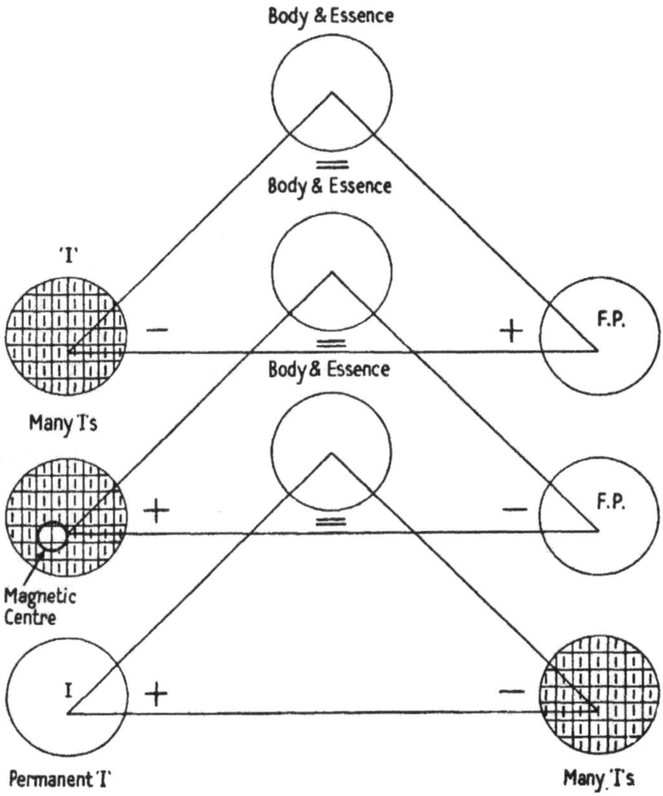

In an ordinary man false personality calls itself 'I' and is active, but after some time, if a man is capable of development, magnetic Centre begins to grow in him. He may call it 'special interests', 'ideals', 'ideas' or something like that. When he begins to feel this magnetic Centre, he finds a separate part in himself, and from this part his growth begins. This growth can take place only at the expense of false personality because false personality cannot appear at the same time as magnetic Centre. When magnetic Centre is active, false personality is passive, but when false personality is active, magnetic Centre is passive.

If magnetic Centre is formed in a man, he may meet a school, and when he begins to work, he must work against false personality. This does not mean that false personality disappears; it only means that it is not always present. In the beginning it is nearly always present, but when magnetic Centre begins to grow it disappears, sometimes for half an hour, sometimes even for a day. Then it comes back and stays for a week!

When false personality disappears for a short time, 'I' becomes stronger, only it is not really 'I', it is many 'I's. The longer the periods for which false personality disappears, the stronger the 'I' composed of many 'I's becomes.

Magnetic Centre may be transformed into Deputy Steward, and when Deputy Steward acquires control of false personality it transfers all the unnecessary things to the side of false personality, and only the necessary things remain on the side of 'I'. Then, at a still further stage, it may be that permanent 'I' will come on the side of the 'I' side with all that belongs to it. Then many 'I's will be on the false personality side, but we cannot say much about that now. There will be permanent 'I' with all that belongs to it, but we do not know what belongs to it. Permanent 'I' has quite different functions, quite a different point of view from anything we are accustomed to.

The name 'permanent I' is not very successful, because it is not permanent for a long time; it only comes and stays when it is necessary, and when it is not necessary it may go away again. So, it is better to say, 'real I'. When this 'I' comes, it controls all other 'I's. It can control everything in a way that no existing 'I's can, so it is quite new in a sense. But when this one 'I' comes, it does not mean that it will stay. First it may not be necessary for it to be there, because smaller 'I's must also learn to act in the right way. Secondly it needs very intensive work, and if work slackens it cannot stay. So, there are many conditions for its presence, but if you experience the taste of it being there once, you will know many things and you will be sure of many things which now you can only surmise.

The Static Triad shows that either personal work or degeneration is going on in relation to different manifestations of false personality, but that body, soul and essence remain the same all the time. After some time, they too will be affected, but they do not enter into the initial stages. Body will remain the same body, essence will change later, but it does not enter into the beginning of the work. According to this system, essence enters only as much as it is mixed with personality. We do not take it separately because, as already explained, we have no means of working on essence apart from personality.

Q. Does this diagram imply that body and essence come in sometimes on the side of false personality, and sometimes on the other, according to which is uppermost?

A. No. If body and essence are normal, they are impartial and do not take one side or the other. But if there is something wrong with them, they are on the side of false personality. But that does not enter into our conversation; we take them as a permanent force. Change takes place at the other two points of the triad.

Q. Docs this diagram mean that Deputy Steward begins to take the place of magnetic Centre when one starts schoolwork?

A. As I have explained earlier, Deputy Steward does not come straight from magnetic Centre, it has to be transformed into different things first. The first thing that shows the right growth of something in the place of magnetic Centre is valuation understanding of the work. There is a long way between the one and the other. In the diagram they are shown to follow one another, but it does not mean that the one follows the other immediately, they are miles and miles apart and there are hundreds of transformations.

Q. What is it that makes 'I' begin to develop and false personality to fade?

A. All changes happen in time. In ordinary life false personality is there the whole time. Then, in time, it will diminish and become less important, will occupy less time. (This is shown in the second stage of the diagram where false personality has become passive and the many 'I's surrounding magnetic Centre have become active.) You cannot diminish false personality in the sense of size, but you can diminish it in the sense of time. Take twenty-four hours how many hours belong to one and how many to the other? Everything that changes in us changes in this way.

Q. I had the impression until now that false personality was the collection of all the many 'I's. This diagram has made things a little obscure to me.

A. Among these many 'I's there are some useful and many passive 'I's which may be the beginning of other personalities. False personality cannot develop; it is all wrong. That is why I said that all work must be against false personality. If one fails in one's work, it is because one has not given enough attention to false personality, has not studied it, has not worked against it. False personality is also made up of many 'I's, but they are all imaginary.

Q. I do not understand what you mean by passive 'I's.

A. Passive 'I's are 'I's which are controlled by other, active 'I's. For instance, good intentions may be controlled by laziness. Laziness is active, good intentions are passive. The 'I' or combination of 'I's in control is active; the 'I's which are controlled or driven are passive. Understand it quite simply. This diagram represents a state, then a slightly different state and again different state. With the help of this diagram, you can see three different states of man beginning from the most elementary. In the most elementary state false personality is active and 'I' is passive. Body, soul, and essence always remain neutralizing. When, after many stages, permanent 'I' comes, the 'I' becomes active, many 'I's become passive and false personality disappears. Many different diagrams can be drawn between these two extremes, and further than that there are several possibilities.

Q. Is there a place in the Static Triad where a group of 'I's, unconnected with magnetic Centre, are active and false personality is passive?

A. When I said that certain groups of 'I's or personalities become active, I meant those that are centered round magnetic Centre. First magnetic Centre itself, and then those 'I's that range themselves round magnetic Centre are opposed to false personality. Then, at a certain moment, magnetic Centre becomes active and false personality passive.

Magnetic Centre is a combination of a certain group of interests or likes. It does not lead you, for leading would mean progress, whereas you remain in one place. But when things come, then with the help of magnetic Centre you are able to see which is which, or whether you like or dislike a thing. You can make a choice. Before one comes into the work, magnetic Centre is a certain point which has transformed itself into a certain group of interests. When one meets the work, it becomes interested in schoolwork, and then it disappears as magnetic Centre, because magnetic Centre is a weak thing, and becomes transformed into what may be called 'work' personality. This diagram is intended to describe the initial stages of the work and so I have put in very few of the combinations which might be shown. For instance, at one of the initial stages we can draw a triad with body, soul and essence at the apex, false personality on one side and many 'I's already divided into certain groups on the other. One of these groups is magnetic Centre, but there are other groups, maybe not attached, but still not hostile to the magnetic Centre, which can exist and eventually develop into something better. The groups of 'I's which are always hostile and always harmful are false personality.

Q. Does the change from one form of the Static Triad to another depend on change of being?

A. Yes, every small change is change of being although this expression is generally applied to bigger, more serious changes. When we speak about change of being we speak about change from men No. 1, 2 and 3 to man No. 4 for instance. This is change of being, but of course this big jump consists of small jumps. The Static Triad is merely an auxiliary diagram. It represents you. It shows the state of your being, what you are at a given moment, and helps you to describe to yourself all the stages you pass through from ordinary mechanical existence to development. In this way you do not describe it in words but give a complete picture of it.

Our aim is to become one, to have one permanent 'I'. But in the beginning work means to become more and more divided. You must realize how far you are from being one, and only when you know all these fractions of yourself can work begin on one or some principal 'I's around which unity can be built. It would be wrong understanding to unify all the things you find in yourself now. The new 'I' is something you do not know at present; it grows from something you can trust. At first, in separating false personality from you, you try to divide yourself into what you can call reliable and what you find unreliable.

When in a state of doubt remember to try and bring up other 'I's which have a certain valuation. This is the only way to conquer doubts. In order to develop you must have some capacity for valuation. The only practical approach is to think of the different sides of yourself and to find the sides that can work and the sides that cannot. Some people have real values, some have false values, and some have no values at all. It is the same with 'I's.

People can spend their lives studying systems and system words and never come to real things. Three-quarters or nine-tenths of our ordinary knowledge does not really exist: it exists only in imagination. But this work must be practical from the first.

You must understand that without work, without the system, one can do nothing. If one begins to work, one has a chance. But even in the work there are dangers, for if people think that they can do something and at the same time refuse to work on acquiring control, if they remain theoretical too long and do not realize that no kind of change is possible without big efforts, if they go on putting off these efforts until to morrow, then this continual hesitation begins to produce an effect and, after some time, there comes a dangerous moment. It does not come in the beginning, but only if for a long time one goes on without making sufficient efforts or without doing anything seriously. Then, instead of one, one can become split into two, so that all features and all personalities are divided into two groups one part useful to the work and helping personal work and another part indifferent or even unfriendly. These two groups can continue to exist side by side, trying not to come up at the same time; one may come in the morning, the other in the afternoon. This is a real danger, because if two parts begin to form like this, the indifference of one spoil the result of the work of the other and in this way development stops. This second part need not necessarily be bad or antagonistic to the work, but only weak, and weakness and strength cannot grow at the same time. So, it is necessary to struggle very quickly and ruthlessly against that, otherwise it may lead to double crystallization.

Q. Would one know if these two groups of personalities were forming in one?

A. If one learns to observe oneself, one can find when it begins to happen, and then one must not let it go on for too long, because it will become every day more and more difficult to struggle with it. But it manifests itself differently in different cases.

Q. Is that a case of acquiring a lot of knowledge without understanding?

A. No. Even understanding is possible in such a case, only *without action*. You see, even knowledge and understanding cannot help if one does not work on being. If will does not grow at the same time, one can understand and not be able to do anything. If people wait too long without making serious efforts or serious decisions, they may have the beginning of this double crystallization. Then they can get no results in their work, and after a time they may even get wrong results.

* * *

CHAPTER VIII

Man's place in the world—Limitations of our perception and thinking— Knowledge is knowledge of all—Principles of relativity and scale—Law of Three—Four states of matter—We are third force blind—Law of Seven—Ascending and descending octaves—Observing intervals— Ray of Creation—Will of the Absolute—Ray of Creation as an instrument for new thinking—Special language—Ray of Creation as an octave— Organic life on earth—Feeding the Moon—Cosmic influences—Mechanical influence of the moon—Influences and state of being—Planetary influences and essence—Liberation from laws— Possibility of development—Man as part of organic life—Study of laws—Justice and injustice—Laws belonging to man—Working against nature—Study of cosmological ideas as help to self-remembering—Law of Three and creation—Passage of forces— Three octaves of radiations—Table of Hydrogens—Different levels of matter—Lateral octave—Possibility of evolution.

We must speak about man's place in the world, because from now onwards we must always study man in connection with his place, since there are many things about us, about what is possible for us and what is impossible, that are connected with this.

In the first lecture I said that we must study man and, parallel with that, we must study the world in which man lives, in order to try to understand why man is what he is and why he cannot be any different. We cannot find answers to all these questions if we study man separately from the world in which he lives. In a certain sense man is analogous to the universe; the same laws operate in him, and we shall find that it is easier to understand some of these laws by studying man, while other laws we can understand better by studying the universe.

But first of all, we must realize the limitations of our perception and our thinking power; so, this study also includes the study of our limitations. The system enlarges our knowledge very much, but it cannot do miracles. If we try to think of the world apart from ourselves and to see it as it is, even from the physical point of view with the help of the telescope or the microscope, we shall realize how limited our capacities of perception are, for they are limited by size. And our capacity for mental seeing is infinitely more limited. Even if we were to come in contact with the source of full knowledge, such as we are we would not be able to take it or use it, for, although we can know more than we ordinarily know, there is a definite limit in us in our mind. So, we must know all our limitations and then, when we know the power of our instrument, we shall know what we can get. The first idea of this system is that, to a certain extent, we can improve this instrument for acquiring knowledge, this is the idea of self-improvement.

If you remember, I said that from the point of view of this system only knowledge of the whole can be regarded as knowledge, for knowledge of a part without its relation to the whole is not knowledge but ignorance. We can have this knowledge, only we do not realize it and do not understand that in relation to everything knowledge begins with knowledge of the whole. Take, for instance, this box of matches. If I look at it through a narrow slit, I shall only see a small part of it and shall never get the idea of the box of matches as a whole. It is the same with everything. Almost all we call knowledge is not really knowledge at all, because it is merely knowledge of a small part without knowing the place of this part in the whole.

There is a certain book of aphorisms which says: To know means to know all. To know a part of something means not to know. It is not difficult to know all, because in order to know all one has to know very little. But in order to know this little one has to know pretty much. So, we have to start with 'pretty much', with the idea of coming to this 'very little' which is necessary for the knowledge of all.

Knowledge of all is possible with the use of two principles: the principle of relativity and the principle of scale. If we speak about the world, it is necessary to know all about the world, and we can know all we need to know about it if we take things on different scales. We can know much more than we know ordinarily if we study things commensurable with us and having a relation to us on one scale, and things which are further removed from us and which have no definite relation to us on another, a smaller scale, in a more abstract way. In this way we can get all the necessary amount of knowledge without learning too much, and this knowledge will include very few useless things, because if we learn everything indiscriminately, we will not know the necessary things.

For instance, you know your own house on a scale proportionate to your body, but the town in which you live you know on a much smaller scale. Some parts you know well, other parts not so well, but there is no part of it you know as well as your own house. And England you know on a still smaller scale, Europe on a smaller scale still and so on.

Now I shall remind you of what I said in the first lecture concerning the study of the world and the two fundamental laws that govern it and shall point out what you must remember and how you must remember it. These universal laws are really beyond our mind, so with all the wish to study them you will not understand much more than words. But even this is useful. With the help of these words, you can reconstruct your views of the universe and put man in the right place in relation to different worlds.

The first thing to remember is what was said about the Law of Three, that everything in the world, all manifestations of energy, all kinds of action, whether in the world or in human activity, whether internal or external, are always manifestations of three forces which exist in nature. These forces are called active, passive and neutralizing, or first, second and third. It must be understood that they do not differ from one another as activity and passivity differ in our ordinary understanding of these terms. Active and passive forces are both active, for a force cannot be passive. But there is a certain difference in their activity, and this difference makes all the variety of phenomena that exist in the world. The three forces work together, but one of them predominates in each combination. At the same time, each force which is now active can become passive or neutralizing the next moment, in another triad. When three forces meet together, things happen. If they do not come together, nothing happens.

From this point of view, matter must also have certain definite denominations according to which force works through it, whether it is organic or inorganic, a chemical element, or a compound. When active force passes through any kind of matter it is called Carbon. When passive force passes through it, it is called Oxygen. When neutralizing force works through it, it is called Nitrogen. And when matter is taken without relation to the force that works through it, it is called Hydrogen. At first these names should be taken simply as labels. Thus, the Law of Three brings relativity into our definition of matter, for instead of one iron we have four irons, instead of one copper four coppers, and so on. Father, mother, son; carbon, oxygen, nitrogen. The family is hydrogen. The beginning of a new family is the son.

In ordinary thinking we realize the existence of two forces action and resistance, positive and negative electricity, and so on. But in this state of consciousness, we do not see that three forces are always present in every event, in every phenomenon, and that only a conjunction of *three* forces can produce an event. Two forces cannot produce anything, they will only turn round one another without any result. It takes a long time to begin to see three forces in things for some reason we are third force blind, although we can observe it in many chemical reactions and biological phenomena. Even when we fully understand that nothing can happen without the presence of all the three elements, in relation to ourselves we are inclined to forget or disregard it. We do not fully observe even two forces and generally expect things to happen when only one force is present. Later you will see that if you want to produce a certain effect or a certain action and one force is missing you can get no result.

In some cases, it may be passive force and then nothing happens, for if there is no passive force there is no material. In another case active or neutralizing force may be missing, and so again you can do nothing.

If you try to find manifestations of the first and second forces, sometimes you can find manifestations of the third. It needs observation, and it cannot be proven except by yourselves. In psychology many things can be explained by the necessity of the third force. This also explains why we cannot 'do'; we cannot bring the third force. And without the third force no action can happen, or it happens in a different way from the way we meant it to happen.

Sometimes we see the neutralizing force, only we are mistaken about its nature. For instance, we often see it as result when in reality it exists before the first and the second. We make many mistakes about three forces, but it is very useful to think about it.

Q. Are the three forces external, outside of oneself?

A. They are in yourself and outside yourself, on our scale, on planetary scale, on universal scale, on all scales.

Q. Could you give us an example of how they work?

A. Suppose you want to study something. You have some material, new ideas and so on, but at the same time you have a resistance to this study, because some 'I's want it and some other 'I's do not want it. They represent active and passive forces. Suppose that this study produces some kind of emotion in you; this emotion works as neutralizing force, and then you can study. If emotion does not come, those 'I's that want it and those that do not want it will continue to argue and nothing will happen.

The Law of Three explains many things that cannot be explained in the ordinary way, because we usually think about only one force. Very seldom do we take the second force, resistance, into consideration, and never the third force. Yet, in any calculation of actions it is necessary to take three forces into account.

Q. Is necessity the third force? So many decisions seem to be settled by necessity.

A. And many others are settled by what is not necessary. People can always do without necessary things, but to do without unnecessary things is much more difficult. So, you cannot say that. But you must realize that you cannot speak about the third force without giving the first and the second.

Q. Can we study the Law of Three to see why our efforts do not succeed?

A. Very useful sometimes. Sometimes you can see that because of not knowing and not complying with the Law of Three people lose all the results of their efforts. Either they do not calculate resistance, or they do not calculate their active force. I am speaking now about a triad where the third force is present. Very strange phenomena happen when the difference between forces is too big, the result appears completely unlike what was expected. Suppose you want to do a certain thing, but you did not calculate resistance. Your intention meets with very strong resistance, and the result, when it comes, is absolutely different from what is wanted.

In the work you can see two forces: the ideas of the system and your own resistance, your own sleep. In each particular case a certain third force enters and either helps one side or another side.

Q. What is the practical value of studying forces?

A. Behind all things there are cosmic laws. You cannot understand why things happen in one way or another way unless you have some idea of these laws.

Q. If you take events instead of matter, can you say that they are of a different kind according to the force that works through them?

A. They are different according to which *triad* works. For instance, we all know how the same sentence, the same words, can have quite a different meaning according to who says it. Or even the same person can say the same words at different times and the meaning will be different.

We can find the teaching about three forces or three *gunas* in Sankhya philosophy, but in the existing literature it has seriously deteriorated, for they speak of each guna or force as remaining always the same, whereas from the point of view of the system, as I said, the activity, passivity or neutralizing power of each force appears only in relation to the two other forces.

There can be seven combinations of forces, one of them incomprehensible to the human mind, since in this triad each force occupies each place.

Triads refer to events, so if we speak of each event separately, whether big or small, we have to understand to which triad each of them belongs. But a succession of events proceeds according to the Law of Seven or the Law of Octaves. The Law of Seven must be understood and remembered from the point of view of intervals. Putting it briefly, the Law of Seven means that no force ever works continuously in the same direction: it works for a certain time, then diminishes in intensity and either changes its direction or undergoes an inner change. In every octave that is, a period between a certain number of vibrations and either double or half that number, there are two places where vibrations or, to be more exact, manifestations of energy going on in space or time, or in both, undergo a certain change, slow down and then start again. If an additional shock does not enter at those places, the octave changes direction. This measured irregularity in the rate of vibrations was calculated and embodied in a certain formula. This formula, expressing a cosmic law, was later applied to music in the form of the major scale. The Law of Seven shows that no force can develop in one direction and shows the places where these changes or retardations occur.

Q. Is it because of obstacles at intervals?

A. It is because of intervals. Obstacles are normal; every energy develops among obstacles.

Q. Does the line always change in one direction?

A. No, in any direction. When things 'happen', one can never be sure of direction. Men 1, 2 and 3 never arrive where they want to; it can only happen by accident. We think that when we do not arrive where we want to, it is an exception; we do not realize that it is a law. We cannot rely on chance to provide the right shocks at the right moments.

Q. Is this process infinite?

A. You cannot imagine a force that works indefinitely. It works according to the amount of energy there is. But again, octaves are different, they may be descending or ascending. An ascending octave is between a certain number of vibrations and double that number.

A descending octave is between a certain number of vibrations and half that number. So, speaking about a succession of events, we have to know ascending and descending octaves. Without knowing whether it is a descending or an ascending octave it is impossible to understand it, and this is what happens in ordinary thinking, because people study ascending octaves and take them for descending and vice versa.

Q. Could you give an example of people taking a descending octave for an ascending one?

A. Suppose we meet savages; we usually think that they are primitive, and from these primitive people there begin to develop civilization and culture. But we do not realize that in most cases they are descendants of cultured people. Very often we take degeneration for evolution.

It is easiest to observe the Law of Seven in human actions. You can see how when people begin to do something study, work after some time, without any visible reason, their efforts diminish, work slows down, and if some special effort is not made at a given moment, the line changes its direction. There is a small but real change in inner strength. Then after some time there is again a slackening, and again, if there is no special effort, the direction changes. It can change completely and go in a diametrically opposite direction, still appearing to be the same thing. There are many phases of human activity which answer to this description. They start one way and then imperceptibly continue in exactly the opposite way. If these intervals are known and if a method of creating some special effort or arrangement is used in these intervals, it is possible to avoid breaks in the octave. Everything goes by octaves; no vibration, no movement, no activity can go on in any other way. Scales vary, so we cannot follow them, but we can see their results, the results of the Law of Seven. Even the inner physical work of the organism is under this law.

With certain kinds of efforts, we can produce these missing semi-tones, fill the intervals and in this way change the work of our machine. For instance, you will see later how the effort to remember oneself changes many things in the chemistry of our organism.

Q. If you discover an interval in a certain action, is it likely to go on repeating?

A. If you could find examples it would be easier to talk. To answer generally, if nothing is done, the interval will increase with each octave, at the same place.

Q. You spoke about octaves of self-remembering. . ..

A. Not exactly. I said that if you work, your work may form itself into octaves and will have intervals. If you do not know where the intervals come, your work will change. But we cannot speak of octaves in relation to self-remembering, because with us it only starts and peters out. If we manage two or three notes, it will be good. We have not got enough initial energy. Yet we must start and start again until we make an octave. We have to begin afresh every day: *do, re; do, re, mi. . . .* For a long time, we can get no further than *mi.*

Q. If you get to *mi*, what happens?

A. Then you stop and go back. For a long time, you will not pass the interval. But after some time of study, you will be able to detect intervals. You will know that in some part of your line of work an interval is approaching.

Q. To see octaves, ought one to try to follow a sequence of happenings in oneself?

A. Not a sequence of happenings, but you can see intervals if you begin to do something, to learn something. You will see how an activity goes on for some time in a particular direction and then deviates from the original course.

Now, having all this in mind, we come to the study of the universe in order to determine what is the world for man.

Man, lives on the earth, but the earth is one of the planets of the solar system, so man belongs also to the planetary world. The earth occupies a certain place in the solar system, so we can say that we also belong to the sun. The sun is one of the stars of the Milky Way, so in a sense we belong also to the Milky Way. Then, ordinary science understands and admits the existence of other galaxies, similar and dissimilar to ours, so we belong also to the world of all galaxies taken together. Astronomically we cannot go any further, but philosophically we can conceive a state of things where everything is one, as an apple is one. This state we call the Absolute. So, all galaxies, our galaxy, our solar system, the planets, the earth, and the moon which is in the sphere of influence of the earth, are all in the Absolute.

The Absolute actually creates only the world of the next order to itself and the Will of the Absolute does not manifest itself beyond World 3. As the number of laws increases, they become more and more mechanical and complicated, and the Will of the Absolute cannot come through the intervening mechanicalness and manifest itself in the lower worlds. But it starts the ball rolling, so to speak. Try to think about it, it is very important.

Q. Why should not the Will of the Absolute fill all?

A. There are things impossible even for the Absolute. You see, we think that if the Absolute is a state of things to which the origin of all things belongs, the Will of the Absolute can do anything. Yet there are some things the Absolute cannot do because he begins by creating certain laws; these laws create other laws, and these yet other laws. The Absolute creates only the first order of laws. If he wants to manifest his will on our level, he will have to destroy all these laws. We are surrounded and controlled by quantities of mechanical laws; when we begin to see that, we realize that it is impossible for the will of the Absolute to enter our level. In order to do that the Absolute would have to destroy all the intermediate worlds, since everything depends on the laws governing them.

A little change would mean the destruction of the whole Ray of Creation.

We can understand this to a certain extent by analogy. If we take man as the Absolute and try to find the ultimate limits that can be reached within himself by his will, even the most superficial knowledge of human physiology will give us an answer to this question. Man's will (taking it as a conditional concept) may govern the movements of the whole body, of separate limbs, of some organs and of breathing. If a man concentrates his attention on the tip of his nose, he begins to feel it. By this concentration he may even provoke a slight sensation in some tissues. But he can in no way manifest his will in relation to some separate cell in his body; cells are too small for this. Man's will can manifest itself only in relation to *tissues*, in relation to cells it can no longer manifest itself.

If we take man as analogous to the Absolute, tissues will correspond to World 3, and cells to World 6.

Or, to take another analogy, if an architect draws the plan of a house and gives it to the builders and contractors, he cannot afterwards interfere with the bricklayers, or with the people who live in the house when built, should he not like the way they behave.

Try to understand that each level brings more laws, independently of the other levels. The architect has made his plan and has finished with the house. Many things did not enter into this plan: the work of the decorators, the people who will live in the house, the cats, dogs, mice and so on. It is a question of understanding the principle. Many things enter on each plane, independently of the original plan

World 1	○	Absolute	1
World 3	○	All Worlds	3
World 6	○	All Suns	6 (3+3)
World 12	○	Sun	12 (3+6+3)
World 24	○	Planets	24 (3+6+12+3)
	▭		
World 48	○	Earth	48 (3+6+12+24+3)
World 96	○	Moon	96 (3+6+12+24+48+3)

There is nothing new in the Ray of Creation, nothing that you do not know, only the facts are differently disposed. Disposing your material in a certain way is necessary for the solution of any problem, and the way it is done includes in itself an understanding of how this problem is to be solved. So, the Ray of Creation is a kind of enunciation of the problem of how to define man's place in the world. This means not only man's exact place but also the relation of this place to as many landmarks as possible.

The Ray of Creation is a help, an instrument or method for new thinking. We know about the division of man into seven categories, and everything else should be divided in the same way. Ordinary thinking is divided into thinking No. 1, 2 and 3. Thinking No. 1 is chiefly imitative; thinking No. 2 is more emotional, based on likes and dislikes; thinking No. 3 is theoretical, logical thinking, which is quite good in its place, but when it is applied to things that are beyond its power it becomes quite wrong. This is all we know in ordinary life. From the Ray of Creation begins thinking No. 4, and this you must try to understand. The Ray of Creation is not another theory, like other theories you know; it is a certain rearrangement of the material you have already. And thinking No. 4 is thinking which, little by little, disposes of all contradictions. In thinking No. 3, whatever line one takes, one immediately finds some other theory which will contradict that particular theory. In thinking No. 4, not at once but gradually, one comes to a certain understanding of the fact that it is possible, to think without contradictions, to understand that contradictions are not really contradictions.

Ordinary thinking has many contradictions. For instance, if we take the world, we either think that there is a kind of divine will which creates and keeps everything, or that things just happen by themselves. Another example of ordinary thinking is will versus mechanicalness, or pre-destination versus accident. When you study the Ray of Creation, you will see that it contains all these things. All these views are right in a sense and the Ray of Creation includes them all. There is a theory that the human mind we know cannot invent an absolute lie. It cannot invent something that has no relation to truth. Everything the human mind can invent will be a partial representation of truth. For instance, if a man tries to draw a new animal, he will have to take parts of known animals, for he has to use the material borrowed from his actual observation of life. The Ray of Creation shows you how all contradictory theories about predestination or freedom, free choice, divine will, mechanicalness and so on can be reconciled in one system, how, in their totality, these views, each of which shows one facet of the truth, do not contradict one another. In one place one thing is right, in another place another thing is right, but each, if applied to the whole, is wrong. Later you will see that certain things cannot be applied to the whole because the whole is not one, it is too varied, has too many faces. The Ray of Creation also shows that.

At present the study of the Ray of Creation and of universal laws is not yet knowledge, it is only language; but with the help of this language, we will be able to talk about many different things for which ordinary language lacks words, expressions, connections between things. In studying this new language, you understand the relation of things to one another, because it binds everything together everything we know or must know or can be interested to know in the world. The value of this language is that in using some term of it you explain not only what this object is and what place it occupies in its immediate surroundings, but you also show its place in the whole universe.

Taking the Ray of Creation as a succession of events, it can be regarded as an octave. It is a descending octave in the sense of expansion and differentiation. The first interval in this octave is filled by the Will of the Absolute. In order to fill the second interval, between planets and earth, a special instrument was cosmically created. This instrument is organic life on earth. Organic life on earth plays a very important part in the Ray of Creation, for it guarantees the transmission of energies and makes the growth of the Ray possible. The growing point of the Ray is the moon. The idea is that eventually the moon will become like the earth and the earth like the sun; then another moon will appear, and so growth will continue up to a certain point. But this is rather beyond us.

Organic life is a sort of receiving apparatus for catching and transmitting influences coming from the planets of the solar system. At the same time as serving as a means of communication between the earth and the planets, organic life feeds the moon.

Everything that lives serves the purposes of the earth; everything that dies feeds the moon. This sounds strange at first, but when we understand the laws which govern organic life, we will realize that it is based on a very hard law, the law that one class of living beings cats another class. This not only makes organic life self-supporting but also enables it to feed the moon and serve as a transmitter of energies. Thus, organic life serves many purposes, those of the greater worlds, the planets, the earth, and the moon.

The question arises: how can we prove it? We can find certain proofs later by analogy with man, because man is built on the same principle as the Ray of Creation. There are many things which we cannot prove in an objective way, but it maybe we can find proofs by studying ourselves.

Q. Why does the soul at death go to the moon?

A. The moon is hungry.

Q. Is not the earth hungry too?

A. The whole surface of the earth, its composition and structure, depend on organic life. The earth receives the body, for that is what it wants. It depends on taste and appetite. The moon wants one thing, the earth another. It is a very interesting idea. Later you will see more clearly how things are connected, how one thing makes another grow. Certain matters pass to the moon in that way which otherwise would not be able to reach it. And they come in an already digested form.

Q. What is the earth? Is it alive? Where does organic life end and earth begin?

A. Organic life is a quite definite thing animals, plants, men and all micro-organisms. As to the earth, it is certainly a living being only on quite a different scale. Nothing is dead in nature. Only some men are dead.

Q. What is the form of communication between organic life and earth?

A. There are many forms of communication. When you inhale air, for instance, this is communication.

We are here on earth as part of organic life. Organic life is under certain influences coming from all the planets and, since we are part of it, these influences affect us too. We are also under certain influences coming from the sun, the Milky Way and, maybe, under the influences of All Worlds, although, naturally, influences of All Worlds on an individual man are very small. We do not know much about influences coming from the moon, but we do know that it plays a very important part in organic life and, without understanding how everything is connected and in what way the life of man on earth is connected with the planets and the sun, we cannot understand man's position and his present life as it is. For instance, without this diagram it is impossible to understand that man lives in a very bad place in the universe, and that many things which we regard as unfair, against which we rebel and try to fight, are really the result of this position of organic life on earth. If we were on the moon, it would be still worse; there would be no possibility of development. On the earth there is a possibility of development, we can develop certain parts in us.

Very little of planetary influences comes to us as individuals. Generally planetary influences are only felt by masses of people; thus, they are responsible for wars, revolutions, and things like that. An individual man is very little under planetary influences, because the part that can be affected by them is undeveloped. This undeveloped part is essence.

To a certain extent man is also under the influence of the sun, and he can be under much higher influences if he develops higher centres and becomes connected with them. So, development means passing from one kind of influences to another kind. At present we are more particularly under the influence of the moon. We have to become more and more conscious to come under higher influences.

Q. In what way are we under the influence of the moon?

A. The moon plays a very important part in our life, or rather the life of organic life on earth. The moon controls all our movements. If I move my arm, it is the moon that does it, because without the influence of the moon it cannot happen. The moon is like the weight on an old-fashioned clock and organic life is like the clock mechanism which is kept going by this weight. The action of the moon on our life is purely mechanical. It acts by sheer weight, and it receives higher energies which little by little make it alive. If you remember the four kinds of energy: mechanical energy, life energy, psychic energy, and conscious energy, then the moon acts with mechanical energy, like a huge electro-magnet, attracting the matter of the soul. When it gets this matter its temperature changes. The moon is in a very low state, much lower than the earth.

All our mechanicalness depends on the moon. We are like marionettes moved by wires, but we can be more free of the moon or less free. When we understand that, we will understand that the way to become more free is by not identifying, not considering, struggling with negative emotions, and so on. At present we cannot move a step without the energy of the moon; the wires cannot be cut at once, for then the marionettes would simply collapse. It is necessary to learn to move first. All sleeping people are under the influence of the moon. They have no resistance, but if man develops, he can gradually cut some of the wires that are undesirable and can open himself to higher influences. In this way he can become free from the moon, if not fully, at least considerably more than he is now.

Q. Do lower influences come from the moon?

A. More mechanical influences. If man is completely under the influence of the moon, he is a machine.

Q. Do you mean that the moon affects us both physically and psychologically?

A. The physical influence is different; this is normal. It is when the moon begins to affect our mind and emotions that it is wrong. It happens only when man is cut off from higher influences; but nothing can cut him off from them except himself.

Q. Could you tell us more about this idea of feeding the moon?

A. First I must ask you a question: what does this idea signify to you? What is the chief principle you see in it?

Q. I do not understand the first principle of it.

A. You see, you can look at it from different sides even when you hear about it for the first time. When you see the right principle, then everything becomes clear. When I first heard it, it certainly seemed very strange, but at the same time I saw that the principle behind it was that everything is connected, that things do not exist separately, that in a certain way organic life connects earth and moon.

Q. Does the moon actually cause human catastrophes by requiring certain food for its own being?

A. The moon does not cause catastrophes; we are guilty ourselves; it is no use trying to accuse the moon. Suppose we neglect to repair a wall and it falls, whose fault, is it? It falls because of physical laws, but at the same time it cannot be the fault of the physical laws. If cosmic influences fall on a right soil, there are no catastrophes, just as a wall does not fall if we repair it. But of course, there may be big catastrophes that are not affected by our attitude.

Q. Why is it that planets affect man in the mass and not individual man?

A. Because the part of man which can be affected is either very small and undeveloped or too covered by personality. Personality reflects all these influences, and man is under the law of accident. If man lived in his essence, he would be under planetary influences or, in other words, under the law of fate. Whether this would be to his advantage or not is another question; it may be better in one case and worse in another, but generally better. Planetary rays cannot penetrate personality.

People in the mass are affected by planetary influences in certain parts of themselves which are always there. Most people in a crowd are men No. 1, that is, men living in instinctive and moving centres. And the chief motive power of man No. 1 is imitation and imagination. When people are under the power of imitation and imagination, they very easily accept mechanical influences; they begin to imitate one another, so it produces a big effect.

When people live as part of the mass, nobody can help them; they are so intermingled that you cannot separate one atom from another. On the level of the mass, they are all the same. People can only expect to meet with favorable influences when they rise from the mass, not before. Influences affecting the mass are only unfavorable; they are influences that keep it down. There are favorable influences that help individuals to get out, but they can only help men who stand a little above the mass. We can expect help, but only on a certain level; for what would be the value of our efforts if someone could take us by the ears and drag us up? If we become conscious, it is the same as having will on a higher level; and if we can 'do', we can isolate ourselves from many of these planetary influences which affect the mass.

Q. Is our aim to develop ourselves so that as individuals we can come under planetary influences?

A. It will not be individual influence, it will be in accordance with your type. Individual men are different according to their essence. Essence or type of man is the result of planetary influences. Planets make us what we are. Different combinations of planetary influences make different essences.

Q. You were saying that we come under cosmic laws to the extent that wars are caused by planetary influences. Is it fate?

A. When I answer about what fate means, I take only what can really be called fate, but for many people fate is much more extended. When they are taken up by some big movement, such as political movements, wars, revolutions, for them this becomes fate. It must be understood why we spoke about planetary influences, why they were mentioned and in connection with what. The chief idea is that planetary influences may be very different. Our state attracts and repels planetary influences. We cannot know what they are, we can only know our state. If you remember yourself, you can attract good planetary influences; if you are mechanical, you attract wrong influences.

Q. Do the many laws under whose influence we are produce the different 'I's in us?

A. Yes, very many. Forces pass through man, and he takes this as his own desires, sympathies, attractions. But it is only forces passing through him from all directions. Starting from World 3, forces reach man and can produce actions, attitudes, or they may be rejected. We can only study the effects they may produce. We are interested in everything from the point of view of our profit, the rest does not interest us. Higher forces or higher influences are normal, cosmic; but we can open ourselves to receive them or shut ourselves off from them. If we are asleep, we are more closed to them, and the more we are asleep the more we are closed. If we awake, we open ourselves to higher influences.

Q. You said we are under the law of accident. From what source of influence does this law come? Can we be free from it?

A. Accident has many different manifestations. The simplest forms begin to disappear very quickly if we are more awake. But you cannot take this literally: this law is very big and many sided. It is a question of degree. Only in the Absolute are things absolute. For us it is a long stairway, and, on each step, one is more free. If you are below, you cannot speak about what will happen when you are at the top. You can only say: 'If I begin to work so as to be free from the law of accident, would my life be less chaotic?' Certainly, if you have a permanent aim, you will be free from accidental aims. Forget about miracles. Each line of effort will bring results on that line, though there are connections.

Q. How can one extricate oneself from bad influences?

A. Before we can even think about 'doing' we must try to understand what these influences are. This is a constant mistake that everybody makes always to think they can 'do'. We cannot 'do', but if we know, we may change something.

Q. As we have not developed our higher centres, how do we receive the influences coming from higher worlds?

A. Our ordinary state is relative; in our best moments we are receptive to higher influences. They reach us through centres. Though we are not permanently connected with higher centres, they influence us if they are not too deeply buried, and something manages to reach us through them.

Q. What is the purpose of man's existence?

A. Man and even mankind does not exist separately, but as a part of the whole of organic life. The earth needs organic life as a whole man, animals, plants. The Ray of Creation is a growing branch, and this communication is necessary in order that the branch may grow further. Everything is connected, nothing is separate, and smaller things, if they exist, serve something bigger. Organic life serves planetary purposes, it does not exist for itself. An individual man is a highly specialized cell in it, but on that scale an individual cell does not exist, it is too small. Our ordinary points of view are very naive and homocentric: everything turns round man. But man is a very insignificant thing, part of a very big machine. Organic life is a particular cosmic unit and man is a unit in this big mass of organic life. He has the possibility of further development, but this development depends on man's own effort and understanding. It enters into the cosmic purpose that a certain number of men should develop, but not all, for that would contradict another cosmic purpose. Evidently mankind must be on earth and must lead this life and suffer. But a certain number of men can escape, this also enters into the cosmic purpose.

So individually we are not important for the universe at all. We cannot speak even about humanity in relation to the universe, we can only speak about organic life. As I said, we are part of organic life, and organic life plays a certain part in the solar system, but it is a very big thing compared with us. We are used to thinking of ourselves individually, but very soon we lose this illusion. It is useful to think about different scales; take a thing on a wrong scale and you lose your way.

Q. Did you say it was intended that some of us should develop?

A. As far as we can see it is under the same law as, for instance, street accidents. It is well known that in every big town a certain number of people will be killed by traffic. Who will be killed is not determined, it need not necessarily be one or another person, but a certain number? In the same way a certain number of people *may* have a chance of escape but there is no *must* about it in this case. This is the difference.

Q. Are we given the possibility, or must we create it in the teeth of circumstances?

A. The possibility is given. Every normal person has this possibility. The rest depends on us. Individually men exist only for themselves. But even for themselves they do not serve any useful purpose. If a man grows and becomes different, he may become important individually in some way, although we cannot know that for certain. But this can refer only to a man of higher development, not to a mechanical man.

Q. Why do the sun, the planets and the moon want to communicate?

A. It is all one thing; only to us do things look separate, in reality they are all linked together like different parts of the body. It is like the circulation of blood in an organism, or the flow of sap in a growing branch. This is why communication is necessary.

Q. How many laws does a man live under?

A. We do not know. We can only speak about the earth, which is under forty-eight laws, but you cannot use the same scale in relation to man. You can only say approximately that organic life stands in the same relation to the earth as the moon and is therefore under ninety-six laws. But this is only the principle. Man is under many more laws.

Q. Could you give an example of the forty-eight laws?

A. It is not a question of a catalogue but of understanding what the idea means. Man is not under one type of law but under many different types. First of all, man like every creature on earth, lives under physical laws, which means that he can live only within certain limits of temperature. Then, there must be a particular amount of humidity in the air, and the air must be of a special chemical consistency for man to breathe. Man is also limited to a certain kind of food which he can digest. These things are all laws for man. Then, coming to quite simple laws, there is, for instance, our ignorance. We do not know ourselves this is a law. If we begin to know ourselves, we get rid of a law. As I said, we cannot make a catalogue of them, for some of them have no names, but some we know. For example, we know that all men live under the law of identification this is another law. Those who begin to remember themselves begin to get rid of the law of identification. So, in order to free oneself from laws it is first necessary to find one law from which one can liberate oneself and get free from it. Then, when one has freed oneself from this law, one can find another. Again, one liberates oneself, and so on. This is the practical way to study laws.

Q. There are so many laws which we cannot help obeying, for instance the necessity to sleep so many hours every night. Is this a way of understanding how much man is a machine?

A. No, not quite, because this law of sleep is a cosmic law. Man is made like that; many cosmic laws maintain this arrangement. But there are laws which hinder us on all sides or keep us in subjection, and which are not necessary at all, there is no beneficial side and no cosmic necessity. We are under too many unnecessary laws, and chiefly the law of our own mechanicalness This is what particularly keeps us down for instance, we live under the law of negative emotions, it is not a necessary law at all, we can live much more happily without negative emotions, although people do not believe it.

Q. Do you mean we must be subject to all these laws?

A. We cannot fall, or not fall, under them, they do not ask us, we are chained They

govern, control, and direct us

Q. Can we get free?

A. We can, on conditions The Ways enter here the four Ways are ways of liberation from unnecessary laws Without schools one cannot know from which laws one can get free or find means of getting free from them the idea is that we are under too many mechanical laws Eventually we can get rid of some of them by becoming subject to other laws. The only way to get out of the power of one law is to put oneself under another law. But this is only the general idea You can be shown the way, but you must work yourself

Q. Does not the acceptance of new laws in a school lead to words and a new crop of academism?

A The outcome of work on oneself is not creation of new laws but liberation from unnecessary laws Discipline, necessary for the period of study, is only a means, not an end in study of oneself, understanding is necessary and being conscious You cannot escape with words This is exactly what is impossible.

Q. Does the possibility of attaining permanent 'I' depend on the number of laws one is subject to?

A. Yes Try to find an analogy to what it means to be under more laws and fewer laws Suppose a man lives an ordinary life, then there is conscription, and he enters military service While he is in the army he is under more laws, when he ends his period of military service he is under fewer laws. Then suppose that while he is in the army, he commits a crime and is sent to prison. He is then under prison laws in addition to military laws, the laws of his country, physical and biological laws and so on This is the kind of analogy we must find to understand the idea for instance, if a man is well, he is under a certain number of laws, if he is ill, he is under more laws.

Q. Not in reality?

A. Yes, certainly, he has to obey his doctor or go to hospital and be under the laws of the hospital

Q. What purpose is there if I have a toothache?

A. I see none.

Q. Is it not part of the cosmic design?

A. No, there is no design. You cannot speak of purpose without scale and relativity It is impossible that the same purpose should apply both on a big and on a small scale. Everything has a cause, but not everything has an aim or purpose, you must not forget the idea of scale.

Q. Nature seems to be very unjust and very cruel to man.

A. What do you call nature? An earthquake is also nature. But for the moment we apply the word 'nature' to organic life. Evidently it was created like it is because there was no other means. If we do not like it, we can study methods of how to run away. We are too small individually to be known by any higher forces So who is just or unjust? We operate with imaginary ideas in a small, limited circle, in definite limited conditions, there can be justice and injustice. But on a larger scale this idea loses its meaning There are many such ideas which have a certain meaning on a small scale but lose all meaning on a larger scale. At the same time this idea of justice is interesting because people lose a great amount of energy on this point. We can stop this waste, but we cannot correct things in the world. All life from beginning to end is an injustice. For instance, we have to die it is most unjust. We divide things into just and unjust, and what right have we? All organic life is based on injustice; it is a self-supporting farm to breed cats and rats. Cats eat rats and rats eat cats. What is justice among cats and rats? This is life. It is nothing very beautiful. Our aim is to get out; it is not our business to feel indignation, that is simply loss of energy. But we must not pretend that facts are different from what they are.

Q. Are you going to put man on the same footing as the rest of organic life?

A. There is no difference, only other units are fully developed, and man is only half developed.

Q. How is it that man, who is but one manifestation of organic life, should be chosen to have a chance of further development?

A. I do not think it is a question of choice, I think this question needs quite a different approach. From this point of view all organic life can be regarded as a long work of experimenting with the idea of producing a self-evolving being. If man can reach a higher state, it is because he is made that way, he is created to be self-evolving. Other beings are only experiments for developing different features, they do not possess all the qualities that man possesses.

Man is a machine, but there are different machines, and machines can be made for a special purpose. If a machine is used for the purpose it is made for, it is in the right place, but if it is made for one purpose and used for another, it is in a wrong place. Man is a special machine, made for a certain purpose; he is made a recipient of certain higher influences coming from worlds 3, 6, 12 and because he can receive these influences from higher worlds, he can become independent of the world surrounding him.

Q. How can man escape from his situation?

A. He can escape from some of the laws. On different levels things are under different laws.

Q. Then is man in a higher state of consciousness subject to fewer laws than we are?

A. Certainly, because most of the laws we have to obey are the result of our sleep and our unconsciousness. Every step we make in becoming more conscious sets us more free. Suppose a man is satisfied with mechanical life; then he cuts himself off from higher influences and receives only influences beginning with world 24. Certainly, he is then in a worse position than a man who receives influences from higher worlds. Laws or influences from worlds 3 and 6 can only come through higher mental Centre and influences of world 12 through higher emotional Centre.

You must understand, besides, that many influences can be received mechanically, but many others need effort. Moreover, influences do not remain as they are in man; they are transformed in him. It all depends on how they are transformed.

Q. Are men responsible for what they do and animals not responsible?

A. Men 1, 2 and 3 are less responsible; men No. 4 and so on are more responsible; responsibility grows. An animal has nothing to lose, but man has. When a man has started to grow, he has to pay for every mistake he makes. If one has no control, as in sleep, one has no responsibility, but if one has even a small possibility of control, a possibility of being more awake or less awake, as in our case, one is already responsible.

Q. That implies justice.

A. No, nobody would call it justice if you had to pay for your mistakes. Most people think that justice is getting what we want and not what we deserve. Justice must mean some co-ordination between actions and results of actions. This certainly does not exist, and cannot exist, under the law of accident and we live under the law of accident. When we know the chief laws, we understand that we live in a bad place, a really bad place. But we cannot live in any other, so we must see what we can do here. Only we must not imagine that things are better than they are.

This question of justice and injustice is a very good subject for thinking, because people spend much energy on this problem. They use the words but do not give an account to themselves why they call one thing just and another unjust. Yet one thing is always connected with another, one thing inevitably follows from another. It is our assumption that there must be justice on each scale. Try to explain what is just and what is unjust. How can you know? People are machines. How can machines be just? It is not a quality that belongs to machines. If they are responsible, like man No. 5, then you can speak about justice and injustice; but if they act in the way conditions and circumstances make them, what can you expect? Very often our idea of injustice is based on a very narrow view. We do not compare things and see that it is the natural order of things. We cannot speak about injustice so long as we think of it as an exception. When we see it as the rule, we may think of how to escape from it. There can be no justice in our present state, no justice in prison. The only thing one can seriously think about when one realizes that one is in prison is how to escape, not sit and cry about injustice in prison. People are machines, they are pushed in a certain way and roll, and when they hit a wall, they stop and then begin to roll back. Justice, like many other things, depends on place. Let us start placing it from the point of view of the system. We start with the division of humanity into different circles. Now we can see where the misunderstanding about justice arises. Justice really begins in the second circle, when people begin to understand one another better and there is more justice in the circle inside that one and still more in the innermost circle. In the outer circle justice can only be accidental, like everything else. Justice, like many other things real and imaginary, such as positive emotion, knowledge of certain things like future life, understanding between people and so on, which we want to find here in the outer circle, exist, if they exist at all, only in the inner circles and are impossible here.

Q. Will things remain as they are unless everyone is conscious?

A. Things will remain as they are, but we can escape. It needs much knowledge to know from what we can escape and from what we cannot escape. But the first lesson we must learn, the first thing that prevents us escaping, is that we do not even realize the necessity of knowing our position. Whoever knows it is already in a better position.

Q. If man is analogous to the worlds, can we understand which are the three laws of man?

A. Yes, we can. If we take World 6, we see that there are six orders of laws, three from the world above and three of its own. So, we can say that the laws belonging to World 6 are half of the totality of laws under which it exists. Now take World 12. Three laws of its own make one-half, equal to the other nine laws which make the other half; and so on, until we come to man. Three laws of man's own make a half of the total number of laws under which man lives. You will see from this that the finer the forces, the less of them comes to man.

Q. Why do they represent half?

A. Because they occupy half the place, and may even occupy the whole, and other forces may not work at all. All depends on which influences we are open to higher or lower.

Q. You said that organic life is governed by ninety-six laws, the same as the moon?

A. The same number, but quite a different manifestation. Organic life is not similar to the moon. The moon is a cosmic body, organic life is a film on the surface of the earth. The number of laws only shows the relation of a given unit to the rest, but not its being and consistency.

Q. Did you say that planets affect situations wars and so forth?

A. Yes, they may create wars. The whole solar system is a unit, so everything in it is connected with cosmic causes and it all affects life on earth. Causes of things that happen on earth are often outside the earth. But when there are causes that can produce wars it depends on the state of humanity at a given place and time. People can show more resistance or less resistance. If people at a certain time in a given country are in a better state, they show more resistance.

Q. Does the earth affect the moon and other planets as well?

A. Yes, but we are only interested in what affects organic life and, through organic life, ourselves.

Q. How can we test the arbitrary statements about the role of organic life and about the moon being the youngest in the Ray?

A. There are no arbitrary statements, it all comes from the system. It is not my system. I have not invented it. Just as a theory it presents no interest: it is interesting only if we realize that it comes from higher mind. I started with the psychological side to give you a possibility to acquire valuation of these ideas. If you have got it, you will be patient with this side.

Q. Are we working against nature? I often get the idea that to a certain extent we are.

A. We are working against nature, but nature is a relative term. In these concentric circles of worlds within worlds, if you work against nature you work against one concentric circle, but it may not be against another circle. It is not all one nature; you cannot work against nature outside of nature; if you go outside of one nature you are inside another nature.

Q. On what evidence is the assumption based that man could revolt from his place in the universe and that this is not another illusion?

A. But man cannot. Man cannot go away from the earth, but he can be under different laws while remaining in the same position and on the same earth. He can be under one set of laws, or another set of laws, and it is possible to observe this if we know what it means. We can observe people living under different sets of laws in ordinary life and when we prove it even in a small way, we can easily understand that it can go further. You must think of what it means to live under different laws. Even such as we are, we have a certain choice, maybe not a full choice, but we can change many things just by choosing rightly.

Q. Must you have a great deal of knowledge before you can choose between influences?

A. This is a very important question because it is not a question of knowledge but of being. Man, lives under influences coming from different parts of the universe. In one state one kind of influence conquers, in another state another kind in the life of the same man he can be one day under one kind of influence and another day under another.

Q. Do we put ourselves under more laws because of our false personality?

A. Quite right, under many quite useless mechanical laws

Q What is the value of studying tables and diagrams?

A. When you started studying the system you must have had many questions and thoughts about the world, about the relation of different things, and about yourself, in the world Diagrams and study of laws give you a new point of view: you had thought of things in one way and now, through these diagrams and principles, you begin to think in another way.

Q. Will this theoretical knowledge of cosmology help understanding to grow?

A. It is not theoretical, it is very practical, and certainly it will help understanding to grow, because it will create a firm ground for it The Ray of Creation is a system of elimination of simplification, it does away with all knowledge that is not practical With the help of the Ray of Creation we eliminate from the universe all that has no personal relation to us, all that cannot be understood practically As I said, in studying the Ray of Creation we use the principle of scale This applies to our perception of things, and yet, from another point of view, it also refers to things in themselves This is what must be understood it is not only subjective, because things on different scales are under different laws. Besides, all big ideas like the Ray of Creation and the fundamental laws of the universe are necessary because they keep our thought in the right channels, they do not let it spread without any results, so they also help self-remembering. If you discard them, if you try only to self-remember and exclude all other ideas it will not come. Now we must speak about the matters from which the universe is made All the matters of the world surrounding us, the food we eat, the water we drink, the air we breathe, the stones of our houses, our own bodies are permeated by all the matters existing in the universe There is no need to study or analyze the sun in order to find solar matter, this matter is in ourselves, it is the result of the division of our atoms In the same way we have in us matters of all other worlds In this sense, man is indeed a miniature universe, he has in him all the matters which compose the universe, the same forces, the same laws which govern the life of the whole world act in him Therefore, as I said, by studying man we study the universe, and vice versa.

But a full parallel between man and the universe can be drawn only if we take man in the full sense of the word, that is, a man whose inherent powers and possibilities are developed an underdeveloped man, a man who has not completed his evolution, cannot be taken as a complete picture of the world, he is an unfinished world.

As has been said earlier, laws are everywhere the same, on all planes. These same laws, manifesting in different worlds, that is, in different conditions, produce different phenomena. The study of the relation of laws to the planes on which they manifest themselves brings us to the study of relativity.

If we take the Ray of Creation, we must remember that the worlds are connected with one another and affect one another in accordance with the Law of Three. In other words, the first three worlds, taken together, produce the phenomenon which influences the following worlds, and so on. In the first three worlds the Absolute is the conductor of the active force. World 3 the conductor of the passive force, and World 6 the conductor of the neutralizing force. In other words, the Absolute is Carbon, World 3 is Oxygen and World 6 is Nitrogen.

If we place the three forces in sequence, according to the order in which they unite, we will get the order 1, 2, 3; but the matters serving as conductors of these forces will, according to their density, stand in the order: carbon, nitrogen, oxygen. So, when the triad begins to form, they stand in the order 1, 3, 2. When matters stand in this order, phenomena are produced. But for subsequent creation, for the formation of the next triad, nitrogen must, as it were, return once more to the third place, to the order 1, 2, 3, and in this way become carbon of the next triad, for the second triad comes from the neutralizing force of the first triad becoming active. This change of place of matters in the triad is a kind of cosmic dance which produces action.

Let us now try to see how forces emerging from the Absolute in order to manifest themselves in World 3 must first pass-through World 6. An analogy shows us quite plainly the necessity of this direction of force. As I said, man's will can influence a fragment of tissue in certain parts of his body. But a tissue is composed of cells. In order to affect the tissue man's will must first influence the cells composing the given fragment of tissue. The tissue is a different world from cells, but at the same time tissues do not exist apart from cells for they are composed of cells.

World 3 is a separate world from World 6, and at the same time it is composed of Worlds 6, that is of worlds similar to our Milky Way. So, in order to influence a part of World 3 (All Worlds) the Absolute must first influence a certain number of Worlds (All Suns) of which World 3 is composed.

Thus, in the passage of forces. Worlds 1, 3, 6 stand, at first, in the order 1, 3, 6, then in the order 1, 6, 3, and then, for a further passage of forces, they must again resume the order 1, 3, 6. In the next triad the Milky Way is carbon, the sun oxygen and the planets nitrogen. Since nitrogen stands between carbon and oxygen, the force coming from the Milky Way, that is from the stars, must first pass through the planets in order to reach the sun.

This may look strange at the first glance, but if we visualize the structure of the

solar system, we shall see quite clearly that it cannot be otherwise. No analogies are needed here. Imagine the sun surrounded by planets moving round it; in the distance, some group of stars from which influences go forth towards the sun. But the sun does not stand in one place; we know that it moves; the planets, rotating round it, move with it in space, forming, each of them by its motion, a spiral round the central rod of the sun, so that this central rod is entirely enclosed in the spirals of planets and no influence can reach it without first passing through the world of planets, that is, penetrating through the rings of the spirals.

Further, planets becoming carbon of the third triad must find corresponding oxygen and nitrogen. In our Ray of Creation, oxygen is earth. But there is no nitrogen in the astronomical Ray of Creation. Therefore, the planets cannot pass their influence direct to earth, and in order to make the passage of forces possible between the planets and the earth, a special contrivance was created which represents the sensitive organ of the earth, organic life on earth.

Organic life on earth is nitrogen of the third triad. Forces coming from the planets fall first on organic life, which receives them and passes them on to the earth.

If we remember the extremely complicated organization of the ends of sensitive nerves in our own organism, for instance the ends of the nerves of taste and smell, we shall not think it strange that man is defined as a sensitive nerve-end of the earth.

Of course, a meadow covered with grass diners in many ways from man; it receives only some planetary influences, and very few of these. Man receives much more complex influences. But people differ greatly from one another in this respect. The majority of men are important only in the mass, and only the mass receives one or another influence. Others are capable of receiving influences individually influences which masses cannot receive, for they are sensitive only to coarse influences.

Organic life on earth, playing the role of nitrogen of the third triad, is by this very fact carbon of the fourth triad in the Ray. In other words, it conducts the active force which meets with corresponding oxygen and nitrogen. Earth is oxygen and moon is nitrogen through which the influences of organic life pass to earth.

Now, if we take the Ray of Creation divided into four triads and bear in mind that the sum total of each triad is a definite hydrogen, we shall get four hydrogens or four definite densities of matter. These four hydrogens can be taken as corresponding to the four fundamental points of the universe. The first corresponds to the Absolute, the second to the sun, the third to the earth and the fourth to the moon.

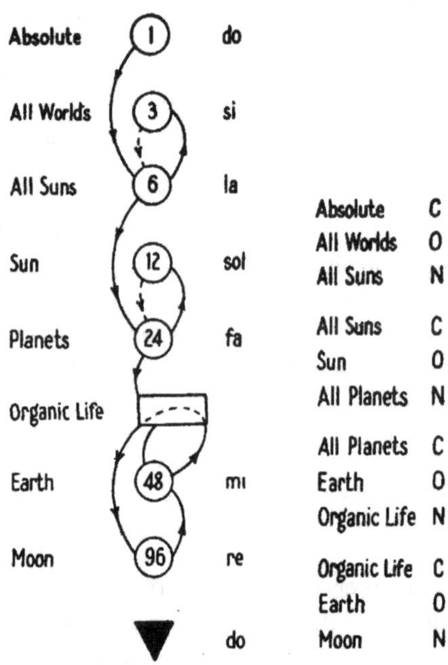

I said that the Ray of Creation can be taken as an octave. After re, represented by the moon, the octave has its *do*, which is also the Absolute. So, there are, as it were, two Absolutes: one begins the Ray, the other ends it. One Absolute is All, the other is Nothing. But there can be no two Absolutes, for, by its very nature, the Absolute is one. Therefore, all includes Nothing, and Nothing includes All. Our dualistically constructed mind cannot take in the identity of opposites. We divide everything, even the Absolute. In reality, what we call the antithesis of opposites exists only in our conception, in our subjective perception of the world. But, even when we understand this, we are unable to express this understanding in words; our language has no words which can include simultaneously thesis and antithesis. Our mind cannot grasp them as one idea, just as it cannot grasp the images of some Hindu gods, combining complete opposites in themselves.

Now we shall examine the passage of radiations between the four fundamental points of the cosmic octave. We take radiations between each two points in the form of an octave and thus obtain three octaves.

Absolute—Sun; Sun—Earth; Earth—Moon.

It should be noted that, although there are six intervals, only three of them require to be filled from without. The intervals between do and si are filled by the Will of the Absolute, by the influence of the sun's mass on the radiations passing through it, and by the influence of the mass of the earth on the radiations passing through it.

Do si	H6	H3	H1	Absolute
la sol	H12	H6	H3	
fa --	H24	H12	H6	
mi re	H48	H24	H12	
do si	H96	H48	H24	Sun
la sol	H192	H96	H48	
fa --	H384	H192	H96	
mi re	H768	H384	H192	
do si	H1536	H768	H384	Earth
la sol	H3072	H1536	H768	
fa --	H6144	H3072	H1536	
mi re do	H12288	H6144	H3072	Moon

All the hydrogens in this Table represent matters with which we have to do in studying man. It has been scaled down twice in order to include only the hydrogens that have relation to man, both to his outer life and the inner life of his organism.

Q. How do these hydrogens connect with man?

A. For instance, hydrogen 768 represents all the food we eat; the air we breathe is hydrogen 192, and our impressions can be 48, 24, 12 and even 6. We have an enormous range of impressions, but we have no choice of air or food. We cannot inhale, for instance, hydrogen 96, for it is fire, incandescent gases. We cannot eat H 384, for it is water, and we cannot live on water. You will see that this Table answers all our requirements; it enables us to speak of all the matters in the human machine and to see their interrelation; and it makes it possible to connect man with the universe, because we can know from which level each matter comes.

This Table of hydrogens shows not only the density of each of them but also, the place of origin of these different layers of matter which are under different laws, as it was explained. Hydrogens which come from planes under a very small number of laws, near the Will of the Absolute, have an enormous power and enormous potential energy.

Thus, we have a scale of twelve densities on which can be placed all matter known to or conceivable by man.

For the lower densities we may find examples both in man and in the world around him. Up to the level of H 96 or even 48, these may be studied physically by chemistry, biology, and other sciences. Above H 48 we can only study psychological effects of their presence or absence knowing the level of hydrogens with which different centres work.

Still higher hydrogens are only potential in man or exist in such small quantities that they are impossible to study. The study of these higher hydrogens in the surrounding world is also beyond the powers of perception of man No. 1, 2 and 3.

Q. How are the three intervals in the three octaves of radiations filled?

A. It is a cosmic arrangement, otherwise the Ray could not exist. They are filled by the forces of nature, just as you will see it in our organism:

some intervals in our organism are filled by nature, otherwise we would not be able to live.

Q. Does a hydrogen consist of three elements as well as three forces?

A. It consists of three forces working through three elements. Three forces cannot work without three elements. A hydrogen is the sum total.

Q. Do impressions generate energy?

A. They are energy in themselves. Every time we get an impression, we receive a certain matter. Matter is not separate from energy: where there is matter, there is energy and where there is energy there is matter.

I want to give you one more diagram that may help you to understand things. I said that organic life is a special adaptation filling the interval between the planets and the earth. It is created in the form of a lateral or an additional octave beginning in the sun, *sol*. *Sol* becomes *do* and produces *si* on the level of the planets, and then three notes, *la, sol, fa*, which are organic life on earth. Then mi of this lateral octave enters into the earth and re into the moon. So organic life belongs not to the main octave but to this special octave which begins in the sun. We do not know what *do* and *si* of this octave mean. Out of all this octave we know only *la, sol, fa* and mi. Even about *re* all we know is that when anything dies whether man or a cockroach, its soul goes to the moon.

do	(1)	
si	(3)	
la	(6)	
sol	(12)	do
fa	(24)	si
la sol fa		
mi	(48)	mi
re	(96)	re

Q. When you say that we know what *mi* is, do you mean the earth?

A. No, all that goes into the earth the physical body, all physical matter at death goes into the earth.

Q. Are souls created for every organism?

A. The body is born and at the same time the soul is born too; it is simply part of the body, invisible, unknown to medicine, physics, and chemistry but without it the body cannot exist. When the body dies, the soul is free and is attracted by this big electromagnet, the moon.

Q. I still do not understand the influence of organic life between planets and earth Does it act in both directions?

A. Try to begin from what you can understand, and later your understanding will increase. No one can understand everything at once to understand means to connect. Organic life transfers planetary influences on earth. As a matter of fact, the process does go both ways, but we cannot see either. We must take it as a theory, but analogies can be found. We can see how organic life transforms influences coming from the sun and what a great part it plays in the structure of the earth's crust. For instance, black soil is the result of earth worms, oil is the result of an agglomeration of fishes and sea organisms, coal is the result of forests; chalk, coral islands, all these are results of organic life which remain in the earth. This shows how *mi* enters into the earth. All this *is mi* of the lateral octave of which *la-sol-fa* is organic life when it is alive This shows how organic life transforms the sun's influences. We do not see how it transforms planetary influences, but we can take the analogy of the sun's influences This shows that organic life is connected with both the planets and the sun and trans forms planetary influences) just as it transforms solar influences.

Q. Is the Ray of Creation mechanical?

A. Not the whole Ray. When it comes to us, certainly all the laws are mechanical on our plane.

Q. How is it possible that a mechanical Ray can create a machine which is capable of achieving a permanent will?

A. You must remember that the Ray of Creation starts consciously, and in the starting point there are evidently plans of everything, or some plans may gradually develop further down. But in the forty-eight laws that work on the earth there are three laws from World 3, which is under the direct will of the Absolute. Laws coming from different planes are not equally mechanical; some are more mechanical, others less. If we take the lateral octave starting from the sun, the octave of organic life we shall see that the sun is much higher than the earth and it is evidently possible to create in this octave possibilities of development. Thus man, if he can be regarded as a seed, has in himself the possibility of growth He is not only what he looks, there is something in him which cannot be seen, this hidden possibility of evolution. We can understand this relation of more mechanical and less mechanical only in ourselves. We know how mechanical we are and that if we work, we can become less mechanical. This is the only way to study mechanicalness.

Q. If man, as part of organic life, fulfils a purpose in the scheme of the universe, what further purpose can he serve by gaining consciousness?

A. That depends on what we want. You may be satisfied with certain purposes of nature, or you may have your own ideas. By becoming conscious you may serve your own purpose, but if you are not conscious, you only serve the purposes of nature. Nature wants man to be as he is in this place. This is the reason why only a few can escape, and they can escape because man is very small.

Q. Then would you say that ninety-nine people out of a hundred have the dice loaded against them?

A. There are no definite statistics about it. A very small minority has the possibility of development.

Q. I have understood that the Absolute can know nothing of man. Is it absurd to believe that there may be deputy powers able to take an interest in man?

A. Not necessarily deputy powers, but maybe special powers. There is no question but that there must be powers which take an interest in man, but we have no direct contact with these powers. We do not know them intellectually and do not know the approach to them. They appear in this small octave which begins in the sun. The sun produces do on its own level and si on the level of the planets. These two notes are the origin of organic life and probably its controlling principle. So, when we know what do and si are we will know about these powers.

There are two things we must always remember about this small lateral octave: first, that it is incommensurable with the Ray of Creation for it is on quite a different scale; second, that we must always remember that we do not know what *do* and *si* of this octave are. When we think that life started here on earth by some process or other, we may think that we know what it is, but when we hear that it does not start on earth, we realize that we do not know.

* * *

CHAPTER IX

Study of man as a chemical factory—Food Diagram—Three octaves of food and their development—First stage with one mechanical shock— Second stage with one conscious shock—Third stage with second conscious shock—Relative value of the three foods—Impressions—Self-remembering —Carbon 12—Laughter—Good and bad impressions—Impressions as different hydrogens—Control of impressions—Work on mi 12—Centres and their speed—Higher centres and their characteristics—Connection with higher centres— Higher centres and drugs—Telepathy—Necessity to increase the production of higher matters—Energy and the storing of energy— Accumulators—Connection with the big accumulator—Yawning— All work must be concentrated on consciousness.

Last time I gave you a scale of matter in relation to man and the human body. Every level represents a certain density of matter and a certain rate of vibrations, or, as it is called in the system, density of vibrations. The top does represent the smallest possible density of matter and the quickest rate of vibrations. Vibrations get slower and slower descending the scale and come to almost nothing at the end, while the density of matter increases correspondingly and comes to its maximum.

Each of these matters represents a very large range. Now we must study man as a chemical factory and see what role these matters play in the human body. Some of these hydrogens we can study physically or chemically while the presence of others we can determine only psychologically. Thus, this table of hydrogens gives us the possibility of studying both physical and psychological manifestations as manifestations of the same order but of different degrees of materiality.

People often ask where man's energy comes from. From this point of view man can be regarded as a chemical factory that receives raw materials from outside and transforms them into other materials of a finer quality.

The three kinds of material which man gets from outside are: the food he cats, the air he inhales and the impressions he receives. Food is always H 768, air is always H 192, but impressions can be very varied. For the beginning of study, for understanding the principle, we take as a standard of impressions H 48. H 48 represents just ordinary colorless impressions without any character. If I see this piece of paper, this is impression 48, nothing more. But actually, impressions can be of very good or very bad quality, we will speak about that later.

From these three kinds of material the machine produces all the matters needed for the work of centres. In the ordinary state the human machine works well enough for maintaining its own life, but as a chemical factory it is unsatisfactory, because it consumes everything it produces; it cannot export or store anything. Yet the development of man depends on storing the higher matters produced by his machine. So, we must think about ways to increase the production. But before we can think about increasing production we must study the factory from the point of view of waste, for there are many leaking parts in the machines, and if we do not stop these leaks, increased production will only increase the leaks. We have already spoken about the leaks, so, although I will now show you how the factory works, and even how production can be increased, the leaks are not shown in the diagram. But they are all in you, and you must remember that you cannot increase production in your present state, for first of all you must stop all the leaks. After this is done, it will be useful to learn practical ways of improving the work of the factory. This is the principle. I will show you three stages or three states of this chemical factory: first, how it works in ordinary man 1, 2 and 3, then how it works with one definite kind of effort and, finally, how it works with a second definite kind of effort.

We take the human machine as a three-storied factory. The three stories represent the head, the middle part of the body and the lower part of the body with the spinal cord.

Food enters the top story and passes to the bottom story as Oxygen 768. In the body it meets with a certain Carbon 192 and, mixing with this Carbon, becomes Nitrogen 384. Nitrogen 384 meets with another Carbon, 96, and with the help of this Carbon changes from Oxygen 384 to Nitrogen 192. It is an ascending octave, so these stages represent the notes *do, re, mi.*

After *mi* there is an interval, and the octave cannot develop any further by itself. It is very interesting that up to this point and one step further we can follow its development with the help of ordinary physiological knowledge. When food enters the mouth, it meets with several different sorts of saliva and is mixed with them in the process of mastication; then it passes into the stomach and is worked on by gastric juices, which break down sugars, proteins and fats. From there it goes into the intestines and meets with bile, pancreatic and intestinal juices, which transform it into the smallest elements. These go through the wall of the bowel into venous blood, which is taken to the liver, where it meets with other carbons which change it chemically, and so to the heart, which pumps the venous blood to the lungs. Here it is oxygenated by the entry of air and returned to the heart as arterial blood. In this diagram all the various matters present in the body which the food meets with up to *mi* are divided into two categories: Carbon 192 and Carbon 96. Venous blood is *mi* 192 and arterial blood is *fa* 96.

At the point when *mi* 192 cannot develop any further, another kind of food enters air. It enters as Oxygen 192, meets with a certain Carbon 48 and with its help is transformed into *re* 96, and this production of *re* 96 gives a shock to *mi* 192 of the food octave enabling it to pass to *fa* 96. Beyond this, physiological knowledge cannot go.

Re 96 of the air octaves meets a corresponding Carbon and produces mi 48; and with the help of the same Carbon *fa* 96 of the food octave transforms into sol 48. Sol 48 can develop further, but *mi* 48 cannot, so the development of the air octave stops at this point. *Sol* 48 of the food octave passes into *la* 24 and *la* 24 into *si* 12 and stops there. Impressions enter as *do* 48, but cannot develop any further, because at their place of entry there is no Carbon 12 to help them. Nature has not provided it, or rather has not provided enough to produce any considerable effect, *so do* 48 does not transform and the three octaves stop at that.

Think about this diagram and connect it with what has been said earlier that nature brings man to a certain state and then leaves him to develop himself. Nature gives man possibilities but does not develop these possibilities. It enables him to live, provides air, for otherwise the first octave could not go on, but the rest he must do himself. The machine is so arranged that air enters at the right moment and in the right consistency and gives a mechanical shock. It is important to understand that the Food Diagram or the Diagram of Nutrition consists of three stages.

The first stage that I have just described shows how things happen in ordinary normal man: the food octave goes on all the way from do 768 to *si* 12; there are three notes of the air octave and one note of the impression's octave. If we want to develop further, we must increase the production of higher matters, and in order to do that we must understand and know how to do it, not only theoretically but in actual fact, because it needs a long time to learn how to use this knowledge and to make the right efforts.

If we know how to bring Carbon 12 to the right place and if we make the necessary effort, the development of the air and impressions octaves goes further. The second stage shows what happens when the right shock has been given. *Do* 48 of the impression's octave is transformed into *re* 24 and *mi* 12. The air octave receives a shock from the impression's octave and *mi* 48 transforms into *fa* 24, sol 12 and even a small quantity of *la* 6. You must understand that the air is saturated with higher hydrogens which, in certain cases, can be retained by the organism in the process of breathing. But the amount of higher hydrogens that we can get from the air is very small. This stage represents the work of the human machine with one mechanical and one conscious shock.

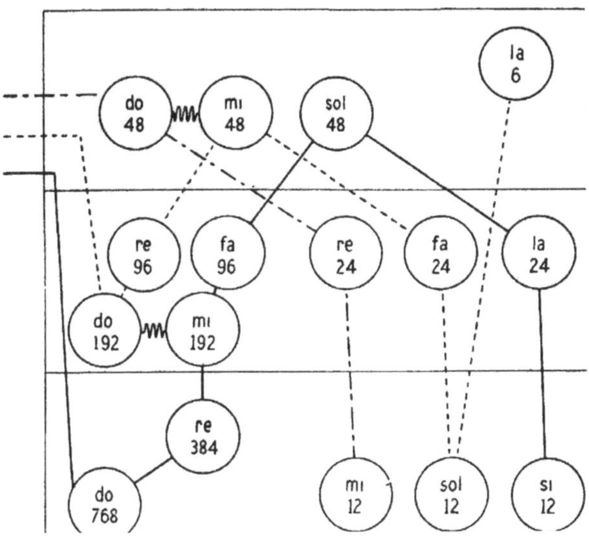

The third stage shows what happens when a second conscious shock is given at the right place. The first conscious shock is necessary at *do* 48. The second conscious shock is needed where *mi* 12 of the impression's octave and *si* 12 of the food octave have stopped in their development and cannot go on any further by themselves. Although there are carbons in the organism which would help them to be transformed, they are far away and cannot be reached, so another effort is necessary. If we know its nature and can produce this second conscious shock, mi 12 will develop into *fa* 6 and *si* 12 into *do* 6. The effort must begin from *mi* 12, so we must understand what mi 12 is psychologically. We can call it our ordinary emotions, that is to say, all strong emotions that we may have. When our emotions reach a certain degree of intensity, there is *mi* 12 in them. But in our present state only our unpleasant emotions actually reach *mi* 12;

our ordinary pleasant emotions usually remain 24. It is not that our intense unpleasant emotions actually are *mi* 12, but they are based on it and need it in order to be produced. So, the beginning of this second effort and preparation for it is work on negative emotions.

This is the general outline of the work of the human organism and of how this work can be improved. It is important to understand where conscious shocks are necessary, because if you understand this it will help you to understand many other difficulties in the Food Diagram.

You must understand, too, that these three octaves are not of equal force. If you take the force of the food octave, you will see that it gives certain results, certain effects that can be measured. Although the matter taken from air plays a very important part, the air octave represents a very small quantity of hydrogens, whereas the impressions octave is very powerful and may have an enormous meaning in relation to self remembering, states of consciousness, emotions and so on. So, we can say that the relationship of the three octaves is not equal, because one has more substance, another less substance.

This is our inner alchemy, the transmutation of base metals into precious metals. But all this alchemy is inside us, not outside.

Q. What causes transformation of food into higher matter?

A. It is mixed with other matters higher than itself and in that way, it rises; then it becomes mixed with still higher matters and rises again, and so on. Take it in a simple way.

Q. It never reaches the level of the highest matter it is mixed with?

A. That does not matter. What matters is that it rises, it becomes higher than itself. Higher matters contain more energy, coarser matters contain less. So, when they mix, higher hydrogens bring their energy into coarser matters.

Q. Can higher matter be produced by prayer and mental exercises?

A. It is not produced out of nothing, but in man's inner alchemy higher substances are distilled out of other, coarser material which otherwise would remain in a coarse state.

Q. Why is it that the first conscious shock comes from impressions?

A. The shock does not come from impressions, this is not quite the right definition. Impressions are a very important food, and in our ordinary state we are starved of impressions. We have enough impressions, but we cannot digest them.

Q. Do we have to produce Carbon 12, or is it in the organism?

A. Generally a man has enough carbons for ordinary normal life, and there may even be a store of them. It does not mean that we have to produce Carbon 12; we must bring it from one part of the machine to another part and this means special effort. We will not know we are doing it, but by making this special effort we will be bringing Carbon 12 from one place to another. But, of course, if there is not enough in the body, we cannot bring it there. If you have money, you can put it in one pocket or another, but if you have none you cannot, it is quite simple.

Q. Is this special effort the general training in the system?

A. The first conscious shock is self-remembering, together with all you are advised to do from the beginning, that is, self-observation, non-identifying and so on. It is all part of this effort.

Q. What is the second conscious shock which changes the character of the factory?

A. If you like, I can tell you what it is, but it will not help, because it is precisely what we cannot do. It is the transformation of negative emotions into positive emotions. It is possible only with long work on self-remembering, when you can be conscious for a long time, and when higher emotional Centre begins to work. This is what brings us to the state of man No. 5, so it is very far from where we are now. Mi 12, combined with a special effort, can produce positive emotion.

Q. It seems to me that to produce any useful results in the direction of being more awake it is necessary for both the conscious shocks to be working?

A. Yes, to produce complete results certainly both shocks must be given, but when the first shock is sufficiently strong it already produces certain results.

But, as a matter of fact, they generally work together, because from the very beginning we must learn not to express negative emotions, and this is already work on the second conscious shock. The first shock is in the nature of self-remembering, and then it produces struggle with negative emotions, so after some time one actually works on both. The more result you get in one, the more you have to work on the other. This explains another principle we meet with in the system that the more one does, the more is expected of one. It is the same in the Food Diagram, the more one tries to work on self-remembering, the more one must be able to control negative emotions, with the idea of being able in the future to transform negative emotions into positive emotions. But this is very far, because one has to have a great deal of material created for self-remembering. All the same, the two shocks are connected and, in a way, the one cannot work without the other.

Q. Does the word 'shock' in connection with the diagrams mean the same thing as shocks in ordinary life?

A. Shocks connected with the Food Diagram must come from you, it is your own action. It is necessary to know the moment and remember to give shocks. And they must be very carefully given, for only the right kind of shock will help in those particular octaves, otherwise they will branch off.

Q. Can you give a practical example?

A. Practical examples are in the Food Diagram. You must try to find analogous things in your own actions. The first shock is provided by nature where air comes in. But at the second interval no shock is provided by nature, and it must be provided by self-remembering. Also, at the third interval no shock is provided, and it must be given in exactly the way we have been speaking about by transforming negative emotions into positive, produced by nonidentification.

The first conscious shock prepares for the second and the second prepares for the first. It is all simultaneous, you do not finish one and pass to the other.

Q. Are shocks necessarily unpleasant?

A. They necessitate effort, but they are not necessarily unpleasant. On the contrary, at the moment of this effort, with the entry of new energy, one may be very pleasantly surprised.

Q. Can the effort to control attention act as the first conscious shock, and does it bring Carbon 12 to do 48?

A. No, it is not enough. There must be self-remembering: actually, self-remembering connected with self-observation, two activities. This is what makes consciousness. One tries to be more conscious of oneself and of one's surroundings of everything.

Q. Could we hear more about what Carbon 12 is? Where does it come from?

A. Carbon 12 may have many different manifestations, but generally we speak about it in relation to impressions. It is probably some energy of the emotional Centre. But the important thing is not the source. What is important is how to bring it. What it is and where it comes from does not matter, because we cannot see it, we do not know where this place is. Normally Carbon 12 comes from the emotional Centre, and Hydrogen 12 is the matter with which the emotional Centre should work. Impressions come in as Oxygen 48 and can be transformed into Nitrogen 24 only with the help of Carbon 12, but it happens that exactly at the place where impressions can be assimilated there is no Carbon 12, or only a little. So, we must bring it there by a special effort, and this effort is self-remembering and self-observation. So, the method is important, not the source. Intensified observation brought about by self-remembering always has an emotional element. When you remember yourself, you bring Carbon 12 to the right place, and it can transform impressions.

I speak in this language because you asked your question in this language, but it can be observed psychologically. Impressions come in and you do not feel them, which means that they come and do not go on. But you can make an effort to remember yourself, and then you begin to notice things. This means that impressions have become 24. Absence of Carbon 12 at the necessary place means that we are not emotional enough. By self-remembering we bring an emotional element to that particular place.

Q. Are the two other Carbons at *mi* 48 and *sol* 48 the same?

A. I think there is a little difference at *mi* 48, although they all have an emotional element. At *sol* 48 the same Carbon works as at *do* 48, but at *mi* 48 it may be instinctive-emotional. It is quite possible that mi 48 works through Carbon 12 from the instinctive Centre which is always there.

Q. What does *mi* 48 represent?

A. This too is arterial blood. It is a recognized fact that blood can be of very different kinds. It can be established physiologically that in different parts of the body blood has different qualities. Chemically it can also be established that its action is different, but what the difference is, science cannot tell. For instance, muscles are fed on blood 96, but brain cells are fed on blood 24, and some nerve cells are fed on blood 12 and even 6.

Q. Do you mean that there is a chemical difference in the blood feeding muscles and brain?

A. It cannot be established, although it is known that there is a certain difference. Generally, the presence of certain matters is recognized by their effect, but they themselves cannot be separated chemically. Science does not know the history of the blood stream: at each point it gives certain things and receives certain things. Before it reaches one or another organ it is one kind of blood, when it leaves it, it is different.

Q. When one has a moment of awareness, does it lead to any immediate alteration in the blood?

A. Yes it does, but that depends on how deep it is and how long. If it is one second, it produces certain alterations corresponding to one second; if it is half an hour, that is another thing.

Q. Can you notice even the result of one second?

A. Sometimes you can if it is sufficiently deep. You can notice the result in the sense that you see more that ordinary sensations become more emotional. But short moments of self-awareness, just on the surface, do not produce much effect, whereas if it is sufficiently deep and long you will have impressions that you will never forget afterwards.

Q. What hydrogen is thought?

A. It can be very different, just as blood is different. It begins with 48 and can go up to 6.

Q. Can thought count as impressions?

A. Yes, but the amount of impressions coming from inside is limited; but the amount of impressions coming from outside is unlimited.

Q. Is everything in the first stage of the Food Diagram entirely mechanical?

A. Certainly it is all mechanical; it is a cosmic arrangement. Man's organism works according to this general scheme, if he does not work on himself and does not try to change his state of consciousness.

Q. In ordinary state one makes no use of impressions?

A. Very little. In this diagram it is impossible to show the small quantity that gets transformed, so we say that impressions octave goes no further. But some pass on, although not enough for development.

Q. As we are now, are all impressions on the same level?

A. Oh no. Impressions can be very varied. In the Food Diagram we take them as H 48 because that represents the great majority of impressions. They are, so to speak, indifferent impressions maybe of one kind, maybe of another; but by themselves they produce no effect. Yet at the same time they are food. They reach us as 48, and in our ordinary state they do not go further. Man would not be able to live in these conditions. But there are some impressions 24 not as many as 48 but a certain quantity of them; and in very rare cases there may be impressions 12 and even 6, but these are exceptional. They do not enter into this diagram because they transform themselves If they come as 24, they may easily be transformed into 12 and maybe further. But they come in a very small quantity.

In ordinary man, who is not learning to remember himself, some of these ordinary impressions 48 are also transformed, but in quite a different way. They are developed further, or helped to develop further, by reactions of a certain kind for instance, by laughter. Laughter, in the sense of humor, plays a very important part in connection with impressions, again remember that I said in an ordinary man. With the help of laughter many impressions 48 are transformed into 24 But this is only because it is necessary for life, for we could not live without impressions. You remember I said that our chemical factory works only for itself It produces all kinds of very precious materials, but it spends them all on its own existence. It has nothing in reserve and nothing with which to develop itself So if man wants to change and become different, if he wants to awaken his hidden possibilities, he cannot rely on the mechanical means of production; he must look for conscious means. But man's organism is such a wonderful invention that everything is taken into consideration, everything has its own key, so to speak.

A function that looks useless, such as laughter, helps to transform certain impressions which otherwise would be lost If there were no laughter or humor on our level, this level would be even lower than it is now.

It can be said that for a man on the ordinary level who does not try to understand what self-remembering means, or who never heard of it, laughter fulfils a certain definite function in the organism It replaces self-remembering in a very small, insufficient way, since it helps quite dull, uninteresting impressions to pass further and become vivid This is the chief function of laughter Of course, there are many different kinds of laughter, some quite useless.

What I just said about laughter and humor refers only to ordinary centres, in higher centres it is no longer useful. It means that a certain impression falls simultaneously on the positive and negative parts of a centre and this produces a feeling of exhilaration It helps to see the other side, increases the capacity of seeing things. But in higher centres there is no need for it. In higher centres we see things not as contradictions, not as opposed to one another, but we see them as they are.

Q. Laughter seems to have a physiological effect.

A. Yes, maybe a contradictory impression that cannot be harmonized produces a tension, and laughter relaxes it.

Impressions 48 enter constantly. As I have said, a certain amount changes mechanically but the greater amount remains unchanged. They can be changed by our becoming conscious or trying to become conscious. If we are more awake, our impressions become more vivid.

Impressions based on or requiring only Hydrogen 48 are impressions we almost miss or notice very little. An impression that attracts attention and leaves a trace already passes to 24. If you try to analyze your past and write down what you actually remember of some particular episode in it, you will see how little you do remember. This is a better way to study the material of impressions.

Q. Is an impression anything I get through the medium of the five senses?

A. An impression is the smallest unit of thought, sensation, or emotion.

Q. I cannot understand how impressions can be food?

A. Taking in impressions means that a certain energy comes in with them. All energy that you receive is food. The food you eat is coarse material, air is finer, impressions are the finest and the most important food. Man cannot live a single moment without impressions. Even when he is unconscious there are impressions.

Q. Are some impressions good and others bad in themselves, or are they what you make them?

A. Some impressions may be bad in themselves; I do not know how impressions can be good in themselves, because if one is asleep the best impressions will produce nothing. So even if impressions are good in themselves, in order to benefit from them, it is necessary to be more awake. But bad impressions can come in sleep, there is nothing to stop them.

Q. I really meant impressions that are pleasant or unpleasant.

A. Many pleasant impressions may be quite bad. Try to understand one thing: impressions can be classified by hydrogens. Every impression is a certain hydrogen. We have spoken of impressions 48, but there may be much higher impressions. On the other hand, impressions can belong also to the lower hydrogens of the third scale, down to the lowest. The most important thing in the division of matters in the hydrogen table is that it shows where each hydrogen comes from. Suppose you have a certain hydrogen to think about. Looking for its position in the table of hydrogens you can see that it has a definite place: it may come from the interval between the Absolute and the sun, or perhaps from a little above the sun, or from below the earth, between the earth and the moon, and so on. This possibility of placing hydrogens is an enormous advantage. At present you cannot appreciate the significance of the fact that in every matter we can know not only its density but also the level it comes from its place in the whole scheme of things. Our science has no approach to this yet and does not realize that matters are different by reason of the place they come from. You must understand that H 12 has an enormous advantage over, say, H 1536, so an impression that comes from 12 is one kind of impression, and an impression that comes from below the earth, say from the moon, is of quite a different kind. One is light matter, full of quick vibrations, the other consists of slow, harmful vibrations. So, if you find that an impression is heavy, unpleasant it is difficult to find the right adjective to describe it, you can tell by this very fact that it comes from some low part of the Ray of Creation. Things that make you angry, make you hate people, or give you a taste of coarseness or violence, all these impressions come from low worlds.

Q. Are we, in normal circumstances, in a position to receive the impressions we need?

A. It depends on what you call 'normal circumstances'. In normal circumstances in the sense of existence, we have enough, otherwise we would die. Since we do not die, it proves that we receive enough. But we are not satisfied with that. We speak about awakening and development, and here a cosmic fact comes to our aid. We cannot improve our food because it is the only food we can eat. We cannot improve air because it is the only kind of air we can breathe. But we can improve impressions. This is our only chance. How can we do that? Not by travelling, or going to the theatre, or something like that, but simply by awaking, or trying to awake.

Q. Is it possible to receive higher hydrogens in our present state?

A. It depends on what your present state is and on how much you have. It is like alchemy; you can make gold only if you have a certain amount of gold. Higher hydrogens have magnetic properties, they attract other higher hydrogens. If we have very little, that can attract only very small quantities, corresponding to what we have. But if we have more, we can get more. Remember the sentence in the New Testament which says that it shall be taken from those who have not and given to those who have. It refers to this.

Q. Can you accept or reject impressions just as you can eat one thing rather than another?

A. You can use some impressions and not others, if you have a certain control, but that requires a certain degree of awakening and a certain training. The more you remember yourself, the more control you will have. If you remember yourself sufficiently, you can stop certain impressions, you can isolate yourself they will come, but they will not penetrate. And there are other impressions to which you can open yourself and they will come without delay. It is all based on self-remembering.

Q. If an impression tends to cause a certain reaction and that reaction is prevented, is that injurious?

A. All impressions must produce some reaction, but you can control these reactions according to the general balance of your work, the tendencies of your life and so on. Any control and experience in this must be connected with work on the lines of this system, and then it cannot be injurious. Nothing connected with self-remembering can be injurious.

Q. At first the effort to remember oneself seems to reduce impressions.

A. They cannot be reduced, they can only be increased if it is self-remembering. If it is thinking about self-remembering, it may appear to diminish certain impressions.

Q. Can you tell us more about different kinds of impressions?

A. You can know much more by observation than by asking questions, because you yourself know what attracts you more, what attracts you less, what repels you, and so on. There are many subjective things: one person is attracted to one thing; another is repelled by the same thing. Certain impressions go to the intellectual Centre, others to the emotional Centre, yet others to the moving or instinctive Centre. Some of them you like more, others less. This is all material for observation. Each Centre has its own apparatus for receiving impressions, but they often become mixed. Sometimes the intellectual or the emotional Centre tries to receive impressions intended for another Centre, but each of them is meant to have separate impressions. For instance, the impression of smell cannot be received by the intellectual Centre, it is received by the instinctive Centre.

Impressions are easier to analyze than food. People can persuade you that something is good food and sell it in a tin, and then you find that you cannot eat it; but by observation, by comparing, sometimes by talk with other people you can understand which impressions belong to higher levels and which to lower.

Q. Are the impressions we must not admit the ones which give rise to negative emotions?

A. You can define it like that, only sometimes they do not immediately give rise to negative emotions.

Q. Even if you can distinguish between one kind of impressions and another, I do not see how you can accept or reject them?

A. By being awake. If you are asleep, you cannot. But when you are awake, maybe not at once, for it needs certain work one time you are conquered by wrong impressions, another time you are conquered, then the third time you manage to isolate yourself. But before that it is necessary to know what kinds of wrong impressions affect you, and then you can find special methods for isolating yourself.

Q. You mean that if you observe you can avoid those impressions which make you negative?

A. I did not speak about things that *make you* negative, but about bad impressions. You change the meaning. I spoke about impressions themselves. As to what can make you negative, that depends on your state. In a certain state anything can make you negative, even the best thing in the world.

Q. Could one stop having impressions if one wanted to?

A. No, certainly not. You cannot stop impressions altogether, but, as I said, you can keep off undesirable impressions and attract to yourself another kind of impressions, for we must already understand that certain impressions we must not admit. There are many wrong impressions which may spoil one's whole life if one admits them for a sufficiently long time, or if one has the habit of looking for certain bad impressions. For instance, people stand in the street looking at a street accident, and then talk about it until the next accident. These people collect wrong impressions. People who gather all kinds of scandal, people who see something wrong in everything, they also collect wrong impressions. You have to think not so much about choosing the right impressions as about isolating yourself from wrong impressions. Only by doing this will you have a certain control. If you try to choose right impressions, you will only deceive yourself. So, although you cannot bring desirable impressions to yourself, you can, even from the very beginning, learn to control them by isolating yourself from certain kinds of wrong impressions.

Again, you must remember that, in order to control impressions, you must already awake to a certain extent. If you are asleep, you cannot control anything. In order to control quite simple, obvious things you must awake and practice, because if you are accustomed to impressions of a certain kind which are wrong for you, it will take some time. One 'I' will know that it is necessary to isolate yourself, but maybe ten others 'I's will like these impressions.

Q. Is the impression that a creation of objective art can produce an example of higher impression?

A. It depends entirely on you and your state. If you are in intellectual Centre, it may produce no impression; if you are in moving Centre, it will produce still less, but if you are in emotional Centre, it can produce an impression.

Q. Does each hydrogen determine the activity of which one is capable?

A. This is formatory. Try to think along the lines that are given. We are speaking about impressions. You do not understand it, and yet you try to bring in more. It means that your mouth is full of food, and you try to put in more and choke yourself. Swallow first.

Q. That is what I find so difficult, I never really follow.

A. It *must* be difficult; all work is difficult. Nothing is easy in the work, but you can get something *because* it is difficult. If it were easy, you would get nothing.

Q. How is it that man, as he is, is able to appreciate the high hydrogens that must be in B influences?

A. Man's centres are made for work with very high hydrogens and for receiving very high impressions He may not receive them, he may live on lower impressions, but he is capable of receiving very fine impressions and he gets these from B influences

Q. Then why is it that some people are born like that, and some are not?

A. People are different, they are not made on the same pattern, besides, there may be many defects due to degeneration, diseases, pathological states All normal people must be able to receive these impressions, but first they must be normal.

Q. When hydrogens are transmitted from higher worlds to lower, are they made lower?

A. No, they can be transmitted in a pure form The question is, can you receive them? They can only be received by certain parts of centres

Q. Can you receive them and then debase them?

A. If one part of you receives high influences and another part low influences, this may create an explosion

Q. Can we in time observe which hydrogen is which?

A. To a certain extent you can After a certain time of observation you will know the difference, for example, between emotions 24 and 12, or between impressions 48 tasteless things and impressions 24 But you must understand that each hydrogen shown in the Table is a *do*, and between it and the next hydrogen there is a whole octave, so there is an enormous distance between one hydrogen and another To understand the principle we create standards for thinking, we cannot begin by studying the whole scale in detail.

Q. What is the point at which the possibility of further transformation of the three octaves of food exists?

A. As I said, the possibility of further transformation exists at the point where impressions enter the body as *do* 48, but ordinarily fail to develop for lack of Carbon 12 at the place of entry in mechanical functioning, the entry to impressions by the senses immediately gives rise to associative thinking or imagination on the level of H 48, or to emotional reactions of a more or less instinctive nature.

Very occasionally in times of emotional stimulation or danger, for instance it may happen that Carbon 12 is brought to the point of entry of impressions Everything is then related to the emotional state, and man has the impression that all he sees is extraordinarily vivid, new and significant But in ordinary man such experiences are accidental, they lead nowhere and are quickly overlaid with imagination The emotional condition which gives rise to them passes, and is replaced by an impulse or desire leading in a quite different direction. Such experiences in ordinary men are disconnected and have nothing to do with the intentional development of consciousness.

With the attempt to self-remember many new sensations begin to awaken in man, particularly sensations connected with his own existence and his relation to the surrounding world. And these in turn may give rise to the realization of the different influences playing upon him and to the possibility of choosing between them.

Q. How do you know when emotional Centre is working with H 12?

A. After a time you will know by a different taste It is the same as knowing the difference between thinking about eating and actually eating with a certain practice of self-observation, we can distinguish each of these manifestations and put labels on them. In the ordinary way we recognize differences in emotions one is more emotional or less emotional. Observing with a certain purpose we shall see how this or that emotion must correspond to a certain density. Only you must not begin with H 12 for it is very unusual. When we know its taste, we will never mistake anything else for it.

Q Must we draw a distinction between impressions and the things which produce then?

A. Yes, a drum is different from the sound of the drum, so you cannot say that the moment you hear it the drum enters into your being So it you want to take it theoretically, you must separate them. But for what purpose? What is important now is to understand that if we do not remember ourselves, we are open to impressions which may be very low on the scale of hydrogens.

Q. But the hydrogen varies according to which Centre the impression is made on?

A. A hydrogen means a certain matter. How can it differ by being in one room or another? I have explained already that each Centre is adapted to work with a certain hydrogen. One Centre needs a lower, another a higher hydrogen. If it uses a wrong hydrogen, that produces wrong work in one or another sense, depending on which hydrogen is used and how it is used.

Usually, centers try to steal better energy, but sometimes they work on worse energy, try to be lazy. Sometimes instinctive Centre tries to work on energy 48, for instance; this leads to very bad work, and one becomes ill. Often illness is the result of that.

Q. Can one control that?

A. To some extent. It has to do with negative emotion. Energy can be distracted from the right places and put in the wrong places by negative emotion. As long as one cannot control negative emotions one cannot control anything else as regards instinctive Centre. There is only one way of saving energy and many ways of wasting it.

Q. Do vivid impressions use a different energy from faint ones?

A. Not use, they bring energy. If you have vivid impressions, it means that certain hydrogens enter into you. Receiving impressions means getting a certain matter into yourself.

Q. When one has a very high impression, why does it often make such a devastating effect?

A. If a really high impression produces a devastating effect, it means that we are in a very bad state; all the machine works wrong, all centres use wrong hydrogens, we are too asleep, have too many buffers. It should not produce such an effect in a normal machine. Higher impressions should produce not a devastating but a liberating effect.

Q. What is the relation between *si* 12, *mi* 12 and *sol* 12?

A. You will understand this later. If you like, I can say that *mi* 12 refers to the emotional centre, sol 12 to the instinctive centre and *si* 12 to the sex centre. We can work only on *mi* 12. We have too little *of si* 12, and *sol* 12 passes higher to a very small amount of H 6 which, though it is so small, keeps the higher centres alive.

Q. What is the characteristic of *mi* 12? How to recognize it?

A. As I have already explained, it is the energy behind negative emotions. It does not mean that all negative emotions reach the intensity of H 12, but they can reach it, and intense negative emotions bum *mi* 12.

Q. Why does one need to study the food factory? Does it hold an important place in the system?

A. A very important place. Again, it depends on what you want. If you want to know yourself with the idea of improving the work of your machine, you must know everything about yourself that is important; and knowing how your machine works and what materials it receives is very important because, with the help of these diagrams, you can understand what you are doing; otherwise, even if you try to do something, you will not know.

Q. It is difficult to see where the third force enters in the Food Diagram. Is it just the result of the other two?

A. Very often it looks like result, but if you think one minute you will see that it is not like that. Take the process of digestion. All the stages of the process are continually going on in the organism. Suppose one is not actually eating at a given moment, but the third and fourth triads of the digestive process are in action; this means that a certain amount of what you call 'result', which is the third force, is already there, for if it were not there, perhaps things which look in the diagram as if they precede that stage, would not happen. It is necessary to understand that not only carbons but also nitrogen's must be there. We cannot determine the moment when the Food Diagram begins. It begins when one is born, or soon after, and then it goes on throughout life. For example, it is well known in ordinary physiology that certain processes in the mouth happen in the way they do because certain other processes in the stomach happen in a certain way. It is all connected and what looks like result is very often the cause.

Well, as I said, what is important to understand first is that this Table of Hydrogens shows from which layer of hydrogens each matter comes. With the help of this Table, you can see that all the hydrogens in our body, what we eat, what we drink, the air we inhale, all our impressions and many other things, all come from different layers of matter in the Ray of Creation. In this way we can see the relation of every action, every thought, every function to a certain part of the universe governed by its own laws. We think it is all on earth, but although things happen on earth their origin is not on earth, it may be above or below the earth. And this is what the Table of Hydrogens shows.

Energies or matters existing in the outside world can only be understood or assimilated by man in so far as he already has corresponding hydrogens in himself. Thus, in order to become receptive to the higher matters or influences he has to produce in himself sufficient corresponding hydrogens to set his higher centres working.

From this point of view self-study becomes the study of the working of different energies in oneself, of their present wastage in useless and harmful functions, and their possible accumulation for the purpose of self-development.

The Study of hydrogens and their relation to one another also helps us to understand centres and their different speeds. Intellectual Centre works with H 48, moving and instinctive centres with H 24, emotional Centre should work with H 12, but it never receives the right fuel and never works as it should. If we could make it work faster, it would make a great difference to our perceptions and other faculties.

Q. I do not understand about the speed of emotions. How can it be measured?

A. By realizing how many different feelings can pass in you during one thought or during one swing of the pendulum.

Q. By speed of emotions do you mean the time between the cause and effect of an emotion?

A. No, it is the quantity of impressions. You put it objectively, but it is subjective; it means that in one thought one can have thousands of emotions.

Q. The rate varies according to the degree of consciousness?

A. Your observation will vary according to the degree of consciousness, but the fact will remain the same. But, as I said, the emotional Centre in us does not work with its proper speed, because mostly only the moving parts of it work and when a Centre works with the moving part its speed is much slower, whereas when it works with the intellectual part it is much quicker.

Q. If we use the emotional Centre at its highest speed, can we have positive emotions?

A. Then we become connected with higher centres and can have positive emotions. But we must be conscious first, because it can happen only when we have a sufficiently complete control over consciousness.

Q. The Food Diagram shows that there is very high matter in man as he is. How does it show itself?

A. Without higher matters man would not be able to live. The soul, which consists of higher hydrogens, must be fed. Essence must be fed. Even personality must be fed, although personality lives on something different. As I said, higher hydrogens can be extracted from air, but impressions special, purified impressions can give much more. The human organism is built on cosmic principles, so quantity is very important.

Q. To me diagrams are only knowledge, I do not get any understanding out of them that helps me to struggle.

A. They cannot help with struggling, but they can help your thinking. Even now, in this initial form, diagrams can help you to solve many of your troubles and problems. They can serve as a formula to find your position in regard to them. They may not give an answer, but they will give you knowledge about where and how you can look for an answer. This is the real meaning of diagrams.

They speak in a language that you learn a little ahead. We will be able really to use this language only when we are able to use higher centres. Suppose you get control over higher emotional Centre. With knowledge of the diagrams, you will be able to interpret many of the new feelings, sensations, ideas that will come to your mind, and transfer this interpretation to the ordinary mind. Without diagrams you will not be able to do it. They are the intermediate language which will connect the language of the higher emotional Centre with our ordinary centres. At the same time this language is a kind of ladder by which we can climb from ordinary thinking to the thinking of higher emotional Centre.

Q. In our present condition, do higher centres function, or merely lie idle?

A. There are three different theories about this. One is that they function and that we could not live without their functioning, but that they are not connected with ordinary centres because of the enormous difference of speed; that it is necessary to eliminate from the ordinary centres all the wrong functions and bring them to their highest possible speed, which can happen only when we pass to another level of consciousness. The second explanation is that higher centres are latent; they are fully developed, but they do not work as they should. The third is that they do not work because there is no fuel for them; that the hydrogens which can serve as fuel for them can be produced only in another state of consciousness. They are in a state of sleep, but when we produce enough material for them, they will awake. All these explanations are right, and they all come to the same thing. We have to become conscious and control our lower centres in order to bring them to their best possible state. Then there will be no difficulty in making contact with higher centres, because even in our present state, very occasionally, very rarely, we have glimpses of higher states, at least some people have. So, the important thing for us to realize is that higher centres will not keep us waiting when we awake. The thing is to awake and pass to another level of consciousness; then higher emotional and, later, higher mental Centre, will respond at once.

If higher centres were working in us as we are now, we would be in a bad way. We would just be conscious machines without a possibility of being anything else because will can only be created by effort. We are such as we are in order to become different. We are very unsatisfactory, but, because of that, we can become stronger and more conscious. If we were connected with higher centres in our present state, we would go mad. Such a connection would be a great danger so long as we can have negative emotions. For this reason, there are automatic brakes in the machine making the connection impossible. First, we must prepare lower centres and change the state of our consciousness.

Q. Have higher centres characteristics which we may regard as extraordinary?

A. Yes. For instance, what is called magic may be the manifestation of a world of a higher plane on a lower plane. Suppose higher emotional Centre manifests itself on a lower level, it will be a miracle.

It is very necessary to understand the relation in which higher centres stand to lower centres. In our state the intellectual and the emotional principles are sharply divided, but in higher centres this difference disappears. Then the higher emotional Centre does not use words, words are too clumsy, too difficult to operate with, and besides their meaning changes even in one generation and a thousand years produces a complete change of meaning. This is why we do not understand the New Testament— there is no similar meaning of some of the words now, so we cannot even guess what they meant then.

The higher mental Centre is still quicker and does not use even allegorical forms, as higher emotional Centre does. We can say that it uses symbolical forms. It gives the possibility of long thought. It is all in us, but we cannot use it, because we work with a very slow machine. Higher centres do not reach us, the gap is too great between them and ordinary centres. The difference of speed is so enormous that ordinary centres do not hear higher centres. They have many important functions about which we do not know, but we cannot use them as minds, they are too quick, and we are too sleepy. So, if we get a connection with higher mental Centre, it simply leaves a blank.

Q. Are their negative emotions in higher emotional Centre?

A. In higher centres there are no positive and negative parts and, as I said, there is no division between intellectual and emotional. Higher emotional Centre is only called emotional. On higher levels what is emotional is also intellectual and what is intellectual is emotional. Work of higher centres is very different from work of ordinary centres. We can sometimes observe this work and the different taste of it in moments of self-consciousness when we become temporarily connected with higher emotional Centre.

Q. Cannot drugs put us in touch with higher centres?

A. The idea of drugs is not new; drugs were used in ancient and mediaeval times in ancient Mysteries, in magic and so on. It was found that interesting states result from a clever use of drugs. But the system objects to drugs. The use of drugs does not give good results because drugs cannot affect consciousness, they cannot *add* consciousness. By stupefying lower centres, they can put us into contact with higher centres; but it would be of no use to us, because we can remember only as much as we have consciousness. Since we have no consciousness, connection with higher centres will only result in dreams or in unconsciousness.

All these trance states sometimes described in books constitute a very dangerous road. Bringing oneself into a trance is connected with creation of imagination in higher emotional Centre, and this is a blind alley. If you are there, you cannot get out and cannot get any further. Our idea is to control imagination; if, instead, you transform it by certain methods into imagination in higher emotional Centre, you get bliss, happiness, but, after all, it is only sleep on a higher level. Real development must go by two lines: development of consciousness and development of centres.

Besides, such experiments are usually disappointing because as a rule people use up in the first experiment all the material they have for consciousness. The same thing can be said of all stupefying, mechanical, self-hypnotizing methods; they give the same results as drugs, they put ordinary centres to sleep but cannot increase consciousness. But when consciousness is developed, higher centres will present no difficulty. Higher emotional Centre is supposed to work in the third state of consciousness and higher mental in the fourth.

Q. Do you think there is anything in telepathy?

A. For men 1, 2 and 3 it does not exist at all; it is imagination. But men of a much higher development control forces which can produce so-called telepathy, because it is a function of the higher emotional Centre. If one can, even temporarily, control higher emotional Centre, one can produce telepathic effects. But ordinary mind and ordinary emotions cannot do it.

Q. I wonder by what process Jesus was able to expel devils and whether anything in the system could be used for similar purpose? Has it anything to do with higher centres?

A. Jesus probably dealt with big devils. We have to begin with small devils, a kind of vivisection, until we are able to deal with big devils.

I said earlier that so long as certain negative emotions exist in us, higher centres cannot work and should not work, for it would be a disaster In ordinary books on theosophy one finds the idea that many things are hidden because they are dangerous But in reality the danger is not in ideas but in the distortion of ideas People may become dangerous if they hear something and begin to apply it in a wrong sense One can use the forces of higher centres to strengthen one's negative side

Q. Can one damage higher centres?

A. One can, by sleeping too much I mean not in the physical sense, but by being always asleep and irresponsible Then, little by little, the possibility of their awakening is destroyed.

You see, all the time, from different sides, we come to the conclusion that man does not work well. We hear about higher centres, and at the same time we are told that we are not connected with them, that they do not work for us or, if they do, we know nothing about their work. We realize that our ordinary mind is not sufficient for dealing with the problems we want to solve There are many things we want to know, but our mind cannot do anything about it. This simple diagram, and other diagrams we study in this system, show us how to study ourselves, how to improve and what to improve in ourselves. But no improvement is possible until we stop leaks, for it is no use increasing the production of energy if there are leaks everywhere.

Q. How can we stop leaks?

A. By self-remembering. It is necessary to develop consciousness, and this will bring with it the possibility of using better organs of perception and cognition. Without higher centres we cannot do much, and this is why a philosophical approach is not much use. It can invent certain theories and then it stops. It does not develop the higher centres which alone can understand the ideas fully. Philosophy does not touch them.

Q. You stress the importance of preserving energy. Does each Centre have its own storehouse of energy?

A. Yes. I will show you how to begin to think about this. We will take the human machine from the point of view of centres. It is the same machine. Energy created in the organism is kept in a certain big accumulator which is connected with two small accumulators placed near each Centre.

Supposing man begins to think and uses the energy of one of the small accumulators of the intellectual Centre. The energy in the accumulator gets lower and lower, and when it is at its lowest, he gets tired. Then he makes an effort, or has a short rest, or yawns, and becomes connected with the second small accumulator. It is very interesting that yawning is a special help provided by nature for passing from one accumulator to another. He goes on thinking and drawing energy from the second accumulator, is again tired, yawns, or lights a cigarette, and becomes connected again with the first small accumulator. But that accumulator may be only half filled and is quickly exhausted. He becomes connected once more with the second, which is only a quarter filled, and so it goes on until time may come when both accumulators are empty. If at that moment a man makes a special effort of the right kind, he may become connected directly with the big accumulator. This is one explanation of miracles, for he will then have an enormous supply of energy. But this needs a very great effort, not an ordinary effort. If he exhausts the big accumulator he dies, but generally he falls asleep or becomes unconscious long before that, so there is no danger. In ordinary life this connection with the big accumulator sometimes happens in extraordinary circumstances, such as moments of extreme danger.

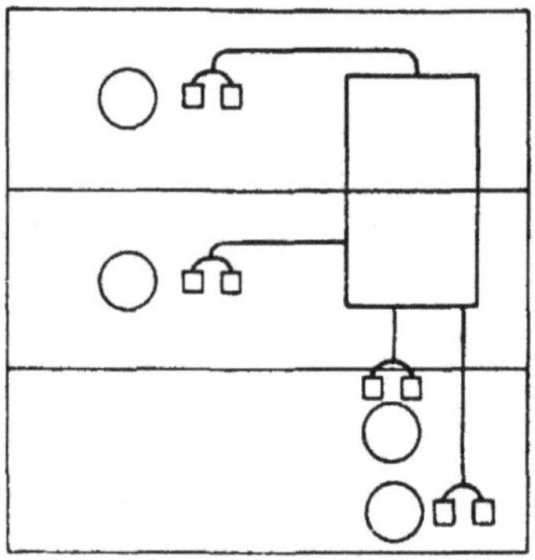

This is why there is this system of small accumulators. If one could be easily connected with the big accumulator one might, for example, never stop being angry for a week, and then one would die. So generally, one does not become connected with the big accumulator until one has control over negative emotions. Emotions are stronger than other functions, so if one were to get into a negative emotion and had unlimited energy it would be too dangerous.

Q. Can sufficient energy be stored in small accumulators?

A. For ordinary work, for ordinary life it is sufficient, but sometimes people who are habitually tired use only half the accumulator and already say that they are too exhausted and cannot do anything. In actual fact, so long as there is anything in the small accumulators, we have no right to be tired. That is why physical efforts are useful. We are afraid of being tired. Of course, we could have much more energy than we have if we did not waste it on negative emotions and other useless things.

Q. To remember oneself one has to have energy?

A. No, that does not enter here, because for this we always have energy. It is not energy that is lacking; it is understanding, knowing how to do it, and a certain laziness which prevents us from self-remembering.

Q. I want to ask about the big accumulator. I do not understand that practically.

A. Efforts! Efforts! The more efforts you make, the more energy you can get. Without efforts you cannot get energy. Even if it is in you, it may be in the wrong place. Do not think about it theoretically; think simply that you have much energy in you that you never use, and you must make more efforts to use it.

Q. What I meant to ask about was what unlocks the energy in the big accumulator and how does it get its energy?

A. That is exactly what I said. Do not think about the big accumulator, think about yourself. Sometimes you must begin with small efforts. If you do not make small efforts, you will never be able to make big efforts. It is quite right that energy is necessary, but the energy is in us. We have enough energy, at least in the beginning, and if we use it for work it is not lost but comes back. If you lose energy on negative emotions, for instance, or on mechanical actions, mechanical thinking, then it is lost. But if you use energy for struggling with mechanicalness you get it back. This is how energy is accumulated.

Q. Can you tell me about the process by which attention is renewed when one controls it?

A. In this case attention depends on the amount of spare energy: if you have energy in reserve, attention will work, if you have no spare energy, it will be exhausted very quickly. So, it depends on the amount of energy, and your reserve of energy depends on how you use it. If you waste it on unnecessary things, then at the moment you need it you will find that you have none. But if you can save it on every possible occasion and use only the necessary amount for every kind of work you are doing, then you will have results. This is why we have to start from the very beginning to struggle with the things that waste it. They must be studied and studied first of all.

Q. Does a person who works in a more balanced way use each accumulator properly?

A. Yes, by training one can do an enormous amount of work, but if a man without training starts doing the same work, he will use too much energy on quite simple movements and will use his accumulators in a wrong way. If you want to think more scientifically about it, you must realize that training, taken in an ordinary sense, prepares accumulators for working rightly. Actually, although

I put only two accumulators near each Centre, there are a great many more. Each Centre is surrounded by accumulators.

Q. Does switching over from one accumulator to another need a moment of consciousness?

A. No, it is automatic. Instinctive Centre knows how to do it and can work quite well, without our being conscious. Consciousness may be necessary for special work in connection with the big accumulator. When we want something extraordinary, something that cannot be got in the ordinary way, it is necessary to invent new methods.

Q. Does the principle of accumulators apply to the ordinary mechanical energy we are using all the time?

A. Certainly. Everything is mechanical. Energy is just fuel.

Q. Then one type of energy is not higher or lower than another?

A. Yes, taken in the sense of hydrogens it can be higher or lower. Different centres use different energy, but fundamentally it is one. You have seen in the Food Diagram how energy is created. There are many variations of hydrogens used for different organs and accumulators.

Q. Can you say that this special adaptation of energy is made in the body?

A. Yes, but at the same time centres have a great tendency to use wrong energy so, this must be kept in mind. But the question of how to make more energy is one thing and the question of how it makes itself, how it 'happens', is another. It is better to divide these things.

Q. If one is tired, and suddenly receives a lot of impressions and as a result of its tiredness goes, is it because one gets energy from them?

A. It is more complicated than that. With new impressions one becomes more awake, and so connections with the big accumulator begin to work better. Direct impressions are not yet energy ready for use; they must be distilled and mixed with other things to produce energy. Impressions that come are undigested food. All the three kinds of food must be digested and mixed in right proportions. But impressions can awake you. When energy in the body reaches a certain pressure, it begins to attract energy from its surroundings.

Q. If one travels, does one get more impressions?

A. The capacity for receiving impressions remains the same.

Q. When a man yawns, does he connect with the other accumulator?

A. Not every time, for one can yawn from imitation. Besides, yawning is pumping energy, it is not necessarily switching over, although a really good yawn may produce a switch over when necessary.

Q. When you say yawning is a pump, where is the energy pumped from?

A. From the organism. It is so arranged that every function has the necessary energy everywhere. There are so many accumulators that it is sufficient to know the principle that there are accumulators. Energy is distributed in the machine in a very complicated way and passes from one accumulator to another, is diluted, concentrated and so on.

Q. Do the small accumulators get filled from the large one during sleep at night?

A. They are refilled constantly. But the big accumulator is refilled during sleep with the energy derived from the three kinds of food. All energies are kept in the big accumulator, either mixed or in a higher form. When a demand comes, a corresponding hydrogen is sent. If energy is produced, it is stored in the big accumulator. If more is produced than is necessary for life, it can be stored in many places.

Q. Can energy be conserved by means of silence?

A. Sometimes, but if you are silent all the time you may lose more energy in silence than in talk. That is why the first principle in this system is discrimination, there are no general rules.

Q. Is it possible eventually to come in contact with the big accumulator?

A. Yes, it is possible, but we are not even on the first step; it may be possible, say, on the twenty-second step, so there are twenty-one steps to climb before we can do that. What can be done now has all been explained, you must try to remember yourself, not identify, try not to express negative emotions and so on. These are the things with which we can start.

Q. Does the energy required for self-remembering come from proper working of centres?

A. Yes, certainly; when all centres work wrongly there can be no accumulation of energy. But this is not sufficient. It is necessary to increase the amount of energy, and it can be increased only by efforts, small efforts, such as struggle with habits, self-observation, trying to control attention and so on. Everyone has some particular efforts he can make; the efforts of one person may be no good for another, or too easy, or impossible.

Q. What regulates the amount of energy that goes into the accumulators of each Centre?

A. Habitual work. Sometimes they cannot be filled, sometimes they refuse to be filled, and sometimes they do not need to be filled. There are many reasons for this, and you cannot control it. But by making efforts, or by remembering yourself, you increase the possibility of control.

Q. Has the big accumulator a large capacity, and is it quickly recharged?

A. It depends. It may be half empty, or filled with bad energy, or it may be full, but we do not use it. It is important to understand that there is a big store of energy in the big accumulator, much of which we never use, it remains dead capital.

Q. If one is more conscious, can one draw more energy?

A. Yes, but a special training is also necessary. If we know how to connect with the big accumulator, we can produce quite different results.

Q. How quickly can it be learnt?

A. I cannot say, it depends on how you study and work. In our attitude to the system there may be a destructive clement that can destroy the result of our work. If one has a right attitude to oneself and to the work, without a destructive element, then it can be attained.

Q. Does it all depend on consciousness?

A. All work is really concentrated on consciousness. In work on center's, we only try to stop definitely wrong work. There are no exercises to increase the work of centres: all the work is on consciousness. When consciousness is increased, centres will adapt.

But *wrong* work of centres must be stopped, for if we remained abnormal and became conscious, our centres would go mad, they would not be able to stand it. But it cannot happen, one cannot become conscious unconsciously. People often ask: what does one gain by becoming conscious? This is because they do not know what the result of consciousness is. When we are conscious, we become connected with higher centres and then the whole picture changes.

* * *

CHAPTER X

We cannot 'do'—Importance of realizing the truth of this idea—Illusion of 'doing' and what produces it—In life everything happens, but in the work we must learn to 'do'—Going against the current—Inner 'doing— A vicious circle and the way out—Co-ordination of centres—'Doing begins with 'not doing'—Inner control—Doing the impossible and what it means —Putting more pressure into one's efforts—Work on will— What is will in the full sense of the word and what is our will?—Our will a resultant of desires—Inner conflict and struggle—Giving up will—We only have short moments of will—Discipline—Necessity of remembering oneself— Consciousness means will—Aim as the controlling factor—Necessity of returning constantly to the question of aim—Self-will and willfulness— Friction—Work against self-will—One can do nothing without school— Necessity of regular work—Cross-roads—Creating moon in oneself-—Centre of gravity—Super-effort— What creates stimulus for work.

We must return to the Inner part of the work to work on oneself. If you think about it, you will realize that the central part of your own work is understanding of the fact that we cannot 'do', of why we cannot 'do' and of what it means that we cannot 'do'. How can you understand that? Either by trying to do what you have never done before or by doing things in another way. Then you will see whether you can 'do' or not. Half of the questions asked are about 'doing', how to change this, destroy that, avoid some other thing and so on. But an enormous effort is necessary to change even one small thing. Until you try, you can never realize it. You see, you do not think enough, observe enough. You can change nothing except through the system. This is generally forgotten. The system shows how things can be changed and done differently and from where one can begin. Even with the system it is tremendously difficult, but without the system it is impossible, absolutely impossible. When you realize that, you will begin to understand the value of the system, because with the system there is a chance, without the system there is no chance at all.

This idea that we cannot 'do' is very important and we must always return to it. If this idea is not clear, or certain features of it are not dear, ask questions about it, because it is necessary to understand and remember it. Everything 'happens'. People can 'do' nothing. From the time we are born to the time we die things happen, happen, happen, and we think we are doing. This is our normal state in life, and even the smallest possibility to do something comes only through the work, and first only in oneself, not externally. Even in oneself 'doing' very often begins by not doing. Before you can do something that you cannot do, you must not do many things which you did before. For instance, you cannot awake by just wanting to awake, but you can prevent yourself sleeping too much and **too long.**

Q. Does one sometimes have a choice between two possible happenings?

A. Only in very small things, and even then, when you notice that things are going in a certain way and decide to change them, you will find how extremely uncomfortable it is to change things.

Q. Why is it that I cannot give up the idea of being able to 'do'? I have proved to myself so often that I cannot.

A. This is the most difficult and the most necessary thing to realize with your whole being, because so long as we think that we can 'do' we shall always put off the things that we actually *can* do if we work. As I said, we can 'do' things only in relation to ourselves, these are the things we have to begin with. But we shall never begin to study ourselves so long as we think we can 'do'. This is one of our greatest illusions.

Q. I can see that I have no choice in larger things, but it seems to me that I can do small things.

A. These small things happen according to certain definite circumstances which control them. You think you control them, but in reality, they happen. We cannot 'do' because we are asleep. How can sleeping people 'do'? It is necessary to be awake; when one is awake, one can 'do'. 'Doing' is magic.

You must understand that nothing happens at the time it happens; the necessity of it happening was created long ago. Things happen by themselves; whether you do or do not do something may have been decided ten years before. Maybe your actions had taken a certain direction ten years previously and that determines what you will do tomorrow, you cannot change it.

We think we can take a certain decision and act accordingly. In reality we are controlled not by internal decisions but by external influences. If the internal decision corresponds to the external influence, we will do it, otherwise we will not. But we can create in ourselves powers to 'do'. Nature has made us machines acting under external influences, but with a possibility to develop our own motor. If there is no inner motor, we will always turn round in the same place.

Q. If a man sets an ideal for himself of how he ought to behave, would this not be what is meant by 'doing'?

A. The question is whether he can do it and whether he does it, because to make plans, to have ideals is one thing and to do it is another thing.

It may be just good intentions. One of the chief features of our being is that we cannot do what we decide.

Q. Sometimes I have found that, with a little extra effort, you can make a great difference to other people in ordinary life. Isn't it doing?

A. It is an illusion, because if a thing must happen you will make this extra effort; if it is not to happen, you will not make this effort. You think you can make or not make this effort, that you can 'do' or 'not do'. But try to think in the right way, that you can 'do' nothing, that things happen mechanically. One thing comes after another and just happens or does not happen, and you cannot help it.

Q. But if you help a poor person to make his life tolerable?

A. If you help a poor person, it happens. If someone takes from this poor person what little remains to him, this also happens. One person will give him a penny, another will take away the last he has. It is first necessary to understand *the principle* that nobody can 'do' anything. If you think of life, not personal life but the life of humanity, wars, revolutions, you will see this clearly. You must try to find a right case for observation, because if you find something too small you will not see it. But if you find the right case, right conditions, right circumstances, you will very soon see whether you can do something or not. The simplest thing is to try and remember yourself. Can you do it or not? People think they can 'do' because sometimes they make certain plans and really get what they wanted. But this only means that they have got into a certain stream of events and things happened to coincide with their plan. When things happen like that, we think that we did it, that we made a plan and did everything according to this plan. In reality it does not mean that we did it on purpose or knowingly and it does not mean that one can choose one stream of events or another stream; it is just accident. In every kind of work, in business, in travel and so on, it sometimes happens that things go successfully, but this only means that at a given moment, in a given place things went mechanically in a certain way nothing more.

It is difficult for us to realize, for example, that when people build a bridge, that is not 'doing'; it is only the result of all previous efforts. It is accidental. To understand this, you must think of the first bridge that Adam built and of all the evolution of bridge. At first it is accidental, a tree falls across a river, then man builds something like that, and so on. People are not 'doing'; one thing comes from another.

Q. I think it is an almost childish question, but I can never see how things cannot be different. One does something and one cannot help thinking that one could do it differently.

A. But if you behaved in a certain way, it means that you could not behave in another way. If you could, you would have behaved differently. We are so accustomed to think that things could be different that we do not try to change the things we could change. We can change to-day, but yesterday is finished If we change to-day, tomorrow things can happen differently. It looks like a contradiction, but it is precisely our belief that things can be different that prevents us from doing what we can to make them different.

Q. When one really begins to understand that one cannot 'do', one will need a great deal of courage Will that come from getting rid of false personality?

A. One does not come to this understanding just like that. It comes after some time off work on oneself, so that when one comes to this realization one has many other realizations besides, chiefly that there are ways to change if one applies the right instrument at the right place and at the right time One must have these instruments, and these again are only given by work. It is very important to come to this realization Without it one will not do the right things, one will excuse oneself.

Q. I do not understand why one should excuse oneself?

A. One does not want to give up the idea that one can 'do', so that even if one realizes that things happen, one finds excuses, such as, 'This is an accident, but tomorrow it will be different' That is why we cannot realize this idea. All our lives we see how things happen, but we still explain them as accidents, as exceptions to the rule that we can 'do'. Either we forget, or we do not see, or do not pay enough attention We always think that at every moment we can 'do'. If you see in your life a time when you tried to do something and failed, that will be an example, because you will find that you explained your failure as an accident, an exception. If the same situation repeats itself, you will think you will be able to 'do', and if you fail again, you will again explain your failure as just an accident It is very useful to go through your life from this point of view You intended one thing and something different happened If you are really sincere, you will see, but if you are not, you will persuade yourself that what happened was exactly what you wanted! When things happen in a certain way, we are carried by the current, but we think that *we* carry the current.

Q. If one feels for a moment that one is able to 'do', say, to put through a particular job in one's ordinary work, what is the explanation of that?

A. If one is trained to do something one learns to follow a certain trend of happenings, or if you like, to start a certain trend of happenings, and then these develop, and one runs behind although one thinks one is leading.

Q. But if one has a right attitude?

A. No, attitude has nothing to do with it, Attitude may be right, and understanding may be right, but you still find that things happen in a certain way any ordinary things. Try to remember instances when you tried to do something differently and see how you always came back to the same thing even if you made a slight deviation enormous forces driving you back to the old ways.

Q. Are all our actions controlled by automatic responses to outside influences?

A. No, we have many things already established, such as habits, usual ways of thinking, associations, buffers, and many other things So it is not simply influences to which we have a natural response. Many things are the result of previous influences

Q. I cannot separate the idea of not being able to 'do' from fatalism When and how have we the power of choice and how do we differ from animals?

A. In the present state we differ very little. Our power of choice begins only when we begin to realize our situation, our mechanicalness, and when we begin to struggle for something else There are possibilities for that, but this is a formatory way of thinking either determinism or freedom Some things are determined, some less determined, some are in our power, if we know how to change them or how to turn them Only, we must know. Everything is relative.

Q. When you said that we cannot help the same things happening, did you mean until our being has changed?

A. I did not speak about work. I said it was necessary to understand that *by ourselves* we cannot 'do' When this is sufficiently understood, we can think about what it is possible to 'do', what conditions, what knowledge and what help are needed but first it is necessary to realize that in ordinary life everything happens. Only when this is emotionally understood is it possible to go further

Q. I do not understand the distinction between what one can and what one cannot 'do'. Why is it that one can struggle with negative emotions, but one cannot make oneself awake?

A. Sleep is the form or the level of our being. One can do something

with the help of the system, if the way is shown, but being awake indicates *the level of being itself*. So, all this struggle with negative emotions, trying to stop unnecessary thoughts, trying to remember oneself, all this leads you to awakening, but you cannot awake before you awake.

Q. But is it their doing when people try to become conscious?

A. Yes; then one sees that one cannot. In trying to become conscious all man's work is his own.

It is only in this system that you are told clearly that you can 'do' nothing All the other systems begin with 'doing' in one sense or another, for they say, do this or do that This system is different It is esoteric teaching, but in it you can begin in the conditions of ordinary life, it is not necessary to go to a closed school or to a monastery. Because of that it is particularly necessary to understand first of all that one cannot 'do' anything and that the only thing one can start to 'do' is trying to remember oneself understanding the one and practicing the other.

Q. I thought perhaps we ought not to take this idea that we cannot 'do' too literally?

A. No, quite literally. Only this refers to people who are not connected with any teaching. When one begins to study certain teachings or systems which give school methods, one has to try to do certain things. In the work we have to 'do', for if we do not try to 'do', nothing will happen. We have to 'do' from the very beginning not much, but very definite things. If you cannot identify it is already the beginning of 'doing'. If you can refrain from talk when you have an inclination to talk, that is already 'doing'. 'Doing' begins with going against the current, first in yourself, in personal things. You can try to remember yourself, then, when you begin to remember yourself, you can get certain results and you will see that you can do more things, but all with regard to yourself. You will be able to do something about negative emotions, for instance, and to think in a new way. But outside you, things will continue to happen.

Q. Would you say that one way of beginning to 'do' would be to alter things in oneself so that things *happen* differently?

A. It is necessary once more to divide people into categories. Men 1, 2 and 3 can 'do' nothing in their case everything 'happens'. If they do good things, it means that they cannot do bad things; if they do bad things, it means they cannot do good things. One thing is no better than another in that sense, because it is all mechanical. But when one begins to work, when one enters a school of any level, one already has to learn to 'do'. As I said, one has to begin with oneself to know oneself, to study oneself, try to eliminate certain things, try to create control over other things and so on.

Q. Have we got to observe how we react?

A. Observing is always useful, but we always react in the same way. We have only five or six ways of reacting: only certain things happen to us, and we always react in the same way to them. But if we try to do all that is advised, and not to do all that we are advised to refrain from doing, things will change in the right way and one day, quite unexpectedly, we will be able to do something we could not have done before.

Q. Can we direct things that happen to us?

A. If we direct things in ourselves. If nothing unnecessary happens in us, we shall begin to be able to control things that happen from outside, but first we must control things in ourselves. So long as things are left to 'happen' in ourselves, we cannot control anything outside. How can it be otherwise? One 'I' decides to control things, but instead all its attention will be occupied with things that happen in us and outside us.

Q. If man can 'do' nothing, does it follow that all he can do is to control his own mental reaction to events outside his control?

A. Quite right. That is the beginning. If he learns to control his reactions, then after some time he will find that he can control more and more, and later it may happen that he will be able to control, again not all, for there is a very large gradation, but certain external events. But certain other external events cannot be controlled because they are of a different size.

Q. If I wish to obtain a particular result and fail, and if I then do the thing differently, will the result be still the same in spite of my effort?

A. You must not deceive yourself. If you do something and the result corresponds to your expectations, it is simply luck, chance that is all. And in some cases, you may do something entirely different and still have the same result.

Q. It seems that one is caught up in a vicious circle!

A. Certainly one is caught, and the system is the way out of this vicious circle, for in ordinary conditions of life one cannot get out.

Q. Would you say a little more about the effort to get out of that circle?

A. If you take all that is given in the right way and work with sufficient effort, the school, or the system, call it what you like, will give you this possibility of getting out. There is no way out without school and without knowledge. Again, if you get the knowledge and do not make efforts, it will be equally useless.

When one is in a school, one is made to 'do', because one cannot make oneself, one cannot create sufficient force. But if one puts oneself in different conditions, it will produce certain results. School is necessary because it is the conductor of neutralizing force. Otherwise, one may have desire, one may make efforts, but one would not know how to start. It seems simple, but it is not simple.

Q. What would be the active and passive forces in this case?

A. Life can be taken as active force, and the passive force, I would say, is in inertia, habits, in all that 'happens'.

Q. How can you distinguish between an effort that is mechanical and an effort that is not?

A. There is no need to distinguish. Make efforts, and result will show.

Q. Do you mean that all I have really done in my life so far is to change one form of sleep for another?

A. It changed itself; you did not do even that. In life one has no control, but in the work one can acquire control. In the work there can be an escape from this state where we can do nothing, and things 'happen'. Without the work there is no escape.

A certain illusion of control is provided in life by ordinary education, but if circumstances change it all disappears.

Q. Then will you tell me please what is the chief thing that is holding me back from escaping?

A. Mechanicalness. In yourself things continue to 'happen', things over which you should have control, but you have not acquired control. There are things in us which can and should be mechanical, such as physiological processes and things like that, and there are other things over which we must acquire as much control as we can because they keep us from awakening. You do not realize to what an extent one thing in us is connected with another. Everything is connected. You cannot do, or say, or even think anything out of the general line of things that happen.

Our four centres, intellectual, emotional, moving, and instinctive, are so coordinated that one movement in one Centre immediately produces a corresponding movement in another Centre. Certain movements or certain postures are connected with certain thoughts; certain thoughts are connected with certain feelings, sensations, emotions everything is connected. Such as we are, with all the will that we can concentrate, we can acquire some degree of control over one Centre, but only one, and even that for only a short period of time. But other centres will go on by themselves and will immediately corrupt the Centre we want to control and bring it again to mechanical reaction. Suppose I know all I should know, and suppose I decide to think in a new way. I begin to think in a new way but sit in the ordinary posture, or smoke a cigarette in the usual way, and I again find myself in the old thoughts.

It is the same with emotions; one decides to feel in a new way about something, and then one thinks in the old way and so negative emotions come again as before, without control. So, in order to change we must change things in all four centres at the same time, and this is impossible since we have no will to control four centres. In school there are special methods for attaining this control, but without a school it cannot be done. On the whole, our machine is very cleverly thought out. From one point of view, it has wonderful possibilities of development, but from another point of view this development is made very difficult. You will understand why it is made like that when you finally realize what consciousness and will mean, and then you will understand that neither consciousness nor will can develop mechanically. Every small thing has to be developed by struggle, otherwise it would not be consciousness or will. It has to be made difficult.

Q. I feel that if I had to do everything instead of relying on accidents nothing would happen to me at all, for my will is too weak.

A. Not doing is in itself a kind of doing. But at the same time, you touch here a very interesting question. When you get control, fewer and fewer things will happen, and you will have to do even small things because they will not happen to you. But this is probably very far.

Q. Would you say that the sense of responsibility that one ought to do something useful in the world is imagination, since you say we cannot do?

A. It may be imagination or imitation, or it may be right. But in that case, we must consider *what* and *how*, and *bow* is more important than *what*. Most people think about what to do but not about how. Often the things they decide to do are impossible, like stopping wars and other such things.

Q. If we try to be conscious and try to see how things really are, would it change our situation so that things do not happen to us, but we do things as we wish to do them?

A. Certainly, this is the aim, but a very far aim. You see, first of all, here is a wrong use of the word 'us'. You must remember that when it was said that things happen to all people and that people cannot 'do' anything, that referred to ordinary conditions in ordinary life what is called normal life. But in this work, we are trying to get out of this 'normal' life, so we already must 'do'. Only we must first learn what we can 'do', because in our present conditions many things will continue to happen; but in certain things we can already have choice, we can show our preference, our will, as much as we can have will. So 'us' cannot be used in the same way as before. But you must understand that at first, the difference is not between 'doing' and 'not doing', but between trying to 'do' and trying to understand, and at present all your energy must be concentrated on trying to understand. What you can try to 'do' has been explained. We are trying to find things we can control in ourselves, and if we work on them, we will acquire control. This is all the 'doing' that is possible at the moment.

Q. Is the full realization that we cannot 'do' anything already a long step on the way to 'doing'?

A. Sometimes the step is too long because every idea prolonged too far becomes its own opposite. So, if you persuade yourself too seriously that you can do nothing, you will find that you really can do nothing. It is a question of relativity. As I said, not being able to 'do' refers to people without any possibility of schoolwork.

Q. I think I need a teacher. I find I can do nothing by myself.

A. A teacher cannot 'do' anything for you. You are given certain tasks and you have to do them. It is always like that. Instead of trying to 'do', try 'not to do'! You learn to 'do' by first learning 'not to do'. You are trying to do things that you consider desirable; try the other way round not to do things that are undesirable.

You see, this self-evolution is not obligatory, not mechanical, there is no guarantee. It depends on effort. People often ask: 'How is it that I have been working so many years and have had no experience of higher centres yet?' And I ask them: 'Have you really been working so many years?' One counts from the time one has heard these ideas, but one does not try to calculate how much one actually worked how many days, how many hours or minutes in each day. If one makes this calculation, one will see that there is no reason to expect any results yet, although one may have heard about it a long time ago.

Q. If we are machines, how can we change our being?

A. We cannot wait until we change. There is one very important principle in the work, you never have to work in accordance with your force, but always beyond your force. This is a permanent principle. In the work you always have to do more than you can; only then can you change. If you do only what is possible you will remain where you are. One has to do the impossible. You must not take the word 'impossible' on too big a scale, but even a little means much. This is different from life; in life you only do what is possible.

It is necessary to put more energy into things into self-study, self-observation, self-remembering, and all that. And in order to put more energy into your work it is necessary to find where it is being spent. You awake every morning with a certain amount of energy. It may be spent in many different ways.

A certain amount is necessary for self-remembering, study of the system and so on. But if you spend this energy on other things, nothing remains for that. This is really the chief point. Try to calculate every morning how much energy you intend to put into work in comparison with other things. You will see that even in elementary things, simply in relation to time, you give very little to the work, if you give any at all, and all the rest is given to quite useless things. It is good if they are pleasant things, but in most cases, they are not even pleasant. Lack of calculation, lack of these elementary statistics is the reason we do not understand why, with all our best intentions and best decisions, in the end we do nothing. How can we do anything if we do not give any energy or time to it?

If you want to learn a language, you must learn a certain number of words every day and give some time to the study of grammar and so on. If you want to learn Russian and begin by learning five words a day, I will guarantee that you will never learn it. But if you learn two hundred words a day, in a few months you will understand Russian. It all depends on elementary statistics. In every kind of work or study there is a certain standard. If you give it a certain amount of energy and time, but just not enough, you will have no results. You will only turn round and round and remain approximately in the same place.

Q. I am one of those people who only learn five words a day, but I have always taken comfort in the thought that it is bound to work in the end.

A. No, it is necessary to put more pressure into it. Notice that even in conversations here only few people speak, the others only want to Listen, for it is more peaceful, more comfortable. Then, you do not follow up thoughts. I give you very very many, but most of them you do not touch. It is laziness of mind, general laziness. This laziness must be overcome. You cannot get anything by being lazy, or by doing one thing and leaving everything else. As it is I give you one line, you miss it. I give you another line, you miss that too. So, in the end we have only missed lines.

As I said, every kind of work, every kind of state, needs a certain definite minimum of effort and minimum of time given to it, and the work we are trying to do needs more than many other things if we want to get even perceptible results. What does it mean to work practically? It means to work not only on intellect but also on emotions and on will. Work on intellect means thinking in a new way, creating new points of view, destroying illusions. Work on emotions means not expressing negative emotions, not identifying, not considering and, later on, also work on the emotions themselves. But what does work on will mean? It means work on one's actions. First you must ask yourselves: What is will in men No. 1, 2 and 3? It is the resultant of desires. Will is the line of combined desires, and as our desires constantly change, we have no permanent line. So ordinary will depends on desires and we can have many desires going in different directions. The line constructed out of all these angles is the resultant. This is our will. It may go in one direction one day and in another direction another day, and we think it is straight. So, it is really the resultant of our blindness.

We have to ask ourselves on what the will of man No. 7 could be based. It must be based on full consciousness, and this implies knowledge and understanding connected with objective consciousness and a permanent 'I'. So, three things are necessary: knowledge, consciousness and a permanent 'I'. Only those people who have these three things can have real will; that means a will that is independent of desires or anything else.

Q. You said no will was possible for us?

A. Will is a relative term: there are different wills on different levels. A mechanical man who never thinks of development has only a multitude of small wills that are quite mechanical. He has a certain desire: one side of him wants to do something and another side is afraid he will be punished if he does it.

A struggle ensues between the different tendencies and the result of this struggle we call 'will'.

Q. Then in order to develop will one must go against desires?

A. First of all you must become one. You are many and you have hundreds of 'I's and hundreds of wills. If you want to develop an independent, will you must become one and conscious. Will depends on unity and consciousness.

Q. If we are determined to do something we do not like, and manage to do it, are we not using will?

A. It may be fear; perhaps you are afraid not to do it, or you may expect some reward either in this life or the next many things are possible. Generally, we are either afraid of something, or expect some kind of benefit from it. As a rule, the term 'will' is used in a relative sense, but when we speak of will, we speak of a certain level. Before we can speak of the possibility of will we must at least have a central point which can control the rest. Will means liberation from the mechanical state.

Q. Can useful unity be obtained by engrossment in some routine work that employs the majority of 'I's?

A. It cannot be called full unity, it is only relative unity, the unity of the 'I's employed in this work. One can train oneself very much by work of this kind, but it cannot touch the whole of you. There is no work that can touch the whole, it will always be only a small part of you.

Q. How can we change or wake if we have no free will?

A. If we had free will we would not be machines. How can a machine have free will? And how can we change? It was already explained that there is a possibility of change, but a very small possibility, and many different combinations of favorable circumstances are necessary in order to begin. Later, with each step, it becomes more and more difficult and requires more and more effort, and then, after some time, it becomes easier. But first a certain combination of circumstances is necessary, and later hard work as well, because school is necessary. Without a school it is impossible to change oneself. Difficulties are so great, and man is so weak that he can do nothing alone.

At present our will belongs to 'I's or groups of 'I's based on one personality out of many. But real will means one will, so it can only belong to a single 'I' or, if you like, to essence. So first we must be one at least at certain moments and then try to work to create will. One cannot become unified at once. Will is bound to come and go; at one moment we shall have will, at another there will be none. It will be a long time before we can speak about anything reliable in us, let alone anything permanent.

Q. How does will grow?

A. It cannot grow without effort. You have to save energy to collect enough for struggle with certain weaknesses. Suppose you realize something is a weakness and that you must struggle with it, but you find that you have not enough energy; you can then try to do some smaller thing which is not so difficult, and, in this way, you will save energy. Generally speaking, we miss the opportunity of making small efforts. We disregard them, do not consider them important enough. Yet we can increase our capacity for making efforts only by making these small efforts which we disregard.

Q. Is creation of unity essentially preceded by inner conflict?

A. By realization of inner conflict. Inner conflicts are constant. Nobody lives without inner conflicts; they are normal and always there. But when we begin to work, conflict increases. When we do not work, we run away, we do not fight. What does 'work' mean? It means struggle with conflicting things. We have a certain aim, but many of our 'I's do not want to go that way, so naturally conflict increases. But the creation of unity is not the result of conflict, it is the result of struggle with conflict. We are many and we want to be one, this is one formulation of our aim. We realize that it is inconvenient, uncomfortable, and dangerous to be so many. We decide to be at least less divided, instead of five hundred to become five. I feel that I must do something, and I do not want to this is conflict, and by constantly recurring it builds up resistance and produces unification.

Q. Does not resistance stop most people achieving anything?

A. Resistance may be very different in nature, because we have many habits, physical and mental, which sometimes we cannot overcome Habits may be so strong that there is no place for anything new There we come again to the question of schools, because by oneself, even if one knows, one cannot overcome either internal or external resistance

Q. If everything is going smoothly and one is not aware of any 'yes' and 'no' conflict, is it a good thing to try and induce it?

A. There is no need The moment one starts working, trying to remember oneself, trying not to identify, to remember the system, at once friction begins Friction creates energy If things are easy, there is no friction but if you put spokes in the wheel of mechanicalness, this creates friction, which creates energy

Q. What would unity mean? Is it unity between centres?

A. Unity is not between centres, because centres are different, but between personalities or groups of 'I's Each Centre has its own work and our centres are too co ordinated, for the work of one Centre mechanically produces work of another Centre This is not desirable at all, and it is partly due to this wrong co-ordination that personalities are not sufficiently connected many of them are quite independent and contradictory

Q. Can desire to develop be called will?

A. Call it desires, this is quite sufficient It is not will. Will belongs to the whole and is another side of consciousness.

Q. In our state of consciousness can we know the difference between desire and will?

A. Certainly, desire is when you do what you want, will is when you can do what you do not want.

Q. How can we make a right use of inner conflict?

A. It is very simple One part of us, magnetic Centre or one personality wants to awake but the larger part of us wants to sleep You must decide on whose side you are, and then help that side. In order to study how to begin work on will, how to transform will, one has to give up one's will This is a very dangerous expression if it is misunderstood It is important to understand rightly what 'to give up one's will' means We have no will, so how are we to give up what we do not have? First you must realize you never agree that you have no will, you only agree in words Secondly, you must understand that we do not always have will but only at times will in our state means a strong desire If there is no strong desire, there is no will and so there is nothing to give up At another moment we have a strong desire that is against work, and if we stop it, it means we give up will. It is not at every moment that we can give up will but only at special moments. And what does 'against work' mean? It means against rules and principles of the work or against something you are personally told to do or not to do. There are certain general rules and principles, and there may be personal conditions for different people.

Q. Should one ask for further personal directions?

A. Yes, but if one asks, one must obey. One is not obliged to do anything apart from following the general rules and principles if one does not ask, so before asking one must think twice.

Q. If one is prepared to obey, will you give directions?

A. If opportunity offers. It must be at a moment when you have will. There must be a definite desire to do something that affects work or other people. Usually we have bad will; we very seldom have good will. If you have good will, I do not speak about it; I simply say, 'Go on, continue, learn'.

You do not know how to think about will. One moment you realize that you are machines, but the next moment you want to act according to your own opinion. At that moment you must be able to stop, not to do what you want. This does not apply to moments when you have no intention of doing anything, but you must be able to stop if your desire goes against rules or principles, or against what you have been told. It often happens that people go on studying and miss these moments. They think they work when nothing happens. We cannot always work equally; at one moment passive study is sufficient, at another moment it is necessary to go against oneself, to stop.

Q. What causes these moments?

A. Desire. As I said, our will is a resultant of desires. It is not a system expression; it is an old psychological definition but a good one. Desires may be very different: they may be intellectual desires, such as desire to know, curiosity, or emotional, instinctive, or moving desires. If one strong desire conquers, it gives direction to desires. I now speak of desires that may have a connection with the work.

Q. We are told to keep rules. This presupposes we can keep them, which would be 'doing'. It seems to me incompatible with the idea that we cannot 'do'.

A. Everything is relative. We can 'do' some inner actions, for we have

a certain control. For instance, we have a certain control of our thoughts:

we can think about one thing or another. This is the beginning of the possibility. If we continue to keep our interests directed in a certain line, our thinking process acquires a certain power and, after some time, it can create at least moments of self-awareness which, when it comes more often and stays longer, can begin to change other things. So, there are ways out of this absolute mechanicalness. But if one is in conditions of ordinary life, without knowing that everything happens, one can do nothing. The real possibility of changing these conditions begins with control of thoughts and control as far as possible of consciousness, that is, with inner work on ourselves. By doing this inner work, by trying to acquire control of oneself, one learns how to 'do'. It does not mean one can 'do', for one cannot; but if one begins, then, little by little, one learns how to 'do'.

Q. Is self-imposed discipline good, or must it be school discipline?

A. Discipline is good if it is discipline. But if it is just an arbitrary invention, then it can give no result. The most important aspect of discipline is not expressing negative emotions and not indulging in negative emotions. Mechanical tasks cannot give any result, but if you catch yourself at a moment of negative emotion and stop it, this is discipline.

If we want to be in the work, we must verify all our thoughts, words, and actions from the point of view of the work. So, if you want to work, you are no longer free, you must lose the *illusion* of freedom. The question is, have you freedom? Have you something to lose?

This is why self-remembering is necessary. Self-remembering is not only elf awareness, but it also means a certain capacity to act in a certain way, to do what you want. You see, in our logical thinking, logical knowledge, we divide consciousness from will. Consciousness *means* will. In Russian, for instance, the same word is used for will and for freedom. Consciousness means will and will means freedom.

Q. Is attention synonymous with will?

A. No, otherwise it would not have been necessary to use two words. But controlling attention is the beginning of will.

Q. You spoke about bringing things under control. What is it in us which controls?

A. That depends on what you want. In every particular line of action aim is the controlling factor. In work on yourself or study you have a certain aim. This aim will control your actions.

But you did not mean that: you asked what is there *in us* that can control. To answer this, I must return again to groups of 'I's, in this case the magnetic Centre. At present, in relation to our personal work, our aim is to be under the control of magnetic Centre and not of stray 'I's, one of them interested in one thing and another in another thing. If every one of them wants to control us, it means that in the end nobody controls; but if we are controlled by magnetic Centre, it already means a certain control.

The determination and definition of aim is a very important moment in the work. It usually happens that one defines one's aim quite rightly, in quite the right direction, only one takes an aim that is very far off. Then, with this aim in view, one begins to learn and to accumulate material. The next time one tries to define aim, one defines it a little differently, finding an aim that is a little nearer; the next time again a little nearer, and so on, until one finds an aim that is quite close, tomorrow or the day after tomorrow. This is really the right way in relation to aims if we speak about them without more precision. We can find many aims that have been definitely mentioned already. 'To be one.' Quite right, a very good aim. 'To be free.' How? Only when one acquires control of the machine. One person may say, 'I want to be conscious'; another may say, 'I want to be awake', or 'I want to have will'. These are all aims on the same line, only at different distances.

Q. I have come to the conclusion that most of my aims are too remote, and I want to work more on the practical side.

A. Yes, because before you can reach remote aims, there are many things you can do here and now, and that is where this system differs from almost all other systems. Nearly all other systems begin with aims at least ten thousand miles ahead which have no practical meaning; but this system begins in this room. That is the difference and that is what must be understood first of all.

Again and again, we must return to this question of what we want from the work. Do not use the terminology of the system but find what you yourself want. If you say you want to be conscious, that is all very good, but why? What do you want to get by being conscious? You must not think that you can answer this question immediately. It is very difficult. But you must keep coming back to it. And you must understand that before the time comes when you will be able to get what you want, you must know what it is. This is a very definite condition. You can never get anything until you can say, 'I want this'. Then perhaps you may get it or perhaps you may not; but you can never get it unless you know what it is. You can formulate it in your own way, and you must be sincere with yourself. Then you can ask yourself: 'Will the system be able to help me to get it?' If we remember our aim, think about it, find more and more reasons why we should work, our will move in one direction and will get stronger. If we forget our aim, we get slack.

I have spoken about the question of aim because I advise you to think about it, to revise what you have already thought about aim and think how you would define your aim now, after a study of these ideas.

I would say that what a man can get, what can be promised him on condition that he works, is that after some time off work he will see himself. Other things that he may get, such as consciousness, unity, connection with higher centres, all come after this, and we do not know in what order they come. But we must remember one thing; until we get this until we see ourselves, we cannot get anything else. Until we begin to work with *this* aim in view, we cannot say that we have begun to work. So, after some time we must be able to formulate our immediate aim as being able to see oneself. Not even to *know* oneself (this comes later), but to see oneself. Man is afraid to see himself. But he can decide to take courage and see what he is.

Q. Is will part of being?

A. Yes, the same as consciousness and understanding. Only, if you work too much on understanding and knowledge and disregard will, then instead of growing stronger your will become weaker, or remain the same as it was. If will remains undeveloped, the development of understanding cannot help much. One can understand a great deal and not be able to do anything about it. So, from the very beginning one must start making serious efforts to develop will. As I said, with our will the will of men No. 1, 2 and 3, we can only control one Centre, using all the concentration possible for us. Yet centres are dependent on one another. Control of more than one Centre can only be obtained if you put yourself under some other will, because your own will is insufficient, and this is why school discipline and school exercises are necessary.

We have no real will; we only have self-will and willfulness. If one understands that, one must have the courage to give up one's will. In a school special possibility to give up one's will are made, so that if you give it up, later you may have your own will. But even without those special possibilities, if people watch themselves and are careful, they can catch moments when strong desire is present and ask themselves what they are to do in the light of the system. Everybody must find what his own situation is.

Q. What is self-will? And what is the difference between self-will and willfulness?

A. There is no particular difference. Both are manifestations of the same thing generally, manifestations of resistance. It is created and controlled by opposition. This will we have, but it does not come from us, it comes from the obstacle. Self-will is when, for instance, someone sees that a man does not know how to do a thing and offers to explain, but the man says, 'No, I will do it myself', 'I will decide it myself', 'I don't want to listen to anybody', and so on. Willfulness is much the same only more general, it can be a kind of habit. It is mechanical will, generally based on wrong assumptions about oneself and one's experience. Self-will is self-assertion. If you compare self-will with a normal action, there is always some opposition in it, you want to do something you should not do. It is very characteristic in work. In studying ideas, you know that certain things you must avoid, but you want exactly those things. If you start with this in thinking about self-will you will find your own examples.

Q. How can we work against self-will? And is it possible for us, as we are, to recognize the moments when we have real will?

A. Not real will; real will is very far off. As I said, all we have is self-will and willfulness, or small wills that change all the time. As to how we can work against self-will: you can study the system. There are certain demands in the system; things you must not do or must do. What can be opposed to self-will? There are only two things opposed to one another: work and self-will. Self-will wants to talk, for instance, and you must not talk about certain things, because if you do, you will only tell lies; there is a rule that you cannot speak about the ideas of the system to people outside before you know and understand them.

A struggle ensues, and the result is according to which of the two conquers. In this way, from the very beginning, you meet with ideas of the work opposed to self-will. If you forget about the work, you are not working against self-will. The only way to struggle against self-will is to remember the work. It may be that at one moment the work does not enter at all, but at another moment it does enter, and in that moment, you can understand what giving up self-will means. Ask yourself: Is it right from the point of view of the work or not? This is struggle against self-will.

In an ordinary man will follows a zigzag line or goes in a circle, this is why it is necessary to subjugate will. This subjugation trains it so that afterwards it can follow a definite line. When it becomes strong enough, it is no longer necessary to limit it. So, will cannot be left as it is at present, for now it runs in all directions. It has to be trained, and in order to train will one has to do many unpleasant things.

Q. Are opportunities for training will always present if you can find them?

A. Yes, as I said, where there is friction. But that depends on what you want on whether you want friction, on your decision, your state, and your position. In the work every moment one has to overcome laziness, inertia, wanting to stop. If one does not work there is nothing to overcome, but if one works at anything one always has to overcome one's desire to stop working.

Q. If I make myself do something I do not want to do, is that friction?

A. Anything is friction if you do it. But it is not enough merely to think about it. Only by friction can you create energy and develop will.

Q. Are vast amounts of internal friction and discomfort always a necessary preliminary to new development?

A. That depends on people. For some people more may be necessary, for some less. Again, it depends on what you want. If you just want to study, it is enough to see, but if you want to change something it is not enough to look at it. Looking at a thing will not change it. Work means friction, conflict between 'yes' and 'no', between the part that wishes to work and the part that does not wish to work. There are many parts of us that do not wish to work, so the moment you begin to work friction starts. If I decide to do something and a part of me does not wish to do it, I must insist as much as I am able, on carrying out my decision. But as soon as work stops, friction stops.

Q. How can one create useful friction?

A. You must start with some concrete idea. If you produce no resistance, everything happens. But if you have certain ideas, you can already resist identification and struggle with imagination, negative emotions, and things like that. Try to find what really prevents you from being active in the work. It is necessary to be active in the work; one can get nothing by being passive. We forget the beginning, where and why we started, and most of the time we never think about aim, but only about small details. No details are of any use without aim. Self-remembering is of no use without remembering the aims of the work and your original fundamental aim. If these aims are not remembered emotionally, years may pass, and one will remain in the same state. It is not enough to educate the mind; it is necessary to educate the will.

We are never the same for two days in succession. On some days we shall be more successful, on others less. All we can do is to control what we can. We can never control more difficult things if we do not control the easy things. Every day and hour there are things that we could control and do not so we cannot have new things to control. We are surrounded by neglected things. Chiefly, we do not control our thinking. We think in a vague way about what we want, but if we do not formulate what we want, nothing will happen. This is the first condition but there are many obstacles.

Effort is our money. If we want something, we must pay with effort. According to the strength of effort and the time of effort in the sense of whether it is the right time for effort or not, we obtain results. Effort needs knowledge, knowledge of the moments when effort is useful. It is necessary to learn by long practice how to produce and apply effort. The efforts we can make are efforts of self-observation and self- remembering. When people ask about effort, they think about an effort of 'doing'. That would be lost effort or wrong effort, but effort of self-observation and self-remembering is right effort because it can give right results. Self-remembering has an element of will in it. If it were just dreaming, 'I am, I am, I am', it would not be anything. You can invent many different ways of remembering yourselves, for self-remembering is not an intellectual or abstract thing; it is moments of will. It is not thought; it is action. It means having increased control; otherwise of what use would it be? You can only control yourselves in moments of self-remembering. The mechanical control, which is acquired by training and education, when one is taught how to behave in certain circumstances is not real control.

Q. Does giving up self-will involve giving up your own judgment?

A. It depends in what. Generally, it means giving up childishness, inefficiency and lying. You have mistaken ideas about what giving up will means. First, you think it is a final action: that you give up will and have no more will. This is an illusion because we have no such will to give up.

Our will lasts for about three minutes. Will is measured by time. If once we give up three minutes of will, tomorrow another three minutes will grow. Giving up will is not one action, it is a continuous process.

A single action means nothing. The second mistake is not remembering certain principles to which you give up will. There are many principles in order to follow which you have to give up your will. The third thing is to avoid thinking in extremes; imagining the most difficult cases. Start with simple, ordinary cases. Giving up will only means remembering about the work. This way you learn how to create will; it is the method of developing it.

Q. Does giving up one's will mean not to act without understanding?

A. You see, this is another of your mistakes. You think that giving up will means *doing* something. This happens very seldom. In most cases you are told *not* to do something. There is a great difference in this. For instance, you want to tell someone what you think of him, but you must not do it. It is a question of training. Will can be grown if a man works on himself and makes his will obey the principles of the work. Things that do not concern the work cannot be connected with it, but the more you enter into the work, the more things begin to touch upon it. However, this needs time.

When their chance comes and people are told to do something, or not to do something, they often go against it for what seems to them the very best of reasons. So, they miss their opportunity. Time passes and later they may see that they have missed their opportunity, but it can no longer be replaced by anything. That is the penalty of self-will.

Q. It seems to me that if you give up self-will you actually get what you desire, for by giving up one's desire, one gets the desired result.

A. Self-will does not include everything you want. If you are hungry and want to eat, that is not self-will. Self-will means preferring to act by yourself and, in our case, not taking into consideration the work and the principles of the work. If my self-will is to swear, for instance, and I give it up because it is against the principles of the work, where is the desired result you speak of?

Some of our desires may be well hidden. For instance, a man may want to criticize someone, and he calls it sincerity. But the desire to criticize may be so strong that he would have to make a really big effort to stop it, and a man cannot make really big efforts by himself.

I must repeat in order to create will, man must co-ordinate his every action with ideas of the work; he must in every action ask himself: how will it look from the point of view of the work? Is it useful or harmful to me, or to the work? If he does not know, he can ask. If a man has been long in the work, there is practically not a single action that is not connected with the work; there are no independent actions in the sense that one can no longer act foolishly and without discrimination. One must think before one acts. This is the only method by which will can be created, and for this method school organization is necessary.

As I said earlier, self-will is always connected with self-opinions, a man always thinks that he knows. Then he comes to a school and realizes that he knows nothing. That is why preparation is necessary for school. One is usually full of self-opinions and self-will.

A man who comes to a school must be ready to accept the teaching and the discipline of the school, or else he will get nothing. He cannot acquire will unless he gives up self-will, just as he cannot acquire knowledge unless he gives up self-opinions.

Q. Must one break self-will oneself, or have it broken?

A. One must break it oneself, and one must have broken it sufficiently to be in a school. One must be sufficiently free from it to accept things without a fight. One cannot keep all the old views and opinions and acquire new ones.

A man must be sufficiently free to give up the old, at least for a time. He must be able to understand the necessity of discipline, for will cannot be created until one accepts a certain discipline.

Without school one can do nothing. One can try and try, and nothing will come of it. When one is already connected with some kind of school, the chief thing is to start with work on giving up self-will. When self-will is sufficiently conquered, then it is possible to speak about different methods of work.

Q. How can I learn to act differently in life so as to avoid the same limited and recurrent emotions which I now feel?

A. To act differently in life is our aim. This is why work is organized, why we have to study different theories, remember different rules and so on. What you speak of is the far aim. We have to work in the system first. By learning how to act in connection with the system and the organization, we learn how to act in life; but we cannot learn how to act in life without first going through the system.

Q. I want to make a decision to work from which I cannot draw back.

A. This is one of our greatest illusions, that we can make decisions. It is necessary to be in order to make decisions because, as we are, one little 'I' makes decisions and another 'I', which does not know about it, is expected to carry them out. This is one of the first points we have to realize, that, as we are, we cannot make decisions even in small things, things just happen. But when you understand this rightly, when you begin to look for the causes, and when you find these causes, you will be able to work and perhaps to make decisions, although for a long time only in relation to work, not to anything else.

The first thing you have to decide is to do your own work and to do it regularly, to remind yourself about it, not to let it slip away. We forget things too easily. We decide to make efforts, certain kind of efforts and certain kind of observation and then just ordinary things, ordinary octaves, interrupt it all and we forget. Again, we remember and again we forget and so it goes on It is necessary to forget less and to remember more, it is necessary to keep certain realizations, certain things that you have already seen and understood, always with you. You must try not to forget them.

The chief difficulty is *what* to do and *how* to make yourself do it. To make yourself think regularly, work regularly this is the thing. Only then will you begin to see yourself, that is, to see what is more important and what is less important, where to put your attention and so on Otherwise what happens? You decide to work, to do something, to change things and then you remain just where you were. Try to think about your work, what you are trying to do, why you are trying to do it, what helps you to do it, and what hinders you, both from outside and inside. It can also be useful to think about external events because they show you how much depends on the fact that people are asleep, that they are incapable of thinking rightly, incapable of understanding. When you have seen this outside, you can apply it to yourself. You will see the same confusion in yourself on all sorts of different subjects. It is difficult to think, difficult to see where to begin to think once you realize this, you start to think in the right way If you find your way to think rightly about one thing, that will immediately help you to think rightly about other things The difficulty is that people do not think rightly about anything.

Q. The thing I find most alarming is the ease with which I fall into a state in which no effort is possible

A. Yes, but if you arrange with yourself to make regular efforts, that will help you to go on This is one of the realizable decisions you can make. In the work you must make only possible decisions, and decisions which have to be remembered.

Q. A few times a year a line of action becomes particularly clear to me. I have been subject to these moments all my life and have come to think it useless to take any serious action without what would ordinarily be called inspiration.

A. There are periods in ordinary conditions when nothing happens, and then there come cross-roads. All life consists of streets and cross-roads. Turning at cross-roads may even become more systematic if one has a Centre of gravity. Then one thing will continue to be more important, and one will always turn in the same direction. But inspiration has nothing to do with it. It is simply the realization of a moment when you can do something.

Q. Sometimes when I am trying to decide whether or not to do something, I find what seem to be good reasons from the point of view of the system both for doing and not doing it.

A. It is impossible to say anything about this in general, it depends on circumstances Sometimes you can decide from the point of view of the system, and sometimes there are things in life you can decide without any relation to it, because you cannot always find a practical use for these ideas before you know them all.

There is an expression in the system, 'to create moon in oneself. Let us talk about what it may mean. It is a symbolical expression, and symbols in the form of diagrams or symbolical expressions are used for very definite purposes.

A symbol expresses many ideas at once. If it meant only one idea, the answer would be simple; but a symbol is used to avoid long descriptions and to put many ideas into one sentence.

How to decipher a diagram or symbolical expression? In order to decipher a symbol, it is necessary to know the order of ideas included in it.

Now, if we ask what it may mean to create moon in oneself, we must first ask ourselves, what is the moon's function in relation to organic life? The moon balances organic life, all external movements are balanced by the moon. What will happen if this function of the moon disappears? Will it be beneficial to an individual man or the opposite?

We must realize that all this refers to being. What are the features of our being? The chief feature of our being is that we are many. If we want to work on our being, make it correspond more to our aim, we must try to become one. But this is a very far aim.

What does it mean to become one? The first step, which is still very far, is to create a permanent Centre of gravity. This is what creating moon in oneself means. The moon is a permanent Centre of gravity which balances our physical life, but in ourselves we do not have such a balance, so, when we create this balance or Centre of gravity in ourselves, we do not need the moon.

But first we must decide what the absence of permanent 'I' means. We have been told about many features of this, but they must be established definitely by observation, and in order to come nearer to the idea of creating moon in oneself we must distinguish what is important and what is unimportant. Then we must begin to struggle against the features which prevent us becoming one. We must struggle with imagination, negative emotions, and self-will. Before this struggle can be successful, we must realize that the worst possible kind of imagination, from the point of view of obtaining a Centre of gravity, is the belief that one can do anything by oneself. After that, we must find the negative emotions which prevent us doing what is suggested in connection with the system. For it is necessary to realize that self-will can only be broken by doing what one is told. It cannot be broken by what one decides oneself, for then it will still be self-will.

Let me repeat. Work on being is always struggle against what you like doing or dislike doing. Say you like roller-skating and you are told to remember yourself. Then you must struggle against your desire to go roller-skating. What is there more innocent than roller-skating? But you must struggle against it all the same. Every day and every hour there are things we cannot do, but there are also things we can do. So, we must look at a day and see what we can do but do not do.

There can be no rule 'You must remember yourself'. If you are told to do or not to do something, and you do not try, it means you do not want anything, you do not want to work.

You have sufficient knowledge. Now it is necessary to push work on being. We always try to escape from doing what is suggested.

Q. What is the purpose of struggling against self-will?

A. You remember how we started. The aim was to create a Centre of gravity, create moon in ourselves. We cannot do it through self-will.

Creating moon in ourselves is connected with the idea of sacrificing suffering. When we begin to sacrifice suffering, we begin to create moon in ourselves. We always want to keep our suffering, yet moon can only be created from our suffering. Only we must remember that giving up suffering is one action and creating moon is the result of a continuous series of actions.

Q. How is it possible to find the 'I's that prevent you from doing the things you are told to do?

A. The first time you find you did not do something that was suggested, find the cause. The second time, find another cause, and so on. Then, as I said, find the negative emotions which prevent you hearing what is said and following it. Either you dislike me that day, or somebody else, or the weather; then you feel justified in doing nothing.

Q. The making of effort is what you call struggle. But what do you call it if one does something without being aware of a struggle?

A. That means it happened. Four kinds of things can happen to us by accident, cause and effect, fate and will. Struggle must be by will, intention. And you must be aware of your intention. You cannot make effort and not be aware of it. What is important is will-action.

Q. In those four categories, will is not often used, is it?

A. Will has to be used. We are never ready for work, but we must work all the same. If we are ready, then we are given other work for which we are not ready. In work one must try to use will in so far as one has it. If one has an inch of will and uses it, it will grow and one will have two inches, then three inches and so on. In the work we must learn to make super-efforts.

Q. What is a super-effort?

A. A super-effort can have many characteristics, but generally it is doing not what you think best, but what you are advised to do. From our own intentions we are ready to do many things, but we are not ready to do or not to do what we are told.

Q. In what way does super-effort differ from an ordinary effort?

A. It differs in degree, but not only in degree. Super-effort is effort made consciously, as much as we can, for a definite purpose which is not required by any external circumstances. We never really make serious efforts; it is all pretense, for we do not know what it means to make efforts. In exceptional conditions, when we are obliged to make efforts, we make them, but not super-efforts. Besides, ordinary efforts one makes in life are necessary, useful.

A super-effort may *look* useless for its purpose.

Q. I feel I am getting into a vicious circle. The more efforts I make, the more I see I cannot 'do'.

A. Then make more efforts and realize it constantly; make it more permanent. You will see that you are not always in the same state. People in ordinary life cannot 'do', but for you it is different, all the time you must try to do. You are always identified, and you must not identify, you must watch your talk, you are constantly negative, and you must struggle against negative emotions, you must remember yourself. All this is doing. You must observe these things and try to change them.

Q. Is it possible to transfer energy where it is wanted? I cannot do it.

A. This is generally connected with control. If you want to acquire control, you must begin from where it is possible. So, you must always study yourself and find weak spots where you can produce control. From another point of view, they can be called 'strong spots', for they are weak from the point of view of mechanicalness. You cannot choose to do one thing before another for preference; one person can begin in one way, another in another way, but everybody must make efforts in some direction and find out what is possible and what is impossible. But for one person it is more profitable to make efforts in one direction, for another person in another.

Q. What creates stimulus for work?

A. Realization of one's present state. When one realizes that one deceives oneself, that one is asleep and one's house is on fire, always, permanently on fire, and that it is only by accident that the fire has not reached one's room at this very moment, when one realizes this, one will want to make efforts to awake, and one will not expect any special reward. Since we do not realize that our house is on fire, we always expect a special reward. What can one do in sleep? One can only have different dreams, bad dreams, good dreams, but in the same bed. The dreams may be different, but the bed is the same.

* * *

CHAPTER XI

Necessity for study of school principles and methods Three lines of work — Right and wrong in relation to the three lines - The need for understanding— Aims and needs of the school—Putting another in ONE'S place — An organization is necessary for practical work— What is 'work'? -Valuation— Working with people Working for the school—Taking personal interest in the organization—The right kind of people— Fourth Way school—Right attitude— Payment—How to pay? —Centre of gravity—Discipline— RULES—Not doing what is unnecessary—Surrendering one's decisions—Meeting Demands-Shocks in school-work— Idea of choice—Physical work—School knowledge— Men of higher mind Can schools influence life?

In These lectures we have spoken about man, not enough, but sufficiently for practical purposes, we have spoken a little about the universe; but I see that the idea of school and schoolwork is still very vague and sometimes mixed with formatory conceptions which do not lead anywhere. The idea of school must be taken simply that is to say, a school is a place where you learn something. But there must always be a certain order in things, and you cannot learn without following this order Speaking of schools connected with some kind of higher schools (without this connection a school has no meaning) I said that in such schools you must work on your being at the same time as your knowledge, because otherwise all your knowledge will be quite useless and you will derive no profit from it Esoteric ideas that are not taken practically become mere philosophy, simply intellectual gymnastics that can lead nowhere.

I have given you all the words necessary for the study of the system and explained the position of this system in relation to other systems. You will remember that I spoke about different ways and from what I said about them it more or less followed that this system belongs to the Fourth Way, that is, has all the peculiarities and features of schools of the Fourth Way Then I said that a school depends on the level of the people who study in this school, and level depends on the level of being.

For development of being school is necessary many people working in the same direction according to school principles and methods. What one man cannot do; many people working together can do. When I met this system, I very soon became convinced that it was connected with schools and in this way had passed through recorded and unrecorded history. During this time methods were invented and perfected.

Schools can be of different degrees, but at present I take as a school every kind of preparatory school leading in a certain direction, and an organization that can be called a 'school' of the Fourth Way is an organization which introduces three forces into its work. What is important to understand is that there is a kind of secret in schoolwork, not in the sense of something actually hidden, but something that has to be explained. The idea is this. If we take schoolwork as an ascending octave, we know that in each octave there are two intervals or gaps, between *mi* and *fa* and between *si* and *do*. In order to pass through these gaps without changing the character or the line of the work it is necessary to know how to fill them. So, if I want to guarantee the direction of the work in a straight line, I must work on three lines simultaneously. If I work only on one line, or on two lines, the direction will change. If I work on three lines, or three octaves, one line will help another to pass the interval by giving the necessary shock. It is very important to understand this. Schoolwork uses many cosmic ideas, and three lines of work is a special arrangement to safeguard the right direction of the work and to make it successful.

The first line is work on oneself: self-study, study of the system and trying to change at least the most mechanical manifestations. This is the most important line. The second line is work with other people. One cannot work by oneself; a certain friction, inconvenience, and difficulty of working with other people creates the necessary shocks. The third line is work for the school, for the organization. This last line takes on different aspects for different people.

The principle of three lines is that the three octaves must go on simultaneously and parallel to one another, but they do not all begin at the same time and so, when one line reaches an interval, another line comes in to help it over, since the places of these intervals do not coincide. If a man is equally energetic on all three lines, it leads him out of many accidental happenings. Naturally, the first line begins first. In the first line of work, you take knowledge, ideas, help. This line concerns only yourself; it is entirely egocentric. On the second line one must not only *take* but also *give*, communicate knowledge and ideas, serve as an example and many other things. It concerns people in the work, so on this line one works half for oneself and half for other people. On the third line one must think of the work in general, about the school or the organization as a whole. One must think about what is useful, what is necessary for the school, what the school needs, so the third line concerns the whole idea of school and all the present and the future of the work. If a man does not think about this and does not understand it, then the first two lines will not produce their lull effect. This is how schoolwork is arranged and this is why three lines are necessary, one can get additional shocks and the full benefit of the work only if one works on three lines.

It we connect the three lines of work with the idea of right and wrong, then all that helps the first line, that is, one's personal work, is right But on the second line you cannot have it all to yourself, you have to think of other people in the work, you have to learn not only to understand but to explain, you must give to others And you will soon see that you can understand certain things only by explaining to others The circle becomes larger, right and wrong become bigger The third line already relates to the outside world, and good and bad become what helps or hinders the existence and work of the whole school, so the circle grows still larger. This is the way to think about it

I particularly draw your attention to the study and understanding of the idea of three lines It is one of the chief principles of schoolwork If you apply it, many things will open up for you. This system is full of such instruments. If we use them, they open many doors.

The first principle of the work is that efforts give results proportionate to understanding If you do not understand, there will be no results, if you do understand, the results will be according to how much you understand So the first condition is understanding, and even before that one must know what to understand and how to get the right understanding. Real work must be work on being, but work on being requires understanding of the aims, conditions, and methods of the work. The aim of the work is to establish a school for this purpose it is necessary to work according to school methods and school rules, and to work on three lines Establishing a school means many things.

There are two conditions in the work with which one must begin, the first, that one must not believe anything, one must verify everything, the second, an even more important condition, refers to doing One must not do anything until one understands why one does it and for what purpose. These two conditions must be understood and remembered It is true that one may realize one does not know anything and does not know what to do Then one can always ask for advice, but if one asks, one has to accept and follow it.

So far you have worked on the first line, you have studied what was given and explained to you, and you have tried to understand Now, if you wish to continue, you must try to work on the second line and, if possible, on the third line You must try to think how to find more work on the first line, how to pass to work on the second line and how to approach work on the third line Without this your study will give no results.

Now ask questions until you are satisfied that you understand about the three lines of work what each line means, why they are necessary, what is necessary for each of them and so on. The profit you may get is always proportionate to your understanding. The more consciously you work, the more you can get. That is why it is so important that all this should be explained and understood.

Q. How does one need three lines of work?

A. In the beginning all depends on the mind, mind must be educated, it must awake. Later it will depend on emotion. For this one needs a school, one must meet other people who know more than one does oneself and one must discuss things with them. Certainly, it you remain by yourself you will forget the things you learn because there are so many momentums in us that things just disappear from our mind. That is why a man cannot work alone and only the combined work of many people together can produce the necessary results. There are many obstacles, many factors which keep us asleep and make it impossible for us to awake. Things WE learn will just disappear if nothing helps them, and what can help them? Only other people around.

First one must work on acquiring knowledge, material, practice. Then, when one has got a certain amount, one begins to work with other people in such a way that one person is useful to another and helps another On the second line, because of a certain special organization, one is in a position to work for other people, not only for oneself And later one may understand in which way one may be useful to the school It is all a question of understanding. On the third line you work for the school only, not for yourself. If you work on those three lines, after some-time this organization will become a school for you, but for other people, who work only on one line, it will not be a school. You remember I said that a school is an organization where you can not only acquire knowledge but also change your being.

A school of this nature is not always the same, it has magical qualities and may be one kind of school for one person and something quite different for another person. You must understand that all you can receive, all ideas, all possible knowledge, all help, comes from school. But the school does not guarantee anything. Take an ordinary university where only knowledge and instruction are given. It can guarantee you a certain amount of knowledge, but even that only if you work. But when the idea of change of being enters, no guarantee is possible, so people may be in the same school, in the same organization, and may be on different levels.

Q. You spoke of the aims and needs of the school. Could you tell us what they are?

A. First we must prepare ourselves for understanding them. We have school ideas, so we must make use of them: that will help us to understand schools. If we do nothing ourselves and talk about schools, it will only create imagination and nothing more. We must draw profit from the ideas we have: if we draw no profit from them, schools will not exist for us. You must have your own aim and it must coincide with the aim of the school; it must enter into it.

Q. Does the difference between the first and the third lines mean that a school has aims apart from the advancement of its members, such, for instance, as perpetuating its own knowledge?

A. Not only. There may be many things because it is taken in a different line of time. In relation to yourself you can take only the present. In relation to school, a longer time.

It may help if I remind you how this work began.

A very long time ago I came to the conclusion that many things existed in man that could be awakened, but I saw that this did not lead anywhere, because one moment they were awakened and another moment they disappeared, since there was no control. So, I realized that school was necessary, and I began to look for a school, again in connection with these powers which I called 'miraculous'. Eventually I found a school and found many ideas. These are the ideas we are studying now. For this study, an organization is necessary, first, in order that people could learn these ideas and, secondly, in order that they should be prepared for a further stage. This is one of the reasons for an organization, and only those people can have a place in it who have done something for themselves already. As long as they are in the power of false personality, they cannot be useful, either to themselves or to the work. So, the first aim of everyone who is interested in the work is to study himself and find what must be changed. Only when certain things are changed does one become ready for active work. One thing must be connected with another. One must understand that personal study is connected with the organization and with the study of general ideas. With the help of these ideas, we can find much more: the more you have, the more you can find. Work is never at an end the end is far. It cannot be theoretical, each of these ideas must become practical. There are many things in this system that an ordinary man cannot invent. Some things one can discover by oneself; some other things one can understand only if one is given them, but not otherwise; and there is a third kind of things which one cannot understand at all. It is necessary to understand these gradations.

Q. It seems to me that what we have been learning so far was theory, and now we need to make it a matter of personal practice?

A. Quite right. Only it is wrong to think that until now everything was theoretical. From the first lecture you were given material for self-observation and for practical work. You must not think that this is the beginning of something new that has not existed before.

Q. What form of work could we have other than lectures and discussions?

A. You must think what you need besides discussion. You need instruction, you need to be shown the way. One cannot find the way by oneself; it is the state of human beings that they can be shown the way, but they cannot find it by themselves.

You see, to put it more clearly, you enter the second line of work in this way: these groups have been going on for some time, and there were people and groups before you. One of the principles of schoolwork is that one can get instruction and advice not only from me but also from people who have been studying before you came, perhaps for many years. Their experience is very important for you, because, even if I wished it, I could not give you more time than is possible for me. Other people have to supplement what I can give you, and you, on your side, must learn how to use them, how to profit by their experience, how to get from them what they can give you.

Experience shows that in order to get what it is possible to get from these ideas a certain organization is necessary, organization of groups of people not only for discussing things but also for working together, as, for instance, in the garden, in the house or on the farm, or doing some other work that can be organized and started. When people work together at anything for the sake of experience, they begin to see in themselves and in other people different things which they do not notice when they just discuss. Discussion is one thing and work is another. So, in all schools there exist different kinds of organized work, and people can always find what will suit them without unnecessary sacrifices, because sacrifices are not expected.

But you must think about it, you must realize that so far people have looked after you, talked to you, helped you. Now you have to learn to look after yourselves, and later you will have not only to look after yourselves but also after new people. This also will be part of your work.

The chief point I speak about is understanding. I mean understanding of the work, of the necessity of work, of the requirements of the work, the general plan of the work, and interest in it all. This is what is obligatory. One cannot understand the methods of the work until one understands its general direction. And when one understands the direction, it will help one to understand many other things that one wants to understand. You see, one cannot avoid one's share in this part of the work. If for one or another reason one avoids it, one cannot acquire any more.

Some people do not understand the very beginning of work; they do not think about work as *work*; they take it in the ordinary way. There is one thing that is necessary, obligatory, after a certain time, and this is *valuation*, because one cannot work without it. On the one hand people want to work, but on the other they want to take things in the same way as usual. But if they want to work, *everything* in reference to the work must be regarded differently, *everything* and they think they can take things in the same way. What I find lacking is work and understanding of work and valuation of work. Valuation is lacking chiefly. Everything is taken for granted, and at the same time it is taken from an ordinary point of view. As a result, nothing changes. Much depends on personal attitude and personal work.

A school for one person is not a school for another.

Q. How can one have the right attitude and valuation?

A. First of all, before beginning to study, one must decide what one really wants to know. It is quite possible that what we study here will not interest one, one may find that one does not need it at all. So, one must try to find more or less what one wants, otherwise one may only waste one's time. This is first.

Secondly, one must understand certain fundamental principles, otherwise one will fail to understand many other things; something will always stand in the way of one's understanding.

A very important principle is that a person cannot study the system alone, and it is necessary to understand why. There are many reasons. The first reason is very simple and obvious, one cannot have a teacher all to oneself. If one finds someone who can teach this system, he will not spend his time on one person. And without someone who can explain things and work with one, one can do nothing. Secondly, if one works alone, or tries to, one cannot put someone else in one's place, and at a certain moment this becomes very necessary in order to pass to the next degree of knowledge and being. You will remember what I said about the staircase in the first lecture, in connection with the explanation of the growth of magnetic Centre and the work following? I said that a man can rise to the next step of the staircase only by putting another man in his place. This means that one climbs up this staircase which represents the difference in levels between ordinary life and what is called the Way. The Way does not begin on the same level as ordinary life, one has to go up higher to reach it. This means that the level of our understanding, our ordinary mind, even our ordinary feelings have to be changed. Only, in thinking about putting other people in one's place, it is very important to avoid one dangerous mistake. Some people are inclined to think that this must be their individual work. They fail to understand that this expression is a formulation of a general principle. It is childish to think that it can be done by one person transmitting these ideas to another. First of all, it is necessary to understand that people cannot do it and, secondly, that it cannot be demanded of them, because individual work can only refer to oneself. Putting people in one's place is schoolwork, that is, the joint efforts of all the people belonging to the school. All *schoolwork* is organized with this purpose in view, the different branches of the work all pursue the same end: to put new people in the place occupied by the people who are there at present and in this way to help them rise to other steps. But nobody has thought about it in the right way. For instance, very few people think about these lectures and about the house in the country: who arranged them and how they are arranged and run.

This is the answer to the question about putting someone in one's place because other people look after you and arrange things for you. They studied the ideas of the system before you and came to a certain point in their study; and now they want to go further. For that they have to help other people to know what they know. They cannot do it by themselves, so they help to arrange lectures and other things for newer people. This is part of the general plan of schoolwork. The principle of the work is that everyone must do what he can. Then, when other people come, it is for them to do what others have done before them. A certain period of effort is necessary, and everyone must share in it.

Q. Why can a man do more in a group than by himself?

A. For many reasons. The first, as I explained, because he cannot have a teacher all to himself. The second, because in schools' certain sharp corners are smoothed out. People have to adapt to one another, and this is generally very useful. The third is that one is surrounded by mirrors; one can see oneself in every person.

Q. But is there a tie between me and other people here?

A. There must be a tie, but the tie is produced by work. Everybody who works creates this tie. We must not expect other people to think about us. They will do so as much as possible, but we cannot take it for granted.

Q. Would you say more on that? Is there any obligation between oneself and the people in this room?

A. That depends on you, on how you understand it, what you feel about it, what you think you can do about it. There are no imposed obligations. Obligations come from work. The more one does, the more obligations one has. If one does nothing, nothing is asked of one. Mr. Gurdjieff explained this in the beginning; he said it was dangerous to do something in the work if you do not want difficult things to be asked of you.

Q. You said that the second line is work with people. I find it easier to work alone.

A. Everybody finds that. Certainly, it would be much better if you could sit here alone and talk to me, without any other people, and particularly 'these' people, because these people are especially unpleasant. We all think that. I thought that when I began to study. It is one of the most mechanical things in the world. The whole work, the whole system is arranged in such a way that you cannot get anything from the first line if you do not work on the second and third lines. In the first line you can get certain ideas, certain information, but after a while you come to a stop if you do not work on the other two lines.

Q. While trying to work on the first line, how can one get an idea of the third line?

A. By working on the first line to begin with, and then getting a picture of the whole, all the ideas of the system and the principles of schoolwork. If you work on what we call the first line self-study and study of the system every possibility in the work enters into it. So, the more time and energy you give to the study of the system the more you will understand what is included in it. In this way, little by little, understanding will come. In the first line you must be very practical and think about what you can gain. If you feel that you are not free, that you are asleep, maybe you will want to be free, to awake, and so you will work to gain that. In the third line you think about the work, about the whole organization. First of all, organization must be the subject of your study, like the Ray of Creation, the idea of organization, the needs of organization, the forms of organization. Then you will see that the organization is your business, not someone else's business. Everybody must take part in it when they can. Nobody is asked to do what they cannot, but everybody must think about it and understand it. What is important in the third line is not so much actual doing as thinking about it. You cannot leave other people to think about it for you. There can be no schoolwork on one line. Schoolwork *means* work on three lines. It must be taken from a personal point of view and understood that only with these three kinds of help can one move from the passive dead spot. Too many things keep you there, you always have the same feelings, the same dreams, the same thoughts.

Q. Is the third line responsible for the progress of the system?

A. Everything is. One line cannot exist without another. One line or two lines is not work. But first of all, understanding is necessary. You can study, time is given for that, but you cannot decide to do one thing and put off another thing.

Q. You say that first we must understand about the third line. But that surely is not yet work?

A. It depends. In a sense, to understand is already work. If not, enough people think about the work as a whole and understand it, it is impossible to continue.

A certain number of people must understand and be able to do what is necessary. You have never realized how difficult it is for the work to exist even in the form it has now. Yet it is possible for it to exist and develop if more understanding and energy is put into it. Then, with right understanding, it will be right development. But you cannot expect someone else to go on putting understanding and energy into it for you.

Q. But the initiative does not lie with me?

A. Certainly it lies with you. Only on the second line it does not lie with you, it has to be organized. You must come to the understanding of the third line yourself, only then will it be third line. It depends on your attitude and your possibilities, and these possibilities cannot be created artificially. If you feel that it is necessary to do something for the work of the school, and if you are able to do it, that will be third line of work. First you must understand what is needed, and only later can you think about what you yourself can do for the organization.

Q. It seems to me that what you want from us is that we should feel that we *are* the organization, or part of it, that it is not something separate from us?

A. Quite right, and more than that. You must understand what a school of the Fourth Way means. It is in ordinary life and therefore it particularly needs organization. Schools of monks and yogis are organized, but ordinary life does not give opportunities for studying the different sides that need to be studied. For this there must be a special organization.

Q. You speak much of understanding recently.

A. Yes, understanding is necessary, and a personal attitude. People do not make the existence of the school a personal concern, and it cannot be impersonal in many cases words stand in the way of understanding. People speak of first line, second line, third line, just repeating words and cease to understand anything. They use these words too easily. It is necessary to have your own personal picture of these lines: first of yourself acquiring knowledge, new ideas, breaking down old prejudices, discarding old ideas which you have formulated in the past and which contradict one another, studying yourself, studying the system, attempting to remember yourself and many other things. You must think about what you want to get, what you want to know, what you want to be, how to change old habits of thinking, old habits of feeling. All that is first line.

Then, when you are prepared enough and have made sufficient efforts for some time, you can put yourself in the conditions of organized work where you can study practically. On the second line the chief difficulty in the beginning is working not on your own initiative; because it depends not on yourself, but on arrangements made in the work. Many things enter into that you are told to do this or that, and you want to be free, you do not want to do it, you do not like it, or you do not like the people with whom you have to work. Even now, without knowing what you will have to do, you can visualize yourself in conditions of organized work which you enter without knowing anything about it, or very little. These are the difficulties of the second line, and your effort in relation to it begins with accepting things because you may not like it; you may think you can do whatever you have to do better in your own way; you may not like the conditions, and so on. If you think first about your personal difficulties in relation to the second line, you may understand it better. In any case it is arranged according to a plan you do not know and aims you do not know. There are many more difficulties that come later, but this is how it begins.

In the third line your own initiative comes in once more, if you have the possibility to do something not for yourself but for the work. And even if you can do nothing, it is useful to realize that you can do nothing. But then you must understand that if everybody came to the conclusion that they can do nothing, there would be no work. This is what I mean by taking a personal picture, not just using the words: first line, second line, third line. Words mean nothing, particularly in this case. When you have a personal picture, you will not need those words. You will speak in a different language, in a different way.

Every line in the work, like everything else in the world, goes by octaves, increasing, decreasing, passing intervals and so on. If you work on all three lines, when you come to an interval in your personal work, another line of work may be going well and will help you to pass the interval in your individual work. Or your individual work may be going well and so may help you to pass the interval in some other line. This is what I meant when I spoke about intervals in connection with different lines.

The one thing to understand in the work is that one cannot be free. Certainly, freedom is an illusion, for we are not free anyway, we depend on people, on things, on everything. But we are accustomed to think that we are tree and like to think of ourselves as tree Yet at a certain moment we must give up this imaginary freedom. If we keep this 'freedom', we can have no chance of learning anything.

Q. About thinking personally, I find when I try to do so I bring it down to a small scale.

A. You mix things, the word 'personal' has misled you. 'Personal' does not only mean your own life and conditions. You must feel it is your own work.

A school can exist only when people feel not outside it but inside, when they think of it as their own house. Then only will they benefit from it and will know what can help the work, what may be useful.

I will give you an example of a personal attitude, you remember the small parable in the New Testament about a man finding a pearl and selling everything to go and buy it. There are also other small parables there which are all pictures of a personal attitude. Imagine a man taking it impersonally, it would be quite different. The New Testament always shows the necessity of a personal attitude, of personal profit.

Many things become possible if we think about them in the right way. Every problem connected with the work, if understood rightly, gives you something, there is nothing from which you cannot get more profit than you do now, the first thing to learn in this system is how to get things, everything you do must be done for a purpose, your own purpose You benefit from all the three Lines, but from each in a different way.

In relation to the third line, it is very important to understand the general idea of why this work exists and how to help it. As I said, the idea is to establish a school, that is, to work according to school rules and principles, first studying these rules and principles and then applying them in practice. Many conditions are necessary for that. One of these conditions is that people are necessary There are people who are prepared, who are capable of developing these ideas, but they do not know them. So, it is necessary to find them, find the right kind of people and give them these ideas.

But for that one must first understand these ideas oneself.

Sometimes I am asked why expansion should be necessary for a system that is meant only for a few It is not difficult to answer this question. It is quite true that this system cannot belong to all; it cannot even belong to many. But *we* must make every effort to give it to as many people as possible. Expansion of ideas of the system will be limited by the nature of the ideas themselves and by people's inertia and their incapacity to understand these ideas. But it must not be limited by *our own* inertia

The system can reach the right people, that is, people who can not only *take*, but also give, only if it is given to a large number of people. If it is limited to a small group, it will never reach the right people small groups, if they think that they can keep the ideas to themselves, will distort and spoil them Distortion can be avoided only if work grows and if many people know about it. Small groups, limited and unchanging, will always add something personal to it. So, the more the work grows, the more each individual can get from it. Another reason why schools cannot exist on too small a scale is that only a certain number of people gives a sufficient variety of types. For successful group-work, variety of types is necessary, otherwise there is no friction, no opposition. People would think they understood one another.

Q. What is the best way to start forming a Fourth Way school?

A. We cannot start. A school starts from another school. If people meet together and say, 'Let us start a school', it will not be a Fourth Way school. But if a school is started, how to continue, how to develop that is what you must think about. And for this you must first understand what work on three lines means and then *work* on three lines.

Q. To some people the system appears as selfish.

A. The system must be selfish in a sense. The first line of work is selfish, for there you hope to gain something for yourself. The second line is mixed, you have to take other people into consideration, so it is less selfish; and the third line is not selfish at all, for it is something you do for the school, not with the idea of gaining something from the school. The idea of gain belongs to the first line. So, the system includes in itself both what is selfish and not selfish

Q. How can one understand the third line practically?

A. When you begin to understand, this marks a definite moment in the work. Suppose you are in contact with a certain school which level, or whether good or bad we do not enter into. In this school you get certain knowledge but what do you give in exchange? In what way do you help the school? That is third line. I am often asked what the third line means, how to understand it and how to start working on the third line. This question never presented any difficulty for me personally. From the moment I met the system I felt that it was bigger and more important than anything I ever knew and, at the same time that it was known only to a small group of people. There were no organizations behind it, no help, nothing. Science, art, the theatre, literature had their universities, museums, books, a large following of people, the help of governments, the help of society, and at the same time all their combined content was very small compared with the system. At best they were only preparation for the system and in spite of this they had all, and the system had nothing.

These were my ideas when I met this system. I decided to work on this line, and *this* was the third line of work.

It is quite clear that the work needs an organization and a place for all the people who want to come, and therefore it is necessary to find people who understand this need and are willing and able to support the work in every way they can. Take as an example an ordinary school. It requires a certain plan and organization, and a certain number of people to run it, and one must know who will do one thing and who will do another.

So, everyone who wants to go on must realize that this work, its existence, and its welfare is *his own business*, that he must think about it, must try to understand its requirements, must regard it as his personal concern that the work should go on, and not leave all this to other people. The most important thing is to make it one's own concern, to think of it as one's own work.

There is a Russian proverb: if you like coasting downhill you must like pulling the tobaggan uphill. If someone says, 'I am interested in the first line but not in the third', it is the same as saying, 'I like coasting down but do not like pulling the toboggan up'.

Try to think that I may go away and the work, as it is now, may disappear. Look at it from this point of view, do not take it as a permanent institution.

Q. I try to take what I can from the work. But how to learn to give back?

A. Sometimes one may be in the position to put the question in this form, but sometimes it is sufficient to understand what *may* be given, not what you can give; to know what is useful and necessary for the work without relation to yourself. Only then can you understand what may be useful at a given moment and see whether you can do something at that moment or not. So, before you can put 'I' into it you must understand what can be done in general, what the work needs. Only later can you put 'I' into it. I do not consider so much what one or another person actually does, but I consider very much what he thinks. This is what is important. If he thinks and feels rightly, opportunity may come. He may not have the opportunity to do anything today, but circumstances may change, and opportunity may present itself. But if he does not care about this side of things, if he does not understand it and does not think rightly about it, he deprives himself of the possibility to gain what he wants to gain.

Q. If circumstances stop this work as it is now, is there a possibility of developing oneself by using what one has heard here?

A. I cannot answer this. I can only say that if people do not work in these conditions how can they work without these conditions? Experience shows that with all possible help a long time is necessary to get some results, so if one is by oneself there is still less chance. It is impossible to say what will happen in one or another case. One has a tendency to forget the most elementary things one has learnt. Even what one thinks one has understood one forgets in a couple of weeks. Then, with the best intentions people distort ideas. Supposing they do not come to any groups, they must continue to think, they have problems, ask themselves questions and have to find answers to them. For instance, one of the usual forms of distortion by people who work by themselves or in separate groups is that they invariably take some kind of explanation as a principle.

But if a man has learnt to remember himself, that is another thing; it is a different state, different conditions.

In the work the first condition is understanding what one wants to gain and how much one is prepared to pay for it, because one has to pay for everything. Sometimes one wants things without realizing what it involves and how much there is to pay. Try to think about it, perhaps you will see what I mean. This means that everything one may acquire needs a certain effort, and in order to make this effort, particularly to make it consciously, one must know why one is doing it and what one can get by this effort. And it is very important to understand too in which conditions one can work and without which conditions it is useless to try to work.

Q. You say one must know how much one is prepared to pay. How can one pay?

A. *Payment is a principle*. Payment is necessary not to the school but to the people themselves, for without paying they will not get anything. The idea of payment is very important, and it must be understood that payment is absolutely necessary. One can pay in one way or another way and everyone has to find that out for himself. But nobody can get anything that he does not pay for. Things cannot be given; they can only be bought. It is magical, not simple. If one has knowledge, one cannot give it to another person, for only if he pays for it can the other person have it. This is a cosmic law. The idea of payment is very strongly emphasized in the New Testament in Matt. xiii in several beautiful parables that I have mentioned. Man has to be a good merchant; he must know what to buy and how much to pay. Things cannot fall from heaven, they cannot be found, they must be bought. What one can get is proportionate to what one is prepared to pay. And one has to pay in advance, there is no credit.

Q. There is no check on the price? You cannot find out whether it is too high?

A. Some people think it is too high, refuse to pay and get nothing.

Q. I do not understand about paying in advance. How is it done?

A. The only way is to pay in advance, but how to do it is another thing, all that we study here is how to pay in advance.

As a general principle, paying in advance means that if you are doing certain work and want to have something connected with it, then if you make it useful for the school, you earn the right to have it.

Payment is a most important principle in the work, and it must be understood.

Without payment you cannot get anything. But as a rule, we want to get something for nothing, and that is why we have nothing. If we really decided to go for this kind of knowledge or even for quite a small thing and we went for it regardless of everything else, we would get it. This is a very important point. We say that we want knowledge, but we don't really. We will pay for anything else, but for *this* we are not prepared to pay anything, and so, as a result, we get nothing.

Q. Has payment to do with some loss to oneself?

A. Loss or effort. You may gain in that way, but you may regard it as a loss. Payment has many sides. The first payment is, of course, taking the trouble to study and understand the things you hear. It is not yet payment in itself, but it creates the possibility of payment. Payment, in the true sense of the word, must be useful not only to you but to someone else to the school. But if you are not useful to yourself you cannot be useful to the school either.

Q. So in order to progress one must make small payments?

A. Or big.

Q. What are they?

A. This is what we are speaking about, you must find it for yourself. It always means a certain effort, certain 'doing', different from what you would do naturally, and it must be necessary or useful to the work.

Q. I do not understand the difference between efforts and payment.

A. Efforts may be payment, but they must be useful, and not only to you. It is necessary to understand the work in general and the needs of the work. When one understands all that, one will find ways of doing something useful. Attitude depends on yourself and on your understanding, opportunity depends on circumstances.

Q. Is there a connection between work on oneself and payment?

A. If you do not work on yourself, you will not be able to pay. This is the connection. Who will pay? False personality cannot pay. So, in the beginning payment means effort, study, time, many things. But that is only the beginning. As I said, the idea is that in the way of attaining *something* in the work one gets only as much as one pay for. It is a physical law, the law of equilibrium.

Q. Is payment sacrifice?

A. Yes, but you have to sacrifice only non-existent things, imaginary things. All our values are imaginary. In the work one acquires new values and loses imaginary values.

Q. Has one to break down every thought one has?

A. You cannot generalize. Some of them may be useful. If all these things could be explained briefly, it would be easy. It is necessary to study many things in order to know what to pay and how to pay. And in life you get credit, but here you get no credit. By paying you must get *something*, but you do not know *what* you will get.

Q. One must be willing to pay?

A. Yes, but it may be difficult, not easy. Generally, paying must be difficult for you and useful for the work. But this is too general an explanation. Often, we cannot define things until we come to facts.

We cannot have old things and new things, there is no room for them, so first we must make room for them. This is so even in regard to ordinary things. If one wants much, one must give much. If one wants little, one will give little. Measure it, then you will understand.

Q. I think perhaps one deludes oneself about wanting to change?

A. Very often. This is a very good observation, because often one persuades oneself that one wants to change but at the same time one wants to keep every small thing, so where is the change? Change is impossible if one wants to keep everything. To think about changing one must also think about what one would give up.

Q. Is there something in ourselves that prevents us from wanting enough to change? If we desired enough, should we get the help?

A. Yes, certainly, but I would not put it like that. You have all the help possible, it is now your turn to work, your turn to do something. Certainly, with different conditions, different preparation, and also different circumstances, things could be better arranged. But the question is not how much is given, but how much is taken, because, generally, only a little part is taken of what is given.

Q. Does it mean that it is important for us to plan our own affairs so that we have more time to devote to the work?

A. I think almost everybody, with the exception of very extreme cases, can give sufficient time to take a certain part in the work without actually changing his life and affairs.

Q. It is not possible for most of us to give up our lives.

A. No. I said that people must *think* about this side of the work, and they must look at the practical side, what is possible and what is impossible. I am perfectly sure that in most cases people can continue to do what they have to do and live as they are accustomed to living. There is nothing in life that cannot become work if one tries to remember oneself, tries not to identify, to understand that everything happens and so on. It is not necessary to change circumstances; on the contrary, changing circumstances is even worse, especially in the beginning Later it may be useful, but not at first.

Q. What did you mean by saying that everything in life can be a possibility to work?

A. I meant that every ordinary occupation in life can become work If one tries to apply the ideas of the work, then, little by little, whatever one does becomes work.

Q. What is a practical application of this system?

A. For instance, the possibility, by self-remembering, of increasing our consciousness. This immediately becomes practical and there are many other things.

Q. I am beginning to understand that most of the work one tries to do for other people in life is useless Would it be true to say that the school teaches one to discriminate as to what work one is really capable of?

A. Yes, certainly, this is one of the most important things But the school does not teach you just to work for people, it teaches you to work for the school, and in this way you learn what you can do and how to do it You must learn first to work for yourself, without that you cannot do anything, you must learn to be useful to yourself, to change yourself Secondly you must learn to be useful to people in the school, you must help them, and then you must learn to help the school as a whole As I said, only when one works on all the three lines can one get full benefit from the school, and in that way one learns what one can do outside the school. Besides, in school one learns cosmic laws and one begins to understand why certain things are impossible

Q. If we are all mechanical, I cannot make out why we try to do anything? If we have a school, what is the object of having it?

A. If there were no possibility to change, there would be no object of having it, but there is a possibility, and this makes all the difference in this system we know that it is impossible to 'do', that everything happens, but we also know that there are possibilities to develop this power to 'do'.

Q. Does work on oneself gather momentum after a time or remain equally difficult, like pushing a cart uphill?

A. I think it becomes more difficult, because it comes to more and more ramifications You start on one line, then after some time you work on three Lines, and each of them divides and divides, and all the time requires attention and effort There is no momentum there. On the other hand, one acquires more energy, becomes more conscious, and that makes it easier in a sense But, by itself, work cannot become easier.

Q. Is it necessary to work for the school before you can make any progress?

A. It cannot be put like that. If you work for yourself and make progress, then the opportunity of working for the school may come, but you cannot make theoretical suppositions. It is your initiative that is the most important thing, both in the first and the third line. You are given material, but the initiative remains with you. But in the second line you have no initiative, or very little.

Let me repeat what I said earlier: you have received these ideas and came here because certain people have worked before you and have put their energy and time into it. Now you must learn to share the responsibility. You cannot continue getting the ideas without sharing the responsibility; this is quite natural. So, if not today, then tomorrow one must 'do'. Do what? One must understand what to demand from oneself. We study school methods, and this is the only way to study them.

Q. Can you give an example of how to share responsibility?

A. No. As I said it is a question of understanding what is useful, what is necessary. Then it is a question of seeing what one can do, if not now, perhaps later. It cannot be given in the form of a prescription.

Q. Is it not true that for one's own benefit one should make payment which is difficult?

A. Yes, but you must find it. Payment is not just making things difficult for yourself without any benefit for anyone else.

Q. Should we avoid looking at the work only from the point of view of our special capacities?

A. Naturally everybody must look first from the point of view of what he can do. But supposing his capacities are not useful, he must then find new capacities which may be useful. People often ask: How to learn to 'do'? By working, by doing all that is possible in connection with the three lines of work. Often, we cannot 'do' because we do not know our own powers. Then we have not the habit of a certain discipline that is necessary in the work. Everything can be learned, but it requires initiative and understanding, and understanding means effort, work.

Q. It seems to me that I have more from the work than I have given. But I have nothing to give.

A. I would not make such a complication out of it. We always have something to give, and we always have something to learn. So long as you are interested and continue to take things, you have a chance to pay. You lose the chance to pay when you take nothing.

Q. I feel that it is part of our concern with the third line of work that we have to try to become man No. 4.

A. That is not third line of work. You do it for yourself, otherwise you cannot do it. All three lines are connected, but the third line is what you do directly for the school, such as you are, without waiting to become No. 4.

Q. But it seems to me that until we reach a higher level of being the understanding of which you spoke would not be for us?

A. No, you are wrong. If you mean by a different level of being having a Centre of gravity, then you are right, but if you mean a different state of consciousness, you are wrong, because if you wait till you have a different state of consciousness, you will get nothing. So, the answer to your question depends on what you mean by change of being. Struggle with false personality is also necessary; because of false personality we can find nothing This means that a certain change is necessary but not a big change.

Q. Would you mind repeating again the characteristics of a Centre of gravity?

A Permanent Centre of gravity comes at a certain moment in relation to the work, when one is already sure what one is doing, and sure of the system, and when this becomes more important than anything else, when it occupies the chief place in one's life This is the moment when permanent Centre of gravity is established. But when one is interested in the ideas of the system, and yet at any moment something else may become more important, this means that one has no Centre of gravity.

Q. Is it possible to look on three lines of work as being three different forces forming a triad?

A. Yes, in a sense, but they always change One is active today but was passive yesterday and may be neutralizing to-morrow. And they are different even in obligations.

You see, like many other things, these three lines of work cannot be denied in words. At the same time the idea is very clear. The moment you understand it you will ask yourself 'Why did I want definitions? It is quite clear without words!' You must try to remember all that was said about it, for many things were already said on this subject. For instance, remember what was said about prison.

I remember a conversation with Mr. Gurdjieff many years ago. He put it in a very simple form. He said: 'One can be useful to oneself; one can be useful to other people; one can be useful to me' He represented the school. That describes the three lines of work. And he added; 'If one is only useful to oneself and cannot be useful to me or to other people, it will not last long'.

Q. But by being useful to oneself one automatically becomes useful to other people?

A. No, it is separate. Only forgetting goes automatically; nothing good happens automatically. It is quite right to get things for yourself, but if you think only about that, you limit yourself. One has to study oneself; one has to work on oneself; so, one has time to study other lines. But after some time, if one does not accept this idea and keeps only to one line, one begins to lose ground.

Q. Isn't the third line rather out of our reach at the moment?

A. No, it is only necessary to understand. Again, one person may be in one position, another in another position, so there are no general laws about it. For instance, I began with the third line; I could do more on the third line, before I could do anything on the first and the second.

Q. Isn't there a sort of organization to help people to work on the third line?

A. Yes there is. But an organization cannot help by itself because each line must be based on some kind of attitude. An organization cannot replace an attitude, but at the same time an organization is necessary for understanding certain things. For instance, one of the most important things in the work is the understanding of discipline. If one understands this idea of discipline, one finds the possibility to work against self-will. If one does not understand it, one will think one works, but in reality, one will not work, because it will only be self-will.

Study of discipline is connected with the second line of work. Without understanding school discipline, one cannot have inner discipline. There are people who could do good work and who fail because they lack discipline. Yet change of being is possible only with schoolwork and school discipline. For a certain period of time, one must have it, and then, later, one can work by oneself. Discipline is connected with rules. Rules are the conditions on which people are accepted and given knowledge in a school. Keeping these rules or conditions is their first payment, and the first test.

One of the most important things in every kind of school is the idea of rules. If there are no rules, there is no school. Not even an imitation school can exist without rules. If it is an imitation school there will be imitation rules, but there must be some kind of rules. One definition of a school is that it is a certain number of people who accept and follow certain rules. Rules are not for convenience, they are not for comfort, they are for inconvenience and discomfort, and in that way, they help self-remembering.

You must understand that all rules are for self-remembering, although they also have a purpose in themselves. If there are no rules and the importance of rules is not understood, there is no work.

The important thing to realize about rules is that there is really only one rule, or it is better to say one principle that one must not do anything unnecessary. Now try to understand that why cannot we 'do' in the right sense? Because we do so many unnecessary things Every moment of our life we do hundreds of unnecessary things, and because of that we cannot 'do' and must first learn not to do anything unnecessary. First, we must learn not to do unnecessary things in relation to the work, and later in connection with our own lives. It may take a long time, but this is the way to learn. You must do this, you must not do that; this is all specifications, but there is only one rule. Until you understand this fundamental rule, you have to try to follow other rules which are given.

Rules are particularly important in connection with organization of groups, because, since people come without knowing one another and without knowing what it is all about, certain rules have to be imposed. For instance, one of the rules that applies to new people is that they should not talk to people outside about what they hear at lectures. People begin to realize the importance of this rule only when this form of talk turns against them, when their friends insist on their talking, and they no longer want to talk. This rule is to help people not to lie, because when they speak about things they do not know, they naturally begin to lie. So, if after listening to one or two lectures, people begin to talk about what they have heard and express their opinions, they begin to lie. Most people are too impatient, they do not give themselves enough time, they come to conclusions too soon and so cannot help lying.

But the chief reason for this rule is that it is a principle of schoolwork not to give ideas but to keep them from people, and to give them only on certain conditions which safeguard them from being distorted. Otherwise, they will be distorted the next day; we have had enough experience of that. It is very important to prevent these ideas from deteriorating because it may be said that a school is something where people and ideas do not die. In life both people and ideas die, not at once, but die slowly.

Another reason for this rule is that it is a test, an exercise of will, an exercise of memory and understanding. You come here on certain conditions; the first condition is that you must not talk, and you must remember it. This helps enormously to self-remember because it goes against all ordinary habits. Your ordinary habit is to talk without discrimination. But in relation to these ideas, you must discriminate.

Q. It seems that in a school nothing is done without reason. Is one reason why this rule is necessary that talking would introduce a new factor, the result of which could not be predicted?

A. Certainly. If people knew what to do without rules, rules would not be necessary. At the same time, it is also a kind of education, because by obeying rules people create something in themselves. There would not be enough friction if there were no rules.

Q. I take it that the main object of rules is to break mechanicalness?

A. Each rule has many objects, but you cannot expect anything from rules alone. They are only a part of the general work, a help.

Q. I find it almost impossible not to utilize the knowledge so far gained to assist one's friends.

A. It cannot be utilized yet, because if you try to do something with the amount of knowledge you have, you will distort it. It is necessary to have more, because only then will you be able to judge whether you can do something with it in a given case or not, whether you can give something to this or that person or not. Now you cannot say.

Besides, everything in this system must be explained fully or not touched at all, and in order to explain one thing you have to explain another. This is the difficulty. Do you see what I mean? For us many things are facts, or at least should be facts. If you tell them to people who have not gone slowly through this study, for them it will be something like faith. They will either believe or not believe, and since these things mostly go against ordinary ideas, it would be much easier for them to disbelieve. So why should we produce more disbelievers? It is impossible to convey these ideas sufficiently clearly to people who do not study them.

Q. It is difficult to discuss something with anyone without it being coloured by what we have heard here.

A. Until it becomes easy you cannot begin to do anything; everything will be transformed into talk and will remain talk. Only when you are able to keep silent, keep something to yourself, only then can you accumulate more knowledge or material. If you make a hole in a balloon, the contents of the balloon will escape. If you make a hole in yourself, something will also escape. Rules are difficult to keep, because by remembering rules and obeying rules you accumulate conscious energy. This is chiefly why rules are made.

One cannot describe rules or give a catalogue of them, but rules can be understood. Besides, emotional development needs discipline. Nothing develops the emotional Centre so much as giving up self-will. Rules are connected with the idea of conduct. When we become men No. 5 our conduct will be perfect compared to what it is now. But we are not men No. 5, so we must have rules. If we remember rules, understand, and follow them, our conduct will be consistent and will lead in a definite direction; it will no longer be the erratic conduct of men 1, 2 and 3.

All the ways need discipline. This explains why one cannot work by oneself. One cannot create discipline by oneself. If one understands this work, then discipline takes the form that one does not decide for oneself but works according to instructions. It takes a long time to acquire will, for self-will has to be conquered first. In the meantime, another will is necessary, the will of the school, of the organization.

Q. I do not understand why rules belong to the second line and not the third?

A. Try to think. There can be no rules on the first and the third lines; there you must do what you can, there must be initiative, work must be free. On the second line there must be discipline.

Q. What is more important on the second line, advantage to oneself or advantage to other people?

A. It is impossible to put it this way. In the second line you must be able to forget your own interests, your own likes, and dislikes.

Q. Are the questions which people ask at lectures, and which are helpful to other people the second line of work?

A. No, work is another thing, you know. It is necessary to understand what the word 'work' means in the system's sense. It does not mean happenings like that, that somebody's question happens to give a useful result. Work always means a line of efforts leading towards a certain definite aim. Not one effort. One effort does not mean work; but a connected line of efforts, an uninterrupted line of efforts, only that becomes work.

Q. If two people help each other, will that be second line?

A. No, as I have explained, in the second line there is no initiative. But there must be a certain preparation for it: one must understand the necessity of working with people. When you begin to understand that it is physically impossible to work alone, that it is only because of these other people that you yourself can work, that will be understanding, but it will not be second line yet. You must understand that the people you meet here are as necessary for you as the system itself. This will be a beginning.

Q. Is there any particular line that will help one to escape from doing unnecessary things?

A. No particular line, all lines that are explained. You must be able to see what is possible. You are given many suggestions and one day you can do better work on one line and another day on another line; there is no special line for all days, for all time. And there is self-remembering, everything that was said about identification, considering, negative emotions, study of the system, many things. You never know which will be more useful at a given time; one moment one helps and another moment another helps.

Q. Does this system involve self-surrender?

A. Not in the usual sense. In the Fourth Way only a special kind of surrender is necessary, in certain kinds of work, in some special situations. For instance, as I have said, one must surrender one's decisions in questions connected with work in the school. This is an example of possible discipline. And one must remember why one is doing it and what one is doing. For instance, in remembering rules, one must surrender a considerable part of one's own judgment and simply remember them. Why? Because one must realize that one does not understand enough. When one does understand, there will be no need to remember rules. So, you see, surrender does not mean blind sacrifice, and it is necessary only in connection with schoolwork, not outside school work.

I repeat: the way to acquire will is to put oneself under a certain discipline and not try to escape. People use in the work the same methods they use in life they adapt. They try to make work as comfortable, or at least as little uncomfortable as possible, and in that way, they lose what the work can give.

Q. I do not see why adapting should not be admitted in the work?

A. You cannot adapt to the work; you have to work in actual fact. Adapting may be right in certain cases in life, but in the work, it is always wrong. Adaptation is not a sure method. You adapt yourself to one state or one set of circumstances, and then it changes, and your adaptation fails. You must find a better method because you never know what will happen next moment. For instance, you sit in your room and decide not to be irritated, then something happens unexpectedly, and you are irritated before you know it.

Q. How can we make this work more real? I realize that it is not what it might be.

A. It is what it is because you are not what you might be. There is a certain principle in the worktime is counted. For every person certain demands are made. If you have only been one month in the work the demands are small; next month they grow, after six months they are bigger, after a year still bigger. If a person does not meet these demands, the bill becomes very heavy in the end. If someone considers that he has the right to be on the level of the first month after being in the work for some years, he cannot pay the bill. Payment means first of all being able to meet demands. Demands always grow, and if you are behind your time things will look below their right level to you, whatever they are in reality, because *you* are below level. But if *you* work, if you grow, you will be on the level of the demands. I am showing you the side from which it is possible to approach this question. Many things are necessary in an organization, understanding first of all, and effort.

Q. I suppose meeting the demands entails giving up some things, but I am puzzled about what they are.

A. Do not worry. When it is necessary to give up something it becomes quite clear. If you do not see what you have to give up it means that it is not the time to think about it yet. Intellectual thinking about it is quite useless, for when you have to give up something it never comes in the form of a puzzle. Maybe someday you will see some particular kind of negative emotion and will realize that if you want to keep it you cannot work. Or it may be some kind of imagination, or something else of this kind. It always begins in this way.

Q. It seems paradoxical that we are trying to get free from laws and are putting ourselves under more.

A. In order to get free it is necessary to submit to many more laws for a certain time, for one can learn to be free only by obeying more laws. There are many reasons for this. One reason is that we are too lenient with ourselves; if we set ourselves a task, after some time we begin to make excuses. And then we deceive ourselves too much.

So, as I said, if people want to continue to study, they must accept certain conditions. This means they must make the study practical. If people do not take work seriously enough, it is a waste of time. You have a right to go away, and I have a right to stop lectures, so there are no obligations on either side. I have other work to do, but my giving up my time to this is necessary, because it is the only way to establish a school. If I can say, 'If I die to-morrow, work will continue', it will mean that a school is established. If it depends wholly on me, it will mean that the school is not of sufficient strength.

Q. In a school is it better to study only yourself and no other people?

A. No, it is necessary to study other people also, but not only other people.

Q. Surely it is easier to be objective about other people than about **oneself?**

A. No, it is more difficult. If you become objective to yourself you can see other people objectively, but not before, because before that it will all be coloured by your own views, attitudes, tastes, by what you like and what you dislike. To be objective you must be free from it all. You can become objective to yourself in the state of self-consciousness: this is the first experience of coming into contact with the real object.

Q. Does one ever learn to administer shocks to oneself in order to work as one should?

A. If you work on three lines, one line will give shocks to another. When you understand, not theoretically but from observation, how one line helps another, you will find out.

Q. What I meant was, when one needs energy quickly for a special purpose, how can one get it? Is it by a shock?

A. A good shock makes energy quickly. But shocks can be of three kinds: somebody else can give it to you, or you can give it to yourself, or it may come accidentally. Nothing else can create energy quickly.

A good shock can make you remember yourself and remember the shock. It may be so good that you will be unable to forget it for some time. that will make you more emotional and the emotional Centre will produce energy.

Q. You said shocks can be accidental?

A. Accidental shocks do not count. Things happen; people find money in the street, but you cannot rely on it. When we speak about 'giving shocks' we speak about conscious shocks.

We must understand how things happen. We start to do something and then come to an interval without so much as realizing the existence of intervals or knowing about their possibilities. This is our situation. Before we come to the possibility of aiming and attaining, we must understand that this is very far from us and we must study intervals in the given examples, such as the food diagram. By studying these intervals and the two conscious shocks which were explained, by learning to produce them, we may come to the possibility of quite a different kind of shock, but not before that. As a matter of fact, if we could produce enough necessary shocks that are strong enough, there would be practically nothing we could not attain. The only thing we need is shocks, but we cannot make them. Even if we think of them, we are not confident enough, we do not trust ourselves, do not know for certain that this shock will produce the desired effect. That is why organized work includes in itself many shocks, so it is not left to ourselves. We are so fast asleep that no shocks wake us, we do not notice them.

Q. Does the realization of mechanicalness give one choice in one's actions or must one wait for will?

A. I would say it gives choice. At the same time, it is wrong to think that when realization comes it already brings the possibility and the power. One can know and not be able to do anything. It is a most difficult and unpleasant situation if one begins to see things and is unable to do anything. That is why in some cases it is better not to begin working unless one is ready to go on to the end. Otherwise, one may remain between two stools.

The idea of choice is a contradictory idea. From one point of view there is no choice, from a second point of view there is choice, from a third again no choice, and all are true. It is a very complicated idea. For instance, in the work there is choice, but work is connected with life outside. Things may become so bad that there is no choice, and then perhaps there is a moment of choice, but if we miss it, we miss it.

Q. Is there any way to recognize these moments of choice?

A. Only by trying to find these moments in the work, because this system is a method of acquiring new knowledge and power and, at the same time, a means of exercising this knowledge and power. Here we have more possibility to choose. If we exercise it, then perhaps later we will be able to apply it to other things. This idea is connected with cross-roads. Crossroads are moments when one can 'do'.

A moment comes when one can help in this work or not. If an opportunity comes and one misses it, another may not come for a year perhaps, or even longer, if one does not arrange to use organized work which may make permanent opportunities.

Q. Concerning work on the second line, is it necessary to ask for an opportunity?

A. Everybody is given the opportunity, only, an individual person cannot organize work on the second line for himself; it must be arranged.

In this connection it was found by experience that physical work is very useful in school. In some schools there are special physical exercises, but, in the absence of these, physical work takes their place. All this refers to the second line it must be organized work. The idea is this; when a certain number of people work together, in the house, in the garden, with animals, and so on, it is not easy. Individually they can work but working together is difficult. They are critical of one another; they get in one another's way; they take things from one another. It is very good help for self-remembering. If a person is interested in the idea, he can try it, but only if he feels the need of it. You must not think it is some kind of magical help. Work means action. Theoretically, work with other people is second line, but you must not think that being in the same room with other people or doing the same work is already second line. You do not know yet what the second line of work is.

Q. You said once that physical work is the way to make centres work properly. What did you mean by that?

A. Physical work not sport, but hard work, one kind for one person, another kind for another person puts centres right. Centres are connected in a certain way and energies are distributed in a certain way. When people are idle, centres try to do one another's work, and because of that physical work is a very reliable method for making them work better. This method is largely used in schools. In modern life, particularly with some people, wrong work of centres saps all the energy. But of course, even in organized work, if one works with identification, it does not mean anything.

Q. What is the difference between physical work in ordinary life and organized physical work in a school?

A. Working anywhere else is much easier: you give yourself more freedom to choose the way to do it. Suppose you work in your own garden. You will do the things you like doing and do them in your own way. You will choose your own tools, your own time, your own weather, everything. So, you introduce very much self-will into it. In organized work you have not only physical results, but you also struggle with your self will. Work does not cease to be dangerous by being specially organized, however, because in ordinary work will always remain self-will, while in school-work self-will spoils the whole thing, and not only for oneself but also for other people. Self-will always knows better, and always wants to do things in its own way. All organized work is a chance to work against self-will.

Besides, organized physical work needs emotional effort. That is why physical work cannot really be called physical because it is emotional as well. If it were only physical, it would not be so profitable. If there is no emotional effort in the physical work you are doing, you must either increase your speed, or increase the time or the effort in order to make it emotional. Try to do some physical work harder and longer than you can do it with ease and you will see that it requires an emotional effort. This is why physical work is important.

Q. What sort of emotional effort?

A. You will see. We are now speaking of physical work connected with the system, it is under quite different laws; you do it for a different purpose, and you have to remember why you do it.

Q. Do some people need school and others not?

A. School is for those who are prepared for school. The beginning of schoolwork already means some preparation. In school a new octave must begin. What is the duty of this personality which was magnetic Centre? What can be required from it now? Valuation of the work, valuation of the system and of everything connected with the system. If valuation is there, this personality will grow; if it is not there, it will not grow.

Q. Can one be identified with a school?

A. That means losing the school. One can be identified with the school in many ways by liking it too much, or criticizing it too much, or believing in it too much.

Q. Does a school interfere with how you behave outside school?

A. In relation to the school your actions are controlled by rules. Outside school you will find that it is also necessary to apply certain principles which you use in school. If you do not try to apply them whenever you can, it is useless to know them. Then this is not a rule or a principle, you will find even outside school that if you want to do something you must not do some other thing; in other words, you have to pay for everything, not in the sense of taking out money and paying it out, but by some kind of 'sacrifice' (I do not like to use this word, but there is no other). In that way it will involve all your life.

Q. Does the number of people in a school depend on the amount of knowledge produced?

A. No, it depends on the number of people who have a certain being and who can look after other people, teach, and instruct them and so on. You think schools are like mushrooms in a wood, but they are very different from mushrooms.

A school is the result of long work. Even if you take this room and us sitting here talking, it is the result of thirty years' work of many people, and maybe many before them. This must be taken into account.

Besides, knowledge in our sense means knowledge connected with the possibility of development of being. This knowledge must come from another school and must be valuable. Suppose I make you learn by heart the dates of birth of all French presidents, what use will that be? Yet very often this is called knowledge.

Q. Is the reason why this knowledge may not be given without payment because people who take it without payment will twist it?

A. Simply because they will lose it, will throw it away, because valuation depends on payment. You cannot have a right valuation of a thing you do not pay for. If it comes too easily, you do not value it. This is one side, and another side of the question is that if you value a thing, you will not give it away to other people. What does valuation mean? If you realize what effort was put into it, how many people have worked, and for how long, to give you this knowledge, you will not give it away for nothing, because first of all, it will not be useful to them if they have it, and secondly, why should they have it for nothing? It would be the greatest injustice. But this cannot happen because they cannot take it anyway.

Q. As far as I understand, the main object of school is to produce superman?

A. I don't know about this 'producing superman'. This is not a superman farm!

Q. What relationship has the idea of school with cosmic order?

A. This school, a school in which you can be is a very small thing. It may help you, but it is a great presumption on our part to think that it has any cosmic meaning. It is very easy to understand the idea of school if you think simply about it. You want to have certain knowledge, and you cannot get it until you meet a school, I mean a school that has got this knowledge from another school, not knowledge invented by ordinary men. This is the only idea from which you can start.

Q. Some time ago you have mentioned men of higher mind from whom this knowledge comes. Do they actually live, and can we recognize them?

A. We cannot recognize them if they do not wish to be recognized. But if they wish to, they can show that they are on a different level. If we meet people of a higher level, we shall not recognize their being, but we can recognize their knowledge; we know the limits of our knowledge, so we can see when somebody knows more than we do. This is all that is possible for us in our present state. But we cannot see whether another person is conscious or not, or more conscious than we are. He will look the same, or even, and this is particularly interesting, it often happens that people who are more developed may look less conscious and we may take them to be more mechanical than we are.

Q. Do schools exist to have a general effect on other people not in schools, or is it entirely for their own reasons?

A. I would say both, only there is no contradiction between the two things, because how can schools have an influence on people not in schools? Only by preparing them for school, in no other way. You see, the chief difficulty in understanding school systems is that they cannot be diluted too much. If they become diluted, they become their own opposite, they cease to mean anything, cease to have any purpose.

Q. Have not schools in the past influenced humanity?

A. When schools influenced humanity, humanity was very small and schools very big. Now humanity is very big and schools very small. For instance, schools under the name of different Mysteries influenced certain periods of Greek life, but Greece was a very small country. Egypt too was comparatively small, so it could be influenced. But how could this small school influence humanity at the present time? You ask without thinking. I remember Mr. Gurdjieff said that 200 conscious people could influence humanity. We calculated once what this would mean. Suppose one man No. 7 exists in the world, he must have at least a hundred pupils, because he cannot be in contact with lower degrees by himself. So, if there is one man No. 7, he must have at least a hundred men No. 6. Each of these men No. 6 must have at least a hundred men No. 5, so that makes 10, 000 men No. 5. Each of these 10, 000 men No. 5 must have at least a hundred men No. 4, through whom he can have contact with other people, so there must be 1, 000, 000 men No. 4. Each of these men No. 4 must have at least a hundred men 1, 2 and 3 whom he knows and with whom he can work; so that will make 100, 000, 000 men No. 1, 2 and 3. This means that, even if we suppose that a thousand makes one school, there would be 100, 000 schools. Well, we know definitely that there is no such number of schools, so it is impossible to expect a man No. 7, because the existence of a man No. 7 would mean that schools would control life. Even man No. 6 would mean that schools control the world. This implies that men No. 7 and No. 6 would only be in the world in special conditions, and it would be seen and known, because it would mean that life would be controlled by schools. And since we know that if there are schools now, they are very hidden, it cannot be so in our times.

Q. Do you mean that man No. 7 cannot exist on this planet or that he does not exist under present conditions?

A. I did not say he cannot exist. I said we may have reason to think that he does not exist, because his existence would show itself. But it does not exclude the possibility that for some reason men No. 7 may exist and not show themselves; only it is less probable

***

CHAPTER XII

Necessity to distinguish more important from less important ideas of the system—Limitations of being—Possibilities of changing being— Householder, tramp and lunatic—Hasnamuss—Sleep and the possibility of awaking—Realisations and words—How to increase emotional attitude— Sense of proportion—Self-remembering—To know and to see oneself— Being serious—Struggle with habits— Understanding mechanicalness—Efforts—Self-study—Self-observation —Shocks—How to be more emotional?—Putting more pressure into the work—Training the emotional Centre—Positive emotions—Pleasant and unpleasant emotions— Increasing valuation—How new things come—Slowness of understanding— Raising one's standard.

Now it is time for you to think about everything you have heard from the point of view of what is more important, that is to say, to look for the Centre of gravity in all the different ideas you have studied and to try to find the chief points, because, as in everything else, there are more important and less important points. There is auxiliary things which help you to understand the chief points, and there are chief points which determine the whole. It is now time to distinguish between them.

Right questions, right problems are those that refer to *being* and change of being, how to find the weak sides of our being and how to fight against them. We must understand that, before acquiring new knowledge, we must realize our limitations and the fact that our limitations are really limitations of our being.

Our knowledge remains on the same level. It grows in a certain direction, but this growth is very limited. We must see what a restricted field we live in, always deceiving ourselves, always imagining things to be different from what they are. We think it is very easy to change something, but it is only when we sincerely try that we realize how difficult, how almost impossible it is. The idea of change of being is the most important idea of all. Theories, systems, diagrams are only a help; they help concentration and right thinking, but there can be only one real aim, and that is to change our being, for if we want to change something in our own understanding of the world, we must change something in ourselves.

What is interesting in this connection, and what I would like to speak about, is the division of men from the point of view of the possibility of changing being. There is such a division.

It is particularly connected with the idea of the Path or Way. You remember it was said that from the moment one becomes connected with influence C a staircase begins and only when a man gets to the top of it is the Path or Way reached?

A question was asked about who is able to come up to this staircase, climb it and reach the Way. Mr. Gurdjieff answered by using a Russian word which can be translated as 'Householder'. In Indian and Buddhist literature this is a very well-defined type of man and type of life which can bring one to change of being. 'Snataka' or 'Householder' simply means a man who leads an ordinary life. Such a man can have doubts about the value of ordinary things; he can have dreams about possibilities of development; he can come to a school, either after a long life or at the beginning of life, and he can work in a school. Only from among such men come people who are able to climb the staircase and reach the Path.

Other people he divided into two categories: first, 'tramps', and second, 'lunatics'. Tramps do not necessarily mean poor people; they may be rich and may still be 'tramps' in their attitude to life. And a 'lunatic' does not mean a man deprived of ordinary mind; he may be a statesman or a professor.

These two categories are no good for a school and will not be interested in it; tramps because they are not really interested in anything; lunatics because they have false values. So, if they attempt to climb up the staircase they only fall down and break their necks.

First it is necessary to understand these three categories from the point of view of the possibility of changing being, possibility of schoolwork. This division means only one thing that people are not in exactly the same position in relation to possibilities of work. There are people for whom the possibility of changing their being exists; there are many people for whom it is practically impossible, because they brought their being to such a state that there is no starting-point in them; and there are people belonging to yet a fourth category who, by different means, have already destroyed all possibility of changing their being. This division is not parallel to any other division. Belonging to one of the first three categories is not permanent and can be changed, but one can come to the work only from the first category, not from the second or the third. the fourth category excludes all possibilities. So, though people may be born with the same rights, so to speak, they lose their rights very easily.

When you understand these categories and find them in your own experience, among your acquaintances, in life, in literature, you will understand this fourth category of people. In ordinary conditions, in ordinary times, they are just criminals or actual lunatics nothing more.

But in certain periods of history such people very often play a leading part; they may acquire power and become very important people, but we must leave them for the moment and concentrate on the first three categories.

Q. Is this possibility of growth of being connected with willingness to obey certain laws and principles?

A. Not necessarily. There are different ways. On the monk's way, for instance, you have to begin with obeying. There are other ways that do not begin with obeying but with studying and understanding General laws you cannot disobey, because they make you obey. You can escape from some of them only through growth of being, not in any other way

Q. Does it follow, then, that people who have connection with a school, however slight, belong to those who can change their being?

A. Certainly, if they are interested in school and are sincere in their attitude towards school, it shows that they belong to those who can, but you see, in each of us there are features of tramp and lunatic It does not mean that if we are connected with a school, we are already free from these features. They play a certain part in us, and in studying being we must detect them; we must know in which way they prevent our work, and we must struggle with them. This is impossible without a school. As I said before, tramps can be not only rich, but they can also be very well established in life and still be tramps. Lunatics can be very learned people and occupy a big position in life and still be lunatics.

Q. Is one of the features of a lunatic that he wants certain things out of proportion to other things, in such a way that it will be bad for him as A whole?

A. 'Lunatic' means a man who always runs after false values, who has no right discrimination. He is always formatory. Formatory thinking is always defective, and lunatics are particularly devoted to formatory thinking that is their chief affection in one way or another. There are many different ways to be formatory.

Q. Is the tramp side in oneself a sort of irresponsibility that is prepared to throw everything overboard?

A. quite right. Sometimes it can take very poetical forms: 'There are no values in the world' 'Nothing is worth anything', 'Everything is relative' those are favourite phrases. But actually, the tramp is not so dangerous. The lunatic is more dangerous since it means false values and formatory thinking.

Q. What is it that determines which category a man belongs to?

A. A certain attitude to life, to people, and certain possibilities that one has. It is the same for all the three categories. The fourth category is separate.

About this fourth category, I will give you just a few definitions. In the system this category has a special name, consisting of two Turkish words. It is 'Hasnamuss'. One of the first things about a 'Hasnamuss' is that he never hesitates to sacrifice people or to create an enormous amount of suffering, just for his own personal ambitions. How a 'Hasnamuss' is created is another question. It begins with formatory thinking, with being a tramp and a lunatic at the same time. Another definition of a 'Hasnamuss' is that he is crystallized in the wrong hydrogens. This category cannot interest you practically, because you have nothing to do with such people; but you meet with the results of their existence.

As I said, for us it is important to understand the second and third categories, because we can find in ourselves features of them both, especially the third. In order to struggle against the second, that is the tramp, school discipline and a general inner discipline are needed, because there is no discipline in a tramp. In a lunatic there may be a great deal of discipline, only of the wrong kind, all formatory. So, struggle with formatory thinking is struggle against lunacy in ourselves, and the creation of discipline and self-discipline is struggle against the tramp in us.

As to the characteristics of a man in the first category, that is the householder to begin with he is a practical man; he is not formatory; he must have a certain amount of discipline, otherwise he would not be what he is. So practical thinking and self-discipline are characteristics of the first category. Such a man has enough of these for ordinary life but not enough for work, so in the work these two characteristics must increase and grow. A householder is a normal man, and a normal man, given favourable conditions, has the possibility of development.

Q. Is there the possibility of the householder in everybody?

A. Not in everybody. I already said that there are some people who have lost the capacity for practical thinking or the capacity for development. In such a case they are fully lunatics or tramps according to what they have lost.

Q. You mean from birth?

A. That we do not know. We cannot speak about that: we can only speak about results. We know that in the work one must have the capacity for practical thinking and practical attitude, and one must have sufficient self-discipline to accept school discipline.

Q. What do you mean by practical thinking?

A. Just what is called practical thinking in ordinary language, namely, the capacity to calculate things in different circumstances. This same capacity can be applied to ideas of the work, school principles, rules, everything.

Q. It seems that people in the category of lunatics or tramps are further from any appreciation of truth than the householder?

A. There is no guarantee of that. As facts go, they can be exactly on the same level in relation to that, but their potentiality is different. Like many other things, people do not differ as manifestations go; they do not differ one from another among mechanical people. But possibilities are different. One can become different, another cannot; one can change only if a miracle happens, another can change by his own efforts and with certain help.

Q. You say we all have parts of tramp, lunatic and householder?

A. Try not to think about it in these terms. Find your own words, what is meant by 'householder', what is meant by 'tramp', what is meant by 'lunatic'. These words are not a description, they are only a hint at certain possibilities.

Q. If one does not like self-discipline, is this a description?

A. Not a description; only one feature. First of all, the tramp has no values; everything is the same; good and bad do not exist for him; and because of that, or in connection with that, he has no discipline. The lunatic values what has no value and does not value what has value. These are the chief characteristics, not a description. The householder has at least certain values from which he can start and a certain practical attitude towards things. He knows that if he wants to eat, he must work.

Q. About the fourth category of man, who has destroyed all possibility of development, does that situation arise in him because of some form of extraordinary selfishness?

A. Yes, in most cases. It is useful to know about this category only because sometimes these people play a great part in life. But they are already there: we can neither help them nor destroy them.

We must think about our own selves, our attitude, and chiefly about our understanding. Because if we understand, it is already better; we accept such people more easily and know their ways.

Q. Are the distinctions between men 1, 2, 3 and 4 definite, or, like tramps, lunatics, householders, are we a bit of each?

A. You know, you absolutely spoil ideas for yourself when you take them like this and mix them up. These ideas are very important. First you must take one, quite separately, and try to understand it. Then take another and try to understand that one. The division of men Nos. 1, 2, 3 and so on is one thing and it was not given parallel to anything else. You must study it as it is, what is meant by man No. 1, by man No. 2, by man No. 3, what are the various combinations of these, how they are mixed and so on.

Then take this second idea. In order to understand what is meant by householder, tramp, lunatic and the further degradations, so to speak, each must be taken separately. You cannot take them all together and talk about them in one breath. This division was mentioned in connection with the possibility of development. You must realize the enormous number of people who, by the state of their being, are incapable of appreciating any real ideas.

Q. Could a tramp ever be outwardly successful?

A. This word is used to describe people who in the ordinary way are often supposed to be very near the possibility of development, although actually they are very far from it, further than quite ordinary people. People can know many beautiful words, speak very easily and yet be very far from the possibility of development.

Q. What is the significance of the idea represented by these three categories?

A. The important thing is that in each of us, even if we find we have some practical attitudes and certain values, an important part of us also has no values or has false values, like the tramp and the lunatic

Q. What can help us to get more discrimination?

A. Divide in yourself the mechanical from the conscious, see how little there is of the conscious, how seldom it works, and how strong is the mechanical, mechanical attitudes, mechanical intentions, mechanical thoughts, mechanical desires.

Q. What is the best way to work on self-knowledge?

A. You remember I said in the beginning that there are two lines by which our development can and must proceed. The first is the line of knowledge. This is comprehensible, we must increase our knowledge, for we do not know enough either about ourselves or about the universe The second is the line of being, for our being is not what it should be, not only in the sense that we are half-developed beings so that our level can be raised, but also in the sense that certain things in us are underdeveloped even for our present state. I said that the chief features of our being are, for instance, that we are not one, that we are many, that we are not conscious. This is inevitable, but the fact that we do not realize it can be changed: we can know it, for example, we can know that at every moment not a single action, not a single thought comes from the whole but only from a small part of us. We can become aware of it Change of being in most cases begins with our becoming aware of something we were not aware of before. But being itself can grow and develop; our level of being can change, and parallel with that grows our knowledge. Real work is work on being, but knowledge helps. At the same time work on knowledge is also important, and then being helps, because in the state we are in we cannot acquire even much knowledge, it will be broken up and divided between the different 'I's. Sometimes people work for several years, acquire information, but do not work on their being. Then they leave, but they cannot forget the knowledge they acquired, and it works in them, but their being does not correspond to it, and so their knowledge becomes distorted.

As regards knowledge, you must also understand that there are three men in everyone man No 1, man No. 2 and man No. 3. One of them may predominate, but everyone has all three. So even in ourselves we have three categories of knowledge. Part of our knowledge is knowledge of man No. 1; part is knowledge of man No. 2 and part knowledge of man No. 3. When you divide what each of them knows, you will see how a man with a strong predominance can be swayed by it.

Some schools start in a wrong way from the beginning and develop imaginary qualities, such as visions and things like that, for work on being needs constant supervision and knowledge, otherwise many things can go wrong: one can take imagination for the real thing, and if one does not work on being in the right way, one's work can take a wrong turn. This is very important to understand: there must always be these two lines, one helping the other.

Q. You said that one of the features of our being is that we are never one. Surely in the case of identification we are one, we are not many, but perhaps in a wrong way?

A. Yes, but it is only one of the many groups of 'I's; it is not *the whole*. And identification practically excludes all other 'I's. Even at ordinary moments, if you are relatively not identified, one 'I' can be doing something and other 'I's can watch and look in the same direction, at least a certain number of them. But in a state of identification, they are completely shut out: one small 'I' occupies the whole field. This is a characteristic of our being, that one small 'I' calls itself 'I', meaning the whole thing. That is why I say that we always lie to ourselves and to everybody else when we say 'I', because this is not 'I' but only a small thing pretending to be the whole.

Q. What is it in us that makes efforts?

A. Again one of the 'I's or a small group of them. Our aim is to be able to make right efforts of self-study and self-development with a bigger group of 'I's, so that this small group of 'I's that begins self-study may grow and after some time become sufficiently big and strong to control the whole thing and keep the direction. But in the beginning, it has to be educated in all that we call schoolwork by a certain kind of study. If this small group of 'I's with which you begin does not grow, you will not have enough strength to go on. Many people begin this work and then leave it. Nothing can be done about it, and one cannot tell beforehand. After some time, you will see for yourself whether you have enough energy and interest, because work needs energy and effort. You can get neither knowledge nor being by being passive. You have to be active in relation to the work.

The chief thing to remember and think about in connection with change of being is sleep and the possibility of awaking. You must find in yourself certain ideas, certain thoughts which will awake you.

Q. Are their certain ideas that will always awake one, because I find some ideas help a lot one day and not another?

A. Yes, certainly, but you must find things that help more often, certain *realizations*. There is a great difference between realization and words. Once you have realized something, you know that it is true. Then you must not forget it. The chief question must be how to awake. Realize that you are asleep, that everybody is asleep. Then realize that the only way out is to awake. It is necessary to concentrate on one fact sleep and the possibility of awaking. If you think about it and feel it, then the chance appears. Until you come to this realization, there is no chance, really. You can talk about this system, about worlds, hydrogens, cosmoses, and everything else in the same way as you talk about other things, and nothing will happen.

Q. If one has the realization that one is asleep. . ..

A. 'If is already a dream. All dreams begin with 'if. Try to think without it. Yes, this realization is the only thing. It is necessary to find ways to awake, and before that you must realize what sleep is.

Q. How is one to increase one's emotional attitude to the ideas of the system?

A. Compare sleep and awaking. All ideas of the work begin with the idea of sleep and the possibility of awaking. All other ideas, life ideas may be clever, elaborate, but they are ideas of sleeping people. We are so accustomed to these imaginary ideas that, after some time, we take the ideas of the system on the same level as these other ideas that lead nowhere. It is useful to think that every day when you meet here may be the last day. We do not know what to-morrow may bring, but we usually forget this. If you realize it, your emotional attitude will increase by itself, and you will be able to think about what is really important.

Try to think about the relative importance of things. It is very necessary to understand how to approach this problem. How can you think about the importance of something if you have no material for comparison? You must have different things to compare. Try to compare the ideas and principles of the work with things in life.

Q. It seems that the two are entirely different.

A. It will not help you if you say they are different. We want to find for ourselves and not for academic purposes what is more important and what is less important, so it is not the way to begin. You will never get the right proportion, the right material for comparison if you begin in this way. Think and you will see.

Q. My difficulty is that I accept intellectually that something is important and profitable and something else is unimportant and unprofitable, but I have no feeling about it.

A. Realization will bring emotional feeling. It must be realized more often, must be connected with more things. Just try to pass, more or less, the ideas you have heard through your head. Find which of them attract you more. Some remain just words for you, about others you have practical observations or experiences. That will help.

Q. It was said that we have to cut out everything unnecessary in order to progress. I find it very difficult.

A. I think this is the aim in everything. If you are doing something for a certain definite purpose, then certainly the fewer unnecessary things you do the nearer you come to your aim. For instance, if you are hurrying to catch a train and at the same time want to linger over your newspaper, you will miss your train and will not read the newspaper. It is better to take the paper with you and read it in the train. But to cut out everything is impossible, and impossible things are not required. However, the principle remains that we have so many unnecessary things we consider obligatory that we can reduce them a little.

Q. Is it usual that one becomes less interested in life as one becomes more conscious?

A. It depends on what one understands by life, because this expression can have many different interpretations. One may be interested in one side of life which is absolutely incompatible with other interests, or one may be interested in a side of life that can become connected with these other interests.

Q. Desire seems to be essential to becoming conscious, yet cannot desire become an obstacle to consciousness?

A. Desire is a complicated thing, it is really a combination of a whole series of thoughts, feelings, even fears. Desire to be conscious comes when you are afraid of mechanicalness. First one must realize that one is a machine, and then be afraid of it. Then desire will appear.

Q. Lately I have had a rather depressing feeling that in spite of the work I still seem frightfully mechanical.

A. We are certainly mechanical, and we cannot do anything about it at present, until we know ourselves better, not only in general, but personally, individually, for there are many general things common to everybody, and there are many individual features. First, we study the general things, then the individual; and when we know ourselves, we shall understand where to begin. Now we are just trying to do elementary things, more for self-study than for actual results.

Q. How can one cure periods of listlessness, when system ideas have no strength?

A. Everything goes in waves up and down. It is necessary to acquire enough memory and enough elevation, so to speak, in order that at moments of depression one will not lose the thread, will not forget what has been.

Q. But what to put in the place of the feeling of depression which comes when illusions disappear?

A. Depression may be due to other illusions that take the place of the vanished ones. The first illusions were full of hope and the other illusions may be full of despair, that is all.

Q. How can we strengthen and fix moments when emotion is felt and we want to work, and use this at moments when we do not want to work?

A. By trying to connect these moments. When you are in this state of wanting to work, remember other moments when you were in the same state and make a mental link between them.

Q. But will it bring with it incentive to work?

A. In this system incentive must come from the realization of your present situation and of the possibility of change. Or it may be even more simple. Incentive to work may be brought by the realization that it is possible to know more than you know now. The second refers to knowledge and the first to being. Actually, you must have both, and all this must be verified. Very soon after you begin to work, you realize that you begin to acquire certain knowledge that opens new possibilities of understanding. Nobody can escape this if he really tries to work. And after some time, one will notice changes in oneself, which one cannot describe, but which produce quite different attitudes. This is inevitable, so it gives one a definite valuation and a definite understanding that one is getting something and moving somewhere, instead of standing still.

Q. How can one strengthen decisions?

A. It depends on the decision. The first thing is to know what is more and what is less important. If you learn to distinguish this, decision will not be difficult. You must learn to discriminate between mechanicalness and consciousness on our level. Things that are connected with work can be conscious. Things connected with convenience, gain, pleasure, profit are mechanical. Then there is another side. If the result of the decision is really important and is connected with your work, you have a right to ask for advice. In such a case you must particularly try not to decide alone.

Q. I feel that my attitude to the work needs complete revision. The system is only of importance to one 'I', the others do not want to learn or change. Is there some way in which I can be helped to want to work?

A. But who will do this if only one 'I' is interested, and the others are not? You speak as though you were something different from these 'I's. One 'I' may decide, but another will come along and will not know about it. This is the situation, and you must try to do all you can. Do not dream of things you cannot do or try to do more than you can. Nobody can help you to want to work, you must want yourself, but if you do not do what you can, you will lose and work less and less. If you try to remember yourself or to stop thoughts three or four times a day, this will very soon give you energy, only it must be regular. How can we increase our power to work? Only by working, there is no other way. If you learn to make small efforts you will have small results, and if you make bigger efforts, you will get bigger results.

Q. How can one be more sure that there is a concrete advantage in becoming more conscious and less mechanical?

A. You must decide for yourself; find reasons for it. First try to understand what it would mean to be more conscious and less mechanical; then decide. Only then will it have real weight. If I answer, it will be my opinion. There are things that one must decide for oneself, only then can they have real meaning and show real understanding.

We do not know what it means to become conscious. But we do not know our present state either, because we live in illusions. If we were free from illusions, a strong impulse to get out of this state and to change would become possible. One cannot describe fully what this change means, and it is better not to try, for imagination is always ready to work in us and deceive us. Better study the present state. If you do, you lose nothing; for we have nothing to lose.

Q. I feel sometimes that I have no sense of proportion. How can I try to remedy that?

A. But this is the whole thing! This is the aim of all work. All that we do has as aim to have a real sense of proportion. But you cannot have it before you work, so it is necessary to work and then, as a result of work, you will have a better sense of proportion.

Q. I think the greatest difficulty is to find the bridge between our ordinary life and serious work in the system. What is the bridge?

A. There is no need to look for a bridge because this system gives the possibility to begin work at once, just as you are. At the same time, when you begin to think about possible results of work and about what happens without any work, you will see that they are quite different. In one case everything happens, and, in another case, you have to be conscious in order to act according to what you know. There is no bridge between these; what bridge can there be between madness and sanity?

Q. Does change of being free one from external events?

A. That you must find out by experience. The more you become united in yourself and the more you are conscious, the less you will depend on circumstances. You will understand them better, find your way better, and thus you will become more free. As to what happens later, it must be experienced in further stages. It is useless to speak about it theoretically. You can judge now, by everything I say, that I am trying to bring you to practical things.

Q. Self-remembering is much more difficult in some life circumstances. Should one avoid them?

A. It is a mistake to think that life circumstances, that is, external circumstances, can change or affect anything. This is an illusion. As to whether to avoid them or not try to avoid them or try to take them as a role you have to play. However, if you manage to avoid them you will find that nothing has changed; there may be exceptions, but the general balance usually remains the same.

Q. If we are all weakness and no strength, from what source do we draw such strength as is needed even to begin work on ourselves?

A. We have certain strength. If we were only weakness, we could do nothing; if we had no strength at all we would not be interested in the work. If we realize our situation, we already have certain strength, and new knowledge increases this strength. So, we have quite enough to start with. Later, strength comes from new knowledge, new efforts.

Q. I find it very difficult to work in the right way, because I do not see what kind of effort is right at one time and not at another.

A. Trying to remember yourself is always right if you can make yourself try.

Whatever you are doing, just try to realize that you are doing that, or that you are not doing something you have to do. If you try this persistently, it will give results. Effort to remember yourself is the chief thing, because without it nothing else has any value; it must be the basis of everything. Only in this way can you pass from the mechanical to a more conscious state.

Q. I still cannot see in what way self-remembering is distinct from thinking of oneself?

A. Thinking of yourself is another thing. If you want to remember yourself, the best thing is not to think about yourself. As long as you think about yourself, you will not remember yourself. It is difficult to explain the difference in words. It is as though you think about yourself on one basis, and you try to remember yourself on another basis. You realize that you do not remember yourself, that you are not conscious, and by making yourself remember this absence of consciousness you begin to remember yourself. I cannot explain it any better. You do not get the right method at once, but if you try for some time, you will find some particular line of thought that will help you. Then you will discover that if you think about some particular things in a certain way, it will make you remember yourself. And this is the first step to consciousness.

Q. I do not know whether I remember myself or not at certain moments.

A. It is sufficient to know that you do not. Catch a moment when you are particularly far from remembering yourself, at this moment you will remember yourself.

Q. If I say to myself 'I will remember myself. . ..'?

A. Nothing comes; you cannot start that way. Either think of something that will bring it or realize that you do not remember yourself.

Q. I see now, at this moment, that I do not remember myself, but it goes no further.

A. Go deeper. Nothing more is necessary. Realize more and more, deeper, and deeper, that neither you nor other people remember, that nobody remembers himself. This will bring you to it better than anything else. Our difficulty in self-remembering is chiefly dependent on lack of realization that we do not remember ourselves. Later many other things may enter into it, but if you try to have them all at once you will have nothing. Try to observe how your time passes. Say you are in the theatre, or you are here, or you go to see friends, then, when you come home, ask yourself were you aware of yourself, and you will find that you were not. Or if you are in a bus, ask yourself, when you get off, what happened on the way. You will see that you never remember yourself naturally, you have to *make* yourself do it.

Q. Then how do accidental glimpses of self-remembering come about?

A. It may be an intense work of centres, particularly when one function looks at another. When one Centre is observing another Centre, impressions may be strong enough or conflicting enough, or helping enough, to bring about self-remembering. Many things of that kind you can create intentionally, for you cannot rely on being made self-conscious by accident.

Q. I feel it is not enough to be assured that we will know the state of self-remembering by its special taste, and I want to know how we may recognize it intellectually, without risk of interference by emotion or subjective thought.

A. Emotion does not mean interference. Intellectual function can bring you only to a certain stage; further you have to travel on emotion. About self-consciousness, which is a higher state of consciousness, no one can say that it is a definitely possible or easy experience, for it means change of being so it is difficult to tell a mechanical man how he will feel and look at things when he becomes more conscious. He is asleep. How can one say what he will feel or do when he awakes?

We cannot make the first step towards higher states because there are many things we do not want to give up. Each of us knows perfectly well what he has to give up, but no one wants to do it. But in relation to self-remembering it is much simpler; if one really tries all possible means, one will notice a difference between one's state and the state of a man who does not try to remember himself.

Q. When I try to self-remember, sometimes my idea of time changes. Is it an illusion?

A. It is quite possible, but in relation to self-remembering we must not think about additional results, side results. We must only think about the definite fact that we do not remember ourselves, which means that we are asleep, and that we want to remember ourselves, which means to be awake. Maybe the subjective feeling of time and many other things will change, but this is not important. What is important is the fact that we are asleep; and the effort to awake is important.

Q. How can I build up a real direction, a stronger aim?

A. Again the same thing by building yourself; you can be stronger than yourself.

Q. But we are the sum-total of different 'I's. How can one know which 'I' to trust?

A. One cannot know that is our state. We have to deal with what we are until we change, but we work with the idea of possible change, and the more we realize the hopeless state we are in, the more energy we shall have for making efforts to change.

Q. While I find it is only too easy to understand how mechanical I am in most ways; I find it difficult to reconcile my inconsistency with this idea. Is this the result of an imperfect understanding of the simile?

A. No. You see, it is easy to understand mechanicalness with the mind. But to remember it always, to see it in facts, in things, to see how everything happens is always very difficult. It takes time.

Q. Why is it that some recurrent mistakes you may see, but cannot stop until somebody points them out to you?

A. Even that will not help. You can go on doing it every day, until you find the cause. Maybe it depends on some other thing, and this thing on yet another thing and so on. For everything you want to change you must find the beginning. But we do not speak about change now, we only speak about study. Change goes further. Naturally, it you find something very obvious, you must try to change it, but this is mostly for self-observation, because if something always happens in a mechanical way you cannot even observe it.

Q. The most fundamental idea of the system is changing oneself, isn't it?

A. It is first necessary to know what to change. The most fundamental thing is to know oneself, although, as you have heard from the very beginning, if certain things do not change you cannot know yourself, for in our ordinary state we have a very strong antagonism to any change or any kind of work. People who only want to know and do not agree with change never learn to know themselves, just as people who only want to study the system intellectually get nothing and, in most cases, leave very soon. But to know oneself is a long process. First, we must study.

Q. Must we not expect any results from our work?

A. What is the use of working without results? But you cannot expect them too quickly, you cannot expect *immediate* results. You put a twig into the earth, and you cannot expect a big tree next year Growth is a process.

Q. Some time ago you said that before one can know oneself one must see oneself. Does seeing oneself mean a combination of self-observation and self-remembering?

A. No, just having a right picture of oneself. Before you get that, you cannot begin any serious work, you can only study, and even that will be fractional.

Q. It is very difficult to make sure that one is telling the truth to oneself.

A. Yes, that is why I said to *see* oneself first, not to *know*. We have many pictures of ourselves, we must see them, one after another, and then compare them. But we cannot say at the first glance which is right. It can only be verified by repeated experience. This is what, in the first group in St Petersburg, was called taking mental snapshots of oneself in preparation for seeing oneself.

Q. Cannot repeated experience also be wrong?

A. Yes, we can deceive ourselves even in that. But when the emotional element conscience enters, that will be verification.

Q. How does one take those mental snapshots?

A. Without a camera. See how you look, how people see you in one or another set of circumstances. You have to do it yourself, although sometimes it may be useful to ask other people about their impression of you, because everybody has a wrong picture of himself. Everybody stands before a mirror and, instead of himself, sees somebody else. If you do that you will get an idea of your roles. Roles are often divided by buffers, so we cannot look from one role at another.

Q. Does to see yourself mean you both see your faults and also what to do about them?

A. Sometimes it may be like that. But you are again trying to have a definition and an explanation, and I speak about actual practice, not about defining or translating it into words. I mean *actually* to see. Suppose you speak about a certain picture which you have never seen and about which you have only heard. You can know all that is possible to know about this picture, but if you have not seen it, you must first see it for yourself and verify all that you heard. Seeing oneself does not mean seeing always. You can see yourself for a time; then you cease to see.

One cannot speak to a person seriously until he begins to see himself, or at least realizes that he does not see himself and that it is necessary to do so.

Q. You said once that it is necessary to be serious in relation to the work. What does being serious mean?

A. First it is necessary to divide two things: being serious and taking things seriously. In thinking about this, people usually think about how to take things seriously, and which things, but never about what it means to be serious. I will tell you what it means. To be serious means to take nothing seriously with the exception of things about which you know for certain that they are important in relation to what you want. This looks too small, but when you apply it in practice you will see that it is the only solution and the most necessary thing.

You see, people who *are not* cannot be taken seriously from this point of view. One moment they are serious, another moment they forget everything, a third moment they again try to find something, next moment they are quite satisfied with what they have. This means they *are not*; they do not exist. First, they must exist.

Q. You said that certain negative emotions make serious work impossible. Does that mean they must be absolutely exterminated before one begins, and what do you mean by serious work?

A. By serious work I mean not only study but change. First you must study certain things, then you work to change them. But, since even study cannot go on without a certain change, because these two processes of study and change are not fully divided, a more serious study than just at the beginning can already be called serious work. With certain negative emotions serious work is practically impossible because they will spoil all results: one side of you will work and another will spoil it. So, if you start this work without conquering certain negative emotions, after some time you may find yourself in a worse state than before. It happened several times that people made continuation of work impossible for themselves because they wished to keep their negative emotions. There were moments when they realized it, but they did not make sufficient efforts at the time, and later the negative emotions became stronger.

Q. What causes people to make efforts?

A. Two things cause people to make efforts: if people want to get something, or if they want to get rid of something. Only, in ordinary conditions, without knowledge, people do not know what they can get rid of or what they can gain.

Q. Has one to have long training?

A. Everything has its own term of life, and if one waits too long it becomes useless and only bad results can come. Short-cuts come from time to time, but if we miss them, after some time they cease to come. It is necessary to remember all that was said at different times about effort, because effort is the basis of work. Everything we can gain is proportionate to effort; the more effort we make, the more we can expect. We want very big things; we do not realize what enormous things we want. In the beginning efforts are small only because in ordinary life we do not make efforts; everything in life is done to avoid work, so it is difficult to realize and accept the necessity of effort. All our ways of thinking and doing have the tendency to avoid it at all costs.

Q. As regards change of being, it seems to be possible only with the effort to do something different. Therefore, it is a vicious circle, since you cannot do anything different, because your being has not changed.

A. No, this is in life, not in school. It is different in any system or any kind of school. In ordinary life one can change nothing, we make one step to the right and one step to the left, and the situation remains the same. But if one works under school conditions, it is not the same. If one works quickly, change will be quick; if one works very little, change will be proportionate. You cannot buy a big house for a few pennies; you have to pay what it costs. Just think about it in this way: how much do you pay and how much change do you expect? We have talked enough and can understand enough. We must see how much we pay and then we will see how much we can get. We cannot expect more. Is that clear? How many real efforts do we make? If we deceive ourselves, we cannot know, but if we do not deceive ourselves, we can see how much we can expect.

Effort by itself does not help, because you do not know in what direction to make effort. That is why school is necessary. Man, as he can learn many things if these things are shown to him and explained, but by himself, if he gets these things, he will get them wrong and make mistakes, or he will simply not get them. If it were not like that, school would not be necessary some people at least could get these things by themselves. But they cannot; nobody can.

Q. Then one cannot get much from books?

A. One can get some ideas, but a person will get one thing and miss ten other things. As a matter of fact, there are books in which very deep secrets are written, but people can read them and never get these secrets. It is quite safe. Again, this is connected with the fundamental idea that understanding depends not only on knowledge but also on being. That is why one needs a school. In school you cannot deceive yourself, and in school it can be explained to you why you cannot understand. It means there is something in you that you have to conquer in order to understand more. We do not see ourselves, but with help, with study, we can see much more. There are different degrees of seeing.

Q. Surely if one makes a resolution. . .?

A. That is only a word. If you were stronger, you would be able to make resolutions. As you are, you can make as many resolutions as you like, and you will continue to talk about resolutions. The chief thing is our weakness in everything. We can have beautiful plans; we can say that we know what we want; we can even have an aim, but we cannot 'do' anything. This is why we have to learn. We have to learn how to do small things first, step by step. We must begin with small efforts. If we do not make small efforts, we will remain the same one moment there, another moment not there. But if we make small efforts and remember about them, that will give a line, a direction.

Q. What is the best way to make efforts at moments when one feels the desire to change?

A. It is necessary to know in what sense you mean change. Also, effort cannot be described. When one understands one's situation, then inner contradictions and many other things give one a sufficient impulse for making efforts. So, it is the realization of sleep, of inner divisions, buffers, negative ness and the unpleasantness of such things that will give one the impulse.

Q. If I think I have changed a little since I have attended these lectures, would it be imagination?

A. No. Certainly you have changed, because you begin to understand certain things you could not have understood before. But it may not be enough. Every small thing you learn changes something, but maybe more change is necessary. You see, it is always a big change as compared with how things would have been without it; but the change may not be great enough from the point of view of acquiring more change, or of getting something else, because change does not come of itself. It comes as a result of a definite effort in a definite direction. The need for effort always remains. Study is impossible without a certain struggle because there are many mechanical things going on in us that cannot be used in the process of acquiring control.

Q. Where is the hallmark to show that we have changed or not changed?

A. Many things can be said about it. It is a difficult thing to do, but if you could imagine what would happen to you if you were not connected with any kind of work this would answer your question; if you could compare yourself with yourself as you would be.

Q. Wouldn't you develop more and more 'I's as you struggle to change?

A. You will still have many 'I's, they will not disappear, but you will be able to control them and arrange them in a certain way.

Q. We have been told that it is useful to struggle with mechanical habits, but it was also suggested that it is not wise to try and alter things. Can this be explained further?

A. What I said about not trying to alter things referred to people in ordinary conditions of life, without school, without discipline, without methods of the work. I said then that in ordinary life people cannot change anything in themselves, because by changing one thing they unconsciously change another. Without knowing how to do it, it is quite useless. But in the work, particularly after some time, this danger does not exist anymore, because by doing all that is advised one avoids this possibility of wrong change, since wrong change always happens in one of the useless functions. If one changes something in the ordinary way, one either begins to lie more, or identify more or express more negative emotions, because these things are more easily affected. But in the work, we have many safeguards, above all self-remembering, which will stop another mechanical thing taking the place of the mechanical thing you destroy. Besides, you must understand that in order to change something it is necessary to know how things are connected and how to do it, and one cannot do it unless it is explained how to begin. There are definite points where one can begin and in order really to change something one must follow the way that is shown. For instance, it is necessary to change our wrong way of thinking, to make our thinking less formatory. But first we must find examples of formatory thinking. Then we can struggle with the expression of negative emotions, with considering, with imagination all these are ways to struggle with habits. At the same time, you can also struggle with other habits, but your struggle will only serve self-observation, because you cannot change them. You can change them only through the channels that are indicated. To struggle with habits directly and obtain right results more knowledge is necessary, you do not know enough yet.

But it will do no harm because this effort will be balanced by self-remembering.

Q. Why has nobody discovered for himself the points from which to begin?

A. Because one 'I' discovers something, but at that moment another 'I' becomes interested in something else and takes all the energy; then while the second

'I' works, a third 'I' comes along, and so on. Man is always running in different directions. We do not realize how important this is.

Q. I do not see how one is to get anywhere unless one tries to go against habits and to change one's everyday life.

A. Yes, certainly one has to do something about it. The question is what one must change. People always try to change things that are not important, and what is important is disregarded and put off till to-morrow.

Q. Are there any good habits?

A. Habits of moving and instinctive centres can be good habits. Habits in intellectual or emotional centres can never be useful.

Q. Are all habits forms of identification?

A. Some habits are quite ordinary and harmless, but if you begin to put obstacles in their way it will give you good material for self-observation and you will be able to distinguish identification when it enters. This struggle introduces friction, and without friction you would not notice yourself, you would live as though in a thick fog, without noticing it. But the second step depends on your decision, you can be simply irritated by this friction, or you can use it.

Q. Shouldn't we do as little as possible in our present state of consciousness?

A. We must study ourselves. We can do nothing until we know: first we must know what we are and what to do. But in these lectures, I have already given you several things you can do.

One can study oneself as one is. It is very important to study that. And I repeat again, from the very first steps one must try to change certain things, because in our state of chaos we cannot even study ourselves. We have to bring in some order. We want to make an inventory of our house and so we begin to set down what there is in it; but suppose that, while we are doing it, other people in the house keep on moving the furniture, or the furniture moves itself. This is what actually happens, the furniture moves itself, so you must attach it to some definite place.

School knowledge is knowledge acquired through higher centres. So, it is quite a different method. We are given certain principles and certain divisions which are not known ordinarily, and if we begin to study ourselves from this point of view, we will discover many new things. When you are quite certain of these divisions and of these principles, then, observing yourself on this basis you discover things you cannot discover without knowing them. With the ordinary mind we see things only vaguely and they become confused: we cannot distinguish one from another, so we mix things. But if we are told how to do so, we can divide them even with our ordinary mind.

Q. So the observation of man 1, 2 and 3 is more complicated, more roundabout, but not necessarily wrong?

A. Observation may be quite right, but if he does not know how to divide his observations he cannot arrive at right results. Very much is based on right divisions.

Q. Is it good to start making observations of one division first?

A. No, you cannot do that, because you cannot know what you can do best at a given moment. So do what you find you can do best. For instance, you may decide to observe the intellectual function and, instead, you may find yourself in an emotional state. You cannot do one thing and then another and then a third, until you have control. And control comes last.

Q. Is there quite a lot of benefit to be derived by observing other people as well as oneself?

A. Yes, but there are dangerous moments. If one is capable of applying to oneself what one finds in other people, then it may be right, but as a rule one thinks that other people are one thing and oneself a different thing. In that case one may see things in other people and never apply them to oneself.

Q. It seems that self-observation and self-remembering become more difficult under conditions of bodily fatigue or when one is feeling unwell. How can this dependence be overcome?

A. Conditions of our body are conditions under which we live, so we have to observe and remember or not remember ourselves in these conditions if we intend to do it. We cannot begin with changing conditions.

Q. Surely observation is like introspection, it turns everything inwards?

A. No, introspection is the same as imagination, it is uncontrolled. It is useless and does not bring anything. But in observing you know what you are doing and why you are doing it, what you want to attain, what you want to know. It is not introspection; it is studying a very complicated machine. It is really mechanics, not psychology. Psychology comes later.

Q. How is it that one can observe oneself and still go on doing the same silly antics?

A. Because there is not one person but many. One person looks on, and another continues the antics. If you can see the different people in you in one case, it is good. If you can see them in several cases, things begin to become uncomfortable. If you can see them always, it is the beginning of work.

Q. I have observed that I am very unnatural. Does being a little more awake mean, one is then more natural?

A. Not necessarily, because people, as they are in ordinary life, are in a very bad state, so in order to become natural eventually, they first have to become unnatural. You cannot expect to become natural at once. It would be possible if we started on the right level, but we start below level.

Q. Why is it that if one gets out of touch with the system all obstacles come up in their worst form? One is more negative, one does more useless talking and so on.

A. Because of work one gets a sort of new control and at the same time one loses mechanical control. So, if one loses touch with the work, one loses this very small conscious control and one has already lost mechanical control. As a result, one is worse off.

Q. Why is there more resistance in me to work in the system sense than to other kinds of work?

A. Because other kinds of work are mechanical and mechanical resistance is less to mechanical action. But if you take an originally conscious action it meets with all possible resistance.

Q. Can some deep shock that occurs in life be favourable to one's work?

A. Yes, but such shocks cannot replace work. All that can be acquired in the line of development of consciousness can only be acquired by effort.

A shock cannot replace effort; it can act on centres but not on consciousness. Consciousness does not develop or grow by itself.

A shock can for a short time open up higher centres and connect one with them for a moment. It can concentrate for a certain time all the energy in our body that is dispersed everywhere and draw it together. You can then awake for a moment, but as a rule you fall more deeply asleep later. You can even lose consciousness or be in a very low state afterwards. So, no shock can increase the amount of consciousness; this is a very important thing to understand. People usually mix the idea of consciousness and functions. Both must develop, but the development of one does not produce the development of the other

Q. What do you mean by development of functions?

A. If centres are balanced and acquire sufficient speed, they become connected with the higher centres. This is the easiest way to understand it, but there can be other descriptions. In this state of consciousness, we can only be aware of the work of lower centres; in self-consciousness we can be aware of more. But first we must start cleaning.

Q. I understand that no effort to be conscious is ever wasted, and yet that, by being negative, we lose the energy we make. How can both be true?

A. This is a great mistake, for it is quite against the principles of the work to say that no efforts can be wasted. People can make efforts all their life and they can all be wasted if they make them in a wrong way. Take any wrong school with some kind of twisted idea. People belonging to such a school can make an enormous amount of efforts and all of them can be lost. Even in the right way one can make efforts for some time and then, if one stops, all those efforts will be lost. So, efforts can be wasted if they are not followed by a right attitude and by other efforts.

Q. What explains the sense of urgency created in oneself in a better state?

A. In the beginning it is magnetic Centre, for it has a dim realization of the unreality of ordinary conceptions, intentions, possibilities. Then, when one begins to study, at a certain moment realization of sleep becomes emotional and gains strength. Lack of understanding means lack of emotion. Only formatory Centre can work without emotion. Every right realization becomes emotional. One of our obstacles is that we are too dull, not emotional enough. The intellect is a very weak machine. This is why the emotional Centre must be free of negative emotions, because otherwise we use all its energy on them and can do nothing.

Q. Is any energy produced by self-observation?

A. Certainly. Every kind of work produces energy, only some kinds produce a small amount, so that it is necessary to make consecutive efforts for a long time to produce sufficient energy. And some other kind of work may produce much energy at once.

Sometimes an effort may look quite small and be very big in reality, and sometimes a very big effort may be very small.

Q. How can I learn to feel more? I live so much in my head. I get too little out of life and there is a barrier between me and the system.

A. This is everybody's problem, because if people could feel more, many things would be easier for them. But they have been for a long time unconsciously creating so many protective devices against feeling that there cannot be any at present- It is necessary to find a beginning; without a beginning nothing is possible. You must begin somewhere; there are things that are more difficult and others that are less difficult. What you really need is more observation and a certain kind of thinking about your self or about something else. If you persist in this thinking it can make you emotional; only you must find for yourself what it is; it is impossible to give general advice, suitable for everybody. Every person has some points which bring him nearer to an emotional state; it is necessary to find them. Whatever happens later, at present one has to begin in this way.

Q. Before I came to the work, I was full of little enthusiasms. I see that many of them were based on imagination, but now I have almost no feeling at all.

A. As I just said, this is one of our biggest problems, how to make oneself more emotional because we cannot go far on intellect alone. The only thing is effort, effort and remembering different lines of the work, trying not to identify, trying to remember oneself, trying this and that effort, effort... .. If you make sufficient effort, you will become more emotional. But the fact that this is a constant question that people ask or if they do not ask, they feel this problem shows that people do not make enough effort.

Q. You say more effort is needed. Do you mean effort to feel emotion or effort to work?

A. It is simply effort to work. You cannot make effort to feel emotional, no effort will help in that, *but you can make efforts.* If you are doing something, you can do it without effort, trying to do as little as possible, or you can put much effort into it. Emotion can appear only as the result of a certain pressure. In ordinary conditions, in ordinary life, it only happens; something happens and brings you to an emotional state. The question is how to produce emotion, how to make ourselves emotional. And I say that in our present state there is only one thing effort. But not effort to produce emotion. There is no such effort. But very strong continuous effort in any work you do will make you more emotional after some time not at once, certainly.

A certain period of efforts on different lines is bound to increase your emotions.

Q. Why should making efforts be so difficult?

A. Efforts may look difficult because we are not prepared in our mind, we do not think rightly about them. We do not even accept mentally that it is necessary to make efforts. That creates the biggest difficulty. The necessity for making efforts comes as a shock, as a new thing.

Q. I cannot by effort reach a state that sometimes comes accidentally.

A. You say it comes accidentally. If it is what I mean, it comes as a result of your efforts, only it does not come at the time. But if you had not made efforts, it would not have come accidentally, so it is not really accidental. The more efforts you make, the more you will have these accidental moments of self-remembering, of understanding, of being emotional. It is all the result of effort. Only in this case we cannot connect the cause and the effect. The reason why we cannot connect them is probably due to many small things, such as identification, imagination, and things like that. But the cause is there and at a certain moment it will bring a result. We must never expect immediate results. It is necessary to work for a long time to create permanent standards, in order to have immediate results; and even that comes only in very emotional states. If we could by will or desire or intention become more emotional, many things would be different. But we cannot. We are very low emotionally and that is why most of the work we do now, even if we really do it, can have no immediate results. But no right effort is lost, something always remains, only it must be followed by other and bigger efforts. So, the first question is how to become more emotional, and that we cannot do, except indirectly, by making efforts. The second question is how to use emotional states when they come, and that is what we must prepare ourselves for, since it is possible. Emotional states come and we lose them in identification and things like that. But we could use them.

Q. When emotional states come, is the only way to prolong them to self-remember?

A. I said use them. Certainly, if you remember yourself, you will see many ways of using this state when it comes; it is a matter of observation. It will give you a different power of thinking, different power of understanding. It cannot be described because it must be a personal experience.

Q. Can emotions be used to see more objectively?

A. Yes, they can, when you have control of them. Emotions can be used as definite instruments for acquiring knowledge only if you can control them. And what does control mean? It means not admitting identification and considering. Control is the second step; study is the first step.

We speak about emotions, but many of them we know only by name. They are so mixed with other things; we identify with them so much that we do not realize all that we can get from them if we could take them in the right way. All that we call emotions, anger, fear, boredom they can all be turned upside down, and then we will find that they have quite a different taste. All emotions can be useful, they are a kind of windows, or additional senses. Only now we cannot use them, except for creating new illusions; but if we used them for seeing things as they are, we would learn many new things.

Q. How can anger or hate help?

A. By turning it against yourself. Hate yourself, find in yourself what to hate. When one becomes angry with oneself one can see many things.

Q. Then that means self-criticism?

A. More than that; criticism is simply intellectual, but this is *feeling*. All intellectual activity is preparing material, and then the emotional Centre will begin to work with this material. Intellectual Centre cannot, by itself, help in awakening. Only work on the emotional Centre can do this, and we can only awake through unpleasant emotions, awakening through pleasant emotions has not been invented yet. The most unpleasant thing is to go against oneself, against one's views, convictions, inclinations. Awakening is not for those who are afraid of unpleasant things, it is only for those who wish to awake and realize what being asleep means and that much help is necessary, a great deal of shaking. This is the real point, how to provide perpetual shaking for oneself and how to agree to it.

Q. To some extent it seems possible to train the thinking and moving centres, but can you say how we could train the emotional Centre?

A. We can begin in two ways: first, as I have often said already, by not expressing unpleasant emotions. We have proof that it is possible because we see that we do not do so through fear. For example, a soldier does not express his unpleasant feelings before his officer, because he knows that if he does his punishment will be severe. So, if it is possible to refrain mechanically, it is possible to do so consciously. We can act on our emotions by separating mind from emotions. Mind can not only be trained but also taught to stand aside and look at emotions. Then, after a time, the emotional Centre begins to realize that it is not worth while going on if mind does not follow.

Then, as a rule, everyone has about five or six kinds of emotion for certain occasions. So, everyone can know beforehand what will happen, the repertoire is very limited, so we can and must study ourselves from this point of view. It is really much easier than we think, and it is quite possible to foresee in advance the things that will happen. If we talk seriously to ourselves for half an hour, we can stop our emotions, because we know all the associations that will produce them. It would not be easy if our repertoire of emotions were unlimited; but emotions for tomorrow are very limited; you know very well that it would be difficult to think of a new one. But you must know all the associations very well, and you must know the ways by which emotions ordinarily come.

It is the most difficult thing; emotional Centre is the strongest one we have. Reason wants to stop emotion, but it is weak, and emotion is strong. One can stop it only in an indirect way, and not at the moment.

Q. Is it bad to try?

A. No, it is good; then, little by little, you may find out how to stop it, for it can only be done by skill. The only way is to create new attitudes opposed to the emotions you want to stop. Then, in the long run, the attitude may prove stronger than the emotion.

So, there are two ways to stop emotion: first, by being conscious, secondly, by creating right attitudes. But for each particular case a different attitude is necessary, so it is long work. We are not only machines, we are already damaged machines. In order to repair the machine, it is necessary to work hard.

Q. What protective attitude against negative emotions do you suggest?

A. As I said, first trying to remember yourself. If you are conscious of all that is going on in you, you can stop them when they are still small. When they are big, you cannot. Then, in observing yourself, you find things that make you more asleep, more mechanical. You must separate them from things that can be useful.

Q. This is about oneself. But how to protect oneself from the negative emotions of others?

A. Our identification brings to us the negative emotions of other people, it makes us susceptible to them. If you have a definite case, you can visualize the possibility of not being identified, and you will see that you will be less susceptible. But even better than visualizing it, try it in actual fact. The relation of identification to negative emotions is not a theory, it can be easily verified.

Identification is more easy to understand than emotions; there are hundreds of different negative emotions, but identification is always the same. The first step towards non-identification is self-observation. One must watch all impressions the moment they come in. Identification works both in the case of attraction and repulsion.

Q. I see mechanicalness to a greater degree now and this seems to involve me in a greater identification, and fear, and a sense of being caught up.

A. If you mean fear of mechanicalness in yourself, this fear can have a useful purpose, because you already know enough about it, how to struggle with it, how to oppose it.

Q. I have been trying to stop expression of negative emotions in order to struggle with mechanicalness, but these efforts run down very quickly and the need to wake up gets forgotten.

A. This is because you try it on small emotions. If you try not to express serious emotions, you will keep awake longer. If you remembered to struggle with the expression of really strong emotions, at the right moment you would see the difference.

Q. I am puzzled by the question of expressing emotions: if it is beyond ordinary human experience to feel positive emotion, and we are told not to express negative emotions, is it meant that we are not to express any emotion whatsoever?

A. No, it is necessary to navigate between the two. We must be as emotional as possible, for we miss many perceptions, ideas, understandings, because at the moment we are not emotional. Many perceptions come through emotion. We have no positive emotions, but we can say that we have negative emotions and pleasant and unpleasant emotions that are not negative.

Q. Positive means not negative?

A. Yes, and much more besides. An emotion that cannot become negative gives enormous understanding, has an enormous cognitive value. It connects things that cannot be connected in an ordinary state. To have positive emotions is advised and recommended in religions, but they do not say how to get them. They say, 'Have faith, have love'. How? Christ says, 'Love your enemies'. It is not for us; we cannot even love our friends. It is the same as saying to a blind man, 'You must see!'

A blind man cannot see, otherwise he would not be a blind man. That is what positive emotion means.

Q. How can we learn to love our enemies?

A. Learn to love yourself first, you do not love yourself enough; you love your false personality, not yourself.

It is difficult to understand the New Testament or Buddhist writings, for they are notes taken in school. One line of these writings refers to one level and another to another level.

Q. Have you a name for an emotion that is not negative?

A. It can be pleasure or suffering. But both can become negative, for the tendency is there: every emotion can either become negative or give birth to other negative emotions.

Q. Does not instinctive Centre make a good substitute for the emotional? For instance, love of animals and small children. . ..

A. We cannot speak of animals when we speak about man. Instinctive negative emotions have their own place and their own normal causes, but the emotional Centre borrows their results and substitutes imaginary causes. It is very interesting 10 see the lack of symmetry between pleasant and unpleasant emotions. Pleasant emotions cannot grow much, they are limited. Unpleasant emotions can grow. But this refers only to our present state of consciousness; in another state the symmetry is reestablished, for there pleasant emotions can also grow. Of course, we cannot verify this until we are in another state of consciousness. Why can unpleasant emotions grow? Because there are no limits to the abnormal state of the machine. But pleasures are limited by our powers of perception. This is one of the unpleasant sides of our situation.

Q. I think we are so used to judging by results that my difficulty is that I cannot judge whether I have achieved something or not when I make efforts in the work.

A. I quite understand. But you see, it is too early to speak about results. The time will come, it may be very soon, when you will begin to see some results, but not yet. In ordinary conditions we judge by results. If we study a language, we know that after some time we will be able to read short sentences, then small paragraphs, then short stories. But if you take the psychological side of the work, you have to make efforts to observe, efforts to remember yourself, and at first you will see no visible results. Then, after some time, you will see some results, but you cannot bargain about it.

Q. But how can I tell whether I have established something for myself that will take me further?

A. Only you can answer that. It depends on you, how much you understand, how much you are prepared. One day there is one situation, another day another situation. One day one works, another day one can make a small mistake which may make one lose all the results of this work. The next day again one may work. One is changing all the time, so up to a certain definite stage it is impossible to say.

Q. At what stage is it that man cannot lose anything?

A. It is so far that it is useless to discuss it. We can lose everything. But even this ability not to lose comes step by step. At a certain stage man cannot lose one thing, then, further on, he cannot lose another thing, and so on. It comes little by little.

Q. I want to know how to increase my valuation of the work?

A. It is impossible to answer this question, because only you can know how to increase your valuation of the work. You must think; you must compare ordinary ideas with these ideas; you must try to find in what sense these ideas help you. Everything we do in the work has the tendency to increase valuation, so try not to miss anything that is given, because all the ideas have this aim. Every principle will increase your valuation of the work, it cannot diminish it. But there can be no special method for this.

Q. I wonder if as much as one desires other things in life, so much it takes away from one's desire to work?

A. Not necessarily. There are many things we can have in life and yet work. IT is quite wrong to think they are always contradictory though they may be contradictory. One may desire such things in life as make work impossible in one or another way. So, one must learn to choose between desires, for some things are incompatible. It is formatory to divide things into 'things in life' and 'things in the work' and put everything together as you do. You must divide better, see better.

Q. Is there any means of distinguishing between important and unimportant things? My whole life is filled with worrying over the next thing I am going to do, and I lose sight of the general idea of the system.

A. Only experience can show that, and a sincere attitude. If you are sincere, or try to be sincere, and at the same time try to observe these things, after some time you will see that the difficulty of distinguishing becomes smaller and smaller, and you will see what is unimportant. One cannot describe what is important and what is not, because it is subjective; one moment one thing is important, another moment another. Again, personalities enter here: what is important for one personality may be unimportant for another.

One of the first things to remember is about different personalities in you and, particularly when you are in an emotional state, not to think 'I'. Personalities based on likes and dislikes are all wrong; one must always start with the personality based on magnetic Centre. Then you can see other personalities, whether they contradict it or not. This idea of different personalities, the idea that you are not one, that you are many, must always be connected with self-remembering.

Q. I have never been able to get any evidence that anybody has achieved self-remembering.

A. You will not see the evidence. If all other people were able to remember themselves and you were not, it would not help you.

Q. Yes it would because they would have more information.

A. For themselves, not for you. You must prove it to yourself. No one can prove it for you.

Q. Because we work on ourselves, it does not mean that we shall gain higher consciousness, does it?

A. No, it may take a very long time. We want to acquire control of higher states of consciousness, but before that the system speaks of acquiring control over ordinary faculties, over thoughts, over emotions, and in acquiring this control we must eliminate certain things and create the possibility of self-remembering. So first we must acquire control over simple, ordinary things. Only then can we expect more. In this system there are gradual steps, one cannot jump.

Q. I find that I am prevented from thinking practically about the ideas of the system by a destructive attitude which starts by trying to find difficulties and objections. What is the best method of weakening this attitude?

A. By studying. As a matter of fact, this is interesting as an observation, because many people, not necessarily only those in the work, live only on objections; they only think themselves clever when they find an objection to something. When they do not find an objection, they do not feel themselves to be working, or thinking, or anything.

I notice from the questions people ask that they do not understand how new things come. The difficulty is that we are too accustomed to think in absolutes, all, or nothing. But it is necessary to understand that everything new comes first in flashes. It comes and then disappears, comes again, and disappears again. Only, after a certain time these flashes become longer and then still longer.

Q. By what means can we prolong these flashes?

A. By repeating the causes that produced them. I do not want to give an example, because it will lead to imagination. All I will say is that, for instance, by certain efforts of self-remembering one can see things that one cannot see now. Our eyes are not as limited as we think; there are many things they can see but do not notice.

Q. What are our greatest difficulties?

A. Absence of understanding and slowness of understanding because understanding generally comes about two years behind time. Another principle I have already spoken about, and which must be remembered is that work does not wait, it does not remain the same. One year has certain requirements, the next year something else is required, and so it goes on. And generally, it happens that people are ready for the requirements of two years ago. People who wish to continue must raise their standard; and this must not be done at my suggestion: you must think for yourselves in what sense and in what form the standard should be raised. You must think about details things which, to begin with, were only advised, must now become rules for you (but not in the sense of 'school-rules', using the word 'school' in its ordinary meaning). The necessity must be understood. We have come to the stage when we must be serious, and this means self-limitation, limiting false personality. Freedom of 'I' depends on limiting false personality; both cannot be free together, one or another must be sacrificed.

* * *

CHAPTER XIII

Different categories of human actions—Right and wrong use of triads— Study of human activities—Remembering the starting-point— Inner separation—learning to see false personality—Masks—Buffers and weaknesses—Study of methods—Alarms—Impossibility of studying the system from an utilitarian point of view—Philosophical, theoretical and practical language—Three degrees of school—Right thinking—Long and short thoughts—Role of intellect—Different values—Right and wrong curiosity—Critical attitude—Influencing others—Story of the sly man and the devil.

I want to give you some new material to think about. DO you remember the starting point when the idea of triads was explained? It was said that every action, every manifestation is the result of the conjunction of three forces. This is the principle, and we must now try to understand how to begin to study it. In the study of triads and three forces one must be very careful and slow, using the principles given in the system and trying to apply and enlarge them when it is possible. One should particularly avoid hurry and invention.

The first point in understanding the meaning of triads is to remember that manifestations of energy, any kind of action, in the world, in man's activity, inside the human machine or in external events always consists of triads. We spoke of six different triads comprehensible to the human mind, each representing a different combination of forces. In order to limit the question, not to make it too complicated in the beginning, we will consider only human activity. But here we come to a difficulty. We have never thought of activity itself being different. We know the difference between wood and metal, for instance, and we will not mix them. But we do not understand that one action can be as different from another as two different objects. For us, in ordinary thinking, actions are the same, only one starts with one aim and has one result and another starts with another aim and has a different result. We think only about motives, aims, and results, but not of actions themselves.

Q. Is then motive less important than we think?

A. It does not determine the action. You may have one kind of aim, but your action may be of a different kind. This happens very often. People start doing something with a certain aim in view, but their actions are such that not even by accident can this aim be ever attained. It is necessary to co-ordinate aim with action, otherwise you will never attain what you want.

This is what we must understand in relation to our actions, and we must try to find different categories of actions. When we begin to look at human activity from this point of view, remembering that there are different kinds of actions, independently of results, intentions, emotions, material and so on, we will begin to see it. It is not the capacity to see that is lacking, but knowledge of this principle, which is new to us.

We cannot begin at once to look for all the six different triads which can be found in human activity, for they will become mixed in our minds. We must find standards for two, three or four kinds, as much as we can see. Look at your own actions and at those of the people around you and you will see certain differences. It is good material for thinking. All the absurdities of life depend on the fact that people do not understand that certain things can be done with only one kind of triad. They use a wrong triad, a wrong kind of action, and are surprised that the results are not what they wanted. For instance, it is no good trying to teach by beating, or trying to persuade with machine-guns. Find your own and better examples of the wrong use of triads and you will see that certain results can be obtained only by an appropriate action. Observe yourself and life in general; if you turn this study on yourself, you will see, for instance, that if you wish to know or change something in yourself and if you approach this problem in a formatory way, you will never get anything. Formatory thinking is an example of an action that does not lead to understanding.

Q. Can you give an example of different human activities?

A. Take two simple examples in order to understand the idea. To build a house, effort is needed at every moment, every single brick must be put into place with a certain effort; no triad passes into another triad without effort. At last, the house is built and furnished. Then, if you want to burn it, you just strike a match and put it to something inflammable, and the house is burnt. If you go deeper into it, you will see that these are two different activities. You cannot build a house by the same activity as you burn it. In the second case one triad passes into another without any effort, automatically, after the first initial effort of striking a match.

Examples of the third kind of triad, in our experience, can be found only in conscious work, not identified work, or in some activity that has a peculiar quality of its own that cannot be imitated by others, such as artistic creation. Efforts at self-remembering and not identifying belong to this category. If you think about it, you will understand that in order to paint a good picture, for instance, one must use a different triad from the one used in building a house or the one used for burning a house; something else is needed.

Another triad may be called invention, discovery, craft. If you think about these four different activities, they will give you material for observing and comparing. Try to see why and in what they are different.

Q. I do not see the distinction between craft and building a house.

A. In one case only energy, only effort is necessary; in the other something more is needed, some knowledge or capacity for invention.

Q. Did you put efforts at self-remembering with art?

A. Yes, it is the same triad. Simple, blind effort, as in physical work, will not help in self-remembering. Neither will effort in the sense of invention, adaptation, help.

Q. I find it difficult to think of analogies to these activities.

A. Naturally, because you are not accustomed to think in this way. It is quite a new way of thinking. You are trying to think in the ordinary, logical, formatory way, and this is not sufficient. It is necessary to think not about words, but about facts. If you find four different kinds, in what do they differ? They differ in the form of effort.

Q. Is formatory activity destructive?

A. It is not destructive by itself, only deficient. But activities that begin with negative emotion are always destructive, they can be nothing else. Very often people do not realize this.

Q. I do not see how I can ever be sure into which category to place an activity?

A. You know enough to start. For every result there is a certain method. Different methods have different results. If you have a block of wood, you have to deal with it in a different way from dealing with a sick man. It does not matter about placing them in different categories. Example is the beginning of the whole thing. We try to pretend that things are more difficult than they are, but in reality, we know all about it. We know that murder is one activity, and writing poetry is a different activity. We cannot murder successfully with the kind of energy used for writing poetry.

Q. Are there also different types of thinking parallel to different types of activity?

A. Yes, certainly. Every kind of activity has its own way of thinking, although we are not aware of it. But what happens is that people act in one way and think in another. Sometimes the two coincide, but often they are in a wrong relation to one another.

Q. But is not action the result of thought? Does not right thought always mean right action?

A. No, not at all. One can think rightly and act wrongly. Understanding is one thing; will and purpose, effort and decision are another: they are two different degrees of the thing. It may be said that right thinking is a step towards right action, but it does not yet mean that the action is right.

Q. How can one set about using the right triad?

A. At moments of effort, or soon after, you may realize that it is a wrong effort, that you cannot get what you want with it. For every definite aim there is a corresponding effort. If you catch yourself using a wrong effort, it means it is a wrong triad. You may not be able to use the right triad, but you can stop using a wrong one.

What is new about this idea of activities is that they are different *in themselves*. For us action is action. At present it is enough to understand that the results of actions we see in life particularly if we do not like them or find fault with them are often due to wrong triads used to attain a given aim. If we understand this, we will understand that by a given activity we are bound to arrive only where we do arrive and nowhere else. To arrive at some other place, we should use a different activity. But at present we cannot choose because we do not know.

Q. Can one learn what actions to use?

A. Yes, certainly. You can learn from work. Schoolwork can be done in only one way. So, you try one way, another way, a third way and, sooner or later, you come to the right way. In ordinary conditions you cannot see the results of your actions, there are too many possibilities of self-deception; but in schoolwork you cannot deceive yourself. Either you get something, or you don't, and you can get something only in one way. There are other methods of learning about different kinds of action, by intellectual understanding, but we will wait for that. I should like you first to understand the general principle better.

You see, effort, aim, motive, all enter into the word 'action' and the idea of action, so actions are connected with motive but not in the way you think.

A certain kind of result can only be obtained by an appropriate action; at the same time motive also determines action. Motive is sometimes important, but with the best possible motives one can do the worst possible things, because we use a wrong effort, and a wrong effort will produce a wrong result. Suppose you want to build something and use the kind of effort that can be used only for destruction; then, instead of building, you will only destroy things, with the best intentions.

I have given you some examples, try to find parallels. Try to think, for instance, that neither the action that builds a house nor the action that bums it can paint a picture; at the same time the action by which you paint a picture is not necessary for building a house, a much simpler effort is required for that. Only a few people can paint good pictures, but everybody can take part in building a house. Then the same effort which is necessary for building a house is not enough to invent, say, a new kind of electric bell. And the action by which you invent an electric bell will not produce a good picture. Different kinds of action mean different triads, but at present it is better to leave triads and not to think which action means which triad, for it will only make you lose the meaning of the idea. You must only try to see the differences. From ignorance or impatience people often use wrong triads and explain their failure by bad luck, or by the devil, or by accident.

Q. When you carry out a certain action, should you try to think how that particular action compares with the examples you mentioned?

A. We should think by emotional understanding whether the action corresponds to our aim. Then, partly by mind, partly emotionally, we can realize whether the way we are going on can or cannot lead to the desired result. Sometimes we can feel this. Then we can either stop it or try to do it in another way. For instance, you are talking to somebody, trying to persuade this person that you are right about something, and he is wrong. The more you argue, the more he is convinced that he is right. Stop, and you may suddenly see that this person understands you. This happens very often. The more you argue, the more difficult it is for him to understand. Or you may even pretend to agree with him and in that way make him understand what you want. This is only an example, but you can find many examples yourself.

Q. I suppose in a case like that we should be capable of knowing whether to argue or agree?

A. If you do not identify you will see. Arguing is one way to persuade, agreeing is another. Generally, what prevents us from seeing what method to use is identifying. It is a question of approach. Some approaches are right, and others are wrong. If you go on observing, you will see.

Q. As regards the law of three, can one observe it in daily life?

A. Yes, in self-study you can, but with patience. You will see that the system always plays the part of the third force between desire to change and inertia. If we have a sufficient supply of the third force, we are successful. In the work the first force is desire to learn and decision to work, the second is resistance. The more we work, the more resistance grows. Only with the help of the system can we conquer resistance. It is a question of consciousness and will.

Well, try to talk about something else. We cannot hurry with this question of different actions. It is actually beyond our possibilities of understanding at present, but if we go slowly, we may get something out of it. Almost every idea in the system is a test. If one can pass one test, one can go further.

Please ask any questions you like, and I will try to answer them. Many things get forgotten and become dull because we forget the starting point. But the moment we connect things with the beginning, we see why we came, where we are going and what we want to get. We realize then what we have got from the system and see that we cannot expect more because the material we have is not sufficiently digested. We must always remember the starting point, remember that it is connected not simply with words but with search for the miraculous. The system would have no meaning if there were no search for the miraculous.

For instance, I am surprised that you do not ask more questions about separation between 'I' and (for me) 'Ouspensky', because there must be many things that are not clear for you yet. In speaking, in writing, in thinking about the work or the people in the work one must always ask oneself 'Who is speaking?' 'Who is writing?' 'Who is thinking?' If you do that, then, after a little time you will be able to distinguish who is speaking and will begin to recognize the different voices. You must know your false personality and find its features, its faces, manifestations, and voices. You must know what it consists of. Sometimes you can actually hear when false personality speaks. It is not much use going on without that, for you will only go on turning round and round in the same circle and always returning to the same spot. When you can be sure that it is really 'you', you can speak. You must already know and mistrust your false personality.

Q. If we do this, will it increase our progress in the work?

A. Nothing can be guaranteed. It should be important to do that without a question of future reward because the idea of separation is sufficiently important in itself.

Q. How can I put more pressure into my work to wake up my desire to fight false personality?

A. Catch a moment when your false personality wants to do something or does not want to do something and stop her. When you find a conflict between you and her, it will depend on you how you will act. If she starts fighting, this creates an emotional storm. If there is no fight, emotions are asleep. All things come through friction, friction between the place where 'I' can grow and false personality. Work on oneself begins from the moment one feels this division between what one trusts in oneself and what one cannot trust. What one can trust is entirely created by work. Before, it was just an empty place, but if one begins to work, something begins to solidify. But I repeat, one can know it better and trust it more only if one knows one's false personality, otherwise false personality will mix with it and pretend to be real 'I', or the beginning of real 'I'.

Q. Is false personality a kind of mask?

A. People wear one or another kind of mask and believe that they are exactly like this mask when in reality they are quite different. Each of us has several masks, not one. Observe your own masks and other people's masks. Try to realize that in different circumstances you have different masks and notice how you change them, how you prepare them and so on. Everybody has masks but begin with your own. We never study masks, so we must study them; it is very useful. Very often we begin to acquire masks at a very early age; even as schoolchildren we wear one mask with one teacher and another mask with another teacher.

Q. Is it a kind of self-protection, or is it imitation?

A. It is a kind of self-protection, and yet not only that. Sometimes, as you say, it has to do with imitation. You can see fifty or sometimes five hundred people wearing the same mask.

Q. If you took off the mask, what would you find underneath?

A. It is not so easy. You will find that behind this mask there is another mask. Or, if you do not work, it cannot be taken off, it grows to the face. But if you work, this mask is not necessary at all and, without it, life becomes much easier, there is less lying.

Q. Isn't a mask sometimes an ideal which one lives up to? Sometimes it makes you appear better than you really are.

A. Sometimes better. That is why I said it is not only a protection. You see, we want to know ourselves. When we find something in ourselves that we do not know, we have to study it. We think we know ourselves, and now we find that all we know is masks, and that masks change. What they are, how they come, what their purpose is, that is another question. We have to study masks themselves, not the theory of masks. We always try to escape into theories, theories are safe.

Q. Is it possible to see false personality as a whole?

A. It is possible, but not at once. It is necessary to work, to study it in yourself and in other people, then, little by little, you will see it as a whole, but for a long time you will see it only from one side or another side. Even that is better than nothing. But you must realize and never forget that it is there. That is the first aim of schools. If false personality remains on top, you cannot have anything, it will take everything to itself.

Q. About different voices, I notice that my voice changes with different emotions and different people.

A. Who has ears to hear can hear many changes of voice. Every Centre, every part of Centre, every part of a part of Centre has a different voice. But few people have ears to hear them. For those who can hear it is easy to distinguish many things. For instance, if you speak the truth, it is one voice, if you lie it is another voice, if you base things on imagination, yet another. It is quite unmistakable.

Q. Do you mean the intonation?

A. Yes, and also the actual sound of the voice. If you train yourself to listen, the emotional Centre can hear the difference.

Q. You spoke about the possibility of a wrong separation. What did you mean by that?

A. Suppose I call everything I like 'I' and everything I dislike 'Ouspensky', it would be a wrong separation. The 'I' from which I observe is a point, it has no material existence yet, it is only the embryo from which 'I' can grow It I give it material existence, it would be wrong.

Q Should not some weight be given to it?

A. Yes, but only in relation to the work Who remembers the aim, who wants to work is 'I'; the rest is 'Ouspensky'.

Q I feel I have nothing in me I can trust. If I get a moment of understanding, false personality seems to take it and the part of me that understood is gone What can I trust?

A. This feeling that one cannot trust oneself comes at different moments in the work as a delusion, as an excuse, or it comes in the real form. But this is later on, at present it is realization of mechanicalness. For work, a certain time and a certain persistence are necessary. Now you must do what you can, with time you will be able to measure the results of your work

Q. Is vanity an essential of false personality?

A It is one of the features of false personality in one or another sense. In some people it may be the chief feature, and then it is very obvious and visible, but very often these features are behind other things and do not show themselves.

Q. If work against false personality is a process, does it mean that one can go up and down?

A Yes, and you must understand in yourself the power and magnitude of false personality, then you will understand that very often people have nothing else, or even if they have some possibility, it is quite outweighed by false personality. False personality decides everything. In ordinary life false personality controls every moment, except perhaps moments when one reads or thinks of something. But when one works and magnetic Centre begins to grow, sometimes it happens that false personality may disappear for ten or fifteen minutes and give magnetic Centre a chance to manifest itself. That is how false personality disappears. It does not entirely disappear; it just goes away for a time This is what we must try to do, to make it disappear for a time.

Q. Is it only by separation that one can work on identification?

A. Only. Without realizing the difference between 'I' and false personality all efforts only strengthen the weaker side. As I said, this separation is the basis of all work on oneself. Unless this idea is understood, nothing can be attained, in everything one must start from that. This is the real difference between people in the work and not in the work. People who are not in the work think that they are what they are. People in the work already understand that they are not what they seem to be. This separation must pass through many phases, but it must begin.

Q. When I see what a balloon of false personality I am, is the thing to do to try and see how I got that way?

A. You have to study yourself. Only one thing can help and change your position and that is getting to know yourself better. This implies many things. There are different degrees and depths of realization and understanding. When one understands sufficiently one will do something, one will not be able to sit and let things go on by themselves. Try to make your question more concrete: what is it you have been trying to do and what do you find you cannot? Then we can discuss it. Maybe you begin from the wrong thing, in a wrong way.

Q. Can one find responsibility in oneself?

A. Certainly. But in relation to what? You begin certain work; you have a responsibility towards this work at least you should have. But who? If you call everything 'I', you must know by now that there are many 'I's; some have responsibility, others have no responsibility, because they have nothing to do with this work. It is only a question of observation to see that.

Q. I see that it all comes back to the question of how to understand more.

A. I am trying to explain, first, how you should study yourself. You must find your particular obstacle which keeps you from understanding. When you find it, you must struggle with it? It needs time, it cannot be found at once, although in some cases it is so clear that one can see it almost immediately. But in other cases, it is necessary to work before one can see it.

Q. Will group work help in this?

A. You must not put too many hopes in group work, because, although it is useful for showing many things, experimenting, testing and so on, in group work one is in an artificial atmosphere, artificial circumstances. The moment one comes out of a group, one is in natural circumstances. So, group work may show the way, but work must be in ordinary circumstances. What is the use if you are very good in a group, and become identified and a machine the moment you walk out of the group? It will be quite useless.

Q. If someone in a school here has a very bad feature, such as bad temper, is special assistance given to overcome it?

A. Only when one has studied and used all the general methods does one come to special characteristics. It is necessary to place this feature, to find the cause. Causes may be different. Some bad feature may be so strong that it may be the last to go, one cannot tell beforehand. If you begin to struggle with obstacles in the wrong order, you will get no results. At the same time, it is necessary to have it in view.

Q. If it is a negative emotion and you observe and resist it, does it change?

A. It depends on the emotion. In most cases it is simply delayed. We do not know how to resist. There is a special key for every emotion. We must find the master key, and for this it is necessary first to know the machine.

Q. If one feels depressed or irritated, what steps can one take against it?

A. First one must try to remember oneself and, secondly, to remember that what is depressed is not oneself but one's imaginary picture of oneself.

Man's progress begins from the moment he realizes that what he is one thing and his imaginary picture of himself is another thing. When he sees that he is smaller, weaker than he thought, that he is all sham, he is on the way to development. He has practically nothing, but enough to develop.

Q. Since I have no permanent 'I', if I try not to identify with one 'I', do I identify with another?

A. You must understand that you were given certain ideas in the same way as Mr. Gurdjieff explained them, that is, gradually, first giving one aspect of an idea and then another. Many things are explained first in an elementary way, and then more details are added. When we speak of a man who is not in the work, we say he has no 'I'. If a man starts to study and make efforts, this already means a certain state; he has magnetic Centre, and magnetic Centre is the beginning of 'I'. So, he no longer has the right to say that he has no 'I'. Naturally, he cannot say that he has a complete and permanent 'I', but he must already have a line of action, and this must mean an 'I'. It is not yet fully conscious, but it grows.

Q. What are the kind of things to look for in trying to separate false personality from the rest of oneself?

A. It is necessary to understand the features of false personality, what makes it up. You may be able to see it in the glimpses you remember of the age to which you can attribute the beginning of false personality.

There are two things that are permanent in us buffers and weaknesses or features of false personality. Everyone has one, two or three particular weaknesses, and everybody has certain buffers that are especially important, for they enter into all his decisions and his understanding of things. This is all that is permanent in us, and it is lucky for us that there is nothing more permanent, because these things can be changed. Buffers are artificial, they are not organic, they are chiefly acquired by imitation. Children begin to imitate grown-ups and create buffers, and some others are unwittingly created by education. Features or weaknesses can sometimes be found out, and if one knows a feature and keeps it in mind, one may find certain moments when one can act not from this feature. Everybody has many features but two or three are particularly important because they enter into every subjectively important situation in one's life; everything passes through them, all perceptions, and all reactions. It is very difficult to realize what this means because we are so accustomed to it that we do not notice it; we are too much in those features, we have not got enough perspective.

Q. Must the chief feature necessarily be bad?

A. It is chief weakness; unfortunately, we cannot think that our chief feature is strength, because we have no strength.

Q. How can it be weakness if there is no not-weakness?

A. It means mechanicalness. We are mechanical in all things, but in one or two things we are particularly mechanical and particularly blind; that is why they are chief weaknesses, for we cannot see them. Other things, that are not weaknesses, we can see.

Q. What would you call a weakness? Do you judge by ethical standards?

A. No. As I said, a weakness is a thing in which you are most mechanical. Naturally, things concerning which you are absolutely helpless, where you are most asleep, most blind are bound to be your chief weaknesses, because there are degrees in everything. If there were no degrees in our qualities and manifestations it would be very difficult to study. We can study ourselves only because of these degrees. Even features are not always the same; sometimes they are more definitely expressed, and sometimes, in rare cases, they show themselves to us a little, and only in that way can they be found. But features are difficult to see in oneself. You will realize better what being more mechanical and less mechanical means if we take another example, say illness. If we are ill, we become at once more mechanical; we cannot resist the external world and things in it even as much as we resist them ordinarily.

Q. You say we have nothing but weaknesses. Surely desire to be free is not a weakness.

A. There can be one or another kind of desire. Suppose one realizes one's weakness and wishes to get rid of it, and at the same time one does not wish to learn the methods of getting rid of this weakness. This would be a second weakness, helping and protecting the first weakness.

Q. But if one makes constant efforts?

A. Again, that will belong to the other side of you, to what I call 'you'. This 'you' is not a power or a force, it is merely a combination of certain desires, desires to get rid of something. If you realize that something is wrong, and you formulate a desire to get rid of it, then if you can keep your mind on it sufficiently long, it becomes a certain plan of action; and if this line of action is sufficiently prolonged it can attain results. Only, it is necessary to add again that several different lines of action are needed to attain results, not just one line. We have to work at the same time on one thing and another thing and a third thing. If we work on one line, we will get nowhere.

Q. I did not understand it when you said once that we cannot change anything, but we must act differently.

A. Try to think, while we still remain as we are, we have to act differently. You cannot change at once, change is slow. But you have many things to do, and if you do them in a wrong way you will never change. Being a machine is not an excuse, although people use it: 'I am a machine, I cannot change anything', and so they do everything as before. Before you came to the work you explained everything by accident. Now you come to the conclusion that tomorrow will be the same as today unless you change. You cannot change, but you have to 'do'. So, it is necessary to understand on what lines, you must do things differently. Everybody has two or three particular things where he is accustomed to act in a certain way and where he must try to act differently. These things are not the same for different people. You remember what I said about knowledge and being? The idea is to change being at exactly that point which is difficult for every person. One person must understand certain features and avoid them, another must understand what is lacking in him and try to acquire it and so on. That is why school is necessary. We need constant reminding about many things.

Q. How can I make better use of moments when I feel the miraculous-ness of the system?

A. Make more regular efforts, not occasional efforts. You know why I always speak about this? Because it is self-deception to think that one can awake without special and long work. We must realize how difficult it is. Thinking, not thinking, talking, not talking, feeling, not feeling, everything keeps us asleep. Now we speak theoretically about it, but work cannot be theoretical. The fact that one is asleep must become a permanent realization, one must feel it emotionally. But by itself this realization will not make one awake: special efforts are necessary to wake oneself up for a moment.

Q. Is it not necessary to be fairly awake to formulate one's aim?

A. This is another thing. Realizing and understanding are possible in a kind of half sleep; just as one can find one's way home, so we can find the way to our aim. Awakening is a long process.

Q. Is hesitation between two different aims a sign of sleep?

A. Partly of sleep and partly of incomplete understanding. When one knows what is most important, one has no hesitation.

What we must think about now is methods how to awake, which forms of work are best. But what is the use speaking about methods to awake if one does not fully realize the fact of sleep. What do you think about it, what do you feel about the state in which you are, have you any observations? This is very important, because there are many things about which we can speak seriously only if we have no doubts about this point. So, it is necessary to think about this state and its different effects and consequences. If you take one day of your life and try to go over it, you will see that there are many things you would not have done if you were not asleep, because they were unnecessary or wrong, or that you did many other things rather than one particular thing, because for that particular thing it was necessary to be awake. All these conversations, systems, theories can help only if, together with this, you work on yourselves.

Q. One realizes the danger of being asleep, but has one something to compensate for the increasing fear of unpleasantness brought by awakening?

A. If I am asleep and do not know it, the dangers are there just the same, so if

I begin to see the dangers it is better than not seeing them, because then I can avoid them.

Q. I find that when I discover a method to make me remember myself, this works for a few times and then wears off.

A. You must always change those methods; they do not work for long; it is part of our state. Take it as a fact; there is no need to analyze it. The more new and unexpected things are, the better they will work. This is connected with the fundamental principle of all mental and physical life. We observe, in the ordinary sense, only changes in our associations. We do not feel permanent associations; we notice only changes. So, when you are accustomed to them, you have to make some kind of alarm; then you get accustomed to this alarm, and it does not work anymore. If you make your alarm-clock ring permanently, you will notice it only when it stops ringing.

Q. Does the realization of being asleep create its own force for awakening?

A. If one realizes one is asleep, one must study means and methods to awake, but it must cease to be a word; it must become a fact based on observation. Only then is it possible to speak with more precision and more practically about it. When one realizes one is asleep, at that moment one is already half-awake, but it is not long enough; the next moment something begins to turn in one's head and one gets carried away into sleep again. This is why one cannot awake by oneself, why elaborate methods are necessary, one must be shaken and shaken.

Q. And who is to do the shaking?

A. This is the question.

A certain number of people who want to awake must agree among themselves that when one of them is asleep someone else may be awake and will do the shaking. But making such an agreement needs sincerity; those people must really want to awake and must not get angry or offended when they get shaken.

Q. What kind of shaking do you mean?

A. Ordinary shaking. One finds one way, another, another. Alarms are also necessary, but it is even more necessary to remember to change them as often as possible. If one feels comfortable, one is asleep, but if one puts oneself in an uncomfortable position, it helps one to awake. Pleasant things only help sleep.

Q. Can one find one's own alarms?

A. One can try, but it is necessary to have constant change and variation and choose things that will awake one. Otherwise, we can awake for a second, decide to keep awake and imagine we are awake when we are really doing all this in a dream, with dream alarms. This is why constant control is necessary, and constant verification as to whether they really awake one or simply create new dreams, or whether one just does not hear them anymore. There is no reason to take too big a thing; but if one tries to take some small habit and check it, that may serve as an alarm, but only for about a week. Next week another will have to be found, perhaps something in connection with the people one lives with or something like that. One must find many alarms.

Q. I find I am more aware of myself when alone, so I try to see as few people as possible.

A. No, no, you must try to remember yourself in all conditions. If you remember yourself when alone, you will forget yourself when you are with people, and if you remember yourself among people, you will forget yourself when alone. If you limit yourself to one set of circumstances, you lose at once. The best time to try to remember yourself is when circumstances are most difficult, and the most difficult circumstances are not when you can choose to be alone or not alone but when you have no choice. And why are the most difficult circumstances the best? Because then self-remembering gives the best results. In easy circumstances, if you decide to be alone or not alone, you may get some results; but if you find yourself in a most difficult situation and still manage to remember yourself, the results will be quite incommensurable.

Q. Is there any action one could take, besides self-remembering, to discourage inner considering?

A. Do that, and that will show you. It is all the same thing: if you consider, you cannot remember yourself. If you want to stop considering you must remember yourself; without remembering yourself, you cannot stop considering.

Q. Does self-remembering help one to get over such a thing as poor health?

A. I do not know about that. This is a doctor's business, not ours. We are told that it produces certain chemical effects, but not at once. We can study it only psychologically; we do not know about the chemistry, but we can say that we will feel different. Generally speaking, I can say that every time one tries to study the system from a utilitarian point of view, it fails. The system is not made for that. In some cases, self-remembering can produce a physical result one does not expect, but if one tries to work for this result, it will not happen.

Q. But isn't physical health important?

A. Certainly one must try to be more or less healthy, so if one is ill, one must see a doctor about it. The question of health is important, but you cannot put it together with the question of consciousness. To use these ideas in the interests of health would be quite futile, though quite unexpectedly they may help.

Q. Does consciousness require directed attention and will?

A. All these things: attention, consciousness, unity, individuality, will, are different shades of the same thing. We divide them, but they are the same. We may have them all for short moments, but we cannot keep them. If you observe yourself for a sufficiently long time, you will find moments of practically everything. But only *moments*. Our aim is to increase these moments, to strengthen them, to fix them, as you fix a photograph.

Q. How should one do that?

A. All work leads in the same direction. Finding names for the things we do not possess will not help. It is necessary to do something about it.

Q. Do moments of attention depend on absence of distraction?

A. There is always distraction, only we should have control. If we rely on circumstances, work will be in emotional parts of centres, not in intellectual parts. If it is in intellectual parts, it needs directed attention. Our centres are there, fully developed, waiting to be used, but we do not use the higher parts of them.

Q. Does one have to sacrifice anything besides 'all nonsense' in order to attain higher states?

A. 'Nonsense' is perhaps a good word. But when you sacrifice it, it is not nonsense for you. Objectively it may be nonsense, but if you felt it to be nonsense there would be no sacrifice.

Q. There is a conflict in me, and though I know what I want it does not make any difference. I still do the thing that is bad for me.

A. This means that you only *know*. To be able to 'do' is different. Knowledge by itself does not give enough power to do what you want. You have to accumulate energy slowly, chiefly by struggle with imagination, with expression of negative emotions, with talking and so on. This will give you the possibility to do what is better for you.

Q. If you had a different attitude towards things, your emotions would be different, wouldn't they?

A. What different attitudes? And what things? How can I answer? There are millions of things in the world and millions of different attitudes. You see, this is a practical question; it cannot be asked in this language. Try to see how your question will sound to another person, because you know what you mean by different things and different attitudes, but I do not know.

Q. I am asking in connection with right attitudes as a weapon against negative emotions. Does an attitude mean accepting or rejecting?

A. It is not a question of rejecting, it is a question of understanding. When I speak about right and wrong attitudes in this connection, I mean attitudes to negative emotions in general, and negative emotions in general are a subject for conversations about the working of the machine. When you speak about your own observation or your personal work, you must describe which negative emotion you mean jealousy, fear, anger and so on. There can be no generalization, because negative emotions are very different, and attitudes are different. About one you can say one thing and about another, another thing If we take negative emotions all together, they have a certain common quality, but when you speak about your own observations you must take things on a different scale, not speak of attitudes, negative emotions, imagination, identification, as though they were abstract things ten thousand miles away from you It is possible to use these terms for the explanation of general features, but you cannot use them when you talk about your own work. You have a certain personal work to do. You come with a certain aim, you want to get something, and something inside hinders you and yet you speak about attitudes, negative emotions, considering and so on. Speak about real things These terms can be in a book, and you speak as though you were taking phrases from a book, You must understand that in our system or in any system for that matter, whether it is acknowledged or not, there are three different languages, or three ways of thinking philosophical, theoretical and practical When I say 'this is theoretical' or 'this is philosophy' in answer to a question, it means that the language is wrong You cannot ask something *in* a philosophical way and expect a practical answer. An abstract question cannot have a concrete answer.

You must understand that the difference in meaning between these words 'philosophical', 'theoretical' and 'practical' is quite contrary to the ordinary meaning attributed to them. The philosophical is the easiest approach, the theoretical is more difficult and more useful, and the practical is the most difficult and most useful of all. There can be philosophical knowledge very general ideas, there can be theoretical knowledge, when you calculate things, and there can be practical knowledge, when you can observe and make experiments In philosophical language you speak not so much about things as about possibilities, in other words, you do not speak about facts In theoretical language you speak about laws, and in practical language you speak about things on the same scale as yourself and everything around you, that is, about facts So it is really a difference of scale.

Things can be taken on these three scales, and many things change completely according to the scale on which they are taken they are one thing on the philosophical scale, quite different if taken on the theoretical scale, and on the practical scale quite different again. Try to find examples. Some things can be taken on all three scales, some only on two, and some on one Even speaking with oneself one must not mix these three scales, otherwise one will create more confusion than there is already and only understand less and less.

Q. Is an effort to self-remember practical?

A. It may be practical, it may be theoretical, and it may be philosophical.

Q. Objective consciousness seems to belong to the philosophical scale?

A. Quite the reverse: it is very practical. But if you mean for us, then, certainly, objective consciousness is a philosophical idea. At the same time the study of descriptions of glimpses of this state is possible. If one studies these descriptions and tries to find similarities, it can become theoretical.

Q. I should like to understand more about this division. I do not know what is practical.

A. It means what you can do in all senses. Only, 'doing' can be on one scale or another scale Doing is always more important than thinking or talking. So, if we take it that philosophical is thinking, theoretical talking and practical doing, the practical is more important.

Q What is philosophical thinking?

A. Thinking on a very large scale.

A thing may look very beautiful on the philosophical scale, the same thing taken on the theoretical scale may be a very narrow and stupid theory and, taken practically, it may be a crime.

When I first heard about the division into philosophical, theoretical, and practical, I was told that schools of knowledge which came from higher mind could be divided into three classes practical schools were the highest, then came theoretical and last philosophical schools. But ordinarily we understand by practical such things as gardening, making boots and so on by theoretical knowledge we understand mathematics, geology, etc., and by philosophical we understand what we usually want philosophy. But according to this system philosophical schools are merely preparatory schools.

Q When I first came to lectures, I thought the word 'school' meant a school of thought, but now it seems to be just like the school I was in when I was a boy.

A. Exactly. It is not a question of thought; it is a question of doing

Q. Isn't it in a way a school of thought too, since doing must come from thinking?

A. Certainly there must be a certain amount of thinking, for without thinking we can do nothing, but thinking is only an auxiliary process, it is not the aim in a school of thought it is sufficient to think about freedom, whereas we want to be free, we are not satisfied with merely thinking about it.

Q. Would this school be of all three kinds or only one?

A. I think it is better to say all three It has three sides Also, some people take the system philosophically, others theoretically and yet others practically You must not forget that the same thing can be taken in different ways

Q Is, then, this system connected with philosophy?

A. It cannot be quite free from it in some ways it is a legitimate form of thinking. But in thinking of man's development, of man's progress, it is better to look for psychological landmarks and not for philosophical ones.

Psychological landmarks are facts, the others may be imagination. Even if a man's intellect is dealing with big philosophical problems, his being may be on quite a low level. But if a man is more conscious, then all his sides can develop.

Q. Who assesses psychological values?

A. There are definite objective signs by which one can judge, definite inner standards. At a certain point they may become objective. As I said, we do not look for philosophical landmarks, we want psychological landmarks. It is very important to understand this. Philosophical conclusions may be just words, rhetoric, but about psychological landmarks there can be no mistake for oneself.

Q. Is it lazy to use philosophical thinking?

A. Not necessarily. Sometimes there are things you can take only philosophically, others only philosophically and theoretically. There are things to which we have no practical approach and for which we must find analogies. So sometimes it is quite right. But there are things which you can take only practically, for only then can you value them.

Q. You spoke of 'thinking in new categories'. This seems to me as impossible as being able to 'do'.

A. Quite right. At the same time, when you begin to understand different categories, you will be able to think, at least sometimes, in a different way. But this is not the whole description of right thinking. Very often you do not think in right categories because you do not have enough knowledge. Even in our state we can think better or worse.

Q. When I try to think in a new way, I do not know where to start.

A. You have plenty of material this system. Try to reconstruct it in your mind, to imagine that you are explaining to somebody the ideas of this system. Try to reconstruct what this system says about man and the universe. If you do not remember something, ask other people. This is a good exercise. Either you turn your thoughts and control them, or they turn by themselves. If they turn by themselves, you cannot expect positive results. In order that they should give results you have to drive them.

Q. Shall I have to find new words for all system words and ideas when I imagine that I am explaining the system to people outside?

A. You cannot invent new words. There is a definite rule that when you speak of the system you must speak using exactly the same language in which you learnt this system and refer to the origin. There will never by any necessity for you to disguise it.

Q. Is it that we cannot think differently until we remove our old ways of thinking completely?

A. No, you cannot wait for this; you have to do so now. One example of thinking in new categories is that thinking must be intentional. We do not realize that whether something is intentional or unintentional changes everything.

Q. If you try to arrest the mechanical process of thinking and to think in a new way, does not the other way of thinking tend to become mechanical too?

A. Yes, everything has a tendency to become mechanical, so when you are trying to do something in a new way you must watch not only what you intend to do but many other things. Identification must not enter into it, imagination must not enter; you must learn to control associations and have only those you need, rather than letting them control you.

Q. But is there any other kind of thinking besides associative?

A. There is controlled thinking. You can limit your thinking to a certain definite point or aim. Associative thinking is accidental. We can go on thinking by old associations without any attempt to change them, or we can try new associations by introducing new points of view.

Q. About right thinking; when I try to think of something connected with the system, it peters out.

A. For right thinking it is not sufficient just to think about the system, it *is the way* you think that is important. You can think rightly or wrongly about the system or about something that has no relation to the system. So, it is not a question of the subject but of the method of thinking. And the method cannot be described. You must find examples of wrong thinking and examples of right thinking, and then compare them. We must learn to control our mind; we must understand formatory and defective thinking and be able to use our whole brain instead of only a small part. The only thing that can help in this is to remember oneself.

You must try to find some personal connection, some personal interest in the question you want to think about, then that will grow and develop. By personal I mean what you thought before, questions about it which came to you by themselves and that you could not answer, or something like that. And when you find that now you can see more, that may give a push to other things.

Q. In thinking about some idea of the system it is difficult to keep a line of thought compared with the ordinary things that happen in one's head, the material is so limited.

A. No, the material is very big something else is limited. Either desire is limited, or effort is limited, but not the material.

Q. I should like to know the cause of the resistance to keeping out other thoughts that come creeping in.

A. There are two causes, the cause of resistance is one thing and the cause of the thoughts that come interrupting is another. The second shows our ordinary way of thinking, we can never keep a line because accidental associations come in.

Resistance is another thing; it is the result of a lack of skill, lack of knowing how to deal with it, lack of experience of intentional thinking on a certain line. This capacity must be educated.

I can tell you what is lacking in our thinking, but if you have no observations of your own about it, it will mean nothing to you. Each thought is too short; our thoughts should be much longer. When you have experience of short thoughts and long thoughts, you will see what I mean.

Q. I have been struck by the limitations of our thinking capacity. What do they depend on?

A. Only when you have examples of a better kind of thinking in yourself, using higher parts of centres, having more consciousness, will you see on what these limitations depend. We know our mind is limited, but we do not know in what it is limited. When you know these two ways of thinking and are able to compare them you will know where the difference lies and then it will be possible to speak about causes.

Q. Is the development of a man with a very good intellect bound to be quicker than that of another whose intellect is not so good?

A. Sometimes yes, sometimes no; not so much can be done by intellect as by balance of centres and development of consciousness, because even in the ordinary state man 1, 2 and 3 can be more awake or less awake, more conscious, or less conscious.

A man with a good intellect may be quite asleep, and then he may be too sure of his own intellectual achievement and too identified with it to start working. His intellect may stop him. This often happens. Often intellectual development prevents study because a man is too argumentative, demands definitions for everything, and so on. Development of intellect alone is not sufficient, very soon work on emotions becomes necessary.

Q. I noticed that people who have never thought often seem to find less difficulty with the work than others who have thought. Which is better?

A. Both are no good, one who does not think and one who thinks too much.

Q. Does the same thing apply to people who are considered brilliant in life?

A. People who are considered brilliant may be very different, so it is difficult to speak about them all in one category. They may be really brilliant, they may be just pretending to be brilliant, or other people may pretend that they are brilliant. But if you mean people who are very identified with their brilliance, then it may be very difficult for them, only not as a result of their brilliance but as a result of their identification. Sometimes an advantage in life means a disadvantage in work, for the better man 1, 2 or 3 one is, the more self-will and willfulness one has to conquer. The easiest and most advantageous from the point of view of the work is to be quite an ordinary man.

Q. Is it not essential to become successful in life? Or should one be unidentified with life activities, whatever the result?

A. Both are necessary. Success is not dangerous in itself, if only one does not identify with it. The aim is not success or failure, but non-identification. Success may help in many things.

Q. How big a part does intellect play in the system?

A. Intellect plays a very important part because we begin with it. It is the only Centre which obeys itself. But development of intellect can go only up to a certain limit. Possibilities lie in the emotional Centre.

Q. Have we anything to control our thoughts now?

A. If you have interests in the right direction, those interests control all other things to a certain extent. If we are not interested, we have no control.

Q. You said that in trying to think rightly about these ideas you need to use the intellectual part of the intellectual Centre. Can you do that by trying to control attention when you think?

A. No, it is a simultaneous action; you cannot divide it. The fact is that about certain things you can think only in the intellectual part, if you think rightly and formulate rightly what it is you want to think about. Then, certainly, you have to keep yourself on this idea without going into imagination. So, the function itself determines the place.

Q. I have come to the conclusion that I do not know how to think about what I want to think about. Is it because of buffers?

A. I think it is simply that we are not accustomed to think about these ideas, we do not think it is necessary to think about them. If we realize the necessity, then perhaps we will be able to. But buffers have nothing to do with it.

Q. I think that the general experience is that early contact with the system brings more destruction than construction.

A. From my point of view, the idea of construction and destruction is wrong. Nothing is destroyed, but if we imagine that we have something we do not have, then when we start working, we may see that we thought we had something but now find that we have not. This means that it is an illusion, and we have to sacrifice it. We can have real things or illusions. We lose nothing that we really possess; we only lose the idea that we possess something which we do not possess.

It often happens that people become disappointed in the work because, from the very beginning, they start choosing and take some things and not others. So, after some time they do not have the system but their own selection from it, and this won't work. Other people want to understand only intellectually and do not want to make experiments with themselves and observe, but without practical work it is impossible to move.

Q. Shall we be told when we can start practical work?

A. You have been doing some practical work from the very first. If you had done only theoretical work, it would mean you have done nothing. This work is practical from the first.

As I have often said, the first condition is that we must never forget what we want to get. People come to this from different sides. Some want to know. They realize there is a certain knowledge and that, maybe, there are somewhere people who know, and they want to get this knowledge. Other people realize their weaknesses and understand that if they can get rid of them things will be different. So, people come with different aims, and they must never forget the beginning. They can be reminded, but that will not help much if they themselves do not remember.

Q. I wish I could strengthen my aim. I go on reacting in the same way as before and seem to be as mechanical. I suppose it is necessary to try harder.

A. Trying hard will not help by itself; it must be based on understanding. It is more a question of valuation, general valuation, valuation of the ideas. About almost everything you can think in a new way, a better way than before. You can understand and connect together many things you could not put together or understand before you came. Only, unfortunately, you want to keep all the old ways of thinking and have the new at the same time, and so there is no room for the new.

Again, if you have some habits of negative emotion, you cannot remember yourself while you have them; so, in order to remember yourself, in order to work, you must have a little free time. It is not so much that there is no aim as that you do not want to sacrifice anything. You cannot keep everything you possess and have new things as well.

Q. Is it lack of unity in man that makes it so difficult to find the practical connection between the aim of the system *and* the aims of ordinary life?

A. There are no aims in ordinary life; that is where you make a mistake. In ordinary life one aim crosses another aims and destroys it or changes its nature, so that in the end there are no aims.

Q. You say that the man in the street has no aim. But when you get older you do not fly about so much, you become interested in one thing.

A. It is one-sided. There are many other sides of one's being and knowledge that this line does not touch at all. Some people can develop a certain oneness even in life, but these are exceptions. If, as you say, one becomes interested in one thing, only one group of 'I's develops this interest; others do not know about it; only a small minority is concerned. So, there are two questions here: the question of minority and majority and the fact that if a line of interest appears it does not touch many other things and occupies only a small part of one's being. The whole being never takes part in it.

I think that what was said before about this question of values in the work and in ordinary life must be understood better. In ordinary life there are so many imaginary values that it is useful to clarify a little. In life the best things have no meaning; people see what is small but miss what is big. In the work you have to do many different things first in order to feel that you are waking up. Then other things come; everything comes, for this is only the beginning.

Aim is necessary in the work, but it cannot be an arbitrary or invented aim. There can only be one aim to awake, and it can only come when you realize that you are asleep, otherwise there is no necessity for it. All other aims, however, one may formulate them, must be in line with that. Then, when one wants to awake, one begins to see obstacles, one sees what keeps one asleep; one finds a quantity of mechanical functions, talk, lying, negative emotions and so on, and one realizes that all life consists of mechanical functions that leave no time for awakening. One understands then the need to suppress them, or at least to make them less strong; then one may have time for awakening.

Q. My problem is, do I really want to awake?

A. What can I say? Suppose you come to a shop and ask: 'Do I want to buy something here or not?' It is the same in this case. So how can I answer? You must understand that at first you get only unpleasant things. *Maybe* (I only say maybe) the possibility to get something pleasant depends on the capacity to accept something very unpleasant; maybe this is the only chance. And if you agree to have something very unpleasant, you always get more than you bargained for. If you agree to half a pound of unpleasant things, you get twenty pounds. The great question is what is the coin in which we have to pay. Effort is not really currency, yet effort has to be exchanged for something else and something else again, until you get to something that can be currency. It is very complicated. But what frightened you?

Q. Suffering is the word in my mind. I do not think it is in me to face unpleasant things.

A. It is a matter of taste. What does 'unpleasant' mean? It means paying. I quite agree that it is better to get things for nothing, but such a method has not been invented yet. Either one understands this and says: 'I will pay, only I must know how'; or one doubts and says: 'I had better either not pay or pay to myself. Then nothing happens.

Q. At first, I was anxious to work. Now I find there is too much to be done and I feel it is hopeless.

A. Although it seems much in description, it all comes to the same thing. It needs time; it is an organic process. Things have been going wrong for many years, it is necessary to give them time to turn round.

Q. Sometimes I feel very frightened that I do not know what I am doing or what I want. I allow myself to get very negative.

A. First you must not allow; and second, when in a state of doubt, you must remember to try and bring up other 'I's which have a certain valuation. This is the only way to conquer doubts.

Q. There are times when I feel a great revulsion for this work and a longing to escape, because there is something in me which I do not want to give up. How can I struggle with it?

A. Either you have to escape or continue to hesitate until you become sure of one thing or another. You must not do anything while you hesitate; it is very important to remember that. Just as in the case of understanding you must choose only things which you understand better and think about them so, in relation to doing, you must choose things about which you are sure, and not spoil your life by things which you do not understand. If you think rightly, that is to say, if you collect and keep only the things you understand, and try to do things you understand, their number will increase. But if you fill your mind with things, you do not understand, you will never move. This is a very definite part of the system's method.

Many things we know very well but we continue to deceive ourselves, mainly about words. It is very difficult to understand the value of words. 'Poor in spirit' are those who do not believe in words and 'rich in spirit' are those who believe in words. Often people say, 'If I do this and that it will be beautiful'. They do not understand that it is impossible to do exactly as they wish that each thing will be a little different and, in the end, everything will be quite different. Then, when they see that it is different, they say, 'Yes, but the original idea was good'. It was not good. It only looked beautiful as an idea, but in realization it often becomes its own opposite. It will necessarily change because of friction. There are some ideas that can pass through triads and others that cannot, that can exist only in the form of one force, or half a force, or a quarter.

Q. I believe that the understanding we are seeking is attainable only by some. Is it not probable that many of us may get to a blank wall of elimination and no further?

A. Nothing can be guaranteed. But if one wants something and tries to work and does not show some particularly unpleasant feature very difficult to deal with, one has a chance. That is all I can say. One has exactly the same chance as everybody else. One person may have very good and beautiful features, and yet behind this have one small feature that makes work very difficult, more difficult perhaps than for somebody else who does not have such brilliant features.

Q. Is conscience what would help most to know oneself?

A. Yes, it is a necessary element; one has to pass through it. It is the most unpleasant thing in the world, because in the ordinary state we can hide things from ourselves. If we do not want to see something, we just shut our eyes and do not see it. But in the state of conscience our eyes will not shut.

Q. How can one bring the ideas of the system into daily life?

A. By studying yourself and studying the system. Everybody has many personal questions and problems, but at present the system stands apart. Little by little you will learn to connect it with more and more things and after some time ideas of the system will enter into everything.

Q. Is it then a waste of time to talk unnecessarily, to laugh and joke when one feels like it?

A. There is nothing wrong in it by itself. What is wrong is what increases mechanicalness. Passing time in chatting and laughing is one of the most mechanical things. It depends on what you want. If you decide to have a rest, it may really be a rest. But if you cannot stop it, if it gets hold of you, then it is wrong.

Q. I can observe what a great deal of energy I waste in vague imaginings, daydreams and worrying, but I am powerless to prevent this.

A. The whole system is a way of preventing this. But first you must study. You are dealing with a very complicated machine, and you must know it. By studying it one learns what must remain, what must disappear, what helps and what hinders, what one must remove, what one must encourage. People either do not realize that they can change, or if they realize it, they take it too easily. They think it is enough to realize, to decide, and one will change. But realization, by itself, will not produce a change; we have too many tendencies created in us. We must know how to struggle with them.

Q. I am constantly up against my past. The roots are far back.

A. Quite right. Only there is no direct method; we have to begin with today, we cannot change yesterday. Try to change today and this may produce a certain change to-morrow. This is everybody's state, a condition in which we have to start. But it is not an obstacle that cannot be overcome.

Q. I have been very negative lately about the conditions in which I found myself, and I feel I cannot see clearly what attitude I should take.

A. It is quite true that in certain conditions one identifies too much with something and loses the possibility to see the difference of things. Sometimes it is impossible to do anything, and sometimes it is possible to struggle. Besides, we have a tendency to magnify and exaggerate. The conditions may not be so bad. There are many points of view, and only you can decide what the case is really like.

Q. The difficulty is that I do not know what is right and what is wrong in ordinary life, and this acts as a screen or a whitewash over my actions.

A. We cannot say we do not know. We know, or at any rate we should know. Nobody can live without certain ideas of right and wrong. But when you come to the system and understand the basis of it, you see that right is connected with consciousness and wrong with mechanicalness. If people are a little conscious, little as they can be, so to say approximately conscious, they have a better direction. Even standing in the same place, but turned one way or another, makes a difference.

Q. Is it wrong to ask questions to satisfy curiosity?

A. Curiosity is a normal thing, if it is strong enough to make you study and if it is a right kind of curiosity, because there are different kinds. Right curiosity is a very important intellectual emotion.

Q. Where does our curiosity for truth come from? And why are we curious at all?

A. Curiosity is a special emotion which exists in each Centre. In the intellectual Centre it is connected with desire to know. But how do you connect it with the idea of truth? It is simply an intellectual process. Intellectually we distinguish what is true and what is false, and naturally we are curious about what is true and not about what is false, again only in our mind. Although we do not know what truth is, we can know what is definitely not true. Our mind is so made that we can know what is false, although in many cases we cannot say what is true.

Q. What is the difference between desire to know and ordinary curiosity?

A. What makes the difference is on what it is directed. If you want to know your neighbour's business that does not concern you, or if you want to know about triads, these two desires are in different parts of centres. Ordinary curiosity is just weakness, foolishness.

Q. I suppose I lack the right kind of curiosity, because I find difficulty in asking questions. Either I am too lazy, or I think I can answer them myself.

A. If you really want to ask certain questions, you will ask them even if you think you already know the answer. If you try to think, you will have questions; you are bound to have many questions now, only you do not formulate them. It is impossible not to have questions, for there are hundreds of things you would like to know. So, you must think about these things and try to formulate them.

Q. What does it really mean to have unity? I thought it was the same as permanent 'I', but now I am not so sure.

A. It may be the same; it depends where you start from in your understanding. You may make a decision, and then two or three days later act against it and justify yourself. Or you may want to struggle, try not to do something you usually do, and when you find yourself doing it again, you realize that you have no unity. Even in our state we can strive to attain unity, that is, collect ourselves, or we can be dispersed and do nothing about it.

Q. When one is struggling to do a job one does not like, what can one do to do it well, apart from not identifying?

A. At first, when you are trying to do a job of work, you cannot catch the right point from which you can do it, because work of one or another kind can be done only from one point in yourself, and it is sometimes very difficult to find this point. For instance, it is often like that when you want to write a letter, but once you start you may write more than you thought you could. The whole thing is finding the right point of the right Centre. For everything we do there is a certain part of a certain Centre that can do it, or at any rate do it much better than any other part of the same Centre or of other centres.

Q. Does doing a thing well involve some measure of subjection of false personality?

A. To a certain extent it may be understood that way It means that, if one can do something well, one is able to have a certain standard by which one can measure both how other people do things and how one does things oneself and see when one does something in a wrong way. If one has nothing like that, if one can do nothing well, one has no standard.

Q. I have a certain critical attitude to people I see a lot and I tried to stop it, but it has come back again very badly

A. Yes, sometimes it can be a very oppressive thing and more difficult to stop than people think There is only one thing just to look at it from the point of view of personal profit. Does this critical attitude give you anything or not? You will see that it gives you nothing. We often forget this question of personal profit, yet it is not only legitimate, it is the only criterion. Sometimes we spend enormous efforts, time, and emotion on things from which we can get no benefit Perhaps this will help you not to criticize. It is just the same as criticizing the weather.

Q. I often think that things are arranged badly.

A. And you can arrange them better? You can struggle with this way of thinking not at the time when you feel emotionally but later, when you can see better, if only from the point of view that we have to take everything as it is. You cannot change it; you can only change yourself. This is the only right attitude, and if you think sufficiently often about it, this emotional element will disappear and you will see things on the right scale, in right relationships.

Q. Is there a way to prevent expressing annoyance? I lose such a lot of energy by it.

A. And by expressing it you may create cause for another annoyance. Try to catch yourself on that. When you express annoyance, try to see that you do it not because you realize that you cannot help it but because you deceive yourself by thinking that you do it for a purpose, you wish to change things, people should not do this thing and cause you annoyance, and so on But after you have expressed it, it may be worse, they may annoy you even more It is quite useless to produce wrong results If you think about this wrong result, maybe you will find the energy not to express your annoyance, and then the cause may disappear, because what annoyed you before would make you laugh We often think we express negative emotions, not because we cannot help it, but because we should express them. There is always something deliberate in it

Q. But cannot you be rightly angry if something is wrong?

A. The most dangerous negative emotions come from the feeling of injustice, indignation. They make you lose more energy, and they are worse if you are right.

Q. Why is it worse if you are right?

A. Because you justify it. If you are wrong, you can see that it is absurd to be angry. But this is not a complete explanation. Start looking at it from this point of view: remember that there are very big things that are wrong. We usually identify with small things and forget the big. If we begin to think about the big things, we realize that it is no use identifying with one small thing that is wrong. And one small identifying leads to another small identifying. But again, it is not a complete explanation.

Q. Can people have a permanent influence on others?

A. Yes, to a certain extent they can, as much as you permit them. If you let yourself go in this direction and let them influence you, they will have an influence. But if you say to yourself, 'I do not want to be influenced', they will have no influence. Remember, they are machines; can a machine influence you? Yes, if you allow it. Suppose you see a wonderful car and would give your life to have this car, it means that you are influenced by this car. It is just the same with people. You are open to the influence of other people as much as you identify or consider.

Q. In relation to work, can one do people harm by influencing them in a wrong way?

A. Yes, one can with some people, not with everybody. Some people are very easily influenced, so if you give them wrong ideas about the work it may do harm. This is why in speaking with people it is always necessary to be careful not to be misunderstood, not to give a wrong impression.

Q. Would you explain why deep sleep should follow a moment of interest and urge to experiment, and why during sleep all desire to repeat the experiment goes?

A. Every function, every effort, needs energy, and awakening needs special energy. If at the moment of awakening something wrong happens, if there is some kind of identification, or something like that, it produces an enormous waste of energy, and after that one may be asleep for a long time without remembering the possibility of awakening. But only if something wrong happens at the moment of awakening. And in our present state something wrong can happen any moment because we do not know what is happening. For instance, some negative emotion may come in and produce such waste of energy that none will be left for a long time. So, the most important moments to try to remember oneself are moments when one is habitually most identified, for if one can remember oneself at these difficult moments other moments will be easier. But if one chooses only the easiest moments, then at difficult moments one will never be able to do it. It is necessary to try both.

Q. In your view, if a man could live the whole of his life in a state of consciousness, could he do no wrong?

A. We cannot take such extreme cases and speak of 'always'. But if a man were to become even a little conscious, if he were able to control himself occasionally for half an hour or even for a few minutes, it would make such an enormous difference that all we know about ordinary man would be inapplicable to him. About doing wrong, that is a different question. If a man can remember himself even to this extent, you can say definitely that he will do nothing more or less serious without knowing what he is doing, and at a moment when he is doing something particularly important, he will become conscious.

Q. Could you tell me the difference between two men on their deathbed, one of whom has learnt the art of self-remembering and one of whom has never heard of it?

A. No, it needs an imaginative writer to describe this. There are many different possibilities, the men may be very different and there may be different circumstances.

I think I had better tell you a story. It is an old story, told in the Moscow groups in 1916 about the origin of the system and the work and about self-remembering. It happened in an unknown country at an unknown date that a sly man was walking past a cafe and met a devil. The devil was in very poor shape, both hungry and thirsty, so the sly man took him into the cafe, ordered some coffee and asked him what the trouble was. The devil said that there was no business. In the old days he used to buy souls and burn them to charcoal, because when people died, they had very fat souls that he could take to hell, and all the devils were pleased. But now all the fires in hell were out, because when people died there were no souls.

Then the sly man suggested that perhaps they could do some business together. 'Teach me how to make souls', he said, 'and I will give you a sign to show which people have souls made by me', and he ordered more coffee. The devil explained that he should teach people to remember themselves, not to identify and so on, and then, after some time, they would grow souls.

The sly man set to work, organized groups, and taught people to remember themselves. Some of them started to work seriously and tried to put into practice what he taught them. Then they died, and when they came to the gates of heaven, there was St Peter with his keys on one side and the devil on the other. When St Peter was ready to open the gates, the devil would say, 'May I just ask one question did you remember yourself?' 'Yes, certainly', the man would answer and thereupon the devil would say, 'Excuse me, this soul is mine'. This went on for a long time, until they managed somehow to communicate to the earth what was happening at the gates of heaven. Hearing this, the people he was teaching came to the sly man and said, 'Why do you teach us to remember ourselves if, when we say we have remembered ourselves, the devil takes us?'

The sly man asked, 'Did I teach you to say you remember yourselves? I taught you not to talk.' They said, 'But this was St Peter and the devil!' and the sly man said, 'But have you seen St Peter and the devil at groups? So do not talk. Some people did not talk and managed to get to heaven. I did not only make an arrangement with the devil, I, also made a plan by which to deceive the devil.'

* * *

CHAPTER XIV

Personal difficulties—Necessity of finding one's most urgent and persistent difficulty—Negative emotions, imagination, formatory thinking—Creating new points of view—Struggle with identification— Three categories of negative emotions and how to deal with them— Transformation of negative emotions—Irritation—Laziness—Dull negative states—Different forms of imagination—Giving up suffering— Voluntary suffering as the greatest force we can have—The role of suffering in organic life—Man is specially made for evolution— responsibility in personal work—Necessity of working on many lines at once—Formatory thinking and its characteristics —Associative thinking—The need of higher centres to understand truth— Meditation—Right thinking—Imaginary conversations—Different meanings of faith—Life after death

Now the time has come for you to think about personal things that are near and practical We have spoken much about theory and you use too many words without asking yourselves what you mean by them Now we must deal with facts, we must understand where we can start from as we are At any given moment there are things we could control but do not control through laziness, lack of knowledge, suspicion or something else We must think about these things, that would be right thinking.

Try to find your personal difficulties I do not mean difficulties of an external kind, but inner difficulties personal features, personal inclinations and disinclinations, attitudes, prejudices, activities which can stop your understanding and prevent you working.

All the difficulties you can meet with in your personal work can be roughly divided into three categories or classes

First of all, negative emotions for some people this is the first and perhaps the chief point, so they have to begin with the study of negative emotions and study of methods of non-identification Some people cannot stop being negative, generally in some particular direction, and when negative emotions become hardened and permanent, they usually stop every kind of work, everything becomes mechanical, and a person cannot progress.

The second point is imagination, particularly negative imagination, for it is as bad as negative emotions by imagination I do not mean day- dreaming; I mean rather imagining things that do not exist cither in oneself or in other people. Everybody must try to find this kind of imagination in himself and the particular things to which it relates.

The third point is formatory thinking and formatory talking. If one does not have a picture of what is formatory and what is not formatory, one cannot progress. It is necessary to get this picture. It is very useful to find some good examples of formatory thought and to keep these examples in mind. Then it will not be difficult to recognize it when you catch yourself thinking formatorily or hear someone else speaking formatorily.

These are the chief kinds of difficulties you have to find in yourselves. For one person one thing is more permanent: for another person another. Later you will probably discover many more things, but in the beginning, you will find that it is roughly one of these.

One can have a difficulty that is most urgent, and everybody can find which of these three is theirs. You must find what is most pressing to struggle against and concentrate on that. There must be reasons for deciding on one or another, but all three refer to everybody. For most people it is necessary to begin with negative emotions. For some others it is necessary to begin with imagination, for they invent things and so never come to real things. And for yet others it is necessary to struggle with formatory thinking, for if they don't, they will always remain in the same place.

Q. You said there were many ways of destroying negative emotions. What are they?

A. First you must know them. You must know in yourself the most important negative emotion because everybody has a pet one and you must begin with that. You must know where to begin, and when you know that you can study practical methods. But first and last, when you find negative emotions in yourself, you must understand that the causes are in you and not in other people they are internal, not external. When you realize that they are in yourself, results will begin to come according to the depth of your conviction and the continuance of your memory.

You see, what I want you to understand is that each person separately has a certain definite point which prevents him from working rightly. This point must be found. Each person has many such points, but one is bigger than the others. So, each of you separately must find your chief difficulty and having found it, work against it. This may help you for a certain time, and then perhaps you will have to find another difficulty, and another, and another. Until you find your difficulty of the present moment you will not be able to work in the right way.

The first difficulty for everybody is the word 'I'. You say 'I' and do not think that this is only a small part of you that is speaking. But behind and beyond this there must be something else, and this is what you have to find. It may be a particular kind of negative emotion, a particular kind of identification, or imagination, or many other things.

You must understand that all the difficulties people have are such because people are such. Difficulties can disappear or change only when people change. Nobody can make their difficulties easier for them. Suppose a good magician came and took away all their difficulties, it would be a very bad service to them, for people would be satisfied to remain as they are because there would be no reason for them to wish to change. Try to think what makes things very difficult or takes much of your attention.

Q. I think my difficulty is self-pride.

A. Self-pride makes a good servant but a bad master. But how to make it a servant? Only by beating it. Take the example in the New Testament about turning the other cheek. An ordinary person will say that self-pride will not let him. But if you can turn self-pride into a good servant, it will make you do that. And this is important, because to be able to do that means other things as well, a quicker perception, control over the emotional and moving centres and many other things.

Q. I don't quite see how to begin finding my chief difficulty.

A. Everybody must try to find his own difficulty, not somebody else's, and in order to do that one must get rid of one's prejudices and of thinking that ideas are one thing, work another and life yet another. So long as you think like that you will not understand. You must realize that you work here for your own personal aims and that there is no difference between life and work. There are many things that stand in your way in a life sense now, and in order to conquer them and improve matters you must do what the work suggests. The results will be seen in ordinary life, in relation to people, to things and to the work you have to do in life. So, try to ask questions only referring to your own personal difficulties. Abstract things we may admit occasionally but remember that they are not the first aim.

Q. How can I struggle with possessiveness?

A. First of all *minds* must become free from justification of it. Mind must be separate; it must not identify. We have a certain control of mind, to a certain extent we can command here. If you decide not to justify a certain negative emotion, it is already the beginning of the struggle. Then the mind will act on emotions. What is the cause of negative emotions? They are always caused by other people; it is always other people's fault. That must be stopped. You must recognize that the cause of your negative emotions is in you. And you must not find reasons for negative emotions, it is always easy to find reasons.

Q. Should we try to discover what it was in us that was demanding expression of a negative emotion?

A. Very often it is imitation. Somebody else expresses negative emotion and something in you admires him and thinks how beautifully he expresses this negative emotion, and wants to imitate, and you do not know it. It may be many other things, but very often it is imitation.

Q. When you say we must work on fundamental ideas of the system, do you mean like work on negative emotions? Can it be called work if one tries hard to work on oneself in this way?

A. In any case, whatever you call it, you have got to work on negative emotions, first by studying them, then trying not to express them, then going further and finding your own favourite negative emotion. Suppose somebody has no self-pity, then it is easy for him to work on self-pity. but he may have some other emotion, his own particular one, against which it is difficult to struggle. Generally, one has only a few principal negative emotions, although some exceptional people may have more.

Q. I find it possible to struggle with smaller negative emotions, but sometimes they are too strong and there is an explosion.

A. I tried to explain that negative emotions are different, and you cannot use the same methods against all of them. In all cases you must be prepared. It is too late to think when you are already in the negative emotion. You must study identification and be able not to identify; you must be able to think in the right way, not at that moment but before and after. And you must be able to use negative emotions for self-remembering. But before all that you must be able to control the manifestation of negative emotions. If you cannot control the manifestation, you cannot start struggling with negative emotions themselves. But you must understand that you can do nothing when you are in the negative emotion; you can do it before and after. Sometimes, when you are better prepared, you can use them for self-remembering, but that is quite a special thing. In the work everything can be used, all wrong functions can be used, so negative emotions of all kinds can be useful as a help for self-remembering. By that I mean that you can train yourself in such a way that negative emotions will remind you of the necessity of remembering yourself.

Q. Did you say that the intellectual Centre could control the emotional Centre if we knew how. Can you tell us how?

A. The whole thing is to learn how. Find emotions connected with a certain kind of thinking, with certain points of view. If you acquire new points of view, then after some time the emotion connected with the old points of view will disappear. Many emotions depend on points of view. But it is slow work.

Q. Why must it be done slowly?

A. Because nobody can do it quickly. It takes some time to change points of view, to have new points of view established. It means breaking down buffers, and this is a painful thing. Besides, buffers cannot be destroyed at once, because then one will have no control at all. In the ordinary way one controls oneself with the help of buffers. So, buffers must be destroyed gradually, and will must be created at the same time. If a buffer is destroyed, will must be put in its place, otherwise one will not be protected by the buffer and one will have no will, so one will be in a worse state than with the buffer. That is why mechanical systems of self-development are dangerous, because by some mechanical means, without knowing what one is doing, one can destroy one or another important buffer without putting anything in its place and become worse off than before. Means must be conscious, one must know.

Q. Can one always find one's chief negative emotion, or only sometimes?

A. One can if one is sincere about it. It is a question of sincerity, and of a certain effort, but we do not want to make this effort, so we never do. Even if we decide to look for our negative emotions, we concentrate on small emotions. We are never sincere enough to admit what our chief negative emotion is, because sometimes it looks ugly.

When I said it is necessary to find one's chief negative emotion, I meant not the most important but the most persistent. If you find them and try to work on them, it often helps to see against what other emotions you can struggle. There are usually two or three you can struggle with. But you must be more precise and not just talk about emotions in general. General talk about emotions is good for general thinking, but not for acting. You can act only in relation to definite facts.

Q. Are not the most dangerous negative emotions jealousy, fear, hate, anger?

A. No, this is a wrong classification. The most useful classification is by the degree of identification, for it does the most harm. You take these as negative emotions of the first degree, but it is not necessarily true. For some people maybe self-pity is the worst. For another person the worst thing may be the feeling of injustice. You never know which is worst, because it depends on identification and on features, since the capacity to feel certain emotions particularly strongly and identify with them may be the chief feature of false personality. It is different for different people.

Q. Which negative emotions has one to transform?

A. All of them. There is no need to make a catalogue. One must first begin with those, one can tackle, and then pass to more difficult and still more difficult if it is possible.

Negative emotions are an intermediate state between sanity and insanity.

A man whose Centre of gravity is in negative emotions cannot be called sane and cannot develop. He must become normal first.

Negative emotions must be divided into three categories: first, the more usual, more ordinary everyday emotions. You must observe them and must already have a certain control over their expression. When you have acquired a certain control of non-expression of these negative emotions, the question comes as to how to deal with the emotions themselves. You must start dealing with them by trying not to identify as often and as much as you can, for they are always connected with identification, and if you conquer identification, they disappear.

The second category of emotions do not appear every day. They are the more difficult, more complex emotions depending on some mental process, such as suspicion, hurt feelings and many things like that. They are harder to conquer. You can deal with them by creating a right mental attitude, by thinking not at the time, but in-between, when you are quiet. Try to find the right attitude, the right point of view, and make it permanent. If you create right thinking, that will take all power from these negative emotions.

Then there is the third category, much more intense, much more difficult and rarer. Against them you can do nothing. These two methods struggle with identification and creating right attitudes do not help. When such emotions come, you can do only one thing: you must try to remember yourself, remember yourself with the help of the emotion. If you learn to use them for self-remembering, they may diminish and disappear after some time. But for this you have to be prepared.

At present, since you do not know which emotion belongs to which category, you must try to use all three methods for all of them. But later you will see that they are divided into these categories and in one case one thing helps, in another case another thing. In all cases you must be prepared. As I said in the beginning, it will be difficult to struggle with them or conquer them, but you will learn through time. Only, never mix emotions with the expression of negative emotions. That always comes first. As long as you cannot stop the expression, it means that you can do nothing about the emotions themselves. So, before you can do anything else you must learn to control the manifestation of negative emotions. If you learn to control the expression, then you can start.

Q. It seems that the effort to remember oneself makes one more vulnerable and more easily swayed by emotions. How can one protect oneself?

A. One cannot protect oneself in the beginning. One has to risk it if it works that way. Actually, it works both ways: from one point of view, it makes you more sensitive; from another point of view, it gives you more control.

Q. With one's habitual negative emotions, is it some particular feature in oneself that always brings them?

A. Quite possibly, but if you practice non-identifying, you will see that. You identify with many, many things, not only with negative emotions. From morning till night, you pass from one identification to another, but when you try more than usually not to identify, you may notice many negative emotions you have not seen before. Some you may see full-size; of others you may only notice their tails disappearing. If you try noticing and not identifying, it will make you stronger in dealing with emotions.

Q. What is the right way to find interest in things without identification?

A. There is no right way. You must either think about right things or connect everything with self-remembering. If you can think about right things, you can be interested in them without identification, but if you become identified, all thinking disappears, and it becomes just a formatory repetition of words.

Q. One negative emotion which is always happening to me sets me against people whom I think I have neglected or harmed in some way. It is based on identification. I cannot see how to escape from it.

A. It is difficult to say. We are so mechanical that in some cases we are not responsible. At the same time, one has no right to say, 'I am not responsible, so it does not matter what I do'. One must do what one can. But non-identifying will not help in this case. If you feel you have done something wrong, try not to do it again. Very often people give all their energy to thinking about the wrong things they did and next day do exactly the same.

Q. Did you say that negative emotions would be useful if we could be not identified with them?

A. If we could be not identified, we would have different results. That would help very definitely, since it would give orientation to life and many other things, we do not know yet.

Yes, I said *if we could not* identify they would be very useful functions. As they are, they are not useful. All negative emotions that we cannot avoid become useful functions if we use them for self-remembering. Some people manage to do that and get two things at once elimination of the negative emotion and creation of self remembering. If you have a persistent negative emotion and by right thinking connect it with self-remembering, then, after some time, it will help self-remembering, and after some more time, if you persist, the emotion will disappear. So, they can serve a useful purpose if you can use them; but if you identify with them, they are no good at all.

Q. Is there anything one can do about negative emotions when one is in a bad state?

A. One must not believe in this bad state. Equally one must not believe in a good state, that it will always remain. Both bad and good state will change. If one believes too much in a good state, a bad state comes and one is not prepared, and as a result one is too much affected. If one identifies too much with one's bad state, one feels that one can do nothing. Bad state or good state, one has to go on, there is only one way.

Q. Does strong jealousy come under the second category?

A. That is for you to decide. It may have very many different forms and manifestations. Generally, it is based on justification mentally you agree with it, approve it, prepare the ground for it. When you stop preparing the ground, it may disappear or be transformed into something different.

But this is too general a description. There are ten thousand different kinds of jealousy, but the basis of them, almost inevitably, is that you feel you have the right to be jealous. You must always remember that all causes of negative emotions are in us.

Q. Are negative emotions catching? Is that what makes family life so difficult?

A. Yes, it is a definite fact that negative emotions are very infectious, but particularly infectious for yourself. If you have certain negative emotions and admit them, if you do not deny them in your mind they are bound to be repeated and become stronger and stronger.

Q. Self-pity, to me, is not an unpleasant emotion, though I consider it to be a negative one. Should it be stopped?

A. Particularly if it is pleasant. When self-pity is pleasant it is a particularly poisonous emotion.

Q. How can I think rightly about self-pity?

A. In thinking about it you must create in your mind a permanent solvent, an attitude which will break up your self-pity when it appears. Find the comical side of it, the absurd side, find the insane side, do not stand on ceremony with yourself. If you succeed in forming a permanent attitude, then as soon as self-pity appears, pour the solvent over it and it will dissolve. Find what is foolish, what is mad in self-pity, not by analysis but by examples. You will find many features in it if you think and observe sincerely, and if you keep them in mind, self-pity will not dare to raise its head.

Q. But if you find it does not disappear?

A. That means a wrong attitude, and not only attitude. Self-pity is not quite normal, so study it, find all its strange features, try to be ashamed of it, do not think or speak about it as if it were something harmless or pleasant.

Q. I find in myself a very great self-indulgence which I believe is my chief weakness and obstacle in the work. But by my own efforts I do not know how to struggle with it in any but the most feeble way.

A. Very often you cannot fight, or you do not know how to begin to work against some special weakness, but it does not matter. Work against *any* weakness and you will work against *this* weakness. It is a very easy way of justifying yourself to say you do not know how to fight against a weakness. Leave it alone and fight against some other weakness, the result will be the same. In special cases we have to return to some difficulty again and again, but in general all efforts lead in the same direction, whether it is struggle against negative-ness, imagination, or anything else.

Q. Why does giving way to anger give me a definite feeling of exhilaration?

A. First because it is a habit, second because it is easy. Every giving way to a habit gives pleasure. The machine always likes to work by the line of least resistance, but in the work, we must go by the line of strongest resistance

Q. Fear need not be a negative emotion? It may be necessary?

A. It is the basis of many negative emotions. We do not speak about instinctive emotions now Negative emotions of the instinctive Centre are necessary, but others are almost all useless. But even instinctive emotions can lead to imagination. For instance, one may be afraid of snakes and, living in a country where there is only a snake and half, one may pass one's life in fear of snakes This is imagination

Q. Isn't one often afraid of things one knows nothing about?

A. Fear is simply a certain state; it can be without any object. This shows how useless negative emotions are. We often invent objects for an emotion when the emotion is already there. Take envy, fear, suspicion We think the emotion is produced in us by something outside, when in reality it is in us, we only look for an object afterwards, and in this way, we justify it.

Q. I still cannot understand why all causes of negative emotions are in myself.

A. If you observe yourself, you will see Causes outside remain the same, but sometimes they produce negative emotion in you, sometimes not. Why? Because real causes are in you, there are only apparent causes outside If you are in a good state, if you are remembering yourself, if you are not identifying, then nothing that happens outside (relatively speaking, for I do not mean catastrophes) can produce a negative emotion in you. If you are in a bad state, identified, immersed in imagination, then everything just a little unpleasant will produce a violent emotion. It is a question of observation.

Q. But I still do not see how some things, for instance, people's behaviour, could fail to produce negative emotion.

A. They are machines Why should the behaviour of machines produce negative emotion? If a machine hits you, it is your own fault, you must not be in the way of the machine. You may have a negative emotion, but it is not the fault of the machine, it is your own fault. Other people do not have as much power over you as you think, it is only the result of identification. You can be much more free if you do not identify, and sometimes you are more free That is why I say it must be observed. If you observe well, you will see that sometimes you identify more, sometimes less; and because of this, sometimes you are absolutely in the power of negative emotions and sometimes you have a certain resistance. It may take a long time to learn how to resist negative emotions, but it is not impossible. You must understand one thing about negative emotions, we are too much afraid of them, we consider them too powerful. We can show resistance to them if we persist and do not consider them inevitable and omnipotent.

Q. I could see myself losing my temper the other day when I was talking to somebody, but I could not stop it. How can I control temper?

A This is an example of mechanicalness. You cannot control your temper when it has already begun to appear, it is then too late Struggle must begin in your mind, you must find your way to think rightly about a definite difficulty. Suppose you have to meet a certain man who irritates you. Your temper shows itself; you do not like it. How can you stop it? You must begin with the study of your thinking. What do you think about this man, not what you feel when you are irritated, but what do you think about him at quiet moments? You may find that in your mind you argue with him, you prove to him that he is wrong, you tell him all his mistakes, you find that, generally, he behaves wrongly towards you. This is where you are wrong You must learn to think rightly Then, if you do, it will happen like this although emotion is much quicker than thought, emotion is a temporary thing, but thought can be made continuous, so whenever the emotion jumps out, it hits against this continuous thought and cannot go on and manifest itself So you can struggle with the expression of negative emotions, as in this example, only by creating continuous right thinking. To explain what right thinking is in a few words is impossible, it is necessary to study it. If you remember what I said about parts of centres you will come to that, because in most cases and most conditions in ordinary life people think only with the mechanical part of the intellectual Centre, which is the formatory apparatus This is not sufficient It is necessary to use the intellectual part of the intellectual Centre Identifying is the chief reason why we do not use it Trying to self-remember and trying not to identify is the best means of passing into higher parts of centres. But we always forget about identification and about self-remembering.

Q. Can conquering negative emotions, like fear, create energy?

A. Very much so This is one of the best means of collecting energy. All possibilities of development are contained in conquering negative emotions and transforming them.

A man with negative emotions will never do anything

Q. Into what kind of things can negative emotions be transformed?

A. It is better to say they must be conquered. But, if you like, we can say that they are transformed into some kind of emotion mixed with very much understanding, an emotion of higher parts of centres. Almost any negative emotion we have now can be transformed into an emotion of higher parts of centres. But this needs understanding, conviction that it is necessary, and decision to do it.

Q. Is it negative emotions that prevent us from getting into those emotional states?

A. Yes. We have enough money, but we spend it all on unpleasant things. If we save enough, we can use it in the right way. Power to use comes with quantity.

Q. I observe two kinds of indignation in myself one when for example I see a child hurt, and another when something annoys me myself. Are they both equally negative?

A. The more unselfish the indignation is, and the more right you are, the worse it is.

The more energy you lose in it, the more negative results it will produce.

Q. Why am I so much sooner roused into negative emotions during discussions than at any other time? Political discussions, for instance.

A. Because you always think that things can be different When you realize and become firmly convinced that things could not be different, you cease to argue. Arguing is based on the idea that things could be different and that some people could do things differently. Try to think from the point of view that all that happens because it cannot be different; if it could be different, it would have happened differently. It is very simple, but very difficult to realize.

Q. If we see something we do not like in others is it because they are mirrors for ourselves, and we have the same thing in us?

A. Chiefly, yes but it is a great thing to realize that. Maybe people dislike others because they are mirrors of themselves. They do not realize it, but somehow feel it vaguely and it makes them dislike them. However, there is also a principle in the work that before becoming better one has to become worse. It is not only because one notices more, but one actually does also become worse before one acquires more control.

Q. If one always remembered about people that they could not act in any other way, could one then understand them?

A. Naturally you must remember that. And until this remembering is constant, you can understand nothing about them. There are many things like that. All you learn in the system must be in your consciousness at the same time, otherwise every small thing will make you forget everything.

Q. I find I become very negative when given advice and never agree with it.

A. Again it is all based on your attitude: you admit that someone else can affect your emotional state. We should not admit an emotional power like that over us Now, even if you merely think about this advice, you feel annoyed. You reconstruct it. But you should think in quite a different way, it is purely a matter of reasoning. Even if people give advice without thinking, even if you know better, there is no reason for you to lose your temper. You cannot get anything by being annoyed or irritated. You must stop justifying it in your mind. When one stops this justifying, one very often finds that the cause of all these negative emotions is some wrong idea. Everybody can find something wrong in one or another side of his life and generally one tends to put the responsibility on this thing. One thinks that if this thing were right, everything else would be right. Everybody has one, sometimes two or more combinations of circumstances which one blames for everything wrong one does and for all one's manifestations of weakness. But one must understand that absolutely anything in the world can produce this result. Suppose there is some definite thing that is wrong, and I think: 'If it were right, I would be different'. But if it were right, I would be just the same. I speak from experience, because I know people who thought so, and when the particular thing they found wrong was changed, they remained the same and merely found another unpleasant thing instead of the first one.

Q. I find that one of my greatest difficulties is irritation.

A. This is one of the deepest features in people and it affects the whole mass. The most difficult thing in the world is to patiently bear the unpleasant manifestations of other people. People can sacrifice everything else, but they cannot stand that. Irritation is a particular emotion produced by the feeling of mechanicalness of oneself or other people. It does not mean that every mechanical thing causes irritation, but sometimes mechanicalness produces it. If we do not feel the mechanicalness of other people in some particular instance, they may be even more mechanical, but there is no irritation. We are irritated by other people acting as machines because we are machines ourselves. If we cease to be machines, we shall cease to be irritated. This feeling of mechanicalness becomes irritation because we identify with it. If we manage to remove identification, the same thing that we know now as irritation becomes a very useful emotion, a kind of tentacle by which we can feel mechanicalness. You cannot imagine how different quite ordinary emotions become, and often how useful, if we do not identify with them.

Q. How can one best deal with negative emotion when it simply becomes apathy?

A. Very often when negative emotion takes the form of passive resistance you can do nothing at the moment. But you can continue to work. If you can do nothing to-day, there will be to-morrow, and the day after, and next week, and next month. You must prepare for the future, first of all by self-remembering, by remembering why you came, by remembering the first principles. All this apathy and negative feelings come from long sleep. If you continue to sleep when you could try to awake, this sleep will produce one or another negative state.

Q. I have observed in myself a constant desire to be comfortable. Is it general for everybody to feel this?

A. This is one of the most important features of our life. To this desire we sacrifice everything. We are ready to give up everything to go by the line of least resistance. Sometimes this desire becomes so strong that one can be comfortable and nothing else. Even if something is not comfortable, one tries to arrange it so that it should be comfortable.

Q. Is there a way of getting rid of it?

A. What to do is a different question; we must come to it from another side. This desire is a very big thing and every effort against it is important, so every effort must be discussed specially, not all efforts together. Sleep is the most comfortable thing; trying to awake is very uncomfortable. Later, when we partly awaken, we will feel how uncomfortable it is to sleep when anything may happen at any moment. But it is necessary to come to that state.

Q. How can one counteract laziness?

A. By effort. How otherwise? It is difficult to speak in general because there are so many forms of laziness, so many different escapes. We must speak about concrete cases, so only you yourself can answer. Find in yourself different kinds of laziness, then you will see that it is not always the same, in some cases it manifests worse, in other cases less strongly. You need a large quantity of observations, nobody from outside can help you.

Q. Is it any good just wanting?

A. No, that is not sufficient. Suppose one is lazy in one particular thing, but not always equally lazy sometimes more, sometimes less. This is material for observation. Find what makes you more lazy or less lazy, then you will find some causes and will know where to observe further. In many things in us we must find what makes a difference, because nothing in us remains the same for long. Even permanent features manifest themselves differently, one day in one way, another day in another way. It is necessary to find what causes it.

Q. Is there a means of telling the difference between a genuine need for rest and laziness?

A. As in many other things, there are cases when you can say definitely, and you must take only these cases and not think about doubtful ones. If you start with cases where you do not know, you can do nothing. In this system you must start with things about which you have no doubt.

Q. If you are trying to remember yourself, and you get some kind of result, can you be sure that it is not imagination?

A. Again the same answer applies. There will be moments about which you will have no doubt, and there will be moments about which you will know that they are imagination. You cannot be sure about every moment, but about some moments you will be sure.

Q. Can an outside circumstance suddenly wake you up?

A. Yes, but the next moment other outside circumstances come and make you fall asleep again, so there is no profit in it. And the more one kind of circumstances awakes you, the more easily others make you fall asleep. Only this awakening is sure which comes from yourself.

Q. Would a man who is beginning to awake develop a sense of duality?

A. Is that an observation or not? If it is an observation, it is one thing

but if it is just philosophy, it is quite useless. It will not help you if you decide in one way and things happen in another way. You must deal with to-day, and with a possible tomorrow.

Q. I have found that I can have a negative emotion and observe it at the same time.

A. Yes, certainly. You can have violent negative emotions and observe them. Very often negative emotions wake us up to a certain extent, so we can observe them. This is quite right, but it does not diminish them, they become even better if you do this and even more pleasing as a form of sleep. Observation is not the way to destroy negative emotions. If you want to destroy them, there are many methods, but observation is only for study.

Q. Is there any way of dealing with rather vague, dull, negative states?

A. Yes, many ways; sometimes you can struggle with it, but supposing even that your state is so dull that you can do nothing at the given moment, if you make efforts before it comes, while in a better state, that will help. You have to do only what is absolutely necessary at such a time, but you must not identify with your state and must only remember that it will pass, must not believe that it is permanent. Emotionally we always believe in things, the emotional Centre does not know to-morrow; for it everything is the present, everything is permanent. You must not identify with this feeling; you must know that it will change.

Q. Everything that interested me in the work I very soon began to feel as a frightful grind. How am I to avoid this trap?

A. Well, it is a beautiful state for self-remembering you can use it. The more negative you are, the better you can remember yourself, if you realize that you can get out. It must remind you, serve as an alarm, otherwise you will remain in a negative state all the time.

Q. It seems that only when I have observed some stupidity in myself am I able to make stronger efforts.

A. Sometimes it is very useful to see one's stupidity. If one could really see oneself, one would not be able to forget it. But this is connected with consciousness.

Q. I have always been rather adaptable, and that worries me. If I try to make an effort, it is very unpleasant to start with, but later it is no longer an effort.

A. The moment it becomes easy, it is a warning; it means that next time the effort will be more difficult.

Q. I find I can sometimes get out of a negative emotion by allowing myself to get identified with something pleasant.

A. You use the word 'identified' in a wrong sense. You cannot say 'I allow myself to get identified'; you can only say, 'I allow myself to get interested in something'. Yes, it may work for some time, but if you become identified, it will be just the same thing from a practical point of view. Only, in pleasant things you *can* be interested without being identified; in an unpleasant thing you *cannot* be interested without being identified.

Q. I find enjoyment a great difficulty. I enjoy almost everything, and this seems to send me to sleep.

A. Try to remember yourself, then enjoyment will be bigger, fuller and you will profit from it. But if it makes you fall asleep, you must try to avoid it, that is all. Every kind of emotional state can be used for self-remembering, but before you can do that it is necessary to create a capacity for it; and the capacity can be created only by constant, regular effort. If you just think about it once a week, nothing will come of it.

Q. I feel my chief obstacle is imagination, chiefly about myself. Is there any special work against this?

A. Imagination may be very different. If there are special ways, it is only possible to arrive at them through a detailed study. If you ask me in general, I can only answer self-remembering.

If you mean daydreams, they are only half of our imaginings, and the most innocent half. Certainly, they mean loss of time, but we waste time in so many ways that a little more or less does not make much difference. It is much more dangerous if you imagine certain qualities in yourself in other people, in humanity or in nature, and then come to believe in these imaginary ideas and put your faith in them. We are surrounded by these imaginary qualities, and it is with these that we must struggle.

Q. In trying to resist imagination, should one find the cause of it?

A. No, stop it at once. There are always causes. Replace it by something else, some intentional thinking.

Q. Why is it of no value to observe and study imagination as a means to self-knowledge?

A. You will very soon see that it does not give anything. Imagination always turns in the same circle. It is an uncontrolled mind activity, and by imagination we create many false values, keep to them, and use them in our thinking. This is why imagination is dangerous. We do not verify things. We imagine things either because we like them, or sometimes because we dislike them and are afraid of them. We live in an imaginary world.

Q. By escaping from reality?

A. Not consciously escaping, but it happens like that. It is partly due. to mental laziness:

for instance, it is easier to imagine a thing than to study it.

Q. Wouldn't knowing that be an easy way of stopping it?

A. No, you can know it and it will still go on. A special effort is necessary to stop it. We are so mechanical that we can know and still do the same thing,

Q. I feel I cannot wait any longer to try and find a path out of the morass in which I now find myself. The more I see my mechanicalness, the more I see the urgency of so doing.

A. You must realize that a long time is necessary. Years and years have passed in ordinary life. When you hear about mechanicalness and are just beginning to struggle with it, you want results at once. It is necessary first to get accustomed to these ideas. There are no secrets or special methods to make it quicker.

Q. I find it difficult to realize that imagination enters into all our emotions.

A. Every emotion based on identification is imagination. Identification is a sign of imagination. When you find an emotion without identification, you will find an emotion without imagination.

Q. Is thought the only way to test imagination?

A. No, not thought but attention, because imagination is one of the manifestations that go without attention. The moment you turn your attention to it, imagination stops.

Q. Do you mean that one cannot observe imagination without stopping it?

A. You cannot observe it for long. If you just notice it and turn away, it can go on, but if you keep attention on it, it stops. Attention acts like a light, and imagination is like a chemical process that can only go on in the dark and stops with light,

Q. Does it not mean that when you notice it thought comes up?

A. Thought brings attention. Attention is a different faculty, because even though can go on without attention. But thought can work *with* attention, while imagination cannot. Some faculties can work only with attention and some others can work without attention.

Q. What is the difference between ordinary thought and imagination?

A. Intentional or unintentional; controllable or uncontrollable.

Q. Imagination is one of the strongest things in man, yet it is the most useless. Why?

A. It is a bad habit, a form of sleep, a weakness. It is easy, it does not need any effort.

All the rest needs effort.

Q. Is it possible to hope that we can get rid of imagination ultimately?

A. We cannot speak about ultimately, it is too far. The first step is to know how much time is given to imagination; the next step is to give it a little less.

Q. I cannot say whether something is imagination or not and I do not know how to begin to recognize it.

A. Nobody can help you to begin, you must begin yourself. You must catch yourself in some kind of imagination, I do not mean exactly daydreaming. You must have some standard of imagination: then, when in doubt, you can compare. Imagination can take three forms: passive imagination, imagination expressing itself in talk and imagination expressing itself in activity. There are lines and lines of our activity, each quite different from another. Some start with effort and go on with effort. Others may be imagination. One may think it is effort when in reality it is imagination expressing itself in activity which cannot stop and needs no effort. Talking is the same: some people must talk, others must do something, but both are manifestations of the same thing.

Q. I notice that imagining seems to take place in memory, going from one association to another. Is this a correct observation?

A. No. Memory by itself is not responsible for anything. Memory is impartial; it supplies material for whatever you want. You may want it for serious thinking, imagination, expression of negative emotions and so on.

Q. Is memory mechanical?

A. Memory itself is mechanical, but the use of memory, the application of memory, the functioning of memory can be more mechanical or less mechanical. Memory is inscriptions on the rolls of our centres. How to use them, how to find them, how to verify them, that is another thing.

Q. Should it matter much whether one knows the cause of any negative moods one observes: is it enough just to recognize that it is negative?

A. No. Sometimes it is very useful to know the cause, because when you want to fight with it, you cannot fight unless you know the cause, and the cause is generally in your own imagination. All the causes are in you, so it is necessary to know them.

Q. Sometimes when one is unhappy or perhaps feeling negative one is brought back to real issues. Since we have been told to guard against negative emotion, I cannot quite fit that in with the system.

A. You mix the idea of suffering and the idea of negative emotion. It is not the same. Suffering is very useful; you can get many things only through suffering. But when suffering is connected with identification and imagination, it becomes negative emotion.

Q. You say that man must give up suffering and also that he must suffer in order to develop. How can both things be true?

A. Different cases, different days, different moments. These are not two contradictory principles. There is much unnecessary suffering which one does not want to give up. Then there is some inevitable and necessary suffering which one must accept if one wants to get something. On the Fourth Way, not all at once, one has to sacrifice all unnecessary things; wrong theories, talk, imaginary suffering. Imaginary suffering is the chief obstacle.

Q. Then, suffering does not exist?

A. Only a certain amount is real. But we increase it by imagination. Real suffering exists, but it is limited by many things, by time for instance. But nothing can stop or limit imaginary suffering. Real suffering, if it has a cause, may be necessary; it may give knowledge. Imaginary suffering takes away knowledge. Death of a friend, or grief of some kind is real suffering, but if you identify with it, it can produce negative emotion. And, after all, suffering occupies a very small part of our life, while negative emotions occupy the whole of it.

Q. Is pain a negative emotion?

A. Simply suffering pain is not a negative emotion, but when imagination and identification enter, it becomes a negative emotion. Emotional pain, like physical pain, is not a negative emotion by itself, but when you begin to make all kinds of embroidery on it, it becomes negative.

Q. It has been stated, or at least implied, that man loves suffering. Is this strictly true?

A You do not quite understand the meaning of that If you think deeper, you will see that everybody has some kind of suffering, say self-pity. One never gives up this self-pity, it is the man's most cherished possession, he carries it with him, puts it in the best place, he will never try or ever decide in his mind to make an effort to get rid of this self-pity. Everybody has one or two negative emotions he is particularly attached to. He does not say to himself, 'I like, this negative emotion', but he lives in it, is fully absorbed in it, and everything is colored by this negative emotion, so he will not sacrifice it, for many people, to sacrifice their chief negative emotion would mean sacrificing their whole life.

Q. Since man ceased to believe that his sufferings were a direct punishment from God, is he not ashamed of them and resentful of them?

A. Yes, it looks like that, but really, he will never give them up When he decides to give them up, he becomes free of them. It seems a simple thing, but when it comes to practice, he finds that he cannot do it, because his sufferings have already become a habit, and so, although he decides in his mind, he still continues to feel the same. Nevertheless, in order to get rid of unnecessary suffering, the first step is to decide to give it up in one's mind When a man makes this decision, after some time he will give it up, but as long as his mind is hypnotized by this suffering, he will not make the effort

Q. If he gives it up, what will he get in exchange?

A. He will get in exchange absence of suffering That is why he does not want to give it up

Q. What method can one use to sacrifice suffering?

A. Realization of values but there are different kinds of suffering. Sometimes an effective way to destroy suffering is to see that it belongs to the imaginary part of oneself Division into real and imaginary is very useful.

The general idea is that you cannot get anything for nothing, you have to sacrifice something. But what to sacrifice? One person does not want to sacrifice one thing, another person another thing. The answer is: (sacrifice) our suffering negative emotions, negative imagination, and all that. It is a very good sacrifice, only it is very difficult, because one is ready to sacrifice any pleasure, but not suffering.

Q. How can one do it? Does one refuse to think that one is suffering?

A. You refuse to accept your suffering and stop your suffering. It is very simple. Suppose you have a grievance, either you are hurt or offended or something. Try to sacrifice this grievance and you will see how much you are attached to it. Actually, it is a very pleasant feeling when one feels, 'I have nothing to worry about. Nobody is guilty.' But people dislike this because they feel it as emptiness.

Q. I suppose the reward of any development is really suffering, for knowledge brings suffering?

A. I do not see that it is necessarily so. It is true that development means increase of suffering for a certain period, but you cannot regard this as an aim or the necessary result. By itself suffering can bring nothing, but if one remembers oneself in connection with it, it can be a great force. If suffering did not exist, it would be necessary to create it, because without it one cannot come to right self-remembering. But people try to run away from suffering, or try to disguise it, or they identify with it and in this way destroy the strongest weapon they have.

Q. What is useful suffering?

A. Until we get rid of useless suffering we cannot come to the useful. Most of our suffering is absolutely useless; we have too much of it. You must first learn to distinguish what is useless suffering. The first condition of getting free of it is to know it for what it is.

Q. Would you say suffering is to some extent essential for attaining change of being?

A. Certainly, but it depends on what you understand by suffering. We get nothing by pleasure; from that we can only get suffering. Every effort is suffering; every realization is suffering, because there are many unpleasant realizations about ourselves and about other things, and there are many forms of suffering. As I said, some sufferings are unnecessary and useless, with some other sufferings we must learn not to identify, and some sufferings are useful. We judge suffering from the point of view of whether it helps or hinders our work, so our attitude to suffering must be more complicated. Useless suffering is the greatest obstacle in our way; at the same time suffering is necessary, and sometimes it happens that people cannot work because they are afraid of suffering. In most cases what they are afraid of is imaginary suffering. We have much imagination and sometimes giving up certain kinds of imagination looks difficult.

Q. Is suffering, apart from physical pain, possible without false personality?

A. Certainly, but it does not become so insistent. When false personality begins to enjoy it, it becomes dangerous. Most of our suffering depends on identification, and if identification disappears, our suffering disappears too. One must be reasonable; one must realize that it is no use suffering if it is possible not to suffer.

Q. I do not understand how a positive emotion can be rooted in pain, yet some men of vision apparently attained the heights through physical suffering.

A. Through physical or mental suffering it is quite possible, by transformation. Every kind of suffering, theoretically speaking, can transform into positive emotion, but *only if it* is transformed. However, such definitions are dangerous, because next moment someone will understand it in the sense that it transforms *itself into* positive emotion. This would be quite wrong, because nothing transforms itself, it must be transformed by effort of will and by knowledge.

Q. Can grief help a man to a higher state of consciousness?

A. No single isolated shock can help because there are many ties that keep us in our present state. It is important to understand that thousands of shocks are necessary, and for years. Only then can the threads be broken, and man become free.

Q. How can real suffering exist if you say that the emotional Centre has no negative part?

A. In the description of man in this system one comes up against the impossibility of describing things as they are: they can only be described approximately. It is the same as on small-scale maps where the relative size of things cannot be shown. In some cases, in the description of the human machine, the differences are so great that it is better to say that a thing does not exist at all than to say that one thing is big and another small. This refers to the emotional Centre. There are emotions that are not negative, yet very painful, and there is a Centre for them, but it occupies such an infinitesimal part compared with negative emotions that are not real that it is better to say that emotional Centre has no negative part.

Q. How can you explain the great amount of suffering that exists in the world?

A. This is a very interesting question. From the point of view of the work it is possible to find at least a logical form of solution of this problem. In organic life man must be regarded as an experiment of the Great Laboratory. In this laboratory all possible kinds of experiments are made, and they have to be made by means of suffering to bring about some kind of fermentation. In some way suffering is necessary for this; all the cells of this experiment have to suffer, and because of that their tendency is to avoid suffering, to have as little of it as possible, or to run away. If some of these cells break this tendency and accept suffering voluntarily, they can rid themselves of it and become free. Suffering, voluntary suffering can become schoolwork. Nothing is more difficult and at the same time nothing can create so much force as voluntary suffering. The idea of development is to create an inner force, and how can a man put himself to the test without suffering? From one point of view the whole of organic life exists for planetary purposes. From another point of view, it exists only for the sake of those who escape. So, it does not exist for feeding the moon alone. This suffering is the highest product, and the rest are merely by-products; the highest is always the most important.

We are far from understanding the idea of suffering, but if we realize that small things can be attained with small suffering, and big ones with big suffering, we shall understand that it will always be proportionate. But we must remember one thing, we have no right to invent suffering. Also, one has the right to accept suffering for oneself, but one has no right to accept it for other people. According to one's views of life, one helps other people, only it must be understood that helping cannot diminish suffering, it cannot change the order of things.

Q. Should not one work for the relief of suffering?

A. As much as one can, but there is suffering which can be relieved and suffering which cannot be relieved because it depends on bigger causes. Sleeping people have to suffer; maybe there is a great cosmic purpose in this suffering, because only suffering can eventually wake them up. If they can arrange their life so as to be happy and contented in sleep, they will never awake. But all this is only talk, because anyway it cannot be changed.

Q. Is there a definite amount of suffering to be borne in the world?

A. Probably for the purposes of possible evolution everyone must be surrounded by enormous possibilities of suffering. Evolution depends on man's attitude; if he accepts suffering and tries not to identify with it. It may be that this whole law was created so that he could become stronger, because strength can only be created by suffering.

Q. Is it good for one person to suffer for another?

A. No one can suffer for another; if I have a toothache, it will not diminish mine if you have a toothache too.

Q. You say that man is an experiment?

A. Man is specially made for evolution, he is a special experiment made for self development. *Every* man is an experiment, not *all* men.

Now we have to return to practical things and the study of personal work. It is necessary to understand responsibility in personal work, because when a man begins to understand something, to formulate certain wishes in connection with the work, his responsibility towards himself increases. The more one understands, the greater one's responsibility, because if one knows nothing and does not attempt to work, one cannot make a serious mistake. But when one begins to work one can sin against the work, so to speak; and when a man makes mistakes it can stop his personal work. So, his responsibility begins as soon as he begins to work, and it must be understood that this responsibility is very great, because everything counts, everything one says or does, *everything* one does not say or do, everything is counted and is put for or against one. It is not an arbitrary action: it is so in the very nature of things. Things themselves make it so.

In order to do something, to reach something it is necessary to work on many lines at the same time, otherwise one sticks. If you miss one or two lines, you have to go back and start again from the beginning; you cannot choose which lines to work on. Suppose you have to work on fifty lines, and you discard three lines you do not like and work on forty-seven. Then, sooner or later, you have to go back and begin again from the beginning on all the fifty lines, because after some time forty-seven lines cannot take you any further. I mean by those lines trying to remember yourself, trying not to identify, not to express negative emotions and so on. Suppose you accept all those lines and leave out only one, about talking, it will spoil everything. Or if you accept them all, and the next moment forget you will again get nowhere. That is why we cannot get right results. We start well and then the next moment forget and say to ourselves: 'I cannot keep fifty things in my mind at once'.

Q. How can one increase one's sense of responsibility?

A. It must be based on valuation. If you value something, then you have a sense of responsibility.

Q. You said that another of our chief difficulties is formatory thinking. I do not in the least know how to think not formatorily.

A. Think to the best of your ability and compare results when your thinking gives results and when it does not. In that way you will come to a better understanding, at any rate better than just wondering about it. Definitions will not help you: desire for definitions is only an excuse. If you find yourself in a very difficult position, you will think to the best of your ability how to get out of it. Think in the same way.

Q. Before we can think differently, is it necessary to perceive things differently?

A. We cannot perceive differently until we think differently. We have control only of our thoughts; we have no control over perception. Perception depends particularly on the state of consciousness. If one awakes for sufficiently long, one can perceive many things one does not perceive now. It does not depend on desire or decision.

Q. Is all thinking formatory, except when we are trying to self-remember?

A. No, not all, but a great deal of our thinking is formatory. But when we think about serious things, such as the ideas of this system, we either cannot think at all, or our thinking is not formatory. Formatory thinking is always poor, but for some problems it is ridiculous.

Q. You said once that thinking about the big ideas of the system can be a way of stopping identification. I cannot see why this is so and why identification should necessarily spoil thinking?

A. Because identification makes thought narrow and defective, it binds you, you cannot think, you cannot make deductions. It lowers the standard of man's normal intellectual capacity. As to why thinking about the big ideas of the system stops identification, it is because you cannot think about them if you identify with them. Your thinking will produce no effect. When we are studying, trying to understand, this means a new way of thinking. The moment we go back to the old way of thinking, we identify.

Q. You said formatory thinking always concerns itself with opposites; but how can we know anything other than by opposites?

A. Not always, I said it is one of the characteristics of formatory thinking. And when we think, we must think about the subject itself, not about its opposite.

Q. But if I am to know about some particular thing, I must know what it is not.

A. Not at all. You can know what one or another thing is without making a catalogue of what it is not. It is quite a wrong self-accusation to say that you have to use such a clumsy method of thinking, because in that way you would have to think for two years about every small thing. You can think about things without opposites, just about what they are. Formatory *thinking* is not thinking. Never forget that formatory thinking can serve many useful purposes, but it is not for thinking.

Q. People No. I live all their lives with formatory apparatus. Does that mean they have no growth of being at all from the beginning of their lives?

A. Not only men No. I but also No. 2 and No. 3 can live only with formatory apparatus. The great majority of people use nothing else. Certainly, they have a certain growth of being only it is, so to speak, not individual, it is mass growth, in the sense of a child and a grown-up man. But their being does not grow beyond a certain level, and we are interested in growth of being towards man No. 4.

To grow up in the ordinary way is natural; but this does not change the level of being. And even this natural growth of being can be arrested.

Q. I have noticed that if I ask a question, while it is being answered, my mind is working and, as a result, I am not listening. What is this due to?

A. Quite right. This is simply associative thinking, mechanical thinking. Naturally, if you ask a question and want to know the answer you must stop associations and take in what is said, and only then think about it and compare. If you do not stop associations, the answer comes to you mixed with your own thoughts, not exactly what was said. So, you never get the right answer. Struggle with associative thinking is a definite line of work. If you study something, listen to something or are trying to understand something, you have to do it with a free mind. If you go on with your own thoughts at the same time, your mind will never be free to follow.

Q. Why is one inclined to ask 'why' rather than 'how'?

A. Because it is easier, more mechanical, we are more accustomed to it. To ask 'how' needs thinking; you have to formulate your question in the right way. And 'why' can be asked without thinking.

Q. It was said that one of the methods of struggling with negative emotions is thinking differently. I do not quite understand what thinking differently means.

A. It means to take some subject which produces emotion and think about it, trying not to justify yourself or to accuse other people. That will be different thinking. Although there are negative emotions that cannot be destroyed in this way, for they need stronger methods, this method must be tried first in every case.

Q. I find that most of the time trivial thoughts occupy my mind. Would it be a good plan to study some difficult language, Russian for example, about which one could think while doing purely mechanical work?

A. For what purpose? After some time, you will have wrong thoughts in Russian!

Q. Is there any way in which we can remember more clearly what we have understood when we were in a better state?

A. It is a very important thing, but I do not know of any special method. These moments must be connected. Look backwards, try to compare. This is particularly important in relation to some definite question. For instance, you may understand something you had not understood half an hour ago; but perhaps in the past there have been moments when you also understood something in this connection. Try to remember these moments and connect them.

Q. Does understanding of an idea or a term vary in relation to the degree of being?

A. Certainly. People understand according to their level, their capacity, not according to the meaning of things.

Q. My difficulty is that no idea is completely clear to me.

A. It is impossible to make it clear with formatory thinking and words. People think they understand a thing when they give it a name, but they do not realize that this is artificial. When you can feel a thing and when you can verify it by higher consciousness and higher mind, then only can you say that it is really true and that it really exists. And schools do not deal with ordinary intellectual ideas. This means that these ideas, as for instance, the idea of self-remembering, are not clear without higher centres, for without higher centres one cannot come to the truth. Schools are the work of higher centres; they give us something which we cannot attain by ourselves, because we can only use the ordinary mind. And the ordinary mind has definite limits and cannot jump over them. It can accumulate material, forget it, accumulate again, and forget again, and reduce the system to just nonsense by going too straight in one direction.

When you find yourself in a state approaching higher emotional Centre, you will be astounded how much you can understand at once and then you come back to your normal state, and you forget it all. By persistent self-remembering and by certain other methods you may come to the higher emotional Centre, but you will not be able to retain what you have understood then. If you write it down, it will have no sense when you read it with the intellectual Centre later.

Q. Sometimes when I have tried to self-remember I have a strange feeling about inanimate objects, as if they had a sort of awareness that was them.

A. Discount the possibility of imagination. Let us say simply that you feel something new in things. But when you begin to explain it, you begin to imagine. Do not try to explain, just leave it. Sometimes you can feel strange things in that way, but explanations are always wrong, because you feel with one very good apparatus and explain with another, a very clumsy machine that cannot really explain.

Q. It all seems to come back to the same question, how to be more emotional.

A. You cannot try to be emotional, the more you try, the less emotional you will be. You can try to be conscious, and if you become more conscious, you will become more emotional. You must think about how to get more energy to be conscious. That would be a right question, and the answer would be that first you must stop leaks and try to get more energy by following all the indications you get from the work, all of them. Do not only concentrate on one; you can always find something that you did not do.

Q. Sometimes I feel that I have the capacity to concentrate, but I do not know what to do. I only think about small things, and it disappears again.

A. You have always more than enough material for work on yourself.

you can never be at a loss as to what to do. Try to stop thoughts, that is easy and useful. If you have no energy to do that, you must accumulate energy by struggle with mechanical habits and things like that. That will accumulate enough energy for this effort to remember yourself or the effort to stop thoughts.

Q. Is meditation, as advocated in Indian books, the same as self-remembering?

A. They speak of meditation, but they also say that one must work under a teacher. We read and remember one thing and forget another; we think we can study meditation or meditate ourselves. If you can remember yourself, you can meditate; if not, you cannot. Self-remembering means control of thoughts, a different state. Meditation is an action of a developed mind, and we ascribe it to ourselves. It would be very good if we could meditate, but we cannot; self-remembering is the way to it. You cannot begin from the end; you have to begin from the beginning like in everything else. What does 'meditation' mean *for us*? Thinking about the system; trying to connect ideas and reconstruct the system. This is 'meditation', not simply thinking about one word or one idea.

Q. In trying to think about some definite idea of the system I always think the same thing I thought before. I cannot help it.

A. This is a technical side. You must try different ways. You can either concentrate on one or another side of the subject, or take one or another point of view, or try to explain to someone else. If it is difficult to think on some definite subject, you can always imagine that you are explaining this subject to some person. But again, you must imagine yourself explaining it to different people, people with preparation or without preparation, a religious person, a scientifically minded person and so on. You have to explain differently according to who you are explaining to. Then it is always very useful to separate what you knew before from what you have learnt from the system. This is very important. If you do not separate, you will always mix things in your thinking. It is necessary to know what you knew before, what you read somewhere and what you got here.

There is yet another thing you can do, you can try to write a programme of thinking for yourself. Find your own subjects you would like to think about, or subjects which you think may be useful to you, or subjects which you do not understand but would like to learn to think about. All this is useful. Then, if you have time, think about them two or three times a day.

Q. I have tried these imaginary conversations you suggested but have not been able to make them last long enough.

A. These imaginary conversations must go according to plan; you cannot start them just from any point. You can invent some sort of situation and make yourself speak to some imaginary person, or to someone you know, and explain some particular subject to him according to the kind of person he is. This may help. But do not try to give a lecture, a lecture is bound to turn formatory.

Q. My difficulty is talking within my mind. Will these imaginary conversations help me to work against this habit?

A. Yes, that may be useful, or you can think about the ideas of the system, set yourself definite tasks. Another approach is to see whether this mental talking is useful or useless. It may be useful, but mostly it is useless. Like all mechanical habits it is very difficult to struggle with. You do not notice it, or you may have been talking to yourself for two hours before you notice, so you must have a better watchman to ring the bell when you begin. This means being more awake.

Q. I feel one might achieve something if one could remember more of the system at one moment instead of just fragments.

A. Quite right. That is why you will see after some time that it is useful to work with new people and explain things to them, because you cannot have a sufficiently large part of the system before your eyes if you do not repeat it all, and you can only do this when you have to explain things to new people and answer their questions. It is not necessary to give lectures or have large groups; something useful can be done with one, two or three people.

Q. Lately I have been more dissatisfied than usual with myself, and the lack of results obtained from my efforts. What is to be done?

A. You must not let yourself identify with these negative feelings and disappointments; it is the worst possible thing. Think about something cheerful. For instance, you can take any subject in the system and compare how you thought before about it and how you think now. You will see that you have gained one thing, and another thing, and a third thing. That will help you to struggle on.

Q. In the example of the eye of a needle in the Gospels does it mean that when identification ceases a person has a chance?

A. It may be simply wrong valuation; or it may be too many words, a great load of words, so that a man cannot pass through.

Q. In our present state, can we know real love, loyalty, or devotion?

A. For us, these things are relative. We can have them more or less. But we cannot know them in any absolute way.

Q. I find it difficult to understand that faith has no place in this system. Surely it is necessary to believe that the system has possibilities of making you more conscious.

A. That will not help, quite the reverse. You must try to verify it, and base your attitude on facts, not on belief. If you do even one-tenth of what is suggested, very soon you will have facts, and then you must base your attitude on these facts, not on theories. Faith is a passive thing. We have to verify everything, accept nothing on faith. For faith there are other ways, but in the Fourth Way faith would be weakness trying to escape work. Instead of trying to know, we would believe. Only what man himself finds to be true can serve as a sufficient foundation.

We must understand that faith, in the true sense, is a certain state that is more than emotional. It is a positive emotion and, taken in this sense, it means a higher level which we, being men 1, 2 and 3, have not reached, and so we do not know what faith means, it is only a word for us. Faith must be directed to big things, not applied to small things of ordinary life. When people use what we call 'faith' in cases when they must *know* it is just laziness.

There can be one faith and another faith, it can be on different levels. According to the division of men into seven categories there can be seven kinds of faith, so it is difficult to speak in these terms.

Q. Why should I want to make myself different if I do not believe there is a reason?

A. Not believe but know. If you merely believe, you will do nothing. If you find out your state, you will try to get out. But this will be based on facts, on observations, not on belief.

Q. What Centre is used for faith?

A. Real faith is a higher emotion, belonging to the higher emotional Centre. In our ordinary emotional Centre, there can only be imitation faith. Real faith means not only emotion, but also knowledge.

Q. I had an idea that work on oneself was work towards salvation, towards immortality.

A. Big words. But if you said it is towards not making fools of ourselves, I would understand you. We constantly make fools of ourselves because we are asleep.

Q. *Isn't* there a part of ourselves which survives bodily death?

A, this is a very interesting and very important point. You ask so simply about after death, as though one could know about it. All experience of all mankind (I do not mean imagination) shows; hat we cannot know what happens after death, otherwise we would have known something positive about it. Since we know nothing, it proves definitely that in this state of consciousness, with ordinary centres, we cannot get at the truth, we can only make theories. First try to understand that our capacity of cognition, our capacity of knowing, is limited by our state of consciousness. In this state of consciousness, we can only know certain things and have answers only to certain questions. If we want to know more, we find that we cannot; in practically every line of study we come sooner or later to a dead wall. In some cases, this wall remains in exactly the same place, as in the case of life after death, we know no more about it than man of the Stone Age. We can only think that if we acquire a higher state of consciousness and use higher centres we may get a concrete answer to that question. We can know our life only from birth to death. If we want to know what was before and what will be after, if there is a before and after in relation to that we can only hope that in a better state of consciousness, using an improved machine, we will be able to understand. We ask ourselves these questions and we do not realize that we cannot have an answer such as we are. There are many questions like that.

It is necessary to realize and remember how many are the things we come up against in our thinking which are really insoluble for our mind. When we realize that, it will help us to see that we must begin with possible problems. Many people, I do not mean necessarily in the work, but even in the work, many people spend all their mental energy on these insoluble problems. They invent all kinds of solutions, try to think in this or that way about them, but it is all quite useless. You can understand one thing if you understand another thing, and a third thing if you have understood the first two. There are ways for everything, but some problems we can approach with the ordinary mind, while other problems we must put off and wait till we are more conscious and are able to use better machines for thinking.

In ordinary thinking, in ordinary philosophy and psychology, this question never arises, or if it does, it arises in so vague and confused a form that it does not help. But we know more divisions, more steps, and we must use this knowledge. It will help us to think more practically and to avoid useless abstractions and trying to solve problems which at present we cannot solve.

* * *

CHAPTER XV

Idea of esotericism—The logical method and the psychological method of thinking—Explanation of the psychological method—What the idea of esotericism implies—Certain kinds of esoteric ideas become accessible only at difficult periods—Necessity of being united— Materiality of knowledge —Great knowledge and how it differs from ordinary knowledge— Accumulators of knowledge—Schools—Can one affect external events?— Study of life—Big events of life and their influence—Subjective ways and objective way—Attitudes as a means of changing influences—Assessing events in life—Gradual disappearance of B influences—The reason for the decrease of influence of esoteric circles—Lack of preparation—The system and how it is taught—Different scales—Death of schools, and conditions necessary for their existence—Relation of the system to Christianity— To die and to be born—Prayer—Suggestions concerning the study of the Lord's Prayer.

I have given you a General Idea of the fundamental principles of the system and up to now the Centre of gravity of our work at least of practical work was in ourselves. Today I want to show you a larger view.

It is necessary to understand the idea of esotericism and to realize why certain people can understand this idea while other people cannot. We must know what esotericism means, what is included in it, what is excluded by it, what is connected with it, and what can serve as a kind of test or touchstone for recognizing people who can understand it.

For some people the idea of esotericism appears absurd, impossible. For them esotericism not only does not seem valuable but does not even appear as possible truth. But for others the idea of esotericism is necessary and important. The cause of this is to be found in the difference of method. All ways of thinking can be divided into two categories: logical thinking and psychological thinking, and the capacity or incapacity to use the psychological method of thinking makes an enormous difference. The logical method is better than no method, but it is very limited. It is useful in law courts, but for understanding it is not sufficient. For logical thinking esotericism is impossible, because it cannot be demonstrated or formulated, but for psychological thinking, which sees the psychological nature of things, the idea of esotericism follows from many facts we can observe. So, the psychological method may bring one to the idea of esotericism and may lead to proofs of its existence certainly subjective proofs, but still proofs. And this in its turn may bring a man to the realization of the necessity of systems or teachings of an esoteric origin. It gives him the possibility of understanding the ideas of such systems and leads to the realization of the necessity of three lines of work and to an understanding of them.

First, we must try to understand the difference between the logical and the psychological methods, and to establish what each of them is.

The psychological method cannot be denied but we can find examples of its application, of its working. We can see how the psychological method opens new ways of thinking, how by using it we begin to understand many things.

When, by means of the psychological method, we have made a general survey of the teachings which prove to have an esoteric origin, we shall more or less know the qualities of teachings which can be called esoteric and shall be able to think in a right way about this system and apply its principles in practice.

The psychological method starts with two admissions. The first is that things have their inner meaning. The second is that things are connected, that they only appear to be separated. Things depend on one another, they stand in a certain relation to one another, whereas the logical method takes each thing separately. So, the psychological method studies everything first from the point of view of its inner meaning and, secondly, it finds similarities in the dissimilar. The basis of this method, and the chief difference from ordinary methods, is the realization of the relativity of mind, the understanding of the type and kind of mind used and realization that in one state of mind things can be understood in one way and in another in another way. For the logical mind everything is certain and unique. But the psychological method shows that everything, every conclusion, every deduction is a mental picture and is merely the result of the working of our mind. For distinguishing, comparing and finding the relative values of things and seeing which is higher and which lower, you can start only with this realization of the possibility of different minds. When you compare ideas, let us say certain ideas of the New Testament, of the Upanishads, or some attributed to Pythagoras or Plato with scientific ideas or philosophy, sometimes you can experience this realization of minds on different levels.

What I want you to understand is that, even using ordinary knowledge, you can come to the relative value of ideas and see that the starting point is the realization that our ordinary mind *is not the only one that exists.*

See if you can find some examples of the psychological method; if you cannot do so now, you must try to find, later, examples of cases when you had new possibilities of understanding.

Q. Do you mean that one is not guided by the external similarity of facts?

A. This is one aspect. If you meet with it, you will know what is psychological method, and what is not.

Q. Is the psychological method the use of the intellectual part of the intellectual Centre?

A. No, not quite. The more centres and the more parts of centres you use, the better the psychological method. It means using all the powers you have. Logical method means the use of only the mechanical part of intellectual Centre.

Q. And is the esoteric method the use of higher centres?

A. No, it is the use of the system. You cannot use higher centres, but you can use the system.

Q. Is psychological thinking only possible when all our functions are working rightly?

A. We must start as we are. We cannot wait till we change, because if we do, we will never change; and if we change mechanically, we change only for the worse.

Q. What are the first things to learn in trying to think psychologically? I feel it is more than I can accomplish.

A. When you say it is more than you can accomplish you think about the completed process. And I speak about the process itself, about beginning to work. If you say this is beyond you, you can do nothing and so, naturally, nothing happens. It is again this habit of thinking in absolutes.

Q. What are the essential features of esotericism?

A. It is difficult to speak about essential features because it depends on how you take this word. The word 'esoteric' means inner. Esotericism includes in itself the idea of the existence of an inner circle of humanity. You remember how humanity was described as consisting of four circles esoteric, mesoteric and exoteric, which constitute the inner circle, and the outer circle in which we live. The idea of esotericism implies transmission of knowledge; it presumes the existence of a group of people to whom a certain knowledge belongs. This must not be understood in some mystical way, but more definitely, concretely. There are a great many differences between the inner and the outer circles. For instance, many things we want to find or create can exist only in the inner circle, such things as positive emotions, understanding between people, certain kinds of knowledge; all this belongs to the inner circle. I think this is sufficient for understanding the idea of the inner or esoteric circle.

Q. I understand that the primary feature of esoteric knowledge is that it is hidden, and one would not be likely to find it. So how can we recognize esoteric knowledge or an esoteric school?

A. We are studying a system which is supposed to be esoteric, so with its help we will be able to recognize it. And although esoteric knowledge is hidden from ordinary life, it can be found. It is not hidden absolutely, so that nobody can find it, otherwise it would have no meaning. This would be contrary to its aims and would spoil the results of its existence. The only meaning of hidden knowledge is that it can be found; the important thing is how to recognize it. With the help of these ideas, comparing what can be found in the ordinary intellectual way and what cannot and then comparing it with the system, we shall be able to establish with a certain degree of probability the level of the knowledge we meet with.

If we take history in the ordinary way as a series of separate events, we shall not find proofs of esotericism. One thing will follow another, on the surface and without apparent connection. But if we know that things are connected, and look for connections, we shall find them hidden beneath the surface. For instance, many big historical changes came apparently from nothing, with no antecedents, no origin. In ancient Greece there is nothing on the surface to explain the seventh century B.C. In the eighth and ninth centuries there was apparently nothing leading up to it; there was no direct line of development. In the same way Gothic art seemingly came out of nothing. It had no history, it appeared instantly.

In prehistoric art too, that is, in all that belongs to more than ten thousand years ago, there is nothing on the surface to explain the big Sphinx, for instance. It is both bigger in concept and higher in level, and, so to speak, more clever (though this is not the right word) than anything we know. Who made it? Why are such works of art found in the desert?

Then again, take literature, especially that of the East. We can find such things as the great Indian poems and the New Testament which are of a higher level than anything else we know. There is nothing similar to them, nothing ordinary can explain them, all these things are absolutely unique. If they are taken separately and presupposing that they have no inner meaning, they cannot be explained. But if we try to use the psychological method, we shall find the connection.

Try to think about esotericism, how it is possible, in which form it can exist, in which form it cannot exist. You can read of secret societies in the East, or in Tibet, of the existence of secret libraries, of groups of people living in hidden places and preserving ancient knowledge. This is a crude form of thinking. There is nothing impossible in the idea that there are groups of people of this kind. But the idea of esotericism is more subtle. It does not require secret societies. The idea of secret societies is a simplified form of thinking. It is quite possible that there are people here on the earth who possess much greater knowledge than we do, but if they have this knowledge, they have no need of secret societies. They need not live in the mountains; they can live anywhere.

Q. Is it necessary to know an esoteric doctrine to recognize the presence of esoteric ideas?

A. No, you can recognize esoteric ideas by means of the psychological method. Only with the psychological method can you find more in the system which you know.

Q. What must one know to use the psychological method?

A. The psychological method requires no special knowledge. What is necessary is simple thinking, but not the narrow ordinary thinking. Logical thinking is narrow, but psychological thinking is broader thinking, comparing not two things but maybe as many as five. Logical thinking always deals with two: one must be true, another false. For the psychological method it is not necessarily so; both may be wrong, or both may be right.

I will give you an example of the psychological method. In 1915 I gave in St Petersburg a public lecture on Life after Death. I tried to bring together all the existing ideas about life after death: the positivist, scientific idea of death as disappearance, the religious understanding of death connected with the idea of an immortal soul, heaven as reward and hell as punishment; the spiritualistic understanding of the idea of survival; the theosophical idea of reincarnation, the Buddhist idea of recurrence; and many others. What is interesting is that they are all right; they only look contradictory. Logically they contradict one another, but from the point of view of the psychological method they complement one another.

In order to illustrate this, I asked the question: how can all these ideas be right since they look so different? It is because there is a law we do not understand. The human mind cannot invent anything absolutely wrong. The normal mind, working freely and not tied to some presupposed truth, always arrives at some kind of truth.

A complete lie can be invented only by an insane mind or a mind working in chains.

Q. Should one know other esoteric teachings and find connections?

A. Only in a general way, to find the place of this system. You do not know enough to compare and find connections. When you think about this system and read something that reminds you of it, you take only one or another idea; you do not compare all ideas. Parts can always be analogous, but such comparing can be useful only when you can see the whole behind the parts and then you may find that the two have nothing in common, because in order to be similar everything must be similar. Suppose one point in one system is similar to one point in another, but these points are surrounded by fifteen other points that have no similarity, this makes them essentially different. We cannot do it yet; we are not accustomed to finding the relation of a part to the whole in ordinary thinking. We think that parts can be compared and that parts can be right or wrong without relation to the whole.

Q. But if you find two systems of philosophy that have points or peaks which resemble one another?

A. How do you know they resemble one another? You only know words.

you do not know what is behind these words. Words do not guarantee the meaning. This is why it is recommended for a long time not to try to find parallels and to study this system separately from anything else. Later, when you know more, you may try to find parallels.

Q. What guarantee is there that there are no new ideas in this system brought in since its origin?

A. This is very clear. If the principles are kept, they eliminate wrong ideas. Formatory ideas cannot exist side by side with esoteric ideas.

Q. What arrangements can be made to ensure that the ideas can be kept pure?

A. Ideas become distorted when people begin to invent their own explanations and theorize; but so long as they work sincerely and try to verify everything that comes into their minds and work according to the principles and rules, distortion is not at all necessary. In the organization of schoolwork every measure is taken against distortion, and if it happens it is only because people forget these precautionary measures. Distortion is generally the influence of formatory Centre, for when people begin to work with formatory Centre and nobody corrects them, there is no idea in the world that cannot be distorted in twenty-four hours.

Q. If that is the scale of distortion you mean, I certainly distort the ideas for myself.

A. For yourself it does not matter, you have a chance to correct it. Everybody distorts them in the beginning until they have the whole range of ideas but understanding one part corrects one's understanding of another. You cannot understand the whole thing and misunderstand the parts, and if you can think rightly of the whole, you will understand every part. Besides, your questions show whether you think rightly, and if you think wrongly, it is corrected.

Q. Different people want different things. How should we understand the meaning of schoolwork?

A. School-work has many different parts, all of them to help you to awake. Every individual must have his own aim. If the aims of individuals fit in with the aims of the school, they work in the school. If they do not fit in, they leave.

You may start with the idea of acquiring knowledge. If you find new ideas, you will begin to value them. The word 'work' is often used without discrimination.

Q. But you use it yourself!

A. I mean it. I want to show you that the only way for you is to understand the psychological method, the idea of esotericism, the proofs of its existence and to have a certain understanding of the system. After that you can start to work. The system is a living thing, an organic thing that grows and opens up new horizons.

You see, we live in a very peculiar time and the work is very important, in that, apart from other points, it gives the possibility to remain sane or to become sane. The further we go, the more we talk about these ideas, the more we are apt to lose sight of the meaning of the whole thing. We take for granted that we have these ideas, we talk about them, we want to get something from this teaching, but we do not think about why we are able to have these ideas and speak about them.

The teaching itself, certain kinds of teachings, certain kinds of ideas become accessible to people only at certain moments, at very difficult periods. These are not the ordinary kind of ideas that you can get at any time and any moment Quite the opposite, the very fact that we can have these ideas shows that it is an extremely difficult time. It would have been much easier to work with these ideas, say, thirty or forty years ago, but in reality, one thing depends on another, for if times were not so difficult, we would not have had them.

So, if we keep this in mind, even this realization alone will by itself bring us to the right attitude, it will always remind us that we have to take these ideas seriously, that nothing in relation to them can be taken from the point of view of ordinary likes and dislikes or ordinary attitudes of right and wrong. In present times it is impossible to foretell what the future may bring, so we must have a particular appreciation and a particular regard for these ideas and this system and try to do not only what is right at a given moment, personally, individually, but what is right in connection with the whole thing; not merely think of personal aim but of the whole tradition connected with this work.

And certainly, first of all, unity is necessary, because it is possible to satisfy the needs of the work itself only so long as we are all ready to go the same way. If there are different opinions and one thinks it best to go to the right and another to the left, nobody will do anything right, for there will be no direction. If one person thinks one thing and another person another thing, both will be wrong; it is not that one will be right and another wrong Actions must be connected, they must agree with one another. There cannot be a rule that everyone must agree with and understand everything in his own mind, but there can be no difference in actions.

Circumstances are not in our hands, they may change, may take one or another turn. But the whole principle of imitating schoolwork is that there cannot be differences of opinion as regards actions, because otherwise how can we work?

I only wish to show you that in dealing with the principles of the system and organization of the work we must never forget that we are dealing with a very big thing, and we have against us very big things. If we keep this in mind, we will find the right way. If we forget this, nothing will come of it.

Q. What do you mean by imitating schoolwork?

A. I used this word not in the sense of imitating external methods but in the sense of inner imitation which can be done only on the basis of a certain organization.

People in the work must be united. The more we are united, the more resistance we will show to all kinds of unfavorable influences and the more we can get out of them, because we will be, as it were, in the middle of a big accumulator full of all kinds of energies. If we are closed, we will be able to get energy out of this big accumulator; if we are full of holes, we will be unable to keep any of it.

You see, I must explain to you one idea. Everything in the world is material and limited, only materiality is different. There is a limited amount of sand in the desert and of water in the sea. Knowledge is also material and therefore limited. It is very useful to remember that the knowledge necessary for change of being exists only in a very limited quantity. Knowledge is substance. For a certain definite period, say a hundred-year humanity has a certain amount of knowledge which can be used. If too many people want this knowledge, they will have so little that nothing can be done with it. But since very few want it, those who want it can get it.

Q. I do not understand this about knowledge. Is not knowledge consciousness?

A. No, consciousness is another thing, although this is true in the sense that a higher degree of consciousness in itself includes knowledge. It does not include all knowledge, but the knowledge you already possess. In a state of consciousness, you know at once all that you know; in this sense you can say that consciousness is knowledge, but by itself consciousness cannot give more knowledge, although one can look at this question from different sides.

As to the idea of great knowledge, higher or esoteric knowledge, we must first of all understand that all our ordinary knowledge, including scientific knowledge, is always knowledge acquired with ordinary mind. All methods of scientific investigation are the work of ordinary mind, but there is another knowledge which is acquired by a higher or a more developed mind, and this knowledge will diner from ordinary know ledge, because knowledge acquired with ordinary mind is always limited by methods of investigation, by eye and ear, for, after all, the most complicated instruments that can be used in scientific research have to be verified by eye and ear. This knowledge is a very narrow knowledge not based on understanding of the whole, whereas great knowledge is knowledge based on understanding of the whole by a more developed mind. Thus, there are different degrees of knowledge which are so different that they cannot really be compared. If you learn the multiplication table, this kind of knowledge not being limited in amount, you do not take it away from anybody. Nor, in the case of esoteric knowledge, do you in fact take it away from others, but this is because there are very few people who want it.

It is difficult, at first, to accept the idea that knowledge is material, but if you think about it, perhaps you will begin to realize it. Let us take it like this: knowledge can exist in different solutions, in a very weak solution or in stronger solutions. When I speak of knowledge, I speak of a stronger solution which is very limited. We think that if we do not know something, it is because we do not know where to learn it. We do not realize how many things there are that we cannot know. Because of this it is difficult for us to understand the materiality of knowledge and what controls its distribution. Just as there are accumulators in the body, so there are accumulators of knowledge in life. At certain periods of history certain knowledge was collected and kept there. If you find such an accumulator, you will get the knowledge. What are these accumulators? They are schools, even the old schools that no longer exist. Man cannot develop without tapping these accumulators, but if he does, he can get energy from them, real energy, such as centres get. Man 1, 2 and 3 will get only coarse energy, the energy that man No. 5 can get will be finer. When it is said that knowledge is limited, it refers to knowledge in these accumulators.

Q. Has this knowledge got form and weight?

A. Form not necessarily, but weight yes, not in the ordinary sense but in the sense of density. In ordinary language too some words have weight while some have no weight at all.

Q. How can we work to find this accumulator? Does it refer only to schools, or is it also something within ourselves?

A. You can work to come into contact with it just by learning what you can learn. It refers to both, to oneself and to schools.

Q. Does a man with greater knowledge have a responsibility towards those who have less? I mean a man who has esoteric knowledge.

A. Esoteric knowledge means school, so a man who has esoteric knowledge is a man who comes from a school or who is in a school. His responsibility is towards the school. When a man acquires school knowledge, he acquires responsibility. But it is impossible to discuss this question in general, for there may be many conditions we do not know. For instance, certain knowledge may be given only on certain conditions.

Q. What a slender thread our connection with esoteric knowledge is, since it depends on you being with us to impart it.

A. It is necessary to understand that our connection with esoteric knowledge cannot depend on a person. Suppose you know a person who is connected with an esoteric school, but you cannot understand his ideas. Then your connection with esoteric school does not exist, and if this person dies, the connection disappears absolutely. But suppose during the time he was alive you understood his ideas, then you are connected, and if he dies you remain connected. So, you can be connected with esoteric circles only through ideas, not through people.

Q. Could the people in the system have any effect on events in life?

A. How do you see it yourself? In what way?

Q. I cannot see how they can, except for individuals to become conscious.

A. For every individual? How can you make them conscious if they do not want to? This is a characteristic example of how we think. We think that we are asking practical questions. If one asks, one must see some point of application. Suppose people could affect events, suppose there was such big magic they must spend a certain amount of energy. And you do not know the amount of energy necessary to produce an effect against the current, even the slightest effect. Our time is very bad, very unpleasant kinds of events happen. In order to stop a typical event on a big scale the whole energy of the solar system is necessary. Can you command it? And the second thing is: do you know what is better? How can, you be sure? I do not speak now about whether it is possible or not, but even if it were possible, do you have the energy and do you know what is better? We are people 1, 2 and 3; how can we know what is right? We have only just started to study a system that is supposed to bring man to a higher level. This is very useful material to think about.

Q. I find that I still cannot give up the idea of our being useful to some sort of conscious work which is going against the general madness.

A. But this is imagination, because first of all, we must be useful to ourselves. How can we be useful to some bigger kind of work if we cannot be useful to our own work? We must first learn to be useful to our own work, and then if there is a larger work, we may be useful to it. Besides, what does being useful mean? You will remember about being connected with the third line of work? A person cannot do more than he can; there may be different circumstances, capacities, and conditions, so being useful cannot be taken as an obligation. But one must think about it and use the opportunity when it comes. One thing, however, must be taken as a rule to do nothing against the interests of the work. It does not mean that everybody can actually help at every given moment, and this is not expected or required. But everybody must be prepared to do what he can and what circumstances allow when the opportunity comes, and certainly to do nothing *against* the third line of work, for one can do many things to harm it. In the beginning, when we spoke of A, B and C influences we did not specify what they were, we merely took them as influences. Now we must try to divide these influences into classes, and the practical side of this study will be how to control these influences, how to be receptive to certain influences and not be receptive to the influences we do not want.

In other words, we must study life. Our study of ourselves will continue, but it is necessary to begin to study external things as well, try to understand them and form a right opinion about them. We will not be able to go far if we do not learn to discriminate between external events, events on a big scale, and find what is good and what is bad from the point of view of possible evolution. If we find in external events something that helps evolution, that will bring us to the question: how can individual evolution, that is, evolution of a small number of people, affect the general state of people? If we look at external life now and ask ourselves how we can regard it from the point of view of the existence of esoteric circles of humanity, we will see that the state of humanity is far from favorable, because, although we know that everybody cannot be in esoteric circles, there can exist in life definite influences coming from these circles. But we can say positively that we cannot see any signs of a control of things by the esoteric circle's life goes on by itself.

Roughly speaking, man's situation can be described like this: he is a machine governed by various currents coming from the big machines that surround him. What are these big machines? All big events, wars, revolutions, civilizations, religions, science, art, inventions of the last century, all these things produce different influences that act on man.

Then in connection with schools it was explained that the possibility of escape is only in schools, that is, with the help of C influences. But what is the situation of people who do not know any school, for the possibility of schoolwork is very small and very rare? Does it mean that it is absolutely impossible to attain anything without school, or is there such a possibility? You remember I spoke of the three traditional ways and the Fourth Way. These four ways are called subjective ways. These ways are supposed to produce certain effects. But some people, maybe very few, may develop to a certain extent even without schoolwork. This is called the objective way; but it is a slow way. Subjective ways are short-cuts, they are for people impatient of ordinary slow work, even if there is a certain progress. So theoretically you can get possibilities of development living quite an ordinary life, without C influence, using only the material provided by B influences. You remember about B influences: religion, philosophy, art, science? On the whole, if people can absorb enough of this material, it should be sufficient for development, but even at best it is slow and uncertain development. All schools, all ways are for impatient people; that is why they are called subjective ways. So, the answer to this question is both yes and no; some people can develop without schools, and some cannot, because it is a question of different types of people. Besides, the objective way also needs conditions; it does not mean that all people who are not in the work can develop. In a sense the objective way is even more difficult than schoolwork, because there one has no possibility of verifying whether what one decides to do or not to do is right or wrong. In school one can verify; but verifying is one thing and doing is another.

Q. So it is not impossible or improbable for a man to develop without the help of a school?

A. Only to a certain extent, and that also with the help of a school, only without his being aware of it. For there are many things in which the help of schools can be found generally in religions, philosophical systems and so on.

You remember I said before that there are different schools: one person needs one kind of school, another person another kind. There are no universal schools suitable for everybody. At the same time, you must realize that the chance to meet some kind of school is very rare, I mean to meet a school in real life, not in books or in theory and if one meets a school, generally there is no other. If one finds this school too difficult and begins to look for another school, then, supposing even that one does meet another, one will find the same difficulty there. There can be no difference between schools in this respect, because differences are created by the relation of a man's state to school. So, it will always be the same whatever school a man finds.

I remember being told a story once by a man who said it had been his own experience. Some disciples of a school which was half-Yogi, half-religious, found the school too difficult, so they came to another school. To their surprise they were immediately given the same task to do, but with some additional difficulty.

One of them asked the man who gave them the task how he knew whether it meant that schools communicated with each other when a man left. The teacher answered: 'It is not worthwhile communicating when a man runs away from one school and comes to another. As soon as I saw you, I realized the kind of task you had been given and could only give you the same but perhaps a little more difficult.' So, you see, there is really no choice.

Q. What will happen if one acquires change of being without school?

A. If one gets being or knowledge so to speak undeservedly, it is generally incomplete and worse than nothing, with the exception of very rare cases in the objective way; but the latter happens so seldom that it is no use speaking about it. Certain examples of wrong ways will be explained later, because in understanding the wrong way we can understand better the right way. For instance, efforts can be made on the basis of fear, but it will not be a right effort, because right effort should be based on understanding, not on fear.

To return to our situation, we must remember all that we have heard and understood about attitudes. Our attitudes are like wires which connect us with events, and certain currents produced by the nature of these attitudes flow through these wires, and the nature of the current determines the kind of influence we receive from a given event. If a certain event produces an influence on us, this influence can be changed by our attitude.

We must create a certain understanding of external things. This means we must judge them not by personal sympathies and antipathies but, as I said, from the point of view of their relation to possible evolution, that is, we must judge them from the point of view of a possible increase of the power of esotericism, because evolution of mankind means an increase of the power of esoteric circles over life.

I said that at every moment one is surrounded by a great many big moving things which always affect one whether one is aware of it or not. They *always* affect one in one way or another. One may have very definite attitudes towards such things as wars, revolutions, events of social or political life and so on, or one may be indifferent, or negative, or positive towards them. In any case, being positive on one side means being negative on another, so it does not change anything. Right attitude includes understanding the quality of a thing from the point of view of evolution and of obstacles to evolution, meaning by 'evolution' conscious, voluntary, and intentional development of an individual man on definite lines and in a definite direction during the period of his earthly life. Things that do not help are simply not considered; however big they may be externally one does not 'see' them. And if one does not consider or see them, one can get rid of their influence. Only, again, it is necessary to understand that not considering wrong things does not mean indifference, because people who are indifferent do not consider things, but are affected by them all the same.

I repeat again, it is necessary to think about things using the ordinary emotional and ordinary thinking faculty and to try to find in what relation they stand to what we call evolution, that is, increase of the influence of inner circles and growth of the possibility for the right kind of people to acquire the right kind of knowledge. We have to understand the weight of things. You remember, it was explained about words that they have different weight, and it is necessary to feel their weight. It is the same with events. Just as in ourselves there are many imaginaries, invented things, so there are also in life. Because people believe in them, they produce an effect. In this sense almost the whole of life is not real. People live in non-existent things and do not see the real things; they do not even bother to think about them, being completely satisfied with the imaginary.

Try to concentrate on the question of what is important and what is unimportant; we must learn to distinguish these things. So far, with the help of the work, we could define good and evil in relation to ourselves. Now we must come out of our shell and try to look around, using the same methods and the same principles. If we use one type of principles for ourselves and another for external things, we will never get anything out of it. We do not think sufficiently of the relation of this work to life in general, we do not give account to ourselves of the position it occupies as regards life. I do not say you can answer this question, but you can think about it, see it from one angle or another angle. Unless you think about it, things will not be in their right perspective for you, and you will not understand the work in the right way. The work is a small thing, and enormous things belong to life. I do not mean by these wars and revolutions and things of this kind, but things belonging to everyday life. You will see that it occupies no position at all and need not exist from the point of view of life.

At the same time the work is the most important thing for those who understand it. So, we must make it go on and not expect any help from life. We must go against life, do everything ourselves. We cannot think that there is plenty of time, that if we do not do something now, we will do it next year, for next year things may be different.

Analysis of events in life can be based on the idea of influences A, B and C. We can ask ourselves, how many influences of the third kind, that is, influences conscious both in their origin and action, do we see? We must admit that we never see them. If we are looking for something, we meet only with certain manifestations of influence B, and every influence B is surrounded by all possible dangers and all kinds of forces trying to destroy it. Many influences B are disappearing under our eyes; things that could be found not so long ago cannot be found any more. How many influences B of the past reach us? They do not live long, they have a short life, with the exception of two or three which are surrounded by such a tangle of mechanical adaptations that they almost become influences

A, they survive only in this form. All mechanical forces tend to destroy them because in their origin they are opposed to mechanical forces.

Q. What is the connection between civilization of the world and personal evolution?

A. We do not realize that the beginning of many activities in life is the work of conscious people. We think that all the work we see was begun and continued by people such as we are, by sleeping people. But sleeping people can only accidentally invent something useful, and they invent both useful and harmful things with equal pleasure, they cannot distinguish the one from the other. If we accept the word 'civilization,' it is the work of sleeping people, so there is no guarantee: there may be civilization today and barbarism tomorrow.

Supposing that what you or someone else calls civilization destroys influences B and you find yourself surrounded by influences A, you will have no chance. And, indeed, what we ordinarily call civilization does destroy influences B. Revolutions destroy, wars destroy, civilizations destroy—everything destroys esoteric influences. For instance, schools have always been destroyed by wars; that is a well-known fact. Schools cannot be established permanently. It is not exactly that wars intended to destroy schools, they did it by the way. War is one of these institutions in the life of humanity which make work impossible and destroy schools. Schoolwork needs a certain amount of normality in life; if life becomes too abnormal, schoolwork becomes impossible, and a school disappears.

Q. But people who profit by schoolwork do not disappear; what they learned would not leave them?

A. If they learned enough, they would profit by it, but if they only learned a little, they cannot profit much. There is a certain standard, a certain amount of knowledge necessary, and if you acquire this amount you can continue to work, but if you did not get enough, you cannot. Individual people, if they have reached a certain stage in development of consciousness, can isolate themselves from circumstances and can continue to work so long as they remain alive.

But school is under different laws: it needs an external form. Schools can do nothing about it, they have to take circumstances as they are, both big and small schools, elementary or highly developed. They have to exist in whatever circumstances they find themselves, and if circumstances become impossible, schools become impossible. This must be kept in mind.

There is another thing in connection with this. Religion is a more stable thing. Maybe it was organized in that way in order to exist. But schools cannot be organized in the same way, they need a certain minimum of security to survive.

Q. Why has the influence of the esoteric circles been diminishing lately?

A. People are becoming less and less sane. They need less truth and are more incapable of distinguishing it and more easily satisfied with lies. Interest in these ideas is much less and people's preparation is much less than even thirty or forty years ago. And this is not only the result of political events, although they also have their part in it.

Q. In what sense do you mean people are less prepared?

A. For instance, the idea of esotericism was not explained in St Petersburg; it was supposed to be known. Now it can no longer be assumed that the psychological method of thinking, the existence of esotericism and the need for schools of an esoteric origin is understood. We can never understand the meaning of esotericism and the inner circles of humanity until we understand that life is chaos and that things, instead of becoming more controlled and orderly are becoming only more complicated and less controlled. We take complication for progress. In ordinary life people's actions are not coordinated and results are unforeseen. Each man works in his own direction and the combined results produce things. Results in life are the results of cross-purposes, not the results of intentional actions. It is necessary to understand that this is always so in the outer circle, and it cannot be different. We can do nothing to change this state of affairs. We are corks on the waves which think that they control currents. It is very important to think about that and to look at things from this point of view. If one does not understand the difference between the inner and the outer circles, one will not understand further. What is possible in the inner circles is impossible in our circle.

Q. Should not the present state of the world make more people look for schools? People are frightened, they feel uncomfortable.

A. Why should one discomfort lead to another discomfort? Do you think that will make them come? You expect too much of them. You can say to a man that if he studies the system he will be more awake, but you cannot say he will be better off.

Q. They will get rid of identification.

A. And they will say that they cannot work without identification, and if they are not identified, they will lose all their money. There is no connection between interest in the system and the discomfort of the present situation.

Q. I have been very puzzled by my observation of young people. If they are happy and thoroughly normal, the idea of esotericism does not seem to appeal to them.

A. The idea of esotericism is very difficult. Sometimes one can catch its meaning at an early age, but often one fails to see it from the right angle. We have so many wrong attitudes and wrong ideas that nothing can be expected. I think a person who becomes seriously interested in these ideas is an exception, because people's minds are in such a confusion with absurd and contradictory ideas.

Q. I am only interested in the psychological side of the system, but not in esotericism.

A. But the psychological side is also esoteric. The system gives you nothing that is not esoteric, for the whole of it comes from minds that are not ordinary minds; it comes from people who understood things. Ordinary systems cannot bring about any change. The psychological side of the system is even more esoteric than the other side, or it would have no value. It has value only because it comes from higher minds, from their understanding and their ideas. This must be understood. We got this system somehow. If we suppose it has been created by men on the same level as we are, or that it is a theory, it has no value at all. But it is not a theory; it is supposed to come from school, from men of higher development. If there were no men of higher development, we would have no system.

In the beginning in Russia Mr Gurdjieff always insisted that it was not a system; it was just fragments and one had to make a system out of them. And he insisted that it should be given in this way. Now I make it more of a system, because we have more people. But when it was only a small group it was just conversations and not lectures. In lectures it is difficult to speak in fragments, but on the whole, it is still fragments, all the same. These fragments are on different scales, so you must understand much to put them together on the right scale. The same words and the same theories are used in different diagrams, for instance all on quite different scales.

Q. Can you give an example of what it means that it is taught in fragments?

A. Many things are taught like that: all about building up energies, the psychological side, the explanation of how the machine works, the side concerning the world and so on. It is very important to understand this. Only when you begin to understand how the scale changes will you be able to understand the system. As I said, it is taught in fragments each of which is on a different scale. You have to put them together and at the same time correct the scale. It is like several geographical maps, each on a different scale, cut into pieces. You have to see which piece fits which, where the scale is very different and where it is less different. This is the only way to study this system.

Q. Do you mean we cannot talk about the worlds unless we reduce them to our scale?

A. No, what I meant is quite different. Of course, we reduce everything, but what I meant is that we have to study things on different scales, and we must remember this and realize the relationship of different scales and the fact that things change with change of scale. Also, we must bear in mind that, about many things, we believe that they mean something, when actually they mean nothing at all. The system teaches us to find the difference between realities and imaginary quantities (and even worse than imaginary).

Q. I feel we have only half the knowledge of the system we could have.

A. Much less than half. Such as we are, we can only get fragments but sufficiently big to build something out of them. We must try to understand the structure. When you have all the fragments before you, you may see certain connections, and when you find these connections, you may see many other things.

Q. Have you altered the teaching much?

A. I have not altered it. But I prefer sometimes to start from a different point. In this system, as in any organic system, one can start from any point, this is not an alteration. Everything else remains the same, but I prefer to start with the psychological side.

Q. Have the people in the inner circle any control over people in the outer circle?

A. Yes, but with many reservations. The conscious circle cannot act directly, but only through B influences. Influences C can appear only if influences B are accepted and if people look for them. Men in the inner circle cannot have control over people who do not wish to know them. They cannot use violence, because it would mean a wrong triad, a wrong activity. For every kind of result there is a special triad. For instance, if people wish to acquire control; they can achieve it only in one way. If they act in another way, they will get the opposite result. Wars, revolutions and so on never give the desired results, but always the opposite results, because wrong triads are used. If people of the inner circles wish to influence other people, they can produce good results only if there is understanding, and only with people who wish it. This is a useful question. Try to think about it.

Q. You spoke of the insecure times we live in. Will the school take precautions to protect itself? I understood you to say that a school is not under the law of accident.

A. I meant that a school cannot be formed by accident, but it can be destroyed by accident. It cannot be formed mechanically, but it can be destroyed mechanically. Take some work of art, it will not be created purely mechanically, it will be made by some special triad, but it can be burnt like anything else.

Q. If schools are real living things, why do they die?

A. What do you mean by saying that schools are living things? It is vague and indefinite. But if we take it literally it will make it quite clear why schools die. All living beings die sooner or later. If people die, schools must also die. I have explained that schools need certain conditions. If these conditions are destroyed, the school is destroyed.

Q. But the ideas may remain?

A. Ideas cannot fly, they need human heads. And a school does not consist of ideas; you always forget that school teaches how to improve being.

Q. Were no ideas written down in the past?

A. Certainly there were, but ideas can be written down in different forms; they may be written down in such a way that nobody can read them without explanation from those who know or without change of being. Take the Gospels, they are written in different ciphers; one must know the key to decipher them, otherwise it would be just a story, doubtful historically and producing many wrong effects.

Q. Will the system give the key to the Gospels?

A. Some keys, but you cannot expect all the keys. Many of the keys can be got only with change of being, they cannot be only a matter of knowledge. Again, you forget about being. Change of being means connection with higher centres. Higher centres can understand many things which ordinary centres cannot.

Q. Then the New Testament must have misled many people?

A. The New Testament is written for schools and for different levels. In schools every word is explained. Every sentence in the New Testament has dozens of meanings, that is why there are so many things in it we do not understand. We are trying to pass from the level of man 1, 2 and 3 to the level of understanding of man No. 4; other people may be trying to pass to the level of man No 5, yet others to the level of man No 6 and so on and they all read the New Testament So we cannot expect, on our level, to understand all of it, since it is written in a very clever way. When somebody said it is under seven locks, he was quite right One must find one key and use it and then, with its help, one will find a second key, and so on, but one will not understand it until one has opened all the seven locks So if we understand all that is possible to understand on our level, we may get the possibility of understanding more.

Q. Can a school reach a higher level than the school it started from?

A. Yes, if it works according to methods and principles of schoolwork, it can grow. But again, you must remember that the level of the school depends on the level of being of the people who constitute it

Q. Was self-remembering a feature of the old esoteric knowledge?

A. Always, everywhere. Only sometimes, for instance in religious schools, it is called by a different name It is not arbitrary, self-remembering is a necessary stage in man's development, not an arbitrarily imposed task. One has to pass through it, and one can pass through it only in one way

Q. Did Christ at any time speak about it, and in what words?

A. Almost on every page, in different words, for instance, 'Watch', 'Do not sleep'. He spoke about it all the time.

Q. How should one consider church religion?

A. We cannot discuss religion, because it is quite a different thing, different elements enter into it Every religion is based on faith and, as I said already, faith does not enter into our system All we can say is that religions are on different levels, as I have explained in the first lectures Religion is a relative term All people are divided into men of different levels and all religions are divided in the same way Each religion has all the degrees. This is one of the very important things to understand We only know the horizontal divisions, historical and geographical. But there exist other divisions. There are religious ways, and religion does not contradict any other system, the difference lies in different levels Suppose you know religion No 2, it is not sufficient if you want to study yourself and become No 4 And suppose you find that this system is on, a certain level and do not know of a religion of a sufficiently high level, then conflict is possible Conflict is possible only between different levels.

Q. I feel since I met this system that I seem to understand the Prayer Book and the Bible better Can it help us by giving a better understanding of the teaching of Christ?

A. I already said that this system is not a religion You can improve your mental machine and your capacity for understanding, and you can make your emotions better but whether the system can help you in this direction I cannot say. Later you may be able to see the connection between the ideas of the system and the esoteric parts of religion. But we do not know esoteric religion, so we cannot speak about it.

A very similar question was asked Mr. Gurdjieff in St Petersburg Someone asked in what relation this system stood to Christianity Mr. Gurdjieff said many things about how different people understand Christianity differently. And then he said: 'If you like, this is esoteric Christianity'. And he added: 'What from your point of view is the most important thing in Christ's teaching? It is action: do this, do not do that. The question is can you, do it? You must decide for yourself whether you can understand it better now or not, but you must take Christianity as a teaching of action, not as a mental teaching.

If you take the Christian teaching without the modern sentimental attitude, you will see that it is the most exclusive of all religions. It is constantly repeated and repeated that only a few have a chance difficult way, narrow way, only a few can pass through, and so on.

Q. One cannot help thinking that the Absolute is one name for God.

A. No, you are quite wrong The Absolute is the principle that lies in the beginning of things and behind everything. I never connected the Absolute with God in the religious sense God in religion can do many things for you, but the Absolute can do nothing for you. So, it is not God in that sense, you cannot pray to the Absolute. If you take a religious question, follow the religious explanation. If you see a difference, keep them separate.

Q. Is it a fact that there are higher forces one can contact when one is in a better state?

A. In every situation, in every question we must keep to what we can know, to what we can be sure about, and we can be sure that most of our time we are in a state in which we cannot be in contact with higher forces, Either we are fully asleep and no higher forces can penetrate to us, or we are negative so that everything that comes to us is transformed into one or another kind of negativeness. In such a state, what can we expect?

Q. Are there many esoteric teachings or only one?

A. Every teaching of an esoteric origin agrees fundamentally with the others. In order to be true, the teaching must be one of many. If it is unique, it means it is invented

Q. In the New Testament we are very often told to watch and pray. What is it in the system which corresponds to prayer?

A. Whose prayer? If a machine prays, what can be the result? Which prayer? Prayer does not necessarily mean petition. Most prayers have as their aim keeping the mind on certain ideas, a form of meditation.

Q. Do you think that self-consciousness can be achieved by prayer? And if so, how should one pray?

A. If one could really pray continuously, it would create self-consciousness. The whole thing is that we cannot.

A man decides to pray and five minutes later it becomes a mechanical repetition of words If one could pray, prayer could do it, but one cannot, because *one is not* Man could do many things if *he was,* that is, if he was permanent As it is, one starts, another continues.

Q. Is true prayer contact with higher powers?

A. I will not argue against it, but we know quite concretely that in ordinary centres we only have the powers that belong to them At the same time we learn that higher centres have many powers that ordinary centres do not have So I can answer in the language of the system that if this contact is possible, it is only possible through higher centres Our problem is how to approach higher centres We cannot have contact now, but higher centres may have Nobody can guarantee it, because even our expectations may be wrong In any case we know and some people have had their short experiences of it, that higher centres have new powers, so all we can do is to try to become connected with higher centres by studying how to become conscious When we become conscious, we shall have contact with higher centres, and then we may have new powers and new knowledge

Q. But do we not already have flashes of higher emotional Centre?

A. Some people do, but they are only flashes which they cannot control. Only man No. 5 can control these things, and we are but men No 1, 2 and 3

Q. According to some esoteric teachings the mind of a man is like a pool When it is calm, he can see things clearly and listen to 'the voice of the silence'.

A. There are many dangers in that It is so easy to mix the real 'voice of the silence' with an imaginary voice, so easy to mix truth with imagination It may be the way for some people, but it is not the way for us We want to know more precisely how to evolve, so for us all such definitions are dangerous, for there is no instrument by which we can separate the imagination in them from reality That is what you must remember in *this* system that you learn how to separate the imaginary from the real from the very beginning, when you learn to distinguish in *yourself* imagination from reality Then later, on higher levels of consciousness, you will be able to separate it in the objective world Many of these mystical ways only increase confusion Instead of bringing man nearer to truth, they lead him further from it

Q. Then should man continually seek irritations?

A. Why irritations? You take that for granted and then try to find opposites You can try all your life and get nothing, if you work in the wrong way but you must try, in the right way, to remember yourself, not to identify, to gain control Nobody has enough control. We are not masters of ourselves, and this is why we cannot begin to do this and not do that. We have to study first and understand first. We must study ourselves, and sometimes we can turn one little thing and another little thing, and in this way, we begin to change. One cannot start with this big calm. One can want to be calm, if one is not calm, but that is the same as speaking of such Christian principles as loving your enemies.

Q. Is not the A B C of all esoteric knowledge the death of the seed?

A. We may take it like that. As a matter of fact, in connection with this there is another thing which may perhaps explain our situation. I remember long ago Mr. Gurdjieff said about this expression repeated two or three times in the New Testament, that in order to germinate and produce a plant a seed must die, that it was not complete in relation to man. In relation to man, it must be amplified. Speaking in general about the work, about its possibilities and about the direction of the work, Mr. Gurdjieff explained it to us like this. First, we must realize that we are asleep; secondly, we must awake. When we are awake, we must die; when we die, we can be born. This is the process in detail and the direction. It is useful to think about it, useful to understand what sleep means, what to awake means, what to die means and what it would mean to be born. Suppose we want to be born. We cannot be born until we die, and we cannot die until we awake. We cannot awake until we realize that we are asleep. So, there are definite steps.

Q. What does to die mean in the sense in which you speak?

A. 'To die' means to die, to disappear, not to be, not to exist. It is useless to die in sleep, because then you cannot be born. You must awake first.

I have been asked many questions, some of them very naive, by different people who have tried to understand the Lord's Prayer and who came to me asking me to explain what one or another phrase in it means. For instance, I have been asked what 'our Father in heaven' means, who are 'our debtors' and what are 'our debts' and so on, as if the Lord's Prayer could be explained in 'plain words'. You must understand first of all that ordinary, plain words cannot explain anything in relation to the Lord's Prayer. Some preparatory understanding is necessary, then further understanding may come, but only as a result of effort and right attitude.

The Lord's Prayer can be taken as an example of an insoluble problem. It has been translated into every language, learnt by heart, repeated daily, yet people have not the slightest idea of what it really means. This failure to understand its meaning is connected with our general inability to understand the New Testament. If you remember, in another conversation, the whole of the New Testament was given as an example of objective art, that is to say, the work of higher mind. How then can we expect to understand with our ordinary mind what was formulated and given by higher mind?

What we can do is to try and raise our mind to the level of thinking of higher mind; and although we do not realize it, this is possible in many different ways. In mathematics, for instance, we can deal with infinities with infinitely small and infinitely large quantities which mean nothing to our ordinary mind. And what is possible in mathematics is possible for us if we start in the right way and continue in the right way.

One of the first things which must be understood and remembered, before a study of the Lord's Prayer is possible, is the difference between the religious language and system language.

What is religion? This word is used very often; there are people who use it every day, but they cannot define what is meant by religion.

In the system we have heard that religion is different for different people, that there is religion of man No. 1, a religion of man No. 2, a religion of man No. 3 and so on. But how can we define the difference between them? Before coming to definitions, we must understand first of all that the most necessary element in all religions known to us is the idea of God, a God with whom we can stand in a personal relationship, to whom we can, as it were, speak, whom we can beg for help, and in the possibility of whose help we can believe. An inseparable part of religion is faith in God, that is, in a Higher Being, omnipotent and omnipresent, who can help us in anything we wish for or want to do.

I do not speak from the point of view of whether this is right or wrong, possible, or impossible. I simply say that faith, that is belief in God and in his power to help us, is an essential part of religion.

Prayer is also an inseparable part of any religion; but prayer can be very different. Prayer can be a petition for help in anything we may undertake, and also, through schoolwork, prayer can become help itself. It can become an instrument of work which can be used for reviving ideas of the system, it can be used for self remembering and for reminding us about sleep and the necessity for awakening.

At the same time, the expressions of religious language cannot be translated exactly into the system language. First, because of the element of faith in religion, and secondly, because of the acceptance in religion and religious language of facts and assertions which in the system are regarded as illogical and inconsistent. Nevertheless, it would be wrong to say that religion and the system are incompatible or contradictory; only, we must learn not to mix the two languages. If we begin to mix them, we shall spoil any useful conclusions that could be made on either of the two lines.

Returning to the idea of God, an idea which is inseparable from religion and religious language, we must first ask ourselves how religions can be divided in a general or historical way. They may be divided into religions with one God and religions with many gods. But even in this division it must be remembered that there is a great difference between the ordinary understanding of monotheism and polytheism and the system understanding of the same ideas. Although there are certain differences between gods as, for instance, in Greek mythology in the ordinary understanding of polytheism all gods are more or less on the same level. From the system point of view, which includes the idea of different scales and different laws on different levels, one has quite a different understanding of the interdependence of gods.

If we take the Absolute as God, we can see that it has no relation to us. The Absolute is God for gods; it has relation only to the next world, that is, World 3. The World 3 is God for the next world, that is, World 6, and also for all the following worlds, but in a lesser and lesser degree. Then the Galaxy, Sun, Planets, Earth, and Moon are all gods, each including in itself smaller gods. The Ray of Creation as a whole, taken as one triad, is also God: God the Holy, God the Firm, God the Immortal.

So, we may choose on which level we wish to take our God if we want to use the word 'God' in the religious sense, that is to say, in the sense of a God having immediate access to our lives. From the system point of view, we have nothing to prove that any of these worlds may have a personal relation to us; but there is a place for God in the system.

In the lateral octave which begins in the Sun as 'do' there are two quite unknown points about which we have no material for thinking. The octave begins as do in the Sun, then passes into si on the level of the Planets. On Earth it becomes *la-sol-fa,* which constitutes Organic Life including man. When each individual being in the human, animal and vegetable kingdom dies, the body or what remains of the body goes to the Earth and becomes part of the Earth, and the soul goes to the Moon and becomes part of the Moon. From this we can understand *mi* and *re* but about *si* and do we know nothing at all. These two notes may give rise to many suppositions as to the possible place of a God or gods having some relation to us in the Ray of Creation.

Now, remembering all that has just been said, we may come to the study of the Lord's Prayer.

The first thing is to discover *why* and *when* it was given. We know that it was given to replace many useless prayers.

The next thing is to note many interesting features in the Lord's Prayer itself and in its very special construction; and from our understanding of this construction, and particularly from our knowledge of the Law of Three, we may be able to realize that, from the system point of view, there is a possibility of the development of understanding through our understanding of the Lord's Prayer.

Like many mathematical problems, the study of the Lord's Prayer must begin with a correct disposition or arrangement of the separate parts of the problem. We notice at once two interesting things: first, that the Lord's Prayer is divided into three times three, and second, that in the Lord's Prayer there are certain keywords, that is to say, words which explain other words to which they refer. We cannot call the division into three times three triads, because we do not know their relation to one another and cannot see the forces. We can only see that there are three parts.

If you read the first three petitions together as one part, you will see many things which you cannot see if you read them in the ordinary way.

1. Our Father which art in heaven hallowed be Thy name

2. Thy kingdom comes

3. Thy will be done on earth as it is in heaven.

In the first petition, 'Our Father which art in heaven hallowed be Thy name', the immediate question is, who is 'our Father'? The keyword is 'heaven'. What does 'in heaven' mean? If we try to answer this question from the point of view of the Ray of Creation, we may be able to understand something. We live on the Earth, so 'heaven' must mean higher levels, that is, the Planets, the Sun, or the Galaxy. The idea of 'heaven' presupposes certain forces, or certain mind or minds on those higher levels to which, in some way, the Lord's Prayer advises us to appeal; 'heaven' cannot refer to anything on the level of the Earth. But if we realize that the cosmic forces connected with the Galaxy, the Sun or the Planets are too big to have any relation to us, then we can look for the place of *our* 'Father in heaven' in the *do or* si of the lateral octave or we can again leave it to higher regions.

In the words which follow there is nothing personal. 'Hallowed be Thy name' is the expression of a desire for the development of the right attitude towards God, and for a better understanding of the idea of God or Higher Mind, and this desire for development obviously refers to the whole of humanity.

The second petition, 'Thy kingdom come', is the expression of a desire for the growth of esotericism. In "*A New Model of the Universe*" I tried to explain that the kingdom of heaven could only mean esotericism, that is to say, a certain inner part of humanity under particular laws.

The third petition, 'Thy will be done on earth as it is in heaven', is the expression of a desire for the transition of the Earth to a higher level, under the direct will of Higher Mind. 'Thy will be done' refers to something that may happen but has not yet happened. These three petitions refer to conditions which may come but which have not yet been fulfilled.

The first petition of the second part of the Lord's Prayer is:

'Give us this day our daily bread'.

The word 'daily' does not exist in the oldest known Greek and Latin text. The correct word, which later was replaced by 'daily', is 'super-substantialism' or 'supersubstantial'. The correct text should be: 'give us to-day our supersubstantial bread'. 'Supersubstantial' or 'spiritual' as some people say, may refer to higher food, higher hydrogens, higher influences, or higher knowledge.

The two following petitions in this second part,

'Forgive us our debts as we forgive our debtors', and 'Lead us not into temptation but deliver us from evil' are the most difficult to understand or to explain. They are particularly difficult because their ordinary meaning, as generally accepted, has nothing to do with the real meaning. When people think about the words, 'forgive us our debts as we forgive our debtors' in the ordinary way, they immediately begin to make logical and psychological mistakes. First of all, they take for granted that they can forgive debts, and that it depends on them whether they will forgive or not forgive; and secondly, they believe that it is equally good to forgive debts and to have their own debts forgiven. This is a fallacy and has no foundation whatever. If they think about themselves, if they study themselves, if they observe themselves, they will very soon see that they *cannot forgive any debts just as they cannot do anything.*

In order *to do* and in order to *forgive* one must first of all be able to remember oneself, one must be awake, and one must have will. As we are now, we have thousands of different wills, and even if one of these wills wants to forgive, there are always many others which do not want to forgive and which *will* think that forgiveness is a weakness, an inconsistency or even a crime. And the strangest thing is that sometimes it is really a crime to forgive. Here we come to an interesting point. We do not know whether it is good to forgive or not, whether it is good to forgive always, or whether in some cases it is better to forgive and, in some cases, better not to forgive. If we think more about it, we may come to the conclusion that even if we could forgive, perhaps it would be better to wait until we knew more, that is, until we knew in which cases it is better to forgive and in which cases it is better not to forgive.

At this point we should remember what has been said about positive and negative attitudes and we should realize that positive attitudes are not always correct, negative attitudes are sometimes necessary for a right understanding. So, if 'forgiving' always means having a positive attitude, then forgiving may sometimes be quite wrong.

We must understand that to forgive indiscriminately may be worse than not to forgive at all; and this understanding may bring us to the right view of our own position in relation to our own debts. Suppose for a moment that there actually was some benevolent and rather stupid deity who could forgive our debts, and who would really forgive them and wipe them out. It would be the greatest misfortune that could happen to us. There would be no incentive for us to work then, and no reason to work. We could go on doing the same wrong things and having them all forgiven in the end. Such a possibility is quite contrary to any idea of the work. In the work we must know that nothing will be forgiven. Only this knowledge will give us a real incentive to work, and at least prevent us from repeating the same things which we already know to be wrong.

It is interesting to look at schools from this point of view and to compare schools with ordinary life. In life people may expect forgiveness, or at least hope for it. In school nothing is forgiven. That is an essential part of a school system, school method and school organization. Schools exist precisely for not-forgiving, and because of this fact one can hope and expect to get something from a school. If things were forgiven in schools, there would be no reason for their existence.

The inner meaning of 'Forgive us our debts as we forgive our debtors' actually refers to influences, that is to say, influences from higher levels. We can attract to ourselves higher influences only if we transfer to other people the influences we receive or have received. There are many other meanings of these words, but this is the beginning of the way to understand them.

The third petition of this second part is:

'Lead us not into temptation but deliver us from evil'. What is our greatest temptation? Most probably it is sleep so, the first words are understandable 'help us to sleep less or help us to awake sometimes'. The next part is more difficult. It reads: 'But deliver us from evil'. Possibly it should be '*and* deliver us from evil'. There are many interpretations of this 'but', but none of them is quite satisfactory as translated into ordinary language, so I shall leave it for the present.

The chief question is, what does 'evil' mean? One possible interpretation is that in relation to the ordinary temptation, which is only sleep, it means letting oneself fall asleep again when one had already begun to awake. It may mean giving up the work when one has already understood the necessity for working, giving up efforts after one had begun to make efforts and, as has already been mentioned, starting to do stupid or even harmful things, such as going against school rules and justifying oneself for so doing. Many interesting examples of things of this kind can be found in the actions of people who leave the work and particularly in their explanations of their doing so.

Finally, the third part of the Lord's Prayer should be taken as referring to a future order of things and not to the present order.

1. For Thine is the kingdom

2. the power

3. and the glory forever Amen,

presupposes that the desire expressed in the first part of the Prayer has already been realized, has already taken place. Actually, these words can only refer to the future.

In conclusion, the whole of the Lord's Prayer can be taken as one triad. It cannot be taken in the sense that one part is active force, another part passive force and a third part neutralizing force, because all relations probably change with the change in the Centre of gravity of attention. This means that, by itself, each of these three divisions or parts can be taken as one force and that together they can make a triad.

These very big ideas are put in the form of a prayer. When you decipher this idea of prayer, prayer in the sense of supplication, disappears.

Q. What is the difference between forgiving and being forgiven?

A. Subject and object. But we cannot be forgiven. We did something and, according to the law of cause and effect, a certain result will be produced. We cannot change the law, but we can become free escape from it. We can change the present, through the present the future, and through the future the past. We must pay our debts. By paying them we change the past, but there are different ways of paying.

Q. What are the different ways of paying our debts?

A. Mechanically or consciously. We pay them in any case: by waiting for the results of causes and paying thus, or by changing the past and paying in another way. Today is the result of some past. If we change today, we change the past.

Q. Is changing the past struggling against the way things go?

A. This is the beginning only. Positive emotions and higher influences are necessary. We cannot change anything without them. There are several stages. This does not come at once; it is necessary to work. I have put some principles; it is necessary to see how we can reach this.

There are many interesting things in this. For instance, there is no word 'I' or 'me' in the Lord's Prayer. That means there can be no personal favors, all people stand in the same relation to higher forces, all need the same things.

* * *

CHAPTER XVI

The idea of recurrence can only be regarded as a theory—Different relationship of people to the possibility of recurrence—Three successive stages—Why the possibility of receiving C influence must be limited—Remembering past lives—Theory of reincarnation as a simplification of the idea of recurrence—Impossibility of finding proof-—We are limited by the state of our being—Different kinds of essence as the strongest argument in favour of pre-existence—Why schools cannot recur—Study of recurrence in one life—Eternal recurrence is not eternal—Possibility of variations— Chances are limited and time is counted—Self-remembering and recurrence —Personality and recurrence—Study of children's minds—Origin of the idea of recurrence—Three dimensions of time—The idea of recurrence and the system—Parallel time—'Limitations of our mind—Growth of tendencies and recurrence—Possibilities of meeting a school next time— Being prepared—Is the starting-point the same for everybody?—School and the demands made in it—Death of essence—Recurrence and date of death— Recurrence of world events—The only thing is to awake.

A New Model of the Universe, long ago, that even in ordinary life people may be very different in relation to recurrence. Some people may have exactly the same recurrence, other people may have different variations or possibilities; some may go up and others may go down, and many other things. But this is all without relation to the work. In the case of people who come nearer to the work, it may be possible, though only theoretically, to study three successive recurrences. Let us suppose that the first is when one comes close to the possibility of meeting with some kind of ideas of higher mind; the second, when one definitely comes in contact with C influence; and the third, which would be the result of it.

The interesting thing is that, after the second, the possibilities of recurrence greatly diminish. Before one comes into contact with C influence, they look unlimited, but after this contact the possibility of recurrence is reduced. If we understand that, we will be able to speak about recurrence with a certain amount of reason and profit; otherwise, if we take everything on the same plane, it will be just theoretical talk and quite useless.

Q. Do you mean that after coming in contact with C influences the number of chances diminishes?

A. Yes, because C influence cannot be wasted. B influences are practically unlimited; this means they are thrown into life and one can take or not take them; they do not diminish. But C influence is limited. Try to answer this question for yourselves and you will understand why the possibility of receiving C influence must be limited, because if one does not make use of it, what is the good of wasting it?

Q. Does it mean if we worked in the right way our chances would **increase?**

A. No, it does not mean that at all. It merely means that if we do *not* work in the right way, we will lose the possibility of these chances recurring.

Without this additional feature I have just mentioned it is quite useless to speak about recurrence even as a theory. In thinking about recurrence, it is useful to think about what is possible and what is impossible; what can happen and what cannot happen. Generally, people either do not accept this idea, or do not know about it, or do not understand it, or else accept too much, put too much into it. So, it is useful to think in what relation we stand to it, and for this we must have a basis from which to start. For instance, it refers to 'remembering'. People often ask about remembering past lives, but they forget that without the work of higher centres they cannot. Very often you hear people say, chiefly in connection with what they call 'reincarnation', that they can remember their lives in previous reincarnations, and they write books about what they were before. This is pure fantasy. You must understand that in our ordinary state we cannot remember past lives there is nothing to remember with. In our mind and centres, it is all new. What may pass from one life to another is essence. So, one can have only such vague sensations, instead of definite recollections, that it is hard to suppose that anyone can remember anything concrete. Only in the first years of life is it really possible, but then one generally does not notice this feeling, or if one does, it creates imagination.

Q. What is the difference between the theory of reincarnation and the theory of recurrence?

A. The idea of reincarnation is a kind of adaptation of the idea of recurrence to our ordinary understanding, because, as a theory, the idea of recurrence is much more difficult for us, it needs quite a new understanding of time. Even educated people need a certain amount of mathematical knowledge to understand the idea of return. Recurrence is in eternity, but reincarnation is in time. It supposes that time exists apart from us and that we continue to exist in this time after death. For instance, in Buddhism they take it that a man dies and is immediately born again, so that one life follows another, because this is easier to understand for ordinary people. But we have no evidence of the existence of time beyond our life. Time is life for each person, and it includes in itself all time, so that when life ends, time ends. So, reincarnation is a less scientific theory than recurrence too much is taken for granted.

Q. But where do all these lives take place?

A. We do not speak about the place, but about recurrence. If you say that you remember that you lived in Rome, for instance, how can you find proof? It is impossible. So, each theory can exist on different planes. The theory of recurrence can exist on a certain plane which requires a certain knowledge and a certain understanding, and then it can be distorted and brought down to lower and lower planes. This can happen with every theory and sometimes in the process it can even become its own opposite. But you must always remember that we cannot prove anything and cannot insist on any particular theory. Only, we must understand each theory within its own limits and its own cycle and see what is possible and what is impossible from the point of view of this theory. If you take a theory and proceed to add one thing and to take away another, that would be wrong. In each theory one must study what it includes, and nothing must be omitted. So, if we find a theory that is philosophically possible, we can look for conditions in which it would cease to be a theory and would become a fact.

Q. Am I wrong in assuming that you yourself are not convinced in the reality of the theory of eternal recurrence?

A. I tried to explain that you *cannot* be convinced of these theories. If you think you can be convinced, it will be just belief. There are whole series of questions and problems about which all we can do is to form theories, without ever being really convinced that one theory is better than another. As a theory I would say that the theory of recurrence is better than the theory of reincarnation, but we have no real evidence as to whether it is nearer to facts or not. And we cannot have evidence because of our state of consciousness. The only possibility, from the point of view of work, is to hope that perhaps, if we change our state of consciousness, our possibilities of observation will increase. In our present state we can have nothing but theories about such things.

We are limited by the state of our being, and the state of being of man 1, 2 and 3 is such that we cannot know these things for certain.

Q. Did you say that one could not possibly remember a former life?

A. Yes. Only essence can remember, and since in ordinary man essence is unorganized and not separated from personality, we do not remember.

At the same time, the fact that one person has one kind of essence, and another kind is one of the strongest arguments for pre-existence, because essence cannot be born out of nothing, it is too definite. But the system takes man only from birth to death.

Q. Where does the part of us which recurs come from?

A. It is you. When we speak about recurrence, we think about *our* recurrence. Where this part comes from, we do not know, and we can spend our whole life on theoretical definitions, but it will not change anything or help our psychological understanding of the idea. I am now trying to establish certain principles which will give us a practical understanding of it. We could find many words, but words will not lead anywhere.

Have you found the answer, why C influences cannot be wasted? Think about that. If you answer this question, you will answer many other questions. And this you do know, put two and two together.

Q. Is it because if such a thing would be liable to recur, again and again you waste it?

A. This is implied, but it is not the answer. Certainly, if it is wasted, and again wasted, what is the use? But there is something you do not see in all this, and yet it is the key to the whole thing. It is very simple, there is nothing mysterious. It is not a puzzle; it is merely a question of thinking.

Try to think like this: take an ordinary school.

A boy goes to school and every year begins to learn the same thing. He studies something for a whole year, then goes home and forgets everything, and has to learn the same thing all over again. Again, he studies it for a whole year, and again goes home and forgets, and again comes back and learns the same thing. What will they say to him at school? This is why schools are not repeated, why there is no recurrence for schools. And this is what people want, they want to learn the same thing again. But next time you must be in a higher school. If you cannot go to a higher school, there will be no other school on this level because you have already passed it.

Q. Would you meet a school through C influence?

A. School *means* C influence. You meet the school through B influences.

Q. You cannot go into a higher class unless you pass an examination?

A. Quite right, but you can pass the examination and forget everything; it happens very often.

Q. But, to a certain extent, you have learnt how to learn?

A. Sometimes, and sometimes not. You learn how to learn, and you learn how to forget.

Q. It seems to me from what you have said that this C influence is transmutation, the power to transmute, and anything less than that is not C influence.

A. Quite right. You are very near, but you can also take C influence simply as a certain amount of knowledge.

Q. Knowledge that can be used?

A. No, that again is a definition. I said knowledge; definitions will not help. It is strange that you do not see it, that you do not catch what it means simply. Transmission of knowledge means C influence, it means a certain work, it does not happen by itself, it means somebody's work, and somebody's work cannot be wasted. If it brings results, it can be continued, but if it brings no result, then naturally it will stop. This explains why the possibility of recurrence must be limited. If one comes to a school and does not profit by being in the school, naturally one cannot come again and again to learn the same thing; one must make something of it. Try to understand it, because without understanding these principles it is impossible to speak about recurrence. All ordinary talks, based on mathematics or anything else, make it too uniform, and recurrence cannot be uniform. You remember we spoke about materiality of knowledge and about the fact that one has very little chance even to begin, because many favourable circumstances are necessary for that. But you must understand that when one begins to get a certain knowledge, chances become smaller and smaller, because if one does not use it, it will be more and more difficult to get, quite naturally. And the same thing applies to every day, every year, to all our life this is what must be understood. The idea of recurrence is useful because it refers to *this life*. If we do not do something to-day, how can we expect to do it tomorrow? If we can do it today, we must; nobody can put it off till tomorrow, because tomorrow we could do something else. We always think we have time.

Q. Does it mean that if we do not listen to what you say today, we will not hear it again?

A. Or maybe you will be here, but I will not be here, how can you know?

Q. Can we only make progress through you?

A. No, you are quite free to find some other place you are not bound at all. If you know somebody else with whom you can make progress, certainly you must use him. One must not lose any opportunity if one has an opportunity.

Q. I meant, are you the only medium here?

A. No, nobody can be the only one. If you know another way, there is another opportunity, but if you do not know of another opportunity, if you know nobody but me, then you must try to get it from me; if you know somebody else, you can get it from somebody else. Is it quite clear? Only remember one thing, it cannot be a theoretical study, we must learn in practice how to do the most important things for us.

Q. Are opportunities always there, only we are too asleep to notice or use them?

A. Opportunities may be different: there are different degrees. If one has not come to the work, one has the opportunity to accumulate knowledge, material, tendencies. They may be not very strong, but they may all lead in the same direction, or they may lead in opposite directions. Then, in what we call 'work', which means influence C or direct knowledge, direct study, opportunities are different, and real opportunities begin only from the moment one uses them.

Q. In the idea of recurrence things happen again. But do schools necessarily appear in the same places? Perhaps in my last recurrence this system never came to England?

A. This is the difficulty about recurrence, because when people hear about it and begin to think, they think in the ordinary formatory, that is, logical way, or very often they think quite illogically, or worse. But even if they think logically, they have not enough material, they do not know enough to think about it. It is necessary to understand first of all that we are speaking about a theory, and secondly, that this theory must be sufficiently full, there must be sufficient material in it. When we think about recurrence, we think that everything repeats, and this is exactly what spoils our approach to it. The first thing to understand about recurrence is that it is not eternal. It sounds absurd, but actually it is so, because it is so different in different cases. Even if we take it theoretically, if we take purely people in mechanical life, even their lives change. Only certain people, in quite frozen conditions of life, have their lives repeating in exactly the same way, maybe for a long time. In other cases, even in ordinary mechanical life, things change. If people are not so definitely governed by circumstances, like great men who have to be great men again and nobody can do anything about it, there are variations, but again not forever. Never think that anything is forever. It is a very strange thing, but it seems as though people who have no possibilities, either owing to certain conditions, or to their own insufficient development, or to some pathological state, can have their lives repeating without any particular change, whereas in the case of people with theoretical possibility, their lives can reach certain points at which they either meet with some possibility of development or they begin to go down. It is either one or the other; they cannot go on remaining forever in the same place and from the moment they meet with some real possibility, they either recognize the possibility of doing something or they lose it and then go down. Just think about it and perhaps you will be able to formulate some questions.

Q. Does the ability to recognize the possibilities depend on change of being, which can only be achieved after a long period of small efforts?

A. There are two things we must understand about this. Things are in a different relationship to possibilities: some things, although they have not yet happened and although it may seem to us that they can happen in one way or in another way, are in reality predestined. Nothing can be changed, because such big causes are moving these things that, although they have not yet happened, they can happen only in one way. In relation to some other things the repetition is not so strict. There are many gradations and, side by side with things that can happen only in one way, there may be other things, which are still to come, which can happen this way or that way. It is necessary to understand this as a principle, to understand why things are different and what is different about them. Take today. Certain things have to happen tomorrow because their causes lie in last year or in ten or twenty years ago. But if the cause of certain things that will happen tomorrow lies in today, then they can happen differently to-morrow if something is done differently to-day. So, it is a question of the nature of the causes and of where they are. You can look at it like this: suppose you see things going on in exactly the same way for a long time, then you cannot expect a sudden change without some particular reason. Other things may be comparatively new a certain tendency has just appeared and so it may easily disappear. But if the tendency has been going on in the same direction for a long time it is difficult to see a possibility of change. That is the only way we can discuss it, for we cannot know anything definite about these things. You must remember one principle in relation to this, things are not the same. If you say that some things can be changed and apply it to everything, you will be wrong, because things are never in the same relationship to the possibility of change.

Q. May the possibility of variation in people's recurrences mean that people born in one recurrence might not be born in the next?

A. This is possible only in some cases, but we cannot go into details of this kind. What I want you to understand definitely is that as long as people are quite mechanical, things can repeat and repeat almost indefinitely. But if people become more conscious, or if the possibility of becoming conscious appears, their time becomes limited. They cannot expect an unlimited number of recurrences if they have already begun to know something or to learn something. The more they learn, the shorter becomes their time. People always forget that there is only a very limited number of chances for everybody, so if one loses a possibility in one life, then next life one will lose it more easily. The closer one comes to the possibility of change, the smaller the number of chances becomes, and if one finds a chance and does not use it, one may lose it altogether. It is the same principle as that which applies to one life. You remember, it was said that in the work, in relation to one life, *time is counted*, and the more seriously people work, the more strictly is their time counted. If you want to work for two months and sleep for ten months, it is counted that you worked for twelve months, even though you actually worked for only two. But the requirements or conditions are for twelve months, and the more one works the more those requirements grow. If one works very little, one may remain in the same relation to a certain idea for a year or two years; one may misunderstand something and not lose much through it because there is still a third year. But if a man has already begun to work in earnest he cannot have three years, because every day is an examination, and he must pass one examination in order to come to another examination. That must be understood, and the same principle can be applied to recurrence.

Q. Is it that if we are completely mechanical, we must recur in exactly the same way, but if we are less mechanical, our recurrences are fewer?

A. It is not exactly like that. As I said, there are many different categories of people. There are people whose lives repeat automatically in exactly the same way. Other people may have different small changes and modifications, all on the same level. Then a third category, to put it very roughly, may have some possibility in the sense that the changes that happen in their lives are not quite aimless, but are nearer and nearer to some B influence. Then the fourth category come nearer to the possibility of meeting a school. The thing to understand is that people are not equal in relation to these possibilities. And, of course, those who have already found some possibility and have discarded it, prove themselves incapable of development.

Q. I still do not understand why time should be limited for anyone who has worked but not for one who has not?

A. For one who has not begun to awake, time is not counted because it does not exist. Everything repeats, always the same thing, again and again. You can take it like this: knowledge is limited, but since such people do not take any knowledge, for them it is not limited. Then, as I said, you can draw a comparison with an ordinary school: it is not possible always to remain in the same class, one must either make progress or go. Certain demands are made, and if people do not fulfil these demands they may lose the possibility. So, if one has begun to work, one must go on. Suppose someone begins to work and then fails. This shows his inability to work, and then what is the meaning of his existence? Try to think about it from this point of view.

Q. Is everyone given access to one of the ways in some cycle or other?

A. I do not know, and we cannot know such things; we can speak only about ourselves.

We have a chance, that is all we know, so we must think about ourselves.

Q. The future in the work seems like walking on a tight rope. Can one hope to attain another level of stability later?

A. Every state has many different forms, and so has the state of sleep. There may be sleep with possibility of awakening, sleep with less possibility of awakening and sleep without any possibility of awakening.

Q. To have memory of another recurrence is it necessary to change something in essence?

A. No, it is necessary to become conscious in this life. You have only this life. You could say to yourself: 'If I lived before, I do not remember it. This means that if I live again, again I will not remember.' If you become conscious in this life, you will remember, and you will remember as much as you remember now. If you do not remember yourself now, then next time again you will not remember yourself, so it will be the same. The possibility of change starts only with the possibility of beginning to remember yourself *now*. All other things are just words.

Q. If personality dies with us, what effect can attempt to weaken it have in future recurrence?

A. There is no need to be very dogmatic about it; when we speak about recurrence, we speak of 'something' that recurs, and this 'something' keeps in itself traces of all the created tendencies. If the tendency of weakening personality has been created, it will continue; and if the opposite tendency has been created, a tendency to strengthen personality, again it will continue. It is quite right that personality dies, but if this 'something' recurs, then the same causes will produce the same effects. If certain new tendencies have been created, they too will have their effect. So, a man who showed a real love of sleep from childhood may fall asleep even earlier.

Q. Then the only thing we can keep is the change, if any, that we make in essence?

A. No, first you must make changes in personality.

Q. But that will not last!

A. It is the only thing we can do. Only very few people can work on essence. It is not exactly an advantage to the people who can, because working on essence is very difficult; but it may happen. Generally, we work on personality, and it is the only work we can do. And if we really work it will bring us somewhere. Sometimes tendencies are in essence and sometimes in personality, but I would not formulate it as 'essence' and 'personality'. I would simply say we have to weaken certain tendencies and strengthen others, weaken mechanical tendencies, and strengthen conscious tendencies. That is the only formulation possible; everything else would be out of place.

Q. It seems to me that personality, physical body, and appearance are too impermanent to recur.

A. Yes, but they were all created by certain causes and, since causes will be the same, they will naturally produce the same effects. One is born in the same circumstances, the same house, from the same parents, and everything will grow the same. There may be some deviations, but in the end, it comes to the same thing. Suppose one is born in a certain town and then one moves out of it for a time. Then, later, one comes back and finds oneself in the same situation as before, as though one had not been away at all. This illustrates what I mean by those deviations. One always returns to the same path.

Q. What is it that wants recurrence so much and yet fears it?

A. That I don't know, it is material for your own study. Certainly, one prefers the idea of recurrence to the ordinary idea of death. At the same time, one fears it because, if one is really sincere with oneself, one realizes that things repeat themselves in this life. If one finds oneself, again and again, in the same position, making the same mistakes, one realizes that to be born again will not help if one continues to do the same things now.

A change can only be the result of effort; no circumstances can produce a change. This is why all ordinary beliefs in the change of external circumstances never lead anywhere: circumstances may change, but you will be the same unless you work. It is the same in recurrence. People's lives may appear completely changed from the point of view of external circumstances, but the result will be the same, the relation of essence to personality will remain. Real change can happen only as a result of school work, or if for several successive lives one only grows the magnetic Centre and does not meet a school, then change will be in the growth of magnetic Centre.

Q. Do you believe that those who attain a sufficiently high state are not under the obligation of recurring?

A. You go too far. Certain religions begin from the idea of trying to stop this wheel of life. But we cannot speak seriously about it, because, as I said, the idea of recurrence is only a theory, so how can we stop what we are not sure exists? If you want to stop a train, you must know that the train is moving. What would be the point of trying to stop it if you are not sure it is moving?

Q. Is the date of one's death predetermined?

A. I cannot say, there are different theories. I think it is safer to say that it is predetermined from one point of view, only so many things enter into it that one's time can be shortened or prolonged so, although it is predetermined, it is not an absolute predetermination. Or it may be better to say that it changes every moment, although it is predetermined. Every moment can bring new factors and make one's life longer or shorter. If nothing happens, then it is predetermined.

Q. Does schoolwork affect the length of one's life?

A. Again you expect too much. Maybe after several incarnations you may find means to prolong your life; but if you expect it at once, you expect too much. In some cases, it may be true, so I think it must be different in different cases.

Q. Does it mean that I am living the same life again? Was I reborn in 1915 and will I again be born in 1915?

A. Always in 1915, that is the only thing that cannot change. And certainly, we are bound to have lived before we could not have come out of nothing, only we do not remember. Even those who think they remember something, remember only as children. But in most cases, they forget.

The study of recurrence must begin with children's minds, particularly before they begin to talk. If people could remember this time, they would remember very interesting things. Unfortunately, when they begin to talk, they become real children and after six months or a year they usually forget. People very seldom remember what they thought before that, at a very early age. But psychologically it is a fact that in very early memories of childhood and sometimes people remember things at the age of a few months, they already have a mentality, a certain understanding of people, places, and things. How can we expect children that have been born so recently to have all this material? Our mentality grows quite slowly, but some children have a grown-up mind. They are not children at all; then later they become children. If they remember their mentality of early infancy, they see that it is the same mentality as grown-up people have. That is what is interesting.

Q. Do you know why a child should remember its grown-up mentality and not its previous child's mentality?

A. We have so little material to judge about it. I speak only about the way it can be studied. Suppose we try to remember our own, trying not to let imagination come in; then, if we find something, that would be material. In literature you find very little, because people do not understand how to study it. But in my own experience I met with some very interesting things. Also, some people I knew had very interesting re collections of the first years of life, and they all had the same impression, that their mentality was not a child's mentality or a child's psychology. Do you see what I mean? They had a ready mind, with quite grown-up reactions and a way of looking at people and recognizing them, such as could not be formed in the course of six months of unconscious life.

Q. Why should it disappear when a child learns to talk?

A. The child begins to imitate other children and to do exactly what grown-up people expect of him. They expect him to be a stupid child and he becomes a stupid child.

Q. How is it possible to know what a baby remembers? I thought that one was born with one's centres completely blank and that one remembered with centres?

A. That is the strange thing. As I said, some people who do not differ much from other people have strange and quite definite recollections even of their first months. They think they saw people as grown-up people do, not as children. They do not make compound pictures from separate elements, they have quite definite impressions of houses, people and so on.

Q. I still do not see how it is possible to remember a previous recurrence. I thought that memory was dependent on the contents of centres which are in personality. How can personality remember recurrence?

A. You cannot remember it if you do not remember yourself here, in this recurrence. We have lived before; many facts prove that. Why we do not remember is because we did not remember ourselves. The same is true in this life. If things are mechanical, we only remember that they happened, only with self-remembering can we remember details. Personality is always mixed with essence. Memory is in essence, not in personality, but personality can present it quite rightly if memory is sufficiently strong.

Q. If we recur into the same circumstances, there seems very little opportunity of having something different at all in our life.

A. In early life there is. We have a long life and in the course of it we can acquire something knowledge, understanding and this understanding can pass into essence. Then, if for the first years of our life we live in essence, this understanding may produce some impression on us, some recollections in essence. As a rule, they disappear at a later age, but children sometimes have them for a fairly long time, till the age of eight or ten.

Q. When I was about three or four, I used to try and remember myself as a sort of game.

A. It is quite possible; it may have remained. You may have tried to remember yourself in a previous life, I see nothing impossible in that.

Q. In connection with the idea of recurrence, does it mean that if we make a bad mistake it goes on recurring?

A. There may be different mistakes, but if there was something deliberate about this mistake, if you made it because you wished to make it, then most probably you will wish even more to make the same mistake again.

Q. Do things like illnesses recur?

A. They may or may not recur. This is connected with rather complicated things. It is necessary to divide illnesses, for they can belong to different categories. Some illnesses may affect essence, others not. Many contagious diseases open accumulators, so they may actually be useful. Then the accumulators may stay open, or they may shut again. Such illnesses may play the role of shocks. They are accidental illnesses, and they may repeat or not repeat. Then there are illnesses belonging to fate, constitutional illnesses.

Q. I do not think I understand eternal recurrence.

A. We speak about possibilities. This is a philosophical conversation; we have not enough material to speak even theoretically. You remember, to speak philosophically means to speak about possibilities. So, if there is recurrence, we speak about the way things *could* happen.

Q. Is one then to consider the whole question as philosophical, or capable of verification?

A. We cannot speak about verification. I think if some people find verification for themselves it will be very subjective. They will not be able to transfer their realization to other people. Other people may or may not believe them, but it will not have the character of proof. But you can verify certain things about recurrence by observing things in this life.

Q. What was the origin of the idea of recurrence?

A. Psychologically, there will be one answer; mathematically, another answer; historically, a third answer. If you mean psychologically, I think it is the very persistent and very definite feeling that children sometimes have that 'it happened before'. For instance, they come to a new house or a new town and have a feeling that all this *has been*. Ordinary psychological explanations by a 'break in consciousness' as it is called and which we can describe much better as passing from one Centre to another, are not sufficient, because they explain some cases but do not explain all cases.

Q. Does it mean that the recurrence has occurred during the existence of that town?

A. Yes, certainly. It is not the same line of time; it is parallel time. The idea of recurrence needs two dimensions of time. The need of three dimensions of time comes only with the idea of work. But the second dimension of time is really very elementary. There can be no doubt about its existence, particularly in modem mathematical and physical ideas. If we accept that the line of time is curved, then curvature has two dimensions, so there are two dimensions of time.

Q. I do not understand rime being two-dimensional.

A. Take a simple thing. You sail in a boat, and you walk on deck while the boat goes along at the same rime. This is the second dimension of your movement. You have one movement you walk yourself, and the second movement is the movement of the boat.

Q. Then a spiral can lead us out of our present circle?

A. I do not think we can speak about spirals from the point of view of the system. But if we do speak about them in relation to recurrence, then in ordinary recurrence there is no spiral at all, it is all on the same level. Recurrences may differ from one another in some details, one may be inclined one way and another more inclined another way, but it is only a small deviation and there is no spiral. The idea of spiral begins with escaping from constant repetition of the same things, or from the moment when something new is introduced.

Q. Is the idea of eternal recurrence part of the system?

A. No, the system can be understood without it, although later some things in the system will be easier to understand if you have some idea of recurrence. The system shows the way to develop but does not say what happens when we do. If we look at the question of survival after death from the point of view of time only from the point of view of time, it is reasonable to suppose that man 1, 2, 3 and 4 has no life after death, that there is nothing permanent in him. He so lacks permanency that he cannot survive the shock of death. If he has something permanent, he may survive. But in my opinion, it is more important to take this question in relation to eternity. This we cannot verify but looking at it in relation to eternity means that there is repetition. Life has to be repeated, there cannot be only one life. Try to understand the design of life. You cannot understand it if you think of a straight line, and if you think of circles, you find that your brain cannot take it in. Everything living organic life, people and so on live and die, and in some mysterious way we do not understand this makes circles; these circles are connected with other circles and the whole design of life is the outcome of it. Everything, every small unit, turns and turns in its circle because everything must go on existing. If a gap appeared, the whole structure would be destroyed.

Q. Is it because we lack the necessary category of thinking that we cannot understand recurrence, since it is in eternity?

A. Yes, if you like. We cannot visualize it, but our higher centres can. If we work, we shall be able to think about it, but only with the help of higher centres not with our ordinary brain. But before that we must make sure that our ordinary centres do all they can, because at present we do not use our ordinary centres to their full extent. Before we can expect to go over to higher centres, we must learn to use fully all the parts of ordinary centres instead of only the mechanical parts.

The idea of recurrence may have many quite obvious faults, but mathematically it is right and is certainly better than any other idea of this nature, because otherwise, without the idea of recurrence, there would be no past. If there is no past, there is no present, and if there is no present, where are we? We cannot live in a world where all the present disappears. Long ago, I wrote about that in Tertium Organum: if we travel by train, we cannot expect all the stations we pass to disappear, and those to which we come to be built anew; they existed before we came and will be there when we have passed. We know that everything dies, so it must be born again; everything is destroyed, so it must be built again; and recurrence is the only theory which can answer.

Q. If every moment is always co-existing, what makes one feel that one is in this moment?

A. The limitations of our mind. Certainly, the idea of parallel time means eternity of the moment, but our mind cannot think in that way. Our mind is a very limited machine. We must think in the easiest way and make allowances for it. It is easier to think of repetition than of eternal existence of the moment. You must understand that our mind cannot formulate rightly things as they really are; we must have only approximate formulations which are nearer to truth than our ordinary thinking. That is all that is possible. Our mind and our language are very clumsy instruments, and we have to deal with very subtle matters and subtle problems. At the same time, we do not realize that by simplifying things, by imagining ourselves in a three-dimensional world, we make this world non-existent. We put ourselves in an impossible position, because if we take, for instance, the ordinary view of the past disappearing and the future not yet existent, then nothing exists. This is the only conclusion from this idea that is logically possible: either nothing exists, or everything exists there is no third alternative, so to speak.

Q. Could you say something about whether it is possible to escape from recurrence?

A. You are making the same mistake as do many doctrines. They begin to think about escape before they are sure of the theory. You must first know that recurrence really exists, by remembering, not theoretically. Then you must get tired of it, bored with it. Only then can you think about escape.

Q. How can one be quite sure it exists?

A. As I said, only by remembering. If you remember that you lived before, what it was like, what happened, then you will know. If you do not remember, you cannot be sure. Theory speaks like that: if you remember yourself in one life, you will remember in the next. If you are unconscious in this life, you will not remember. So first you must become conscious in this life.

Q. If one could escape from the law of recurrence, would one still be at the same time or is higher man able to escape into other times?

A. No, time has nothing to do with it. Time refers only to one life. Out of one lifetime does not exist, that you can call eternity. And what do you mean by escaping? There are many different ways to understand this idea. How can you escape from time? It is part of you; it is the same as escaping from your legs or your head. At the same time the idea of escape has meaning, it means escaping from mechanicalness, being one 'I' always, doing what you want. There are many degrees of escape, but this is the beginning. You take this idea too simply. Try to think about what escape means.

Q. I cannot reconcile the idea that the past is there, really living, with the idea that it comes back again.

A. Do not try to think of it if it is difficult. Leave it. This is why we have to speak about recurrence in simplified forms; our mind cannot think in any other way. This idea is really for higher mental Centre which can think rightly. It is almost useless to talk about recurrence because it becomes philosophy, but there are certain things we can say about it even with our present knowledge, and that is that in relation to school something will remain. Even if one has made a start, one will retain something. One cannot forget about it; maybe one will remember earlier, and this may help one from one cycle to another, so that if one came to a school once, one may expect to meet a school sooner, which may help. So even by being associated with these ideas we have gained something. In any case we begin with the advantages of the system. This is the only thing that is assured; all the rest depends on our work.

Q. How can recurrence be of advantage to man?

A. If one begins to remember and to change, instead of turning each time in the same circle; if one begins to do what one wants and thinks best, then it is of advantage. But if one does not know about it, or even if one knows and does not do anything, then there is no advantage in it at all. Then it means the same things repeated and repeated.

Things repeat in one life, so just remembering how things happened yesterday you can avoid certain things to-morrow. Everyone lives in a certain closed circle of happenings to one person one kind of things happen to another person another kind. You must know your own types of happenings, and when you know them, you can avoid many things.

Q. Having met the system in one recurrence, will one meet it again in the next?

A. It depends on what one did with the system. One could meet the system and say: 'What nonsense these people talk!' It depends how much effort one makes. If one made efforts, one could acquire something, and this may remain, if it was not only in surface personality if it was not only formatory.

Q. Does one necessarily follow some line of action in each recurrence?

A. As I said, all acquired tendencies are supposed to repeat themselves. One person acquires a tendency to study or be interested in certain things. He will be interested again. Another acquires a tendency to run away from certain things. Then he will run away again.

Q. Do these tendencies grow stronger?

A. They may, or they may grow in a different direction. There is no guarantee until one reaches some conscious action, when one has a certain possibility to trust oneself. If we had enough material, we could answer many questions about it. Why, for instance, strange tendencies appear in children, quite opposed to their surrounding circumstances, quite foreign to the people among whom they live. Sometimes they are very strong tendencies that change their life and make them go in totally unexpected ways, when there is nothing in heredity to produce that. This is why it happens in most cases that parents do not understand their children and children do not understand their parents. They never can understand one another sufficiently or rightly. They are quite different people, strangers to one another; they just happened to meet accidentally at a certain station and then they go in different directions again.

Q. When you say, 'study children', what do you mean?

A. That is what is so difficult. If you observe tendencies on a big scale, you can find quite unexpected things. You can say about one or another tendency that it is the result of surroundings or find another reason for it, yet quite unexpected tendencies may appear in young children, not the accidental tendencies that appear and disappear, but such as will continue throughout life. According to this theory, these may be tendencies acquired in a previous life in much later years, and then they appear very early.

Q. From the point of view of recurrence, then, may it not be that some important actions we made in a previous life are responsible for our tendencies now?

A. Quite possibly. Only, there is one thing: this work did not exist before. It may be that some other work did, there may be many different kinds but not this. This work did not exist before, that I am perfectly sure of.

Q. What I meant was that it seems such a huge idea to think that between now and the time we die we make the fatal actions which will give us tendencies for next time.

A. Certainly. Every moment of our lives we may create tendencies we may not be able to get rid of for ten lives. That is why in Indian literature they always emphasize this point. It may be in the form of a fairy tale, but the principle is the same.

Q. You say that this work has not occurred before. Does this mean also that it will not occur again?

A. There is no guarantee. For yourself it will depend on you. Certainly, one thing can be certain it will not happen in the same way. Maybe there will be groups and schools, only not in the same way and not at the same time. Work is the only thing, which is not under the law of recurrence, otherwise it would not be work. If it is a little conscious, it cannot recur in the same form. If we take this particular work, many things in it may happen quite differently. For instance, what happened now at a certain time may begin perhaps twenty years earlier.

Q. If schools do not recur in the same way, does it mean that a person can only meet a school in one life?

A. No, that is introducing another idea. It is more simple than that. Recurrence, if it exists, is mechanical and based on mechanicalness.

A school cannot be mechanical, so it must be under different laws, even if it is an elementary school. If a school existed once in one form, next time it may be not in the same place, the same time, or the same form. How it would change it is impossible to say, but it cannot be the same thing, otherwise it would be mechanical, and if it is mechanical, it is not a school.

Q. Then it means that an individual who came across a school might not find it next time?

A. He may find another, maybe a better one, or he may find nothing. The kind of school one could or could not meet next time depends on many unknown reasons, but only quite petrified things can be repeated again and again without change. Things that are alive can never be the same. You can rely on something like Trafalgar Square recurring, but you cannot rely on schools from the point of view of recurrence.

Q. Then, since schools are not mechanical, if we recur there is no assurance that we should ever find this system again?

A. No assurance, quite right, but there are many sides to it. It is quite true that things do not recur in exactly the same form, but at the same time one cannot lose anything one has acquired. This means that if one loses one possibility one can find another.

One can lose only through one's own fault, not through the fault of things, although it is necessary to understand and remember that possibilities are not unlimited. There is recurrence in a sense, at least there may be, but, as I said, there can be no 'eternal' recurrence in the literal sense of the word for everything, whether big or small. There are different manifestations and what we expect to be eternal *may* not be eternal at all. Everybody has only a limited number of chances. If people live an ordinary life and do not accumulate right influences, do not form a magnetic Centre, then after some time they lose even the possibility of forming one. They may die out because there is big competition. . . .. There are many things we do not know about it all, but the first thing that must be understood about recurrence is that it is not eternal.

I see from people's questions that some of them do not realize how very rare the possibility of development is and how many people there are who never come to it. Neither do they realize how many dangers, both external and internal, surround this possibility. As to the chance of meeting the same school again, I felt that people were even astonished that they might not meet it, that this possibility might not be there forever. Actually, all that refers to schools is bound to be outside ordinary laws, so that nothing can happen in exactly the same way That does not mean there will be no other possibilities, but one must be prepared for them. The school cannot run away from one, the only person that can run away is oneself, but one has to be ready to meet it, one must prepare oneself, even if there are ten thousand lives. Nothing comes by itself. If it comes by itself, one will lose it. One can get only as much as one is prepared for, and one can be prepared only by one's own efforts. In this work there are no guarantees. You do not receive degrees for the length of time you stayed in the work. Every day you go through an examination and every day you can either pass or fail.

Q. As it is so rare and difficult to meet with school, I am so afraid one might recur in conditions that would make it impossible.

A. I think there is very little chance of that because, if we take this theory of recurrence, one will be born in the same circumstances, the same time, the same period. Even if for some reason things are not repeated exactly, you will find something else, especially if you remember something of your past life. In any case there will be more chance than if you did not know anything.

Q. Is it true then that none of us had ever met this system before?

A. I think it is quite true. But possibly you met something similar. However, the fact that I think so will not mean anything to you; you must find out for yourself why I think so.

Q. Is there any certainty that if you start work in one life you will be able to continue it afterwards?

A. Again, speaking theoretically, you will begin from the same place where you left off. The more you get now, the easier it will be to begin. It is the same as taking it from one day to another: the relation is the same. For instance, you begin to learn something today, and tomorrow you continue, you do not need to begin again from the beginning. But if you only pretend to be learning, if you look at the book and let yourself dream instead, then next time you will have to start from the beginning.

Q. Does change of being this time increase magnetic Centre next time?

A. Oh no, magnetic Centre must be made in personality, so you will have to make it again next time. You cannot receive it ready made from past life.

Q. Could a tendency in one recurrence become a habit in the next?

A. It depends on the tendency. If it is mechanical, it will become a habit. If it is conscious, it cannot become a habit, because they are two different things.

Q. Thinking back over my life I see certain cross-roads where some decisions were taken which I think were wrong. Is there any particular thing I can do in this recurrence so as not to repeat the same mistakes in the next?

A. To a certain extent; everything is to a certain extent. If we look back, we may find moments which we can call cross-roads. If we do not study these, we may make mistakes and take for cross-roads points which were not real cross-roads and so miss real cross-roads. One can think, one can change now as regards those particular points, and if it is sufficiently deep, one will remember; if it is not so deep, one may remember. In any case there is a chance that with time one may not do the same thing again, for this question of inevitably turning one way or another way may be more inevitable or less inevitable.

Q. If we can perceive these cross-roads, can we make use of them?

A. There is no question of making use. It is a question of studying them in the past, not in the future. We do not know enough to think about 'doing'. It is only formatory thinking that always starts with the idea of 'doing'.

Q. If we can make any choice, how might that affect recurrence?

A. Recurrence cannot be affected directly. According to the idea of recurrence nothing changes, only you can change. If you change, then many things can change in recurrence. Many ideas and things can pass from one life to another in this way. For instance, someone asked what one could get from the idea of recurrence. If one became intellectually aware of this idea and it became part of one's essence, that is, part of one's general attitude to life, then one would not forget it and it would be an advantage to know it early in the next life.

Q. Is it right to think that we cannot go on living forever, that is, dying and being born again?

A. Quite right. People with a quite mechanical life have a longer time, and people who become conscious have a shorter time; that is the only difference. It looks very unjust, but at the same time mechanical people can get into very unpleasant circumstances.

Suppose that through some external accident connected with historical events, such as wars or something like that, somebody dies very young and continues to die young every time, then only a very exceptional combination of circumstances can introduce a change in his case.

Q. In a case when an accident affects one's whole life, does it recur?

A. Yes, the same kind of accident may repeat itself. You must not forget that we speak only about a theory, but a theory may be better or worse, nearer, or further from possible facts.

In mechanical life even things which happen do not bring any practical change. Things are important only when a man begins to awake. From this moment things become serious. So, are you asking about mechanical recurrence or about the beginning of awakening?

Q. I had in mind the possibility of meeting a school next time.

A. As I said, schools are more free from recurrence compared with things in life. Many things may be repeated exactly as they are now, and some may change. It is the same as when you go about you see different things:

people, trees, buses, cars, houses, lampposts; some things stand still and some move. Wars, revolutions, and other such things are like lampposts, but conscious things are like the light from passing cars. If you go out, you will always see the same lamp posts, but you are not likely to see the same cars.

Q. Is it that opportunity never comes twice?

A. Not the same opportunity, it would be waste of time. When people meet with certain opportunities, they become responsible for the energy spent on them. If they do not use it, it does not recur. Lampposts stay fixed; cars do not stay; they are not made for standing still but for moving. It is useful to think that the same opportunities may not recur next time. We expect things to be the same, but they may be different. It may depend on other people; other people may begin earlier. For example, I began these lectures in England in

1921, but next time I may begin in 1900. You will be prepared only for 1921, but in 1921 there may no longer be an opportunity for you. This should not be taken literally; it is just an example for thinking about.

Q. It is very difficult to think about preparing for meeting the system earlier.

A. You can prepare nothing. Only remember yourself, then you will remember next time. The whole difficulty lies in negative emotions; we enjoy them so much that we have no interest in anything else.

Q. Is the starting-point in the work the same for everybody, or do we have different starting-points?

A. Very, very different; people begin on different levels. We do not know our history in the sense of past lives. Some people have already done some work, although it is impossible to say in what form. Some people only begin while others have already many efforts behind them, so everybody begins differently. But in school all have to go through the same things and sometimes for people who have more material it is more difficult than for people who have less. Individually it is very different. Some people cannot be responsible for some time, others can. Some can work with new people; others must only listen for a long time.

Q. Is it of practical use to think of events of one's life when trying to self-remember, with a view to fixing them for future recurrence?

A. No, this is not practical. First, as I said many times already, it is necessary to be sure about future recurrence; and secondly, it is necessary to be sure of remembering yourself. If you put it in the way you did, it will only transform itself into imagination. But if you first try to remember yourself without adding anything to it, and then, when you can, also try to remember your past life, you remember I spoke about trying to find cross-roads then in combination it will be very useful. Only do not think you can do it yet, because you cannot.

There are many ways of trying to think of your own life in four dimensions. Now we can take it only psychologically, in relation to our own life. Suppose you put yourself back ten years and find that you remember certain moments very well. Then imagine that you know all that will happen, and that you have to live it all over again, knowing it all live through all the mistakes, all the nonsense and so on. Then you will have a different view of the whole thing. Everything is in you now if you study your life by going backwards and then forward again. By using your imagination, you will do it consciously. But you must not try and change anything. Then you will re-live these ten years and see that everything happens in the same way as before, and at the same time you know that everything is to happen in the same way.

Q. How can one remember well enough?

A. It is necessary to find moments you remember well. Some people remember better than others. But for those people who do not remember well it will be especially useful, because all life must be absolutely clear. This is a dissecting-room; only in an ordinary dissecting-room they deal with dead bodies, whereas here you cannot deal with other people until you know everything about yourself.

Q. What do you do when you get to a moment when you forget what happened?

A. There is in us memory of absolutely everything, but it may be what one may call 'frightened'. However, if you insist, then, little by little, things will appear, and you will find that you can think of words, moods, feelings, and people. This shows that psychology cannot be studied apart from yourself. In study of all your life you have a whole museum before you.

Q. You said a few minutes ago that one went on from where one left off in another life. Does it mean that if you become man No. 4 in this life you will be born No. 4 in the next?

A. That I do not know. I think it is better to say that it will be easier to become No. 4. You see, with a big change of being like that of passing from one degree to another degree, one falls under many new laws. How this works, I do not know. We can speak only about our own situation because *that* we know, and we can say that we can expect comparatively small changes more knowledge, more consciousness and, with luck, a little more conscience or hunger. But we cannot speak of big changes such as passing from one degree to another. Still, even a slight change is a change, and it is better to think about small changes which we can measure.

You see, in connection with all these questions, it is very useful to realize we can know. These questions are asked as though we could know the answers, but just five minutes of thinking would show that we cannot, because if we could, probably we would have had the answers long ago. In order to answer these questions practically it is necessary to have a better instrument; if we could use this instrument with a bigger range, perhaps we would have concrete answers, but not with the ordinary brain we have now.

Q. I do not understand the connection between change of state and change of circumstances.

A. They are different. Circumstances change by themselves and state changes only as a result of work, and many causes by which the state can change do not depend on circumstances. One must understand how things happen. It is useful to think about these things, but it is easy to make mistakes. One mistake is that we think things could be different. This is true only of ourselves. All causes governing big external events were created long ago, and it is not really our subject, we have no time to study those things in detail. But we must study ourselves in detail.

Q. If a person ceases to be born in his particular period, what happens to all the other lives with which he is in contact?

A. This is one of the very difficult problems to understand. As far as we can see in this theory, one cannot start being born at once. Being born is also a process like everything else: one fades out little by little, and this fading out does not produce any big effect. Some people can fade out, others have to remain, such as people connected with historical events and things like that. They are in a most unpleasant position, they just turn round and round, and most of them are quite dead.

Q. Is it then impossible for great people in historical movements to escape from life?

A. In most cases it is too late for them to escape; they are dead already, they are almost losing their bones on the way, but they have to continue to exist and turn round. That is one of the mysteries of life, that it is governed by dead people.

Q. I do not see why big historical figures are so important that they must continue to recur even when they become dead? Why wouldn't it be easy to find substitutes for them?

A. Easy for whom? Evidently, they fit into some conditions and so continue to go round in the same way even if they die and people take them for living beings. Perhaps it is their chief feature that they are dead, for then they cannot make a mistake, they do exactly the same things over and over again.

Q. You speak of dead people recurring, but I thought essence could not die?

A. It can die relatively, in the sense that it cannot develop. Mechanically it may exist, but it cannot grow, it can only deteriorate with time. Essence can die in many different ways. It may die only for this life, or it may die completely. It can die completely only as a result of a long period of wrong actions, actions against conscience. Killing essence means killing conscience. Or it can die in this life and be born again, safe, and sane, in the next. For instance, one can fall on one's head and essence may die in the sense that it will not develop any further. But in the next life it will live again. So, in speaking about death of essence we must know which case we mean, accidental or intentional.

In thinking about life, we forget that many people are dead and that sleeping people easily fall under the influence of dead people.

Q. Are most people dead?

A. This question was much discussed in our group in St Petersburg. Some thought that most people were dead, but I was always against this. Everybody is asleep, but even in life you find pleasant people who may not work through laziness, lack of opportunity, or something else. But they are not dead.

Q. How can dead people influence sleeping people?

A. In comparison with sleeping people they are very strong, because they have no conscience and no shame. What makes ordinary people weak? Conscience and shame. Besides, if people are asleep, anything can happen to them, they can be stolen out of their beds.

All people in life are asleep, but not all are dead yet. At the same time, if one cannot accept and use B influence at all, there is nothing to keep one from dying sooner or later. B influences are sent to keep men from dying, even though they are asleep. But if they reject them, there is nothing to prevent their dying. People are not equal in relation to evolution. Some can evolve, others cannot. Either they lost the possibility of evolution, or they have done nothing to deserve it.

Q. Is there any difference between clairvoyance and memory of recurrence?

A. Real clairvoyance, apart from fantastic descriptions, is a function of the higher emotional Centre, which means a function of man No. 5. Everything below that is either lies or imagination. It is quite possible sometimes to have glimpses of higher centres, but it is not reliable, and no one can control it except man No. 5, and he must be a complete No. 5. If a man crystallizes and becomes almost No. 5, but without having been man No. 4, he is not complete and so he cannot fully use these powers. But if one attains the third state of consciousness, this development of consciousness means the functioning of the higher emotional Centre which has a bigger range of vision than our ordinary vision.

Q. Is it possible to have any understanding of recurrence if one cannot grasp questions of dimensions and different times?

A. I think it is possible to understand, but we must first agree about terms. As a theory it has a psychological, a mathematical and what we may call a physical side, and I think the psychological side can be understood without necessarily understanding the ideas of dimensions and space. After all, what is important is not the mathematical side. It is only a theory of life which is, so to speak, mathematically sound. But we cannot speak about it as a fact.

It can be explained in another way. The idea of recurrence can be connected with the life of humanity. Individual time ends and one becomes connected with the life of a bigger entity humanity.

It means only one thing: if man remains mechanical, he can recur ten thousand times and will not profit by it. The fact of recurrence does not change anything by itself. But if one begins to work, it becomes enormous; it is the only principle which can explain certain things. But by itself ten thousand lives or one life are just the same.

Q. Do all events in history come again, such as wars and revolutions?

A. We are now speaking about individual recurrence; we cannot pass straight from that to historical events. At the same time, we can say that these things will repeat. They are produced by mechanical forces and mechanical people, so those people will be in the same conditions as before externally. The thing we must understand is that if nothing changes now, nothing will change again. Suppose there are some people who remember; what can they do? Others do not remember, and they are more sure of their opinions and less inclined to listen to reason. And remembering events depends on self-remembering. If you become conscious now, then if there is a next life, you will remember what happened. If you do not remember yourselves, how can you remember things and events?

Q. Does it mean that the situation of world events will always be the same for me?

A. You must understand that each world, from the point of view of recurrence, is within another world. The situation can change in one of the bigger worlds and affect the world inside it. There are many things in relation to this that our mind is incapable of thinking about in the right way. If we could think more definitely and clearly, we would see more.

There is one thing I want to add in relation to worlds. As long as the Absolute exists, all other things must exist; they have no right to die. Even if they die, they are repeated and repeated as long as the Absolute exists.

But all this is theory. In the system recurrence is not necessary. It may be interesting and useful; you can even start with this idea, but for actual work on yourself it is not necessary. This is why we are not given this idea in the system. It came from outside, from me, from literature. It does fit, it does not contradict the system, but it is not needed because all we can do, we can do only in this life. If we do nothing in this life, the next life will be just the same, or there will be slight variations but no positive change. If recurrence exists, we cannot change it. There is only one thing we can change: we can try to awake and hope to remain awake. If we have to come back, we cannot stop it. We are in a train; the train is going somewhere. All we can do is to pass the time in the train differently, do something useful or spend it quite uselessly

* * *

LIST OF TITLES WITH ISBN NO.

ISBN	TITLE
9788194914129	1984
9789390575220	1984 & Animal Farm (2In1)
9789390575572	1984 & Animal Farm (2In1): The International Best-Selling Classics
9789390575848	35 Sonnets
9789390575329	A Clergyman's Daughter
9789390575923	A Study In Scarlet
9789390896097	A Tale Of Two Cities
9789390896837	Abide in Christ
9789390896202	Abraham Lincoln
9789390896912	Absolute Surrender
9789390896608	African American Classic Collection
9789390575305	Aldous Huxley: The Collected Works
9789390896141	An Autobiography of M. K. Gandhi
9789390575886	Animal Farm
9789390575619	Animal Farm & The Great Gatsby (2In1)
9789390575626	Animal Farm & We
9789390896158	Anna Karenina
9789390575534	Antic Hay
9789390896165	Antony & Cleopatra
9789390896172	As I Lay Dying
9789390896226	As You like it
9789390575671	At Your Command
9789390575350	Awakened Imagination
9789390575114	Be What You Wish
9789390896233	Believe In yourself
9789390896998	Best of Charles Darwin: The Origin of Species & Autobiography
9789390896684	Best Of Horror : Dracula And Frankenstein
9789390575503	Best Of Mark Twain (The Adventures of Tom Sawyer AND The Adventures of Huckleberry Finn)
9789390896769	Black History Collection
9789390575756	Brave New World, Animal Farm & 1984 (3in1)
9789390896240	Brother Karamzov
9789390575053	Bulleh Shah Poetry
9789390575725	Burmese Days

9789390896257	Bushido
9789390896066	Can't Hurt Me
9788194914112	Chanakya Neeti: With The Complete Sutras
9789390896042	Crime and Punishment
9789390575527	Crome Yellow
9789390575046	Down and Out in Paris and London
9789390896844	Dracula
9789390575442	Emersons Essays: The Complete First & Second Series (Self-Reliance & Other Essays)
9789390575749	Emma
9789390575817	Essential Tozer Collection - The Pursuit of God & The Purpose of Man
9789390896578	Fascism What It Is and How to Fight It
9789390575688	Feeling is the Secret
9789390575190	Five Lessons
9789390575954	Frankenstein
9789390575237	Franz Kafka: Collected Works
9789390575282	Franz Kafka: Short Stories
9789390575060	George Orwell Collected Works
9789390575077	George Orwell Essays
9789390575213	George Orwell Poems
9788194914150	Greatest Poetry Ever Written Vol 1
9788194914143	Greatest Poetry Ever Written Vol 1
9789390896301	Gulliver's Travel
9789390575961	Gunaho Ka Devta
9789390575893	H. P. Lovecraft Selected Stories Vol 1
9789390575978	H. P. Lovecraft Selected Stories Vol 2
9789390896059	Hamlet
9789390575022	His Last Bow: Some Reminiscences of Sherlock Holmes
9789390896134	History of Western Philosophy
9789390575121	Homage To Catalonia
9789390896219	How to develop self-confidence and Improve public Speaking
9789390896295	How to enjoy your life and your Job
9789390575633	How to own your own mind
9789390896318	How to read Human Nature
9789390896325	How to sell your way through the life
9789390896370	How to use the laws of mind
9789390896387	How to use the power of prayer

9789390896028	How to win friends & Influence People
9788194824176	How To Win Friends and Influence People
9789390896103	Humility The Beauty of Holiness
9789390896653	Imperialism the Highest Stage of Capitalism
9789390575084	In Our Time
9789390575169	In Our Time & Three Stories and Ten poems
9789390575145	James Allen: The Collected Works
9789390896189	Jesus Himself
9789390575480	Jo's Boys
9789390896394	Julius Caesar
9789390575404	Keep the Aspidistra Flying
9789390896400	Kidnapped
9789390896424	King Lear
9789390575824	Lady Susan
9789390896455	Law of Success
9789390896264	Lincoln The Unknown
9789390575565	Little Men
9789390575640	Little Women
9788194914174	Lost Horizon
9789390896462	Macbeth
9789390896929	Man Eaters of Kumaon
9789390896523	Man The Dwelling Place of God
9789390896349	Man The Dwelling Place of God
9789390575909	Mansfield Park
9788194914136	Manto Ki 25 Sarvshreshth Kahaniya
9789390896509	Marxism, Anarchism, Communism
9789390575664	Mathematical Principles of Natural Philosophy
9788194914198	Meditations
9789390575800	Mein Kampf
9789390575794	Memory How To Develop, Train, And Use It
9789390896486	Mind Power
9789390896585	Money
9789390575039	Mortal Coils
9789390575770	My Life and Work
9789390896035	Narrative of the Life of Frederick Douglass
9789390575152	Neville Goddard: The Collected Works
9789390575985	Northanger Abbey
9789390896530	Notes From Underground

9789390896547	Oliver Twist
9789390575459	On War
9789390575541	One, None and a Hundred Thousand
9789390896554	Othelo
9789390575435	Out Of This World
9789390575015	Persuasion
9789390575510	Prayer The Art Of Believing
9789390575091	Pride and Prejudice
9789390896561	Psychic Perception
9789390575381	Rabindranath Tagore - 5 Best Short Stories Vol 2
9789390575367	Rabindranath Tagore - Short Stories (Masters Collections Including The Childs Return)
9789390575374	Rabindranath Tagore 5 Best Short Stories Vol 1 (Including The Childs Return
9789390896622	Romeo & Juliet
9789390896127	Sanatana Dharma
9789390575596	Seedtime & Harvest
9789390896639	Selected Stories of Guy De Maupassant
9789390575206	Self-Reliance & Other Essays
9789390575176	Sense and Sensibility
9789390575299	Shyamchi Aai
9789390896738	Socialism Utopian and Scientific
9789390896646	Success Through a Positive Mental Attitude
9789390575428	The Adventures of Huckleberry Finn
9789390575183	The Adventures of Sherlock Holmes
9789390575343	The Adventures of Tom Sawyer
9789390896691	The Alchemy Of Happiness
9789390575862	The Art Of Public Speaking
9789390896288	The Autobiography Of Charles Darwin
9788194914181	The Best of Franz Kafka: The Metamorphosis & The Trial
9789390575008	The Call Of Cthulhu and Other Weird Tales
9789390575107	The Case-Book of Sherlock Holmes
9789390896110	The Castle Of Otranto
9789390896745	The Communist Manifesto
9789390575589	The Complete Fiction of H. P. Lovecraft
9789390575497	The Complete Works of Florence Scovel Shinn
9789390896820	The Conquest of Breard
9789390896813	The Diary of a Young Girl

9789390896332	The Diary of a Young Girl The Definitive Edition of the Worlds Most Famous Diary
9789390575701	The Great Gatsby, Animal Farm & 1984 (3In1)
9789390575312	The Greatest Works Of George Orwell (5 Books) Including 1984 & Non-Fiction
9789390575992	The Hound of Baskervilles
9789390896707	The Idiot
9789390896714	The Invisible Man
9789390575657	The Knowledge of the holy
9789390575558	The Law & the Promise
9789390896721	The Law Of Attraction
9789390896776	The Leader in you
9789390896363	The Life of Christ
9789390896196	The Man-Eating Leopard of Rudraprayag
9789390896783	The Master Key to Riches
9789390575268	The Memoirs Of Sherlock Holmes
9789390896479	The Midsummer Night's Dream
9789390575466	The Mill On The Floss
9789390896790	The Miracles of your mind
9789390896660	The Mutual Aid A Factor in Evolution
9789390896448	The Origin of Species
9789390896905	The Peter Kropotkin Anthology The Conquest of Bread & Mutual Aid A Factor of Evolution
9789390896806	The Picture of Dorian Gray
9789390896271	The Picture of Dorian Gray
9789390575275	The Power Of Awareness
9789390896356	The Power of Concentration
9788194824169	The Power of Positive Thinking
9789390575411	The Power of the Spoken Word
9788194914105	The Power Of Your Subconscious Mind
9789390896899	The Power of Your Subconscious Mind
9789390896417	The Principles of Communism
9789390575787	The Psychology Of Mans Possible Evolution
9789390896615	The Psychology of Salesmanship
9789390575732	The Pursuit of God
9789390575398	The Pursuit of Happiness
9789390896851	The Quick and Easy Way to effective Speaking
9789390575947	The Return Of Sherlock Holmes

9789390575138	The Road To Wigan Pier
9789390896981	The Root of the Righteous
9789390575855	The Science Of Being Well
9788194914167	The Science Of Getting Rich, The Science Of Being Great & The Science Of Being Well (3In1)
9789390896011	The Screwtape Letters
9789390896073	The Screwtape Letters
9789390575336	The Secret Door to Success
9789390575695	The Secret Of Imagining
9789390896868	The Secret Of Success
9789390896431	The Seven Last Words
9789390575930	The Sign of the Four
9789390896004	The Sonnets
9789390896516	The Souls of Black Folk
9789390896875	The Sound and The Fury
9789390575244	The State and Revolution
9789390896882	The Story of My Life
9789390896936	The Story Of Oriental Philosophy
9789390896752	The Strange Case of Dr. Jekyll and Mr. Hyde
9789390896943	The Tempest
9789390575916	The Valley Of Fear
9789390575879	The Wind in the willows
9789390896080	The Wind in the willows
9789390575763	Their eyes were watching gofd
9789390575831	Three Stories
9789390896950	Twelfth Night
9789390896592	Twelve Years a Slave
9789390896677	Up from Slavery
9789390896974	Value Price and Profit
9789390896967	Wake Up and Live
9789390896493	With Christ in the School of Prayer
9789390575602	Your Faith is Your Fortune
9789390575473	Your Infinite Power To Be Rich
9789390575251	Your Word is Your Wand
9789390575718	Youth
9789391316099	A Christmas Carol
9789391316105	A Doll's House
9789391316501	A Passage to India

9789391316709	A Portrait of the Artist as a Young Man
9789391316112	A Tale of Two Cities
9789391316747	A Tear and a Smile
9789391316167	Agnes Gray
9789391316174	Alice's Adventures in Wonderland
9789391316136	Anandamath
9789391316181	Anne Of Green Gables
9789391316754	Anthem
9789391316198	Around The World in 80 Days
9789391316013	As A Man Thinketh
9789391316242	Autobiography of a Yogi
9789391316266	Beyond Good and Evil
9789391316761	Bleak House
9789391316778	Chitra, a Play in One Act
9789391316310	David Copperfield
9789391316075	Demian
9789391316785	Dubliners
9789391316051	Favourite Tales from the Arabian Nights
9789391316235	Gitanjali
9789391316068	Gravity
9789391316150	Great Speeches of Abraham Lincoln
9789391316662	Guerilla Warfare
9789391316839	Kim
9789391316822	Mother
9789391316211	My Childhood
9789391316846	Nationalism
9789391316327	Oliver Twist
9789391316853	Pygmalion
9789391316334	Relativity: The Special and the General Theory
9789391316389	Scientific Healing Affirmation
9789391316341	Sons and Lovers
9789391316587	Tales from India
9789391316372	Tess of The D'Urbervilles
9789391316396	The Awakening and Selected Stories
9789391316402	The Bhagvad Gita
9789391316303	The Book of Enoch
9789391316228	The Canterville Ghost
9789391316907	The Dynamic Laws of Prosperity

9789391316006	The Great Gatsby
9789391316860	The Hungry Stones and Other Stories
9789391316433	The Idiot
9789391316440	The Importance of Being Earnest
9789391316297	The Light of Asia
9789391316914	The Madman His Parables and Poems
9789391316457	The Odyssey
9789391316921	The Picture of Dorian Gray
9789391316464	The Prince
9789391316938	The Prophet
9789391316945	The Republic
9789391316518	The Scarlet Letter
9789391316143	The Seven Laws of Teaching
9789391316525	The Story of My Experiments with Truth
9789391316532	The Tales of the Mother Goose
9789391316549	The Thirty Nine Steps
9789391316594	The Time Machine
9789391316600	The Turn of the Screw
9789391316983	The Upanishads
9789391316617	The Yellow Wallpaper
9789391316426	The Yoga Sutras of Patanjali
9789391316990	Ulysses
9789391316624	Utopia
9789391316679	Vanity Fair
9789391316020	What Is To Be Done
9789391316686	Within A Budding Grove
9789391316693	Women in Love